Elements of Crime Patterns

Elements of Crime Patterns is the first detailed compendium of the specific elements and variables of crime patterns. It articulates tacit and implicit knowledge about what crime patterns consist of and contains a wealth of information illustrating what could be in a crime pattern. It details the offender and victim, location and time, weapons, tools, equipment, travel, communication, and methods used to commit crimes. The behaviors in 27 crime categories are succinctly but specifically examined, from robbery, burglary, and cybercrime to sexual assault, terrorism, and drug trafficking. This book serves as an "anatomy book" of crimes and as a type of diagnostic manual. To diagnose crime patterns more accurately, it is wise to obtain a thorough grasp of their possible parts and what these parts might look like. By recognizing crime patterns sooner, we increase the likelihood of preventing crimes, apprehending criminals, understanding problems, and developing more effective crime reduction tactics and policies. So much basic information in one place allows those who work in policing to formulate better questions when working in traditional ways and when interacting with artificial intelligence systems. Novices to the subject will gain foundational knowledge. Experienced police officers, investigators, and analysts will utilize the book as a comprehensive reference tool. Criminal justice students, teachers, and researchers will learn the ins and outs of crime patterns. Instructor resources can be found at routledge.com/9781041217312, offering a syllabus, instructor guides, exercises, case studies, slide decks, and other resources for teaching and training using this book.

Deborah Osborne is a retired US Secret Service Investigative Analyst and a former Crime Analyst for the Buffalo Police Department. As a crime analyst, she read and analyzed the narratives of over 100,000 police crime reports. She co-authored the book *Introduction to Crime Analysis: Basic Resources for Criminal Justice Practice* and wrote *Out of Bounds: Innovation and Change in Law Enforcement Intelligence Analysis* as a research fellow for the Joint Military Intelligence College. Osborne was the co-chair of the International Association of Crime Analysts' certification committee when it first developed certification standards for the profession. She trained analysts and taught this subject at the college level for over six years. She has won awards from the International Association of Crime Analysts and the International Association of Law Enforcement Intelligence Analysts for her contributions to the field.

Elements of Crime Patterns

A Foundation for Theory and Practice

Second Edition

Deborah Osborne

Routledge
Taylor & Francis Group
NEW YORK AND LONDON

Designed cover image: Getty Images

Second edition published 2026
by Routledge
605 Third Avenue, New York, NY 10158

and by Routledge
4 Park Square, Milton Park, Abingdon, Oxon, OX14 4RN

Routledge is an imprint of the Taylor & Francis Group, an informa business

First edition published by Deborah Osborne 2023

ISBN: 978-1-041-21731-2 (hbk)
ISBN: 978-1-041-21730-5 (pbk)
ISBN: 978-1-003-72873-3 (ebk)

DOI: 10.4324/9781003728733

Typeset in Galliard
by Apex CoVantage, LLC

Visit the Support Material: www.routledge.com/9781041217312

To my sister,
and our shared childhood love
of Agatha Christie

Contents

Preface

When my sister gave me the civil service examination announcement for the position of crime analyst, I tried to find out more about what a crime analyst was, but there was nothing to read in my library. Once I was hired as the first crime analyst in the Buffalo Police Department, I found that there were significantly more books about the behavior patterns of birds and other creatures than the specific behaviors in patterns of crime. I wanted to see observational lists, descriptive elements, and documented types of activities to learn what I should be looking for as I poured through hundreds and then thousands of crime reports, looking for patterns. Looking for crime patterns was my job, and I wanted to be good at it. I never found the book I was looking for, and now that I am retired, I decided to write it.

Fortunately for the novice crime analyst I once was, the brain is designed to find patterns – it excels at that job even when we don't have the education to recognize new kinds of patterns. The brain will strive to find patterns.[1]

I found crime patterns easily, but I was not confident of the validity behind my findings. Officers reassured me that, yes, what I found were crime patterns. I was bound to find them in an urban environment as criminals commit serial crimes more than you might think, not the TV maniac serial killer we all know about, but frequent serial burglaries and robberies peppered the city, along with other types of crime series.

I found crime patterns in the newly created crime analyst position because that was a primary part of my job, besides the tasks of conducting basic statistical and geographic analysis. Police officers and investigators are not generally tasked with finding patterns. They run to calls, one by one, and investigate crimes, one by one. Yet early detection of crime patterns could help arrest a suspect earlier, provide the opportunity to predict the next crime or link the offender to a past crime with more information, such as forensic evidence or witnesses. Detecting crime patterns can prevent future crimes by helping officers and the community disrupt the opportunity to commit another crime. Early detection of crime patterns allows police to warn the public of the patterned criminal behavior. Finding patterns was the morally right thing to do to me. I wondered why it was not a central activity of policing. I thought every officer would want to do it.

Like any crime analyst with years of experience, I have countless examples of serial crime patterns I discovered, sometimes identifying them earlier than officers, sometimes at the same time, sometimes later. There were times a pattern went on and on, such as when a burglar struck 25 apartments in an apartment complex, leaving pornography on site. It took too long to link the crimes; report-taking officers didn't include the unusual behavior in their crime narratives in many of the reports. Another time, a pattern was not obvious except for three consistent variables; the robber with dreadlocks rode a bicycle in a specific neighborhood. He used various weapons and displayed inconsistent behaviors, but the crimes in one area of the city (location) and the bike (transportation) and the dreadlocks (physical description) helped link the crimes.

In one rape series, the suspect raped the victim in an elevator and, in his next crime, raped another victim on a stairway landing. This struck me as being something only a human would notice as related crimes since elevators and stairways are seldom mentioned in standardized crime reports, if at all. The relation between the two are clear to see, but not glaringly obvious.

Once I learned how to map crime using Geographic Information Systems (GIS), I found other types of patterns beyond serial crime patterns, those which the same suspect or suspects likely commit. GIS helped identify hot spot crime patterns in the city, which are geographic clusters of criminal activity. There were also patterns of victims, such as the elderly who were targets of springtime traveling criminal scams, people offering to make driveway or home repairs, and then disappearing with the money. There were patterns of certain things being stolen, like catalytic converters, which contain precious metals such as platinum, palladium, and rhodium. Patterns, patterns everywhere.

When I worked as an investigative analyst for the US Secret Service, I found other patterns: patterns of the same counterfeit currency distributed in different locations, patterns of IP addresses criminals used in a cybercrime scheme, travel patterns of specific criminals, and patterns in mortgage fraud transactions.

Before I became a crime analyst, I was a behavior analyst working in the field of developmental disabilities. The wealth of existing literature to support that work was detailed and valuable. I could learn about specific disabilities and psychiatric disorders and how these might manifest in particular problem behaviors. It seemed strange to me that crime analysis had no such equivalents. There was a great deal of theory and research about crime, but not what I was looking for. I wanted details on *modus operandi*, the methods of committing crime, and what to look for in crime data.

When I was a behavior specialist, it was our practice to identify the baseline behavior[2] in a problem, indicating how often the individual's specific behavior was occurring. When I started analyzing robberies in depth, I uncovered a series of ten gunpoint robberies of meat delivery trucks. Still, I had no way of knowing that ten robberies of this type within a month were quite unusual. There was no baseline of modus operandi information; I didn't and couldn't know the normal threshold[3] of any specific crime modus operandi – experienced officers and investigators would see that immediately if they were looking. That information resided only in their minds and was not written anywhere.[4]

It was clear that knowing the most I could about possible modus operandi factors could help me be a better analyst. I started collecting example reports from other law enforcement agencies that had fields of information to capture the methods used to commit the crime. I gathered as much research as I could on the subject throughout the years. I made lists on spreadsheets and thought about writing a book like this one to share the information, but I did not have enough material. I told others in the field about my belief that a book like this was needed, but no one seemed to get what I meant. They just did not see it in their head the way I did. I felt frustrated and gave up on the idea repeatedly. I wished someone else would write such a book and hoped they would. I intermittently searched the Internet looking for the new book I thought should exist.

Enter Open AI ChatGPT and the possibility of asking questions of this large language model (LLM) form of artificial intelligence (AI). Suddenly, I had a tool, a helper for this enormous task that had seemed beyond me. In the first version of this book, which I self-published, I used ChatGPT extensively to answer my questions; it provided me with answers I already recognized as accurate and could not easily recollect on my own. When I did not know if something I wanted to include was true or not, I researched it and verified it. I even asked AI what the pros and cons of writing this book were, and one negative was that it would be too complex and challenging.

AI tools helped me to write about specific crimes the way a behavior specialist might if she were to become a crime analyst. The chapters on crimes in this book provide succinctly presented basics that should be especially helpful for those unfamiliar with certain crimes. I personally worked on crime patterns in most of the types of crimes included in this book. I included as many crimes as possible because, in my opinion, patterns involving repeat offenders can be found in all of them, not just in the incident-based crime pattern analysis that occurs in local-level policing. My federal-level investigative experience taught me that there are patterns in unreported crimes that law enforcement must uncover through investigations and later prove in the court systems. I wanted this book to be helpful to every level of law enforcement.

As I worked on the second edition of this book, I added Claude AI, Perplexity AI, and Google Gemini AI to my cognitive team to help me formulate ideas, develop text, and provide structure. As I expanded the original book, I added example cases and scenarios, brief exercises, and critical thinking guidance to the book.

While using this technology, it became clear how this book could help in another way beyond what I had envisioned – it could help in the future when LLMs would be widely incorporated into law enforcement practice. While the book I imagined was primarily an aid to expand thinking about recognizing and identifying crime patterns, documenting this information for others so that they might ask better, richer questions of AI was a bonus benefit. With the help of LLMs, all sorts of unstructured data will be searched more easily for patterns, but to take optimal advantage of it, the ability to ask questions in new ways must be developed by its users. We are on the eve of a new age in data analysis in policing, where we can bridge the gaps between all sorts of information sources, but only if we can imagine what we want to find. We also need to be able to question what these systems will automatically produce. The new tools will analyze for us, but they will be much more useful if we can interact with them and critically evaluate their outputs. This book may add to your imagination to do so.

In the July 10, 2023, Law Enforcement Analysis Podcasts interview by host Jason Elder, Jakob Lindergård-Bentzen, Program Manager and Senior Advisor for the Danish intelligence-led policing program, stated that when you become an expert and you know what questions to ask the data, you become more exploratory. Becoming exploratory means going beyond using your technical skills to analyze crime. This book's goal is to help you do that. He talked about the need to develop a framework for analysts so that they know the things that will allow them to ask the better questions.[5]

This framework has yet to exist, and it is my hope that this book moves us in the right direction.

Above all, this book is intended to be a thinking resource to supplement your mind when you face the work of looking at crimes. Expanding your knowledge of potential elements in a crime pattern can help you identify what you may be overlooking and learn about aspects you never considered examining. My attempt to document what I observed and learned as a working law enforcement analyst at the local and federal levels, combined with extensive research and ongoing curiosity, should be seen as a beginning step. I invite you, readers, to take the journey further.

Notes

1 Barrett (2009).
2 In behavior analysis, the measured level or pattern of a target behavior prior to the introduction of an intervention. It serves as the reference point for evaluating the effects of treatment or changes in environmental conditions.
3 The minimum level, rate, or number of crime occurrences needed to establish a measurable pattern, justify analysis, or trigger a law enforcement response.
4 Smith (2001).
5 Elder (2023, July 10).

Bibliography

Barrett, L. F. (2009). The future of psychology: Connecting mind to brain. *Perspectives on Psychological Science*, *4*(4), 326–339. https://doi.org/10.1111/j.1745-6924.2009.01134.x

Elder, J. (Host). (2023, July 10). *Jakob Lindergård-Bentzen: Leading with intelligence (No. 167)* [Audio podcast episode]. Law Enforcement Analysis Podcasts (L.E.A.P.). www.leapodcasts.com/e/atwje-jakob-lindergard-bentzen-leading-with-intelligence

Smith, E. A. (2001). The role of tacit and explicit knowledge in the workplace. *Journal of Knowledge Management*, *5*(4), 311–321. https://doi.org/10.1108/13673270110411733

Part I

Overview

1 Introduction

A Starting Point

This book is about the elements and their many relevant variables in crime patterns. No book could possibly include all such details, but this book is an attempt to put as many of them as practical and possible in one place. It should be considered a starting point of detailed capture, in itself an analysis of the elements and variables in crime patterns, designed to expand shared language when we talk about, investigate, analyze, and solve crime patterns.

It is not a book about theory or policy, although in Chapters 5 and 6 it explains how it relates to specific criminological theories and policing approaches. These theories and approaches assume a shared foundational understanding of the elements and variables in crime patterns, yet there has not been any collective effort to describe them in a way that is accessible to both researchers and law enforcement practitioners.

Intentionally, it is a book to aid practitioners in thinking about crime and the many elements and variables they encounter when dealing with criminal behavior in the field. Its level of detail broadens the knowledge of how complex the crime landscape truly is to improve situational awareness of the crime environment we all face.

Neuroscientists have found that much of our thinking is based on predicting what might come next based on what we have already learned. The mind is a prediction machine; what you know is what you will see.[1] This book provides the reader with more in their mental database so that they are more likely to consciously recognize crime patterns variables in general as well as an unfamiliar variable in an emerging crime pattern.

First and foremost, readers of this book should understand that this book is descriptive rather than prescriptive. It contains a multitude of specific variables that can be in crime patterns. It is not presented as a researched theory, an approved new classification system, or the final word on the contents of crime patterns, but it could be a starting point for creating fundamental typologies that inform all crime studies.[2]

Patterns

Dictionaries define the word pattern as the repeated or regular way something happens or is done. The United Kingdom's College of Policing states that pattern analysis focuses on emerging and current trends, linked crimes or incidents, hotspots of activity, or common (of offenders/offending behavior).[3]

DOI: 10.4324/9781003728733-2

The International Association of Crime Analysts (IACA) defines a crime pattern as a group of two or more crimes reported to or discovered by police that may be considered one unique unit of analysis because they share at least one commonality. Commonalities include the type of crime, the behavior of the offenders or the victims, the characteristics of the offender(s), victims or targets, property taken, or the locations of occurrence. The IACA definition refers only to stranger-on-stranger crime, crimes notable and distinct from other criminal activity occurring within the same geographic area, in the same general date range, and of limited duration.[4]

Examples of such patterns:

- two burglaries of jewelry stores in a city during one month in which the suspect(s) broke in through an adjoining wall
- a robbery of a McDonald's on a Saturday night near closing by a suspect with a gun wearing an orange jacket, followed by a robbery of a Burger King a week later with the same variables
- morning thefts of purses in churches in a county when the visitors leave their pews to pray
- the price of copper goes up, and a region experiences a rash of copper thefts

This book presents elements that would help identify criminals who commit crimes using the same or evolving methods. The public is highly aware of the existence of serial killers, but many other crimes occur in patterns involving the same person committing the same types of crimes. The fact that any offender that commits the same crime over again could be thought of as a serial criminal, no matter what the crime types, is a basic premise of this book. It can be argued that this is not a premise shared by current criminological logical theories, and that is a valid argument, but note that this book is not about a new theory or conflicting theory. It is a way to look at information as it applies in the practical aspects of policing. It is a thinking tool.

Recognizing and Identifying

In the context of crime patterns in law enforcement, recognizing and identifying have distinct meanings:

Recognizing refers to perceiving or acknowledging something based on previous knowledge or familiarity. Recognizing involves the capability of law enforcement officers, investigators, and analysts to identify patterns, trends, or behaviors that they have encountered before or have been trained to recognize. It's about seeing familiar patterns and understanding their significance in the context of crime investigation and prevention. Experienced police officers, investigators, and analysts recognize specific modus operandi associated with crime patterns and sometimes even particular criminals. This is their on-the-job learning. By simply reading this book, you will gain similar knowledge.

Identifying goes further and involves determining or naming something or someone based on specific characteristics or information. Identifying means pinpointing a particular behavioral pattern, suspect, element, or variable based on the available data and evidence. It can include identifying modus operandi, suspect descriptions, or evidence linking crimes together. Users of this book can take the specific information contained in it and actively search for existing real-world crime patterns.

Experienced officers, investigators, and analysts may welcome this book more than any reader because it is impossible to remember all the elements, variables, and factors that might be in a crime pattern on any one day. They will recognize crime patterns intuitively, using their expertise, but on a busy day or a day when they are tired, the skill of recognizing and identifying crime patterns may simply be lost in the shuffle. A neutral aid, such as this book, can be a valuable thinking support tool. This book can serve as a creative prompt to look for more possible patterns as well.

Various studies show that a small percentage of criminals commit a large percentage of crimes. Because humans are creatures of habit, in some cases these repeat offenders will have identifiable patterns of behavior. Becoming more aware of the variables involved in their specific patterns will help you link more of their crimes. If you can link them to more of their crimes, when they are arrested more charges may be brought against them, leading to stiffer penalties and more time off the streets.

Practical Information About This Book

Note that the information in this book tends toward the more variables, the better. Information is not organized in order of importance; instead, alphabetization was used in some lists as an ordering convention rather than a rating scale.

Be aware that this book may not include local terminology and descriptive information. For example, when gathering information for this project from police data entry forms, the term "jalousie," which refers to a type of window, was in a Florida data collection report; "jalousie" was unfamiliar to the author, who lives in the northeast United States. As you review the lists and information, you may note things you would add. Feel free to add them to your book notes or create lists of your own.

The book is slanted toward a US audience, but much of the information can be applied to any crime pattern in any country. International readers will find this to be true because criminals have similar behavior around the world. In this second edition, United Kingdom and Commonwealth (Canada, Australia, and New Zealand) equivalents of American terms that are used in crime reports can be found at the back section of the book.

Information may overlap and be repeated; efforts were made to keep that to a minimum. The basic elements will have broad application in many types of crimes. Readers who are assigned to investigate particular crimes are invited to jump ahead to the crimes that interest them, but it is recommended that the basic elements are reviewed first, because efforts were made not to repeat the specifics that were mentioned in the basic elements section.

Each basic element chapter in Part Two provides a crime pattern scenario and a case example taken from real life with example query terms that could be used to search databases or online. Crime type chapters in Part Three contain case scenarios for particular crime types. These chapters conclude with exercises and critical thinking guidance.

The exercises emphasize practical application over theory, focusing on the systematic analysis of behavioral patterns for linkage analysis rather than psychological or sociological interpretation. Each exercise can be completed with pen and paper or basic spreadsheet tools, making them accessible to all readers regardless of technical resources or specialized software. The activities are designed to develop pattern recognition skills through hands-on practice with realistic scenarios, building competency in identifying behavioral consistencies across crime series.

Recommendations for Readers

Police Officers: Use this book to help you recognize new-to-you types of crime patterns and then identify the new crime patterns in your jurisdiction as they arise. Collect more relevant, quality information; aid your agency to have a more accurate picture of the crime in your jurisdiction by incorporating these details.

Investigators: Use this book to help you identify commonalities in unsolved cases and expand your awareness of possible crime linkages and indicators of criminal activities. Search the information you have in your files beyond the computer to look for patterns. Question beyond your policing agency and jurisdiction.

Crime and Intelligence Analysts: Use this book to inform your analytical approach. Look for a wider variety of variables and indicators. Search various datasets to find correlations. Share the book with officers to show the value of detailed information collection and sharing. Communicate with other crime analysts in your region when you identify significant patterns.

Law Enforcement Agencies: Use this book as a guide to understand and respond appropriately and proactively to emerging crime patterns in your jurisdictions. Use it as training material for new recruits or as a reference book for more experienced officers.

Private Security: Use this information to deepen your ability to describe and address the crime patterns you encounter in your work. Share the pattern information in partnership with law enforcement.

Researchers: Criminologists, sociologists, and psychologists can use this book for theoretical development and practical application. This book can serve as a supplemental launching point for the formation of research questions, hypotheses, and methodologies.

Information Technologists: Use this book to understand the nuances of crime patterns. The information contained here can be included in developing information technology that more effectively captures and analyzes relevant information and addresses the users' needs.

Legal Professionals: Lawyers, judges, and other legal practitioners use the book to understand better the context of crimes they deal with. The defense and the prosecution interpret or argue complex cases involving serial or other patterned crimes; this book can help with mentally organizing information to do so.

Policy Makers: Use this information to understand the complex issues in crime patterns better. Create and fund guidelines and systems for information collection, analysis, sharing, and information systems interoperability. Address the obstacles to gathering robust data to serve the societal goal of crime reduction and increased public safety.

Journalists and Crime Reporters: Use the book to understand better the crime patterns they report on, potentially offering more insightful commentary and analysis for their readers or viewers.

Educators: Use this book as a course textbook in crime analysis, intelligence analysis, criminology, sociology, law, and public policy. Use it to develop curriculum and lesson plans.

Students: Use this book to better understand crime patterns, investigations, and criminal behavior.

Community Leaders: Use the knowledge from the book to understand crime patterns in your communities and thus better advocate for effective strategies to reduce crime and improve public safety. Use this knowledge to create community awareness and encourage active participation in community policing initiatives.

Notes

1 Bubic et al. (2010).
2 A typology is a way to group similar things together based on shared features, and this book used that framework to organize information.
3 College of Policing (n.d.).
4 International Association of Crime Analysts (2011).

Bibliography

Bubic, A., von Cramon, D. Y., & Schubotz, R. I. (2010). Prediction, cognition and the brain. *Frontiers in Human Neuroscience*, *4*, 25. https://doi.org/10.3389/fnhum.2010.00025

College of Policing. (n.d.). *Analytical techniques.* www.college.police.uk/app/intelligence-management/analysis/analytical-techniques

International Association of Crime Analysts. (2011). *Crime pattern definitions for tactical analysis* (White Paper 2011–01). Author.

2 Modus Operandi Information

Introduction

The systematic study of modus operandi (MO) – the characteristic methods offenders use to commit crimes – has been recognized as vital to detection and prevention for more than a century. As Raymond Fosdick observed in 1915, beyond eyewitnesses and stolen property, the traces left by a criminal's method of operation often provide the most reliable link between crimes and offenders. Yet even with today's national reporting systems and specialized databases, detailed MO information is inconsistently recorded, unevenly shared across jurisdictions, and too often remains in the memories of individual officers or analysts rather than in accessible records. This chapter examines how MO information has been understood historically, how it is currently captured, and why its systematic use is essential for identifying patterns, linking cases, and strengthening investigative outcomes.

Tracking Modus Operandi

From the 1915 article "The Modus Operandi System in the Detection of Criminals" by Raymond B. Fosdick:

> It is at this point that the scientific thought of Europe is making its first direct contact with the problem of connecting crimes with criminals. The new method involves an intensive study of criminal methods of operation, an exact analysis of the traces which the criminal leaves behind him. Roughly speaking, there are three ways of detecting the perpetrator of a crime: first, his recognition by an eyewitness; second, in case of theft, the tracing to him of stolen property; and third, the traces which he leaves behind him. The first method is unsatisfactory because in most criminal cases the perpetrator is not seen. The police are called in to investigate a crime of which no one knows anything except that it was committed. The second method – the property clue – is difficult to apply because much stolen property is unidentifiable; moreover, it is often easily changed in appearance or passed to innocent parties. The third method of connecting crime with a criminal by the traces which he leaves behind him is far the most reliable and is always more or less completely available. Yet hitherto this means of crime detection has been largely neglected by the police. An occasional detective here and there has used it – that is, he has been sufficiently familiar with the modes and practices of certain criminals or bands of criminals to recognize a fresh crime as being their work. But such knowledge has not been systematized. It has remained the exclusive possession of an officer who could not communicate it to his fellows or to the newly joined recruit. He took it with him when he left the force and it died with him, to be rediscovered laboriously, and after many failures, by his successors.[1]

DOI: 10.4324/9781003728733-3

Over 100 years later, detailed modus operandi information remains in the minds of officers, investigators, and analysts. The term modus operandi (MO) refers to the mode or manner of operating or the method used to commit a crime. While modern information systems capture more and more data for statistical analysis and predictive modeling, it is not the consistent practice of policing agencies to capture detailed modus operandi information regarding how specific individuals committed crimes. Many law enforcement agencies collect some MO information in their crime report databases, usually using drop-down boxes for users to select specific terms for data consistency and uniformity, but there are necessary limits to these data fields. Some police forces have investigative units where MO files are maintained and stored, usually thought of as intelligence files, but access to the files is limited to those whom they deem have the need to know. Crime analysts also maintain systems to track modus operandi, but often they are not accessible to non-analysts.

When someone is arrested and convicted of a crime, their MO information is not included in their criminal record. We do not know whether the convicted robber has a penchant for robbing pizza delivery persons, and if they get out of jail and start robbing the same victims, we can only link them if an officer or analyst in a particular law enforcement jurisdiction remembers the details of why they were arrested in the past. Since many individuals who are arrested go on to commit crimes again when released from incarceration, sometimes the same exact type of crime, it is valuable to know more about what they did before. Because criminals are mobile and do not just commit crimes in one policing agency's territory, finding new ways to communicate such information across jurisdictional boundaries is also needed.

Modus Operandi and Data Systems

The FBI's Uniform Crime Reporting (UCR) Program began in the late 1920s, evolving into the National Incident-Based Crime Report System (NIBRS) in the late 1980s, a system that collects more in-depth modus operandi information than the original UCR reporting.[2]

While NIBRS is an improvement in detail compared to the UCR original standards, with participation required since 2021, participants do not collect the level of detail often needed to link a criminal to their modus operandi in specific crime patterns.

According to the FBI, in 2022, there were 18,878 law enforcement agencies in the United States. Of those over 18,000 agencies, 14,155 provided complete data to the FBI that year.[3]

Gaining compliance for entering data for statistical analysis is a challenge. Thus, requiring more data labor-intensive data entry is not the answer. This book aims to show what could be and have the users of the information decide how they will find new ways to work with qualitative data.

Data quality is an issue in data collection for the programs as well. Imagine you are a police officer on a 911 call and take a police report, with calls interrupting your workflow. It is understandable why an officer may not be able to capture crime details fully in a big city. If they are in a small jurisdiction, they may have the luxury of time to complete a detailed burglary report, but in a big city, it is less likely to be true. Add to that the fact that more information comes in later about a crime as a detective starts working a case. That information most likely never gets added to the initial data gathering used in UCR and NIBRS reporting. This represents a significant knowledge gap that goes unquestioned.

The National Crime Information Center (NCIC) provides criminal histories and other important information to law enforcement agencies, such as missing or wanted persons and stolen property, but does not provide information on modus operandi. The Law Enforcement Information Exchange, or LInX, a regional information-sharing system supported by the US Naval Criminal Investigative Service (NCIS), is another information resource whose police agency participation is optional. Participants can share crime reports in that system and, depending on the quality of the crime reporting, can use the system to uncover some modus operandi variables beyond what the other systems offer.

UCR and NIBRS provide valuable statistics for research and policymaking while NCIC and LinX are operational policing tools. All of these systems fail to address an important need for front-line officers, investigators, and analysts. They don't adequately assist in linking patterned crimes, which is a critical aspect of everyday crime-solving. In addition, not all crimes get reported. In fact, according to the Bureau of Justice Statistic's National Crime Victimization Survey (NCVS), only 46% of violent victimizations were reported to police in 2021, which was higher than 2020 (40%).[4]

The FBI's Violent Criminal Apprehension (VICAP) database collects detailed modus operandi information to link serial rape and murder cases across the United States. It is intended to meet a need this book presents. A 2015 article in the Atlantic magazine criticized it, stating that only 1,400 police agencies out of roughly 18,000 enter data into the system; one reason given was that officers found it cumbersome to enter the information.[5]

A study on the Canadian equivalent program, Violent Crime Analysis Linkage System (ViCLAS), tested inter-rater reliability to determine the extent to which two (or more) different investigators enter the same information about a case into a ViCLAS coding booklet (after receiving the same training), and found a low rate of agreement.[6]

That meant the data in the system were not necessarily reliable. In a doctoral study of discrepancies between database narrative information and MO drop-down box completion in one police department, the researcher found a similar limitation in officers in filing out MO information in their own agency department crime database.[7]

Thus, it would be, for whatever reason, unrealistic to expect that requiring the collection of more modus operandi information would work. If a willingness to participate falls short in collecting detailed data for the egregious crimes of murder and rape, it is unlikely to be any better for other crimes.

The ramifications of missing modus operandi information in law enforcement investiga tions are significant and multifaceted. The absence of MO data hampers the ability of investigators to understand criminal behaviors, allocate resources effectively, and develop accurate offender profiles. The cumulative effect of these data collection challenges creates significant gaps that impact every level of law enforcement operations.

Missed Connections and Overlooked Patterns

The absence of MO means investigators may fail to recognize patterns and connections that could lead to the identification and apprehension of criminals. The absence of MO data increases the likelihood of cases being treated in isolation, limiting the potential for comprehensive investigations, and hindering the development of a clear understanding of criminal behaviors.

MO data help in anticipating criminal activities and allocating resources effectively. Without this information, agencies may be unprepared to respond to emerging trends or targeted criminal activities. Delayed responses can allow criminals to continue their operations, perpetuating a cycle of victimization and hindering the overall effectiveness of law enforcement efforts.

Investigators heavily rely on MO data to identify leads, develop profiles, and narrow down potential suspects. When this information is missing, investigators must rely on other evidence and methods, often leading to increased time and effort required to solve cases. The absence of MO information may result in longer investigation timelines, increased strain on resources, and decreased overall efficiency in resolving cases.

When criminals remain unidentified or patterns go unnoticed, communities may experience heightened fear and uncertainty. The absence of MO data undermines the ability of law enforcement agencies to effectively communicate with the public, provide accurate safety guidelines, and alleviate concerns. This can erode public trust, hinder cooperation between law enforcement and the community, and impede society's overall sense of security.

Accurate perception of crime patterns also involves recognizing that failed attempts at committing a crime may be part of a pattern. For example, a 911 call about a suspicious person lurking in a neighborhood could provide information about a suspect in a specific neighborhood burglary pattern. A traffic stop in the area could also provide important clues. It is recommended, if possible, to expand one's search beyond the crime report to increase the odds of early crime pattern identification.

The solution to crime pattern detection cannot be solely data-driven. The informal exchanges of information through conversations, explorations, and intuitive perceptions are crucial in investigative casework, but researchers and policymakers often do not acknowledge this. It is important to understand that conversations between law enforcement staff are the means that some crime patterns get recognized, especially those involving separate records systems in other jurisdictions. The significance of a crime pattern is determined by its jurisdiction and the individuals that uncover it. Context is crucial.

Studies have shown over and over again that much crime occurs because of offenders who repeatedly engage in criminal activity – they are prolific offenders. In fact, roughly 10–15% of the most criminally active individuals are responsible for about half of all crimes.[8]

Leaders of organized criminal groups are problematic to society but go undetected while they influence the behavior of those repeat offenders who serve under them.[9]

In 1919, August Vollmer, the Berkeley police chief well-known for modernizing policing,[10] wrote the following:

> An old officer in the police service once said,
>
> There is a clew to every crime. Finding the clew proves that you are working, and not playing in your chosen profession. There is a clew to every crime. The most important and easiest to get, though more often overlooked than found. That clew is the method employed by the criminal in securing his ill-gotten loot.[11]

Vollmer was referring to crimes involving property, as opposed to violent crime, and property crime represented 90% of the reported crime in his time. We have similar rates in the United States today. Vollmer revised the "Modus Operandi System" developed by Major L. W. Atcherley, Chief Constable of West Yorkshire Constabulary in England, adapting it to the United States. Vollmer thought that every police agency in the country should adopt the system and that the information could be shared with all agencies through centralized centers in each state, which would then be shared with a national system.[12]

An argument against focusing on modus operandi is based on the fact criminals do change their MO, sometimes becoming more sophisticated over time or intentionally altering their criminal actions so that they might avoid detection. Another argument is that crime is based more on opportunity than the planning and deliberate plotting to act a certain way to commit a crime. For example, someone with a propensity to steal items might steal in the different situations they happen to be in, like taking a wallet from a shopping cart one day and then taking a laptop and change from an unlocked car the next day. Thus, if the opportunities vary, the criminal will vary their method. These arguments are valid, but still some criminals commit their crimes in habitual ways and do not think of being caught.

In the 2023 research article Modus Operandi in Sexual Assaults of Female Stranger Does Not Change Over Time, authors Eric Beauregard, Julien Chopin, and Martin Andresen find that offenders do not change their methods as much as previously thought. More interestingly, the authors' literature review concludes that "there is no single theory explaining the change – or lack thereof – in the modus operandi of criminals, let alone individuals who have committed sexual crimes."[13]

Information

Information crucial to the early identification of crime patterns and efficient response to them is contained beyond law enforcement databases. With the emergence of sophisticated artificial language learning models law enforcement will more easily look through its information-rich environment for patterns beyond those collected in drop-box forms on crime reports. Virtually anything captured in computer files and online will be analyze-able. Investigative reports, witness statements, social media posts, open-source intelligence, audio and video recordings, and the basics of crime reports, criminal records, and arrest data can be searched for links and patterns. It is essential to be aware of the plethora of information sources that can help uncover crime patterns as we move toward that future.

Information Examples

From Law Enforcement and Related Agencies: accidents reports, arrest reports, booking reports, calls for service records (911), case histories, citation records, crime reports, criminal histories, field interview reports, gang intelligence, intelligence reports, investigative follow-up reports, juvenile offender information, known offender files, offender data, organized crime intelligence, parole information, parole release notices, police narratives/synopses, premise hazard information, registered sex offender information, stolen/recovered property data, surveillance information, terrorist/extremist threat intelligence, threat assessments, traffic citations, traffic stop data, traffic tickets, victim statements, victim testimony, witness statements, witness testimony

From Professional Peers: bulletins/reports from regional crime analysis, crime analysis meetings, email discussion lists, regional crime analysis networks, regional intelligence meetings, other law enforcement agency information

From Government/Community Entities: census data, citation records, city records, county records, critical infrastructure information, deeds and tax assessment data, demographics data, drug overdose/death information, fire/rescue data, firearm licenses, hunting/fishing licenses, land use information, liquor license information, motor vehicle registration and licensing data, parks information, probation information, professional licensing information, property ownership information, public health data, public housing information, school information, social services information, tax assessment information, street map data, surveillance information

From Businesses: alarm company information, business information, business licensing information, business listings, business open-source information, business websites, critical infrastructure information, pawnshop data, commercial/private security information, telephone records, surveillance information

From the Community Members: anonymous tips, citizen complaint information, community organization information, confidential informant information, neighborhood meetings, neighborhood watch information, online bulletin boards and discussion groups, surveillance information, terrorist/extremist threat information, tips from the public

From Open Sources: government websites, national newspapers, news websites, newscasts, online public records, police magazines/newsletters/journals, police websites, public transformation route information, social media sites, sex offender registries, telephone directories, regional newspapers, websites

Limitations on Researchers

Researchers cannot study every aspect of crime patterns because much of the critical information – such as detailed modus operandi (MO), suspect data, and investigative findings – is restricted to law enforcement. As a result, they often work with delayed or anonymized datasets that limit their ability to identify the same connections officers, investigators, and analysts see in real time. This means researchers have limitations in exploring details that would be useful for understanding a fuller picture of how crimes are linked. To address this, some researchers embed within law enforcement agencies, where they can access more complete data under strict controls. Sometimes crime and intelligence analysts help bridge the gap by working with researchers studying longer-term crime problems.

Exercise

Select a public location where you can observe people engaging in similar activities (coffee shop ordering, library book selection, or parking lot behavior) and spend 30 minutes documenting the behavioral patterns of different individuals performing the same task. Note consistent methods, sequences, preferences, and decision-making patterns then identify which behaviors could potentially link multiple observations to the same person and which details might be missed or inconsistently recorded by a busy observer. This exercise demonstrates the challenges law enforcement faces in systematically capturing detailed modus operandi information while highlighting how behavioral consistency can reveal meaningful patterns even in routine activities.

Notes

1 Fosdick (1915).
2 FBI (n.d.a).
3 FBI (n.d.b).
4 Bureau of Justice Statistics. (2022).
5 Miller (2015, June 30).
6 Snook et al. (2012).
7 Casella (2012).
8 Frith (2025).
9 Ratcliffe and Kikuchi (2019).
10 Dinkelspiel (January 27, 2010).
11 Vollmer (1919, p. 229).
12 Vollmer (1919, pp. 229–274).
13 Beauregard et al. (2022).

Bibliography

Beauregard, E., Chopin, J., & Andresen, M. (2022). Modus operandi in sexual assaults of female strangers does not change over time. *Sexual Abuse: A Journal of Research and Treatment*. Advance online publication. https://doi.org/10.1177/10790632221139174

Bibel, D. (2015). Considerations and cautions regarding NIBRS data. *Justice Research and Policy*, *16*(2), 185–194. https://doi.org/10.1177/1525107115623943

Birks, D., Coleman, A., & Jackson, D. (2020). Unsupervised identification of crime problems from police free-text data. *Crime Science*, *9*, Article 12. https://doi.org/10.1186/s40163-020-00127-4

Bureau of Justice Statistics. (2022). *Criminal victimization, 2021*. U.S. Department of Justice, Office of Justice Programs. https://bjs.ojp.gov/library/publications/criminal-victimization-2021

Casella, S. E. (2012). *A behavioral approach to modus operandi: Incident form completion and its effect on predictive analysis* (Publication No. 25) [Doctoral dissertation, Western Michigan University]. ScholarWorks. https://scholarworks.wmich.edu/dissertations/25

DeLang, M., Taheri, S. A., Hutchison, R., & Hawke, N. (2022). Tackling UCR's missing data problem: A multiple imputation approach. *Journal of Criminal Justice*, *79*, 101882. https://doi.org/10.1016/j.jcrimjus.2022.101882

Dinkelspiel, F. (2010, January 27). *Remembering August Vollmer, the Berkeley police chief who created modern policing*. Berkeleyside. www.berkeleyside.org/2010/01/27/remembering-august-vollmer-the-berkeley-police-chief-who-created-modern-policing

Federal Bureau of Investigation. (n.d.a). *About the Uniform Crime Reporting (UCR) program*. https://ucr.fbi.gov/leoka/leoka-2010/aboutucrmain

Federal Bureau of Investigation. (n.d.b). *Crime data explorer*. U.S. Department of Justice. https://cde.ucr.cjis.gov/LATEST/webapp/#/pages/home

Federal Bureau of Investigation, Criminal Justice Information Services Division. (2021). *National Incident-Based Reporting System user manual (2021.1)*. U.S. Department of Justice. https://bjs.ojp.gov/sites/g/files/xyckuh236/files/sarble/data_common/nibrs-user-manual-2021-1041521.pdf

Fosdick, R. B. (1915). The modus operandi system in the detection of criminals. *Journal of the American Institute of Criminal Law and Criminology*, *6*(4), 560–568. https://doi.org/10.2307/1132736

Frith, M. (2025). The longitudinal concentration of offending among individuals and families. *CrimRxiv*. https://doi.org/10.21428/cb6ab371.bfac7b78

Kaplan, J. (2021). *National Incident-Based Reporting System (NIBRS) data: A practitioner's guide*. https://nibrsbook.com/

Liao, D., Berzofsky, M. E., Heller, D. C., Barrick, K., & DeMichele, M. (2015). *Treatment of missing data in the FBI's National Incident-Based Reporting System: A case study in the Bakken region*. Proceedings of the Survey Research Methods Section, American Statistical Association. www.asasrms.org/Proceedings/y2015/files/234045.pdf

Miller, T. C. (2015, June 30). Why can't the FBI identify serial rapists? *The Atlantic*. www.theatlantic.com/politics/archive/2015/07/vicap-fbi-database/399986/

Osborne, D., & Wernicke, S. (2003). *Introduction to crime analysis: Basic resources for criminal justice practice*. Haworth Press.

Ratcliffe, J. H., & Kikuchi, G. (2019). Harm-focused offender triage and prioritization: A Philadelphia case study. *Policing: An International Journal*, *42*(1), 59–73. https://doi.org/10.1108/pijpsm-08-2018-0118

Snook, B., Luther, K., House, J. A., Bennell, C., & Taylor, P. D. (2012). The violent crime linkage analysis system. *Criminal Justice and Behavior*, *39*(5), 607–619. https://doi.org/10.1177/0093854811435208

Tilley, N. (2013). *Analyzing and responding to repeat offending* (Problem-Solving Tools Series, No. 11). U.S. Department of Justice, Office of Community Oriented Policing Services. https://popcenter.asu.edu/content/analyzing-and-responding-repeat-offending

Vollmer, A. (1919). Revision of the Atcherley modus operandi system. *Journal of the American Institute of Criminal Law and Criminology*, *10*(2), 229–274.

3 The Anatomy of a Crime Pattern

Introduction

This book examines crime patterns the way anatomy texts explain the human body: by naming parts and describing how they work together. A crime pattern is not just offenders, victims, locations, times, or methods in isolation, but a functioning system in which each element shapes and is shaped by the others.

This chapter introduces the basic elements of crime patterns and explains how they interact as a system. Later chapters break these elements into specific *variables* for detailed analysis, and Part Three applies the same framework to particular crime types. Using this "anatomical" perspective, combined with systems thinking, provides a structured way to see how offenders, victims, opportunities, and environments connect to form patterns that can be recognized, tracked, and disrupted.

The Basic Elements

Every crime pattern contains identifiable parts. These parts can be described through variables that help in recognition, linkage, and analysis.

Offender Variables

- Physical description: vague or specific (height, build, clothing, facial features).
- Offender Characteristics: manner of speech, odor unusual gait, habits.
- Forensic evidence: DNA, fingerprints, digital traces, tool marks.
- Lifestyle/employment: routines, occupations, or activities that may influence crime involvement.
- Group affiliation: gang membership, organized networks, co-offenders.

Victim Variables

- Physical description: vague or specific (height, build, clothing, facial features).
- Vulnerabilities: age, disability, isolation, lack of guardianship.
- Lifestyle/employment: activities or roles influencing risk (e.g., prostitutes, executives).
- Victim – offender relationship: stranger, acquaintance, family, intimate partner.

DOI: 10.4324/9781003728733-4

Vehicle Variables

- Type of vehicle (car, truck, motorcycle, bicycle, etc.) and identifiers (color, make/model, license plate, condition, modifications).

Modus Operandi (MO) Variables

(Broken into their own detailed chapters later but listed here for overview.)

- Deception
- Approach and escape
- Entry, search, and exit
- Tools and equipment
- Signature behaviors
- Weapons
- Force and physical trauma
- Knowledge and skills
- Group affiliation
- Travel
- Communication

Location, Time, and Opportunity Variables

- Location: single site or multiple; public versus private; accessibility.
- Time: specific moment, recurring window (e.g., midnight–2 a.m.), seasonal/weekly patterns.
- Conditions: lighting, visibility, presence of guardians, routine activities.
- Opportunity factors: distracted victim, lack of surveillance, low police presence.

Property Variables

- Type of property (cash, goods, vehicles, data, etc.) and condition of property (stolen, damaged, destroyed).
- Illicit commodities (drugs, weapons, contraband), how they flow (move across neighborhoods, jurisdictions, or borders), and their markets (resale, barter, online markets).
- Concealment method (disguising, hiding, etc.).

Crime Type Variables

- Primary crime type (burglary, robbery, fraud, etc.), secondary crimes (related or supporting crimes such as car theft to support robberies), specialization versus diversification (offenders may repeat one type or mix offenses).

About Crime Patterns

All crime patterns have at least one offender who commits the crimes.[1]

Do not assume there is only one offender without supporting evidence such as victim or witness accounts or surveillance footage. If there are witnesses of any sort, you will have a physical description. This may be very vague or extremely specific. The physical description variables in this book can also be applied to victims to determine whether there are similarities in appearance. Offender characteristics like a manner of speech or an unusual gait can be important to note. Forensic evidence offers scientific clues for identifying the offender(s).

All crime patterns have a victim. Sometimes, there are multiple victims in one crime incident. Victim vulnerabilities may play an important role in a crime pattern, such as those of being elderly, handicapped, or living in an isolated area. Non-person victims, like businesses or community areas, also experience vulnerabilities, such as robberies at banks (where individuals walk in without barriers) or drug dealing in public parks (where there may be no barriers to the activity).

The lifestyle and employment of both offender and victim may contribute valuable information for recognizing essential aspects of the crime pattern. For example, a prostitute may be targeted for sexual violence or a business executive may be targeted for business email compromise.

The victim-offender relationship is vital to note, although most crime pattern analysis focuses on stranger-on-stranger crime, particularly in property and street crimes.

The vehicle description of the vehicle used by an offender before, during, or after a crime can be important information for linking crimes or apprehending the offender.

The offender's modus operandi offers clues to linking the crimes to a real-life pattern. In this book, those aspects are broken down into specific chapters: deception; approach and escape; entry, search, and exit; tools and equipment; signature behaviors; weapons; force and physical trauma; knowledge and skills; group affiliation; travel; and communication. The factors that apply will depend on the type of crime(s) involved in the pattern and the behavioral choices made by a particular offender. These variables primarily help link crimes when the offender is unknown.

All crimes in a pattern occur at a location, sometimes more than one, in time, sometimes within a time range, and under conditions. The opportunity to commit the crimes must be present. For example, a distracted woman may have her purse snatched on an empty street, or a lonely person may fall prey to an internet romance scam. The purse snatcher saw the opportunity afforded to them because the woman was not paying attention, and no one was around. The internet scammer preys on the opportunity the lonely victim offers when they want love enough to overlook suspicious requests for money.

Many crime patterns involve property that is stolen. Sometimes, the pattern involves damaged or destroyed property, such as in vandalism or arson. Some crime patterns involve illicit goods that are moved across jurisdictions or internationally (commodity flow). Markets for stolen property and illicit goods commonly factor into crime patterns, particularly theft and organized crime. Concealment methods may also share similarities in a pattern of crime.

The specific crimes in a crime pattern have their own modus operandi variables. There are 27 chapters on a variety of crimes in this book that delve into aspects of the variables specific to the crime chapter.

In general, it is assumed the crime pattern will contain one primary type of crime, but serial offenders can commit a variety of crimes even when they have a specialty. For example, a burglar may also steal in ways that don't involve breaking into a building, and a robber may steal cars to commit their crimes separate from the robbery crimes.

Just like the human body with its various anatomical parts, a specific crime pattern can be viewed as one "system" that contains a number of other parts that make it whole.

Systems Thinking in Crime Patterns

A crime pattern can be thought of as a complex system, similar to how the human body is composed of interrelated organs and functions. Each element (offender, victim, location, modus operandi, timing, property, opportunity) is not isolated but interdependent. The pattern only exists when these parts interact.

Example: A robbery pattern is not defined just by the offender but by how the offender selects victims, the locations chosen, the weapon used, and the timing. Each element interacts to create a repeatable structure.

Systems thinking emphasizes flows:

- Inputs: offender motivation, target vulnerabilities, environmental opportunities.
- Processes: offender decision-making, planning, preparation, and execution.
- Outputs: completed crime incidents, patterns of victimization, forensic traces, property movement.

Like a biological system, crime patterns have "feedback loops" where each completed crime may shape the offender's future actions (e.g., success reinforcing the method, failure leading to adaptation and modified method).

Systems thinking requires understanding interconnectedness, how one change in a variable affects the whole:

- A change in victim availability (e.g., reduced nightlife during a curfew) shifts offender opportunity recognition.
- Altering police visibility (patrols, surveillance) influences offender tactics or locations.
- Market demand for stolen goods often fuels the offender's choice of property crimes.

Thus, no element can be studied in isolation; each is part of a dynamic network.

Criminal systems are adaptive based on feedback:

- Positive feedback loops: An offender's successful robbery reinforces the same time/place/method, leading to repetition.
- Negative feedback loops: Increased law enforcement or community reporting may disrupt patterns, forcing offenders to shift tactics or locations.

This mirrors living systems where survival depends on adjusting to the environment.

Just as the human body contains circulatory, respiratory, and nervous systems, a crime pattern contains subsystems:

- Offender system: motivation, skills, group affiliation, travel, concealment.
- Victim system: vulnerabilities, routines, lifestyle.
- Environmental system: locations, timing, situational opportunities.
- Transactional system: stolen goods, intermediaries, financial activities.

Together, these subsystems create the holistic pattern that may be recognized.

A key principle in systems thinking is emergence, seeing that the whole is more than the sum of its parts. A single burglary is not a crime pattern. But repeated burglaries, linked by offender methods, victim type, or location, reveal an emergent structure: the pattern.

Defining system boundaries is also critical: Is the "system" just one neighborhood, one gang, or a national commodity smuggling network? Boundaries determine how analysts interpret data and what interventions are possible.

Using a systems perspective allows officers, analysts, and investigators to:

- Recognize leverage points – strategic intervention points where small changes can produce significant effects across the entire system (e.g., disrupting stolen property markets may collapse a burglary pattern).

- See interdependencies (e.g., victim lifestyle and offender travel patterns overlap at specific times/places).
- Anticipate adaptation (patterns evolve when enforcement pressure changes).

Applying systems thinking challenges the paradigm of a narrow focus on single incidents and instead equips law enforcement to disrupt or dismantle "systems" of crime. The whole point of identifying a crime series or larger crime pattern is to find ways to do that. This book provides the articulated foundation of elements and variables needed in order to more fully understand and address specific crime systems.

Addressing Limitations and Ethical Considerations in Pattern Recognition

The Limitations of Pattern Recognition

Crime pattern recognition in policing is an imperfect science that requires careful application and constant scrutiny. While identifying behavioral consistencies across crimes can provide valuable investigative leads, investigators and analysts must recognize that correlation does not equal causation, and similar patterns do not automatically indicate the same offender. The human tendency to see patterns where none exist (apophenia) can lead investigators to force connections between unrelated crimes, potentially misdirecting resources and even implicating innocent individuals. Every pattern identification should be treated as a hypothesis requiring verification through additional evidence rather than as definitive proof of linkage.

Error Rates and False Connections

Research in behavioral linkage analysis noted significant error rates even when using sophisticated statistical methods. These errors occur in two directions: false positives, where unrelated crimes are incorrectly linked, and false negatives, where related crimes are missed. Factors contributing to these errors include incomplete data, offender behavioral changes over time, copycat crimes, and the prevalence of common criminal behaviors that appear similar but stem from different sources. Geographic proximity, similar victim types, or matching temporal patterns might reflect environmental opportunities rather than a serial offender. It is important to weight multiple variables together and seek corroborating evidence beyond behavioral similarities.

Ethical Considerations in Pattern Analysis

The systematic analysis of crime patterns raises important ethical questions about surveillance, privacy, and presumption of innocence. Pattern recognition can inadvertently lead to demographic profiling when certain communities or populations appear repeatedly in data. This risk is particularly acute when patterns correlate with race, ethnicity, socioeconomic status, or mental health conditions. Remember to distinguish between environmental factors that create crime opportunities and assumptions about group criminality. Additionally, the increasing use of algorithmic pattern detection introduces concerns about transparency and accountability. Human oversight remains essential to contextualize patterns and prevent automated bias from directing investigative resources.

Practical Safeguards

To minimize errors and ethical concerns, agencies should implement several safeguards. First, pattern identification should trigger further investigation, not immediate arrest or prosecution. Second, practitioners should document their reasoning, including alternative explanations for observed patterns. Third, regular audits should examine both successful and failed linkages to improve methodology. Fourth, training should emphasize the probabilistic nature of behavioral analysis and the dangers of confirmation bias. Finally, multidisciplinary review teams can provide crucial oversight, ensuring that pattern recognition enhances rather than replaces traditional investigative methods.

Exercise

Break this crime series into system parts:

> Over the course of six weeks, five late-night armed robberies take place at gas stations located along a major highway. In each case, a male offender wearing a ski mask enters between midnight and 2 a.m., displays a small handgun, and demands cash from the clerk. He usually takes cash and cartons of cigarettes before fleeing in a dark-colored sedan, which is briefly captured on surveillance footage. The victims in all incidents are lone employees, typically young males working overnight shifts. Each targeted location is a 24-hour gas station positioned close to a highway exit, with low police presence during those hours. After the third robbery, clerks began hiding larger bills, resulting in smaller gains in the last two incidents.

Consider the offender system (skills, tools, travel, and methods), the victim system (vulnerabilities, routines, and roles), and the environmental system (locations, timing, and opportunities). Think about the transactional system (property stolen and how it may be used or sold) and identify feedback loops (e.g., how both offenders and victims adapt after each event). Does this crime series represent only the highway corridor, or could it extend into nearby towns or even across jurisdictions? What would happen to this pattern if gas stations installed time-locked safes?
Optional: Make a chart or diagram for the anatomy of this crime pattern.

Critical Thinking Guidance

Just as the human body is made up of organs that only function properly when working together, the anatomy of a crime pattern is more than a list of parts. Offenders, victims, locations, times, and methods are like interrelated organs that form a larger system. Each part gains meaning through its connection to the others: an offender's choice of victim depends on opportunity, which is shaped by environment and routine, while the offender's modus operandi both influences and adapts to those conditions. A true crime pattern emerges only when these parts consistently interact over time, creating feedback that reinforces or alters the offender's behavior. Thinking in terms of anatomy helps us name and describe the parts, while systems thinking can help us work with the reality that the whole pattern is greater than the sum of those parts.

Note

1 Since in frontline policing the offender is often referred to as the suspect, this book occasionally uses the terms interchangeably.

Bibliography

Amissah, M., Gannon, T., & Monat, J. (2020). What is systems thinking? Expert perspectives from the WPI Systems Thinking Colloquium of October 2nd, 2019. *Systems*, *8*(1), Article 6. https://doi.org/10.3390/systems8010006

Bennell, C., & Canter, D. V. (2002). Linking commercial burglaries by modus operandi: Tests using regression and ROC analysis. *Science & Justice*, *42*(3), 153–164.

Cabrera, D., & Cabrera, L. (2023). Developing personal mastery in systems thinking. *Journal of Systems Thinking 3*(1), 1–39. https://doi.org/10.54120/jost.0000043

Clark, R. V., & Eck, J. E. (2016). *Crime analysis for problem solvers in 60 small steps.* Office of Community Oriented Policing Services. https://portal.cops.usdoj.gov/resourcecenter/content.ashx/cops-w0047-pub.pdf

Eck, J. E. (2003). Police problems: The complexity of problem theory, research and evaluation. In J. Knutsson (Ed.), *Problem-oriented policing: From innovation to mainstream* (pp. 79–113). Criminal Justice Press.

Snook, B., Cullen, R. M., Bennell, C., Taylor, P. J., & Gendreau, P. (2008). The criminal profiling illusion: What's behind the smoke and mirrors? *Criminal Justice and Behavior*, *35*(10), 1257–1276.

Taylor, S., Calvo-Amodio, J., & Well, J. (2020). A method for measuring systems thinking learning. *Systems*, *8*(2), Article 11. https://doi.org/10.3390/systems8020011

Tilley, N. (2013). *Analyzing and responding to repeat offending* (Problem-Solving Tools Series No. 11). Problem-Oriented Guides for Police Series. Office of Community Oriented Policing Services, U.S. Department of Justice. https://popcenter.asu.edu/content/analyzing-and-responding-repeat-offending

Woodhams, J., & Toye, K. (2007). An empirical test of the assumptions of case linkage and offender profiling with serial commercial robberies. *Psychology, Public Policy, and Law*, *13*(1), 59–85.

4 Linking Crimes

Introduction

We link crimes to determine whether separate offenses were committed by the same offender or group, with no single universal method for doing it. In practice, law enforcement may use informal observation, structured analysis, or a combination of both, while academic research uses formalized approaches, such as comparative case linkage or formal case linkage. Commercial software may also incorporate these methods through built-in algorithms, scoring systems, or predictive analytics. Whatever the approach, effective case linkage depends on a detailed awareness of the elements and variables described in this book, since these form the foundation for recognizing meaningful similarities and differences between cases.

Comparative Case Linkage: Structured Pattern Analysis

Comparative case linkage systematizes the pattern recognition process by establishing uniform comparison points across multiple cases. Rather than relying on chance observation, this approach examines every case using the same analytical framework.

The method focuses on several categories of variables. Crime type, date, time, location, target information, and basic modus operandi details are often included.

Temporal (time) variables may include frequency and rhythmic elements that might indicate when offenders are most likely to act. A burglar who consistently strikes during the first week of each month demonstrates temporal consistency that extends beyond simple scheduling coincidences.

Location may be a spot on a map, but geographic patterns encompass crime locations and their spatial relationships. Analysis might reveal that an offender operates within specific distance parameters from anchor points,[1] follows particular travel routes, or maintains buffer zones[2] around certain areas. These patterns often reflect the offender's familiarity with geographic areas and personal movement habits.

Methodological patterns involve breaking down criminal techniques into component elements. Two burglaries involving crowbar entry might seem similar on the surface, but detailed analysis might reveal differences in search efforts or tool usage that distinguish between offenders or link cases more definitively.

Target selection patterns examine both what offenders choose and what they avoid. This analysis often requires looking beyond successful crimes to include attempted offenses or situations where offenders approached but didn't complete crimes.

A version of comparative case linkage (also called comparative case analysis) is used by many who are tasked with linking crimes, but they may not be calling it that.

DOI: 10.4324/9781003728733-5

Formal Case Linkage: Quantitative Connection Assessment

Formal case linkage protocols provide structured methods for evaluating the strength of potential connections between crimes. This approach uses standardized documentation and analysis techniques to move beyond subjective assessment toward measurable evaluation.

The process begins with systematic case coding. Criminal behaviors are broken down into specific, measurable variables that can be consistently recorded across different cases and analysts. A robbery might be coded across variables including approach method, weapon handling, verbal behavior patterns, victim interaction styles, and departure procedures.

Similarity assessment examines degrees of correspondence across multiple variables simultaneously. This analysis goes beyond simple matching to evaluate how closely cases align across different behavioral dimensions. Two cases might share some characteristics while differing in others, requiring careful evaluation of overall similarity patterns.

Variable weighting[3] accounts for the fact that different behaviors carry different significance for linkage purposes. Common behaviors shared by many offenders provide less linking value than rare behaviors displayed by few individuals. Formal protocols incorporate these differences by assigning weights based on behavior frequency within the relevant offender population.

Threshold determination[4] establishes the level of similarity required to conclude that cases are linked. These thresholds balance the risks of false connections against the possibility of missing genuine links. Different crime types and investigative contexts may require different threshold levels.

The formal approach also incorporates negative evidence, significant differences between cases that might argue against linkage. Analysis weighs both similarities and differences to reach conclusions about case connections.

Police Versus Research Perspective

Police Perspective: Practical Pattern-Finding

For officer, investigators, and analysts working in policing agencies case linkage is not about proving scientific certainty but about spotting workable patterns. Police deal with incomplete reports, time pressure, and shifting priorities, so the value of linkage lies in identifying similarities that may connect cases, guide interviews, or direct surveillance resources. Even when patterns are uncertain, they can still provide leads worth pursuing. In this sense, linkage analysis functions as an investigative aid, not as evidence intended to withstand courtroom or scientific scrutiny.

Research Perspective: Scientific Reliability

Academic researchers approach linkage differently, emphasizing measurable accuracy, error rates, and standardized methods. The goal is to determine whether similarities between cases reflect true behavioral consistency or random coincidence. Scientific protocols require structured coding, statistical weighting, and validated thresholds to minimize false linkages. While this level of rigor strengthens reliability, it is often removed from the practical realities of everyday policing.

Three Methods

In law enforcement, there are no standardized terms or universally accepted processes for linking crimes into patterns using modus operandi (MO) data. As a result, the methods used by law enforcement can vary widely. Three common approaches reflect different forms of reasoning: inductive, deductive, and abductive.

Inductive Reasoning (From Cases to Patterns)

One approach begins with a specific type of crime, such as robbery or burglary, and searches for similarities across incidents. Investigators compare characteristics (like method of entry, weapon used, victim type) across multiple events to infer whether they may be connected. This process moves from particular observations toward broader generalizations, gradually building the possibility of a crime pattern or series.

Deductive Reasoning (From Offender to Cases)

Another approach starts with a known or suspected offender. Once the individual is identified and their behavioral traits or MO are established, investigators use that general knowledge to narrow down which unsolved crimes might be attributed to them. Deduction works from the general to the specific, applying what is already known about the offender to test possible links to specific cases.

Abductive Reasoning (From Hypothesis to Exploration)

A third, less frequently documented method begins with a hypothesis or exploratory question and then searches for possible supporting evidence. Abduction starts with an incomplete idea or "best guess" and seeks the most plausible explanation. For example, an analyst might hypothesize that robberies of delivery drivers are occurring within their jurisdiction. They could test this idea by searching databases for terms such as delivery, food, pizza, or related words within robbery reports. Unlike induction or deduction, this is a proactive, exploratory method that emphasizes generating and testing hypotheses when patterns are not immediately apparent.

Another Reasoning Method: Retroduction (From Observed Effects to Underlying Causes)

Retroduction is a reasoning method that asks: "What underlying mechanism or condition must exist for this to happen?" While related to abductive reasoning, retroduction focuses specifically on identifying the deeper structures or causes that generate crime patterns, moving beyond the surface-level similarities examined through induction, deduction, or standard abductive approaches.[5]

Example in practice: If a series of robberies occurs at gas stations near highway exits, induction might notice the pattern of location, and abduction might hypothesize offender travel routes. Retroduction goes further by reasoning that the offender likely lives or works along that highway corridor because such a pattern requires familiarity and accessibility.

Role in crime linkage: Retroduction helps analysts avoid stopping at surface similarities and instead consider what social, geographic, or situational conditions make a series possible. It is especially useful in linking crimes across jurisdictions, where underlying drivers (drug markets, offender mobility, logistics) are less obvious from single incidents.

Distinction:

Induction: builds generalizations from observed cases.
Deduction: applies general knowledge about an offender to specific cases.

Abduction: generates hypotheses to test for plausibility.
Retroduction: seeks the hidden mechanisms or causes that explain why the pattern exists at all.

Practical Application

Part Two of this book provides tools for applying abductive reasoning in practice. By using suggested phrases, keywords, or conceptual prompts, analysts and investigators can explore their data for hidden or emerging patterns that may not yet be recognized. Each chapter in this section ends with an example case and a list of possible query terms. These terms are primarily designed to illustrate deductive reasoning – showing how known offender characteristics can be used to identify related crimes – but they can also support abductive reasoning when used more broadly to test hypotheses or explore new possibilities in the data.

Anomalies

An anomaly is something unusual or out of place that doesn't fit the normal pattern of a crime. Spotting an anomaly can help in linking crimes together much faster. For example, if a burglar always leaves a certain mark at the scene, uses an uncommon tool to break in, or steals the same unusual item, that detail stands out. Even if two crimes happen in different neighborhoods, the same odd detail can connect them. This means that paying attention to small, unusual details can be just as important as looking at the bigger picture. Recognizing an anomaly early helps identify pattern sooner, link cases that might otherwise look unrelated, and focus their efforts on stopping the offender before more crimes happen.

Indicators

Some of the 27 specific crime categories included in Part Three of this book do not generate crime reports and thus they cannot be examined for links. These criminal activities operate below the threshold of formal reporting for extended periods before (or ever) generating police reports. Organized criminal enterprises, ongoing fraud schemes, and developing drug operations may leave traces in various data systems before being detected through traditional crime reporting. Crime indicators are included in the chapters involving crimes that often do not generate enough police reports to note a pattern. These crime series may also cover wide geographic areas that do not easily allow for crime report comparison.

Crime indicators provide methods for recognizing and identifying patterns that suggest criminal activity may be occurring or developing. Indicators can appear in financial records, communication networks, transportation systems, or business activities rather than traditional crime data.

Financial indicators include transaction patterns that don't align with legitimate business activities, fund movements that follow unusual routes, or discrepancies between apparent income and expenditure patterns. Analysis requires distinguishing between unusual but legitimate financial activity and potential criminal enterprise indicators.

Communication indicators encompass patterns in phone usage, travel coordination, meeting arrangements, or network structures that might suggest criminal organization. Analysis often focuses on communication patterns and network relationships rather than content.

Geographic indicators include transportation patterns, facility usage, or business clustering that might facilitate criminal operations. Understanding these patterns requires knowledge of both legitimate business operations and the ways criminal enterprises might mimic or exploit legitimate activities.

Effective indicator analysis requires understanding the base rates of various activities in legitimate contexts to distinguish between normal variation and potential criminal activity indicators.

Crime Script Analysis: Process-Based Examination

Crime script analysis examines criminal activity as multi-stage processes rather than isolated incidents. This approach views crimes as sequences of actions that unfold over time, with each stage presenting distinct analytical opportunities. Criminology views crime script analysis as a practical framework that helps understand the process of offending and identify intervention points for prevention. In Part Three of this book, crimes by type are presented using generalized crime script analysis to illustrate how readers may potentially link crimes by looking beyond the incidents.

This framework divides criminal activity into preparation, execution, and aftermath phases. Each phase contains multiple steps that reveal different aspects of offender behavior and thinking patterns.

Preparation scripts detail how offenders plan and organize their criminal activities. This includes target selection processes, tool acquisition, surveillance methods, risk assessment procedures, and contingency planning. Analysis of preparation scripts often reveals similarities in thinking patterns and approach strategies that might not be apparent from examining only the crime execution phase.

Execution scripts break down the actual commission of crimes into sequential actions. This includes approach methods, victim or target interaction, property acquisition procedures, and exit strategies. The sequence and timing of actions often reveal behavioral consistencies that persist even when surface details vary.

Aftermath scripts examine post-crime behaviors including evidence disposal, benefit realization, and risk management activities. These behaviors frequently provide may reveal connections between cases through shared approaches to post-crime challenges.

Script analysis identifies both functional elements that serve practical crime commission purposes and expressive elements that fulfill psychological needs. Expressive elements often prove particularly valuable for linkage analysis because they reflect deeper behavioral patterns that tend to remain consistent across incidents. Examples of expressive elements displayed across multiple crimes include: using the same verbal threat each time, offering a cigarette to the victim, and removing a trophy from the scene.

Challenges in Linking Crimes

There are a number of challenges to linking crimes by the elements and variables provided in this book.

Limited Data: The availability and accessibility of relevant data can be a significant challenge. Serial crimes and other crime patterns are often spread across different jurisdictions, and the data related to these crimes are stored in disparate databases or not adequately shared between agencies. Limited data hinder the recognition and identification of patterns.

Data Quality and Consistency: Even when data are available, it suffers from quality and consistency issues. Incomplete or inaccurate data can lead to false patterns or make it difficult to identify genuine connections between crimes. Inconsistent data formats, terminology, and classification systems across different databases can also complicate the analysis.

Complex Patterns: Serial criminals can exhibit complex patterns that are difficult to detect or analyze. They may and do change their methods to commit crimes, making it harder to link them together.

Data Volume and Scale: The sheer volume of data generated by different sources, including crime reports, witness statements, CCTV footage, social media, and forensic evidence, is overwhelming. Processing and analyzing large datasets in a timely manner pose significant computational and resource challenges. Yet, these sources contain valuable cues for linking crimes.

Bias: Officers, investigators, and analysts have preconceived notions or biases that can affect how they collect and interpret the data. For example, they may overlook some information. They may focus too much on certain types of crimes or locations and miss patterns in other areas. We all have biases. The only way to transcend them is to become more aware of them.

Limited resources: Law enforcement agencies often do not have the resources to collect and analyze all the data they need. This could be due to budget constraints, a shortage of personnel, or other logistical issues. It takes time to gather detailed information about a crime occurrence, and police officers are often short of time in an urban high-crime area.

Lack of Standardized Protocols: Law enforcement agencies often do not have standardized protocols or frameworks for identifying and analyzing serial and other crime patterns. There may be no standard protocols for collecting the information needed to do so. The absence of clear guidelines can lead to inconsistencies in approaches and make it challenging to compare and share information effectively.

Multidimensional Data Analysis: Patterned crimes involve multiple dimensions, such as time, location, modus operandi, and offender/victim characteristics. Analyzing and correlating these different aspects to identify patterns sometimes requires sophisticated analytical techniques and tools. Law enforcement agencies may lack the necessary staff, expertise, tools, and resources for complex data analysis.

Privacy and Legal Considerations: Personal data and privacy concerns can pose challenges when analyzing crime patterns. Striking a balance between privacy protection and effective pattern detection is crucial but challenging.

Lack of Interagency Collaboration: Crime patterns often span multiple jurisdictions, requiring collaboration between different law enforcement agencies. However, interagency collaboration is difficult due to jurisdictional boundaries, differences in systems and protocols, and information-sharing barriers. Overcoming these challenges and fostering effective collaboration are crucial for identifying and tracking serial crime patterns.

Real-time Detection: Timeliness is imperative in detecting serial crime patterns to enable proactive law enforcement actions. The main reason to identify a serial criminal is to end the crime series. Developing real-time monitoring and detection systems that can process and analyze incoming data in near real-time is a technological and operational challenge.

Exercise: Script Analysis Practice

Choose a routine activity that someone in your household performs regularly (making coffee, walking the dog, or getting ready for work) and observe it on three different occasions. Break down the activity into preparation, execution, and aftermath phases as described in crime script analysis. Document which steps remain consistent across all observations (functional elements needed to complete the task) versus which steps vary or seem unnecessary but still occur (expressive elements that reflect personal preferences). Consider how an investigator might use these consistent behavioral scripts to identify when the same person performed similar activities in different locations or contexts.

If you work in a law enforcement agency, examine a crime and identify preparation, execution, and aftermath phases as described in crime script analysis.

Critical Thinking Guidance

In evaluating crime linkage, base rates[6] are critical: behaviors that occur frequently across cases provide limited evidentiary value, while rare or distinctive behaviors offer stronger linking potential. For example, if many crime reports describe a suspect with black hoodie, a black hoodie in crime reports does not mean the crimes are linked – it becomes a less valuable variable to search for when linking crimes through data analysis. A few urban crime reports describing a bow and arrow used as a weapon would be quite rare and thus more likely linked.

Notes

1 The central location that is significant to an offender's activities, such as their home, workplace, or another familiar site, from which they travel to commit crimes.
2 The area immediately surrounding an offender's anchor point where they avoid committing crimes to reduce the risk of being recognized or caught.
3 Giving more or less importance to certain factors (variables) when analyzing data, so that the most relevant ones have a stronger influence on the results.
4 Setting a cutoff point or limit that decides when something is important enough to be noticed, included, or acted on in an analysis.
5 Jang et al. (2025).
6 The frequency or percentage of mistakes that occur in a process, test, or analysis.

Bibliography

Bruce, C. (2024, March). *Identifying crime patterns: Inductive and deductive approaches* [Webinar transcript]. International Association of Crime Analysts.
Burrell, A., & Bull, R. (2011). A preliminary examination of crime analysts' views and experiences of comparative case analysis. *International Journal of Police Science & Management, 13*(1), 2–15. https://doi.org/10.1350/ijps.2011.13.1.212
Center on PBIS. (2022). *Tier 3 brief functional behavior assessment (FBA) guide*. Center on PBIS, University of Oregon. www.pbis.org
Chainey, S., & Berbotto, A. A. (2021). A structured methodical process for populating a crime script of organized crime activity using OSINT. *Trends in Organized Crime, 25*(3), 272–300. https://doi.org/10.1007/s12117-021-09428-9
Davies, K., & Woodhams, J. (2019). The practice of crime linkage: A review of the literature. *Journal of Investigative Psychology and Offender Profiling, 16*(3), 169–200. https://doi.org/10.1002/jip.1531
Dehghanniri, H., & Borrion, H. (2019). Crime scripting: A systematic review. *European Journal of Criminology, 17*(5), 655–673. https://doi.org/10.1177/1477370819850943
Halford, E. (2023). 'Two sides of the same coin' – A proposed model for delivering a whole system serial crime reduction plan. *Policing: A Journal of Policy and Practice, 17*(2), paad026. https://doi.org/10.1093/police/paad026
Jang, M., Sebire, J., & Stubbs, G. (2025). Detective reasoning in criminal investigation: Integrating abduction, retroduction, deduction, and induction into the national decision model (NDM). *International Journal of Police Science & Management*. Advance online publication. https://doi.org/10.1177/14613557251344042
Johnston, J. M. (1996). Distinguishing between applied research and practice. *The Behavior Analyst, 19*(1), 35–47. https://doi.org/10.1007/bf03392737
King-Parker, M., Bartels, R. M., Onwuegbusi, T., & Dickinson, P. (2024). Examining burglary scripts in community-based samples. *Deviant Behavior, 45*(11), 1584–1609. https://doi.org/10.1080/01639625.2024.2315109
Porter, M. D. (2016). A statistical approach to crime linkage. *The American Statistician, 70*(2), 152–165. https://doi.org/10.1080/00031305.2015.1123185
Tuominen, N. (2025, March 12). Critical thinking for intelligence analysts & police officers: A path to improved criminal justice. *Journal of Applied Operational Intelligence, 1*(1), 63–72. https://doi.org/10.5750/jaoi.v1i1.2263

Tonkin, M., Woodhams, J., Bull, R., & Bond, J. W. (2012). Behavioural case linkage with solved and unsolved crimes. *Forensic Science International*, *222*(1–3), 146–153. https://doi.org/10.1016/j.forsciint.2012.05.017

Wieten, G. M., Bex, F. J., Prakken, H., & Renooij, S. (2020). Deductive and abductive reasoning with causal and evidential information. In H. Prakken, S. Bistarelli, F. Santini, & C. Taticchi (Eds.), *Computational models of argument: Proceedings of COMMA 2020* (Frontiers in Artificial Intelligence and Applications, Vol. 326, pp. 383–394). IOS Press. https://doi.org/10.3233/FAIA200522

5 Dependent Criminological Theories

Introduction

Criminological theories assume we already possess a comprehensive understanding of what constitutes meaningful crime pattern elements and variables, when in fact no such systematic foundation exists. This chapter examines how Crime Pattern Theory, Environmental Criminology, Rational Choice Theory, and Routine Activity Theory depend on modus operandi (MO) data and how incomplete information can undermine their effectiveness.

By expanding understanding of both the potential applications and scope of these frameworks, academics and practitioners can better appreciate why establishing foundational knowledge of crime pattern elements and variables is essential to the field's scientific and operational validity.

Crime Pattern Theory

Although this book examines crime patterns, its focus on cataloging specific elements and variables differs from Crime Pattern Theory's emphasis on spatial and temporal clustering of criminal events.[1]

Crime Pattern Theory asserts that criminal events cluster in predictable patterns based on offenders' activity spaces and awareness of opportunities. Activity spaces refer to the geographic areas within which an individual conducts their regular activities (such as home, work, school, shopping, leisure, and social interactions). These areas form a mental map or routine path network that significantly influences where crimes are likely to occur, especially for offenders.

Key Elements of Activity Space

Nodes: These are the central locations of routine activities such as home, work, gym, favorite hangout spots.

Paths: The routes people take between these nodes. Offenders often become familiar with these paths and may identify suitable targets along them.

Edges: The perceived boundaries of an individual's activity space. Crime is less likely to occur outside of these boundaries due to unfamiliarity and increased risk.

This theory requires detailed MO data, such as offender movements, accurate time frames and locations, target choices, and victim-offender interactions, to construct reliable patterns. Incomplete MO data limit understanding offender behavior and reduce the accuracy

DOI: 10.4324/9781003728733-6

of predictive analytics and preventative strategies, often allowing ongoing crime patterns to remain undetected.

Example: ATM Robbery Series

Complete MO Data Scenario

A series of ATM robberies occurred consistently during late-night hours along main commuter routes. Detailed MO data (including robbery times, precise ATM locations, offender approach methods, and victim selection patterns) enable analysts to identify the offenders' "activity nodes" (key locations like nearby gas stations, convenience stores, or transit stops). Police deploy targeted patrols around these nodes, disrupt the offenders' travel paths, and successfully apprehended the suspects.

Incomplete MO Data Scenario

Without detailed MO information (timing, precise locations, offender travel paths), police broadly disperse resources citywide or merely around known ATM locations without understanding specific offender movements. Such generalized responses miss the actual offender activity nodes and paths, enabling continued crime.

Application of Crime Pattern Theory

Crime Pattern Theory emphasizes the offenders' routine movements between activity nodes (homes, workplaces, recreational spots) and crime targets. Its utility lies in recognizing offenders' routines, predicting where and when they might strike next based on known MO details. Accurate MO details help analysts map these routines and identify specific pathways for intervention, while incomplete data obscures these patterns, leaving critical nodes unidentified and interventions unfocused.

Environmental Criminology

Environmental criminology studies how physical and social environments facilitate crime occurrence and criminal behavior.[2] It can be considered a subset of Crime Pattern Theory. In environmental criminology, pattern recognition is the outcome of examining spatial-temporal (space and time) clusters, location characteristics, and environmental factors that facilitate crime. Accurate MO data, including precise locations, timing, offender methods, and victim selection, are critical to mapping crime hotspots and identifying environmental influences. Incomplete MO data related to locations and location characteristics reduce the ability to pinpoint environmental risk factors. Decisions based on inadequate data lead to imprecise crime prevention strategies and inefficient resource allocation.

Example: Residential Burglary Hotspots

Complete MO Data Scenario

Police use precise MO details such as exact entry points (rear windows), times of incidents (weekday afternoons), offender approaches (back alleys), and victim selection (houses near highways), to identify and predict burglary hotspots. Officers increased targeted patrols, and city officials improved lighting and installed security cameras in the identified areas, significantly reducing burglary incidents.

Incomplete MO Data Scenario

Conversely, burglary reports lack critical details such as entry points, offender methods, or precise timing, and hotspot analysis becomes generalized. Without knowing the burglars' preferred approach routes or victim selection criteria, police allocate resources broadly across large residential areas, diluting their effectiveness and failing to prevent future incidents efficiently.

Application of Environmental Criminology

Environmental Criminology posits that crime occurs where motivated offenders find attractive targets in settings lacking adequate security or surveillance. In the burglary scenario, accurate MO data (entry points, timing, offender routes) allows analysts to identify environmental vulnerabilities such as easily accessible back alleys, poorly secured rear windows, and proximity to escape routes (highways). Recognizing these environmental facilitators helps law enforcement and community stakeholders directly intervene by altering environmental characteristics (installing lights, security cameras, physical barriers) to disrupt offender activity. Conversely, incomplete data obscure these critical environmental factors, preventing precise, effective preventive measures.

Rational Choice Theory

Rational Choice Theory posits that offenders weigh risks, efforts, costs, benefits, and rewards before committing crimes. Detailed MO data about offender techniques, planning levels, victim selection, and target vulnerabilities significantly enhance the analysis of decision-making processes. Incomplete MO data weaken the assessment of offenders' perceived risks and benefits, hindering the development of effective deterrent strategies. Detailed MO data help determine the evolution and adaptation in crime patterns as offenders learn and adjust methods.

Example: Carjacking in Urban Settings

Complete MO Data Scenario

Detailed MO data indicate offenders deliberately targeted drivers who stopped at specific intersections late at night, typically choosing isolated locations with poor lighting. Understanding these rational offender choices enables law enforcement to strategically station patrols at high-risk intersections, enhance lighting, and use visible deterrents to disrupt offender decisions.

Incomplete MO Data Scenario

Lacking specific details about offenders' target locations, timing, or victim characteristics, law enforcement might broadly patrol urban areas without affecting the offenders' rational assessment of specific intersections as low-risk targets.

Application of Rational Choice Theory

Rational Choice Theory hinges on understanding offender decision-making processes, the careful weighing of risks, efforts, and benefits. Detailed MO information allows Rational Choice Theory to be effectively applied, providing insights into offenders' calculated evaluations of crime opportunities. Missing or incomplete data hamper efforts to disrupt offender decisions and reduce criminal behavior through targeted interventions.

Routine Activity Theory

Routine Activity Theory emphasizes the convergence of motivated offenders, suitable targets, and lack of capable guardianship.[3] It demands comprehensive MO details about target vulnerabilities, offender methods, guardian presence, and offender-target intersections. Missing or incomplete MO data restricts the identification of specific vulnerabilities and opportunities, impairing crime prevention measures and law enforcement responsiveness.

Example: Bike Thefts on College Campuses

Complete MO Data Scenario

Detailed campus crime data showed bike thefts consistently occurred in locations lacking surveillance, mostly during class hours when students were predictably occupied elsewhere. Accurate MO data (exact timing, precise locations, victim behavior) allowed campuses to increase surveillance, install additional bike locks, and encourage students to park bikes in secure locations, dramatically reducing thefts.

Incomplete MO Data Scenario

Without specific timing and location data, campuses might broadly implement ineffective strategies, like generic security patrols, not aligned with thieves' predictable routines or locations.

Application of Routine Activity Theory

This theory highlights crime as occurring when motivated offenders encounter suitable targets without adequate guardianship. Precise MO details enable targeted enhancement of guardianship and reduction of target suitability at exactly the right places and times. Without comprehensive MO data, effective interventions become impossible.

Why Routine Activity Theory Matters Here

Routine Activity Theory's effectiveness depends on accurately identifying when and where offenders, vulnerable targets, and lack of guardianship intersect. Detailed MO data reveal these intersections clearly, guiding precise prevention strategies. Incomplete data undermine understanding of offenders' routines and vulnerabilities, making interventions less targeted and ultimately less effective.

Exercise

Choose one criminological theory (Environmental Criminology, Crime Pattern Theory, Rational Choice Theory, or Routine Activity Theory). Write a short essay evaluating the impact of incomplete MO data on the practical application of this theory, using specific examples from one or more real-life cases found through online searches. Identify some specific MO variables that would be most critical for the chosen theory

Critical Thinking Guidance

Academics often present crime analysis as a science, drawing parallels to epidemiology[4] and emphasizing large-scale data, population-level patterns, and statistical rigor.[5] This perspective is valid when the goal is to understand broad crime distributions, social risk factors, or neighborhood trends. At that level, crime analysis can function as a science because it generates generalizable insights about crime as a social phenomenon. But when analysis shifts down to the level of the individual case, the comparison to science no longer holds. Linking a set of burglaries, connecting assaults with a consistent modus operandi, or ruling out a suspect's involvement is not scientific research – it is diagnostic reasoning applied to unique circumstances.

At the case level, law enforcement practitioners are not testing hypotheses with representative samples or seeking universal laws. They are working with fragments: incomplete witness accounts, surveillance stills, timelines, and behavioral details. Their task is to make informed judgments about whether cases connect, whether a suspect is viable, or where an offender may strike next. This work is more like medical diagnosis than scientific experimentation. Just as a physician applies general medical knowledge to treat one patient, law enforcement professionals apply criminological and investigative knowledge to interpret the evidence of one case or a series.

It is important to be clear: this casework is not and cannot be "science" in the strict academic sense. If it is mistaken for science, its value is often underestimated. A crucial contribution of officers, investigators, and analysts at this level lies in skilled interpretation, experience-based reasoning, and timely decision-making. These are not universal findings for journal publication. They are professional judgments that keep investigations moving and communities safer. Recognizing this distinction prevents a common misunderstanding: crime analysis is both a science and an applied practice, but the case-level work belongs to the realm of diagnosis, not scientific generalization.

Notes

1 Brantingham and Brantingham (2021).
2 Wortley and Mazerolle (2016).
3 The presence of a person or thing that can prevent a crime by watching over people or property.
4 The study of how diseases or health-related events spread, who they affect, and what factors influence their patterns in populations.
5 The careful and precise use of statistical methods to make sure research results are accurate, reliable, and not due to chance or error.

Bibliography

Brantingham, P. J., & Brantingham, P. L. (2021). Crime pattern theory. In *Oxford research encyclopedia of criminology and criminal justice*. Oxford University Press. https://doi.org/10.1093/acrefore/9780190264079.013.254

Brantingham, P. J., & Brantingham, P. L. (1993). *Environmental criminology*. Waveland Press.

Clarke, R. V., & Felson, M. (Eds.). (1993). *Routine activity and rational choice*. Transaction Publishers.

Eck, J. E., & Weisburd, D. (1995). Crime places in crime theory. In J. E. Eck & D. Weisburd (Eds.), *Crime and place* (Crime Prevention Studies, Vol. 4, pp. 1–34). Willow Tree Press.

Felson, M., & Cohen, L. E. (1980). Human ecology and crime: A routine activity approach. *Human Ecology*, *8*(4), 389–406. https://doi.org/10.1007/BF01561001

Scott, M. S. (2015). *Identifying and defining policing problems* (Problem-Oriented Guides for Police, Problem-Solving Tools Series, No. 13). U.S. Department of Justice, Office of Community Oriented Policing Services. https://popcenter.asu.edu/content/identifying-and-defining-policing-problems

Sherman, L. W. (2015). A tipping point for "totally evidenced policing". *International Criminal Justice Review*, *25*(1), 11–29. https://doi.org/10.1177/1057567715574372

Wortley, R., & Townsley, M. (Eds.). (2016). *Environmental criminology and crime analysis* (2nd ed.). Routledge.

6 Dependent Policing Approaches

Introduction

Policing approaches, regardless of their theoretical or operational emphasis, increasingly depend on the systematic collection and interpretation of MO details. From strategic models like Intelligence-Led Policing to spatial tactics like Geographic Profiling, the ability to detect, analyze, and respond to patterns is only as strong as the data describing those patterns. This chapter examines eight policing approaches, providing brief definitions and theoretical examples of each to illustrate how precise MO data underpin their effectiveness.

Predictive Policing

Predictive Policing uses statistical models and historical crime data to forecast where and when future crimes are likely to occur, enabling proactive resource allocation and crime prevention.

Application Example: Residential Burglaries

A police agency implements a predictive policing program to combat residential burglaries. Analysts input MO data including entry points (rear windows), time of day (midday), target home characteristics (single-family homes), and accurate locations into predictive models. The system identifies high-risk areas with narrow patrol time windows. Directed patrols in those areas result in a measurable decline in burglaries over the next three months.

MO Relevance: The predictive model requires detailed MO variables to generate reliable risk maps. Incomplete data would have led to broad, ineffective predictions.

Evidence-Based Policing (EBP)

Evidence-Based Policing emphasizes interventions that have been scientifically tested and proven effective, focusing on measurable outcomes rather than tradition or anecdote.

Application Example: Domestic Violence Risk Reduction

Domestic Violence Risk Reduction: A police department participated in a study on reducing domestic violence recidivism. Officers collected rich MO data during initial incidents, including threat types, presence of children, prior history, and offender demeanor. Researchers used these data to create a risk assessment tool that guided police responses and social

DOI: 10.4324/9781003728733-7

services. High-risk cases received immediate intervention and follow-up visits. Repeat incidents declined, and victim support services increased.

MO Relevance: Empirical evaluation and tailored intervention would not have been possible without detailed, structured MO data feeding the research process.

CompStat (Comparative Statistics)

CompStat is a performance management system that uses timely information, rapid deployment, effective tactics, and relentless follow-up to reduce crime and achieve department goals.

Application Example: Subway Assaults

A major city's CompStat program identified a rise in assaults on subway platforms. Weekly reviews highlighted specific MO variables: time of day (late night), offender behaviors (intoxicated, targeting lone riders), and station types (transfer hubs). Commanders shifted patrol schedules and initiated targeted enforcement in vulnerable locations. Assault rates dropped within weeks.

MO Relevance: MO elements, particularly time and behavioral patterns, were keys to identifying trends and deploying resources effectively.

Intelligence-Led Policing (ILP)

Intelligence-Led Policing emphasizes analysis and intelligence to guide objective decision-making that prioritizes crime hotspots, repeat victims, prolific offenders, and criminal groups.

Application Example: Gang Violence Reduction

ILP is used to address a rise in gang-related homicides. Analysts gathered highly detailed MO data, including the names of gangs involved, timing of retaliatory shootings, types of firearms used, and victim affiliations. By synthesizing this intelligence, the department identifies high-risk individuals and rivalries likely to escalate. Targeted interventions focus on disrupting gang leadership, conducting precision patrols in hotspots, and initiating community outreach in vulnerable neighborhoods. As a result, gang-related homicides significantly decline.

MO Relevance: The success of this ILP strategy depended entirely on the accuracy and granularity of MO data. Without precise information about gang member behavior and conflict dynamics, intelligence products would have lacked focus and impact.

Problem-Oriented Policing (POP)

Problem-Oriented Policing is a systematic method[1] for analyzing and addressing the underlying conditions contributing to recurring crime and disorder, moving beyond incident-level responses to solve complex community problems.

Application Example: Open-Air Drug Markets

A police department faced persistent problems with open-air drug markets. Using the POP model, officers and analysts collect detailed MO data on dealer behavior, customer patterns, transaction locations, and peak activity times. These data reveal that specific street layouts, low visibility, and poor lighting enables drug sales to flourish. Working with city planners and local residents, the police redesign the environment, adding street barriers, enhancing lighting, and adjusting traffic patterns. Surveillance and police presence is increased at key hours. Over time, drug markets are disrupted, and the quality of life is improved.

MO Relevance: The intervention's success hinges on detailed analysis of behavioral and environmental MO variables. Generalized data would have failed to identify the specific facilitators of the crime pattern.

Community Policing

Community Policing emphasizes collaborative partnerships between police and communities to proactively identify and solve problems through trust-building, mutual respect, and shared problem-solving strategies.

Application Example: Neighborhood Burglary Prevention

In response to repeated residential burglaries in a low-income neighborhood, a police department launched a community policing initiative. Officers held community meetings, conducted door-to-door outreach, and collected MO data from both crime reports and residents' observations. Residents provided specific information about suspicious behaviors, common entry methods, and times when homes were most often left unoccupied. The department used this intelligence to increase patrols at vulnerable hours, educate residents on home security, and establish a neighborhood watch program. Over the next six months, burglaries in the area declined by over 40%.

MO Relevance: The initiative succeeded because officers incorporated non-traditional MO data from residents – such as observed behavior and household routines – into their prevention efforts. Without community input, these nuanced insights would not have been available through formal reports alone.

Geographic Profiling

Geographic Profiling uses the locations of related crimes to determine the most probable area where an offender resides or operates, based on spatial behavior theory and crime site patterns.

Application Example: Serial Arsons

A law enforcement agency uses geographic profiling to investigate a series of arsons in residential neighborhoods. Analysts enter MO data (exact locations, times of night, building types, and ignition methods) into geographic profiling software. The resulting profile identifies a high-probability zone within a 1.2-mile radius. Surveillance efforts focus on that area and eventually catch the offender attempting another arson.

MO Relevance: Geographic profiling would not have succeeded without detailed MO data. Specific timing, location type, and ignition method were all necessary to form a viable spatial pattern.

Behavioral Analysis/Criminal Profiling

Behavioral Analysis examines crime scene behavior and victim-offender interactions to infer offender characteristics such as psychological traits, criminal history, and geographic familiarity. It is sometimes called criminal profiling.

Application Example: Serial Sexual Assault

In a large city, a series of sexual assaults occurs in with strikingly similar elements. Behavioral analysts review detailed MO data including approach method, control techniques, victim demographics, language used by the offender, and post-assault behaviors. These details enable the development of a behavioral profile suggesting the offender was local, had prior offenses, and targeted specific victim types. Investigators narrow down suspects based on these traits and apprehended the offender through combined surveillance and DNA evidence.

MO Relevance: Without rich, consistent behavioral MO data, the offender profile would have been too vague to guide investigative direction effectively.

Conclusion: Why MO Data Are Central to All Policing Approaches

Across all policing models, from tactical interventions[2] to strategic frameworks, the quality and completeness of MO data directly affect operational success. These approaches rely on data that is consistent, structured, and detailed. Missing MO elements reduce pattern clarity, obscure offender behaviors, and limit the potential of both human and algorithmic analysis. Conversely, when crime pattern data is robust, law enforcement agencies implement specific policing approaches more effectively.

Exercise

Each approach in this chapter relies on certain types of information. Pick one approach and make a short list of the kinds of details (about offenders, victims, places, or times) it would need to work best. Which of these details do you think would be hardest for police to collect, and why? Discuss.

Critical Thinking Guidance

The policing approaches outlined in this chapter demonstrate a common thread: their effectiveness rises or falls with the quality of the MO data that supports them. Predictive systems, intelligence products, spatial analyses, and community-based strategies all require detail, precision, and consistency if they are to generate actionable insights. Yet in practice, law enforcement often works with partial, inconsistent, or poorly structured data. When that occurs, even the most advanced models and frameworks risk producing generalized outcomes that lack operational value.

The lesson is not simply that "more data are better," but that structured and standardized data is indispensable. Just as medicine and meteorology evolved by formalizing classification systems for symptoms or weather patterns, policing can only advance when MO variables are codified and consistently applied. A shared framework enables meaningful comparison across cases, agencies, and jurisdictions, while also opening pathways for integration with emerging analytic technologies. Recognizing MO details as the foundation of all dependent policing approaches reframes data collection from a routine administrative task into the central pillar of scientific and operational progress in the field.

Questions to Consider

Each of the policing models in this chapter relies on pattern identification as part of its implementation. But how are patterns recognized and identified without first having a classification system for what makes up a pattern?

What might happen if different units, agencies, or systems each used their own informal or inconsistent typologies?

In medicine, the diagnostic process depends on recognized categories of symptoms and conditions. In meteorology, weather forecasting depends on the classification of cloud types, atmospheric patterns, and pressure systems. In each field, the typology came first, and only then could prediction, analysis, and strategy evolve.

How might law enforcement benefit from thinking about crime elements and MOs in a similarly standardized and structured way?

Could the formalization of more crime pattern variables open up possibilities for shared databases, better AI integration, or cross-jurisdictional intelligence?

Notes

1 POP uses the SARA framework (Scanning, Analysis, Response, Assessment).
2 Specific short-term actions taken by police or other authorities to stop, reduce, or control crime in a particular area or situation.

Bibliography

Cordner, G. W. (2020, May). *Evidence-based policing in 45 small bytes (NCJ 254326)*. U.S. Department of Justice, National Institute of Justice. https://nij.ojp.gov/library/publications/evidence-based-policing-45-small-bytes

Eck, J. E., & Clarke, R. V. (2005). *Crime analysis for problem solvers in 60 small steps*. U.S. Department of Justice, Office of Community Oriented Policing Services. https://cops.usdoj.gov/RIC/Publications/cops-w0047-pub.pdf

Goldstein, H. (1990). *Problem-oriented policing*. McGraw-Hill.

Meijer, A., & Wessels, M. (2019). Predictive policing: Review of benefits and drawbacks. *International Journal of Public Administration*, *42*(12), 1031–1039. https://doi.org/10.1080/01900692.2019.1575664

New Jersey State Police. (2006, September 26). *New Jersey State Police practical guide to intelligence-led policing*. Center for Policing Terrorism, Manhattan Institute.

Office of Community Oriented Policing Services. (2014). *Community policing defined (COPS P157)*. U.S. Department of Justice. https://cops.usdoj.gov/RIC/Publications/cops-p157-pub.pdf

Perry, W. L., McInnis, B., Price, C. C., Smith, S. C., & Hollywood, J. S. (2013, September). *Predictive policing: The role of crime forecasting in law enforcement operations (NCJ 243830)*. RAND Corporation. www.ojp.gov/pdffiles1/nij/grants/243830.pdf

Petherick, W., & Brooks, N. (2020). Reframing criminal profiling: A guide for integrated practice. *Psychiatry, Psychology and Law*, *28*(5), 694–710. https://doi.org/10.1080/13218719.2020.1837030

Police Executive Research Forum. (2013). *Compstat: Its origins, evolution, and future in law enforcement agencies*. U.S. Department of Justice, Bureau of Justice Assistance. https://bja.ojp.gov/library/publications/compstat-its-origins-evolution-and-future-law-enforcement-agencies

Ratcliffe, J. H. (2003). Intelligence-led policing. *Trends & Issues in Crime and Criminal Justice*, (248), 1–6. Australian Institute of Criminology. www.aic.gov.au/publications/tandi/tandi248

Ratcliffe, J. H. (2007). *Integrating crime and intelligence analysis: Enhanced information management for law enforcement leaders*. Police Foundation.
Ratcliffe, J. H. (2016). *Intelligence-led policing* (2nd ed.). Routledge.
Rossmo, D. K. (2000). *Geographic profiling*. CRC Press.
Sherman, L. (1998). *Evidence-based policing*. National Policing Institute. www.policinginstitute.org/publication/evidence-based-policing/

Part II

Basic Elements

7 Forensic Evidence

Introduction

Forensic evidence is any information or material (physical, biological, or digital) that can be scientifically examined and used in court to help show what happened or who was involved in a crime. As an element of a crime pattern, forensic evidence provides the most reliable means to identify an offender. When present, it can offer an objective, scientifically verifiable connection between specific crimes and specific criminals. Such evidence may be left at one crime scene but not another or collected at one crime scene but not others in a series of crimes. The modus operandi information is essential when forensic evidence clearly identifies an offender because the MO information in that crime can be compared with MOs in similar crime occurrences where no forensic evidence was obtained.

Forensic evidence gathering is useful in crimes beyond murder and rape. Studies demonstrate that it can help solve crimes such as arson, assault, burglary, and robbery. Since sending evidence technicians to every crime scene is not practical or affordable, numerous crimes that could be linked by forensic evidence go unsolved.[1] Because forensic evidence is not available for many crime scenes, modus operandi information becomes even more valuable as a means to link crimes.

Many people think of fingerprints and DNA when they think of forensic evidence, yet it has evolved as technologies change. For example, investigating the travel and communications of criminals may involve non-traditional forensic evidence such as computer files and histories, cell phone and cell phone tower records, CCTV camera evidence, and GPS data.

Crime-Specific Forensic Evidence Examples

- Homicide: Collection of blood, tissue, and hair samples; fingerprint analysis; ballistics analysis; DNA profiling; analysis of weapon or tool marks; autopsy and toxicology reports.
- Sexual Assault: Collection of bodily fluids; hair and fiber samples; DNA profiling; analysis of clothing and personal effects; documentation of physical injuries.
- Robbery and Burglary: Fingerprint analysis; footprints and tire track analysis; collection of tool marks; hair and fiber analysis; DNA profiling; analysis of surveillance footage.
- Assault: Collection of blood, hair, and tissue samples; DNA profiling; documentation of physical injuries; clothing analysis; fingerprint analysis.
- Arson: Collection of fire accelerants; analysis of burn patterns and fire debris; electrical system examination; collection of samples from the origin of the fire.

DOI: 10.4324/9781003728733-9

- Drug Offenses: Analysis of drug samples; collection of paraphernalia; fingerprint analysis; financial investigation; DNA profiling on related equipment.
- Fraud and White-Collar Crimes: Forensic accounting; analysis of financial records and documents; computer forensics; fingerprint analysis; handwriting analysis.
- Cybercrimes: Computer forensics; analysis of digital data; network analysis; malware and virus analysis; email and social media account investigation.
- Vandalism: Paint and graffiti analysis; fingerprint analysis; footprints and tire track analysis; collection of tool marks.
- Terrorism: Analysis of explosive materials; collection of debris and shrapnel; ballistics analysis; DNA profiling; analysis of electronic communications.
- Human Trafficking: DNA profiling; fingerprint analysis; analysis of personal effects and clothing; documentation of physical injuries; financial investigation.
- Environmental Crimes: Soil and water sample analysis; examination of industrial records; analysis of chemical substances; wildlife forensics.
- Auto Theft: Fingerprint analysis; collection of glass fragments; footprints and tire track analysis; DNA profiling; paint analysis.
- Child Abuse: Documentation of physical injuries; analysis of clothing and personal effects; DNA profiling; hair and fiber analysis; psychological assessment.
- Stalking and Harassment: Analysis of electronic communications; computer forensics; handwriting analysis; phone record analysis.

Forensic Variable Examples

Evidence left at the crime scene example variables: ammo shells, cans/bottles, cigar/cigarette, food/food wrappers, matches/lighters, notes, prints, tool marks, tools, weapon.

Forensic physical evidence example variables: audio recordings, ballistics, biological material, bite marks, blood, blood spatter, bloodstains, body fluids, bones, bullets, cash, casings, chemicals, clothing, contracts, cutting instruments, diaries, disposable gloves DNA, documents, drugs, gasoline residue, explosives, explosive residue, fecal matter, fibers, fingerprints, fire debris, firearm, footprints, fragments, glass shards, gun, gunshot residue, hair, handwriting, instruments, letters, metal particles, paint chips, poison, pollen, powders, pry marks, saliva, semen, shoe prints, signature (in writing), skin cells, small particles, soil, stains, threads, tire tracks, tool scratches, tool marks, tools, trace evidence, urine, vaginal fluids, vegetative material, videos, weapons.

Forensic digital evidence example variables: Bluetooth, browsing history, CCTV camera videos, cellular data, cloud services, computers, digital photographs, emails, GPS/location data, internet activity, internet history, metadata, mobile phone data, photographs, sat nav data, search terms, smartphones, social media activity, surveillance videos, tablet, texts, videos, Wi-Fi.

Crime Pattern Scenario

Serial Commercial Burglary Pattern – Technology Store Targets

A pattern of six electronics store burglaries over two months shared several forensic elements that created strong linkage opportunities. Distinctive pry mark patterns from a specific crowbar type and latex glove prints provided physical evidence connections. DNA evidence was recovered from only two scenes – saliva on a discarded energy drink and skin cells on broken glass – but tool mark analysis definitively linked all six incidents to the same implements.

Digital evidence included GPS tracking data from stolen devices that revealed a common disposal route leading to the same electronics resale area. The combination of DNA from two scenes, tool marks from all scenes, and digital traces created a comprehensive forensic foundation that guided investigators to focus on offenders with access to specific tools and familiarity with electronics resale markets. This pattern demonstrates how multiple types of forensic evidence can compensate for gaps in individual categories while reinforcing behavioral consistencies across the crime series.

Example Case

In 2005, Thomas Sweatt was convicted for setting a series of fires in Maryland, the District of Columbia, and Virginia in 2003 and 2004. He set 45 residential fires using incendiary devices, the components of which were a one-gallon plastic jug, a plastic bag, a cloth material used as a wick, and gasoline as an accelerant in the devices.[2] Often victims were at home and the devices placed near the front door or inside in a stairwell. He was linked to the fires through DNA evidence found at scenes where DNA on Marine dress cap and trousers, some DNA on a charred sock and a single hair on a juice jug in a distinct black plastic bag that all matched his genetic profile.[3]

Example Query Terms: device near a door, near front door, stairwell, victim at home, occupied home, gasoline, ignitable fluid, juice jug, plastic bag.

Exercises

1. DNA evidence is collected via sexual assault kits (SAK) in some cases involving sexual assault, yet historically, in many jurisdictions, there is a backlog of testing these kits. How does this impact on linking crimes? Why does modus operandi information become more valuable in this scenario? Find a solved serial rapist pattern (suspect apprehended) and explore these questions.
2. Visit a public space where people regularly handle objects (library, coffee shop, or bus stop) and spend 20 minutes observing what physical traces people might leave behind. Note items touched, materials that could transfer between people and surfaces, and digital devices used. Create a list of potential forensic evidence categories you observe, then consider: which traces would be most useful for linking someone to multiple visits to this location? How might environmental factors (weather, lighting, cleaning schedules) affect evidence preservation? Finally, think about which traces would be easiest and hardest for someone to avoid leaving behind.

Critical Thinking Guidance

Critical thinking in the use of forensic evidence requires recognizing both its strengths and its limits within crime pattern analysis. While DNA, fingerprints, and digital traces can provide powerful links between crimes and offenders, evidence is often partial, absent, or subject to error in collection and interpretation. Investigators must guard against assuming that one type of forensic evidence is conclusive on its own, or that missing evidence automatically indicates offender skill. Instead, each piece of forensic data should be weighed alongside other elements of the crime pattern, including modus operandi and environmental context. Careful analysis means considering alternative explanations, documenting both supporting and contradictory findings, and remaining aware of biases that can distort judgment. In practice, forensic evidence should be treated not as a stand-alone answer but as one part of a larger system of interconnected variables that together shape the recognition and understanding of crime patterns.

Notes

1 McEwen (2010, December 13).
2 U.S. Department of Justice, U.S. Attorney's Office for the District of Maryland (2005, September 12).
3 The Washington Post (2005, April 28).

Bibliography

Brown, C., Julian, R., & Howes, L. M. (2023, November 8). "Strands in a cable": Effective investigator decision-making using forensic identification evidence in volume crime investigations. *Policing and Society*. Advance online publication. https://doi.org/10.1080/10439463.2023.2279063

Federal Bureau of Investigation. (2024, July 10). *FBI marks 100 years of fingerprints and criminal history records*. www.fbi.gov/news/stories/fbi-marks-100-years-of-fingerprints-and-criminal-history-records

Forensic Science Regulator. (2020). *Cognitive bias effects relevant to forensic science examinations* (FSR-G-217, Issue 2). Crown Copyright. https://assets.publishing.service.gov.uk/media/5f4fc26ce90e074695f80977/217_FSR-G-217_Cognitive_bias_appendix_Issue_2.pdf

Lopez, B. E., McGrath, J. G., & Taylor, V. G. (2020, October). Using forensic intelligence to combat serial and organized violent crimes. *NIJ Journal*, (282). National Institute of Justice. https://nij.ojp.gov/topics/articles/using-forensic-intelligence-combat-serial-and-organized-violent-crimes

McEwen, T. (2010, December 13). *The role and impact of forensic evidence on the criminal justice system: Executive summary*. National Institute of Justice, Office of Justice Programs, U.S. Department of Justice. www.ojp.gov/pdffiles1/nij/grants/231977.pdf

National Institute of Justice. (2022). *Forensic science strategic research plan 2022–2026*. U.S. Department of Justice. www.ojp.gov/pdffiles1/nij/304856.pdf

National Research Council. (2009). *Strengthening forensic science in the United States: A path forward*. The National Academies Press. https://doi.org/10.17226/12589

Peterson, J., Sommers, I., Baskin, D., & Johnson, D. (2010). *The role and impact of forensic evidence in the criminal justice process*. California State University, Los Angeles, School of Criminal Justice & Criminalistics. www.ojp.gov/pdffiles1/nij/grants/231977.pdf

Rossmo, D. K. (2006a, September). Criminal investigation failures: Avoiding the pitfalls. *FBI Law Enforcement Bulletin*, *75*(9), 1–8.

Rossmo, D. K. (2006b, October). Criminal investigative failures: Avoiding the pitfalls (Part two). *FBI Law Enforcement Bulletin*, *75*(10), 12–19.

The Washington Post. (2005, April 28). Pants left behind yielded pivotal link. *The Washington Post*. www.washingtonpost.com/archive/politics/2005/04/28/pants-left-behind-yielded-pivotal-link/

Tièche, C. C., & Dubach, M. (2021). Efficient DNA sampling in burglary investigations. *Genes*, *13*(1), Article 26. https://doi.org/10.3390/genes13010026

U.S. Department of Justice, U.S. Attorney's Office for the District of Maryland. (2005, September 12). *"Serial arsonist" Thomas Sweatt sentenced to life in prison for setting 45 residential fires in Maryland, District of Columbia and Virginia* [Press release]. www.justice.gov/archive/usao/md/news/2005/SweattSentencePR.pdf

Wallenborn, J. K. (2022). Why sexual assault kits were not tested: A systematic review. *Criminology, Criminal Justice, Law & Society*, *23*(3), 22–44.

8 Physical Description

Introduction

Physical descriptions are a foundational element in crime reports and can lead to crime pattern identification in crimes involving victims or witnesses, as well as those involving CCTV or other types of videos. These descriptions assist in linking cases and identifying suspects. In rarer instances, the descriptions of victims can be significant in case linkage efforts.

Thinking more critically about detailed physical description information can distinguish one series from another or tie seemingly unrelated incidents together. This chapter prompts readers to consider the collection of appearance-based data and to consider how improved documentation can strengthen investigations.

Physical Attributes Variables

These basic categories of offender physical description are standard in police crime reports:

Age: estimated/exact age range of the offender.
Sex: gender of the offender (male, female, or unknown)
Race/Ethnicity: the racial or ethnic background of the offender
Height: approximate height of the offender
Weight/Build: estimated weight and/or build of the offender
Hair: offender's hair color
Eyes: offender's eye color
Scars, Tattoos, or Marks: if observed

Additional description information is gathered by many agencies, such as unusual physical features, complexion information (light, medium, dark), and hair details (color, length, style). Any unique or notable physical features that may help identify the offender, such as birthmarks, missing teeth, or distinctive facial characteristics, can link crimes together in a pattern.

The following list provides basic and additional variables to consider when searching for patterns of crime based on physical description. Variables like one another are included to give as many information-gathering and search terms as possible.

Age: infant, toddler, child, school-age, adolescent, teenager, young adult, adult, middle-aged, senior, elderly
Sex/Gender/Orientation: male, female, homosexual, intersex, nonbinary, straight, transgender

DOI: 10.4324/9781003728733-10

Race: White/Caucasian, Black/African American, Asian, Hispanic/Latino, Native American/Alaska Native, Native Hawaiian/Pacific Islander, other/mixed race

Physical Build: tall, short, thin, average, athletic/fit, stocky, thick, obese, overweight, heavy-set, slender, muscular, medium, average

Hair Color: black, brown, blonde, blue, gray, green, orange, pink, purple, red, sandy, white, salt and pepper (mix of gray and dark hair), multi-colored

Hair Length: bald, bald/shaved, balding/receding, bun, buzz cut, collar-length, long, longer than shoulder-length, medium, pigtails, ponytail, shaved, short, shorter than collar-length, shoulder-length, tied-up, waist-length

Hair Texture: coarse, curly, fine, frizzy, kinky, straight, wavy

Hair Style: afro, bald, bangs, bob, braids, center part, cornrows, crew cut, dreadlocks, fade, fringe, layered, mohawk, pixie cut, receding hairline, shaved, side part, side-swept bangs, updo, widow's peak (V-shaped hairline)

Facial Hair: beard, beard with exposed chin, clean-shaven, Fu Manchu style, full goatee, goatee without mustache, sideburns, stubble, unshaven

Eyebrows: arched, bushy, micro-bladed, none, sparse, straight, tapered, tattooed, thick, thin, unibrow (connected eyebrows), unusual, well-groomed

Eye Color: black, blue, brown, dark, gray, green, hazel, light

Eye Shape/Size: almond-shaped, bulging, close-set, deep-set, hooded, large, prominent, small, sunken

Eye Features: bags under eyes, colored contact lenses, crossed eyes, droopy eyelids, crow's feet, eye prosthetics, eye twitching, glasses, marks near eyes, patch over eye, scars near eyes, sunglasses, tattoos near eyes, wrinkles around eyes

Eyelashes: curled, false eyelashes, long, mascara-worn, missing, short, sparse, straight, thick

Eye Expression: alert, angry, bloodshot, cold, dilated, dull, fearful, glassy, intense, narrowed, piercing, sad, squinting, teary, watery, wide-eyed

Lips: bow-shaped, dark, full, large, light, lip-filler, narrow, pale, plump, small, thin, thin upper lip, wide

Teeth: braces, bridges, bad, broken, brownish, buck teeth, cavities, chipped, crooked, crowded, crown, decayed, dental implants, dentures, discolored, fillings, gaps, gold, gold-capped, good, grayish, grills, jewel-studded, large, missing, off-white, orthodontic appliances, overbite, partial plate, pointed canines, protruding teeth, protrusion, restora tions, retainers, rounded incisors, silver, small, stained, underbite, white, yellow

Tongue: tongue piercings, unusual color, unusual size

Ears: attached lobes, deformed, detached lobes, large, pierced, protruding, scarred, small

Jawline/Chin: cleft chin, double chin, pointed, rounded, strong jawline, square jawline, weak jawline

Skin Tone: fair, dark, ebony, jaundiced, light, medium, olive, pale, tanned, yellowish

Skin Texture: acne-marked, blemished, blemishes, dimpled, dimples, freckled, freckles, moles, pock-marked, rough, scarred, smooth, wrinkled

Skin Condition: blemished, bruised, burn mark, discolored, dry, irritated, oily, pock-marked, psoriasis, rash, scaly, sunburned, wounded

Nose: average, bulbous, crooked, downturned, flared, large, large nostrils, pierced, small, small nostrils, straight, upturned, wide

Cheeks: dimpled, fat, high cheekbones, hollowed, rosy, sunken

Forehead: high, low, narrow, receding hairline, wide, wrinkled

Neck: hanging jowls, protruding Adam's apple

Fingers/Hands/Nails: distinctive rings, long nails, missing finger, missing fingernails, missing parts of finger, painted nails, polished nails, short nails, tattoo on hands, tattoo on finger
Other Features: facial asymmetry, deformity, unusually large hand/feet, unusually small hands/feet
Scars: cultural scarification patterns, noticeable scars, unusual scars, identifying scars
Marks: beauty marks, birthmarks, freckles, moles, permanent cosmetic makeup, piercings, port-wine stain, uneven pigmentation, spider veins, vitiligo
Tattoos: cultural tattoo pattern, gang-related tattoo, specific symbolic tattoo, specific design tattoo, specific word tattoo[1]
Locations of Scars, Marks, and Tattoos: abdomen, ankle, arm(s), back, breast(s), buttock(s), chest, ear(s), face, finger(s), foot/feet, groin, hand(s), leg(s), neck/throat, nose, shoulder(s), thigh(s), tongue
General Appearance: casual, clean, conservative, dirty, flashy, formal, neat, sloppy, unclean, unkempt, well-groomed

Clothing and Accessories Detail Variables

Description of the clothing worn by the offender at the time of the incident can help pinpoint a crime pattern, along with that of any distinctive accessories or items the offender was carrying. Unique or distinctive details about clothes can be important to note.

Crimes might be linked by variables such as the brand and style of sneaker the suspect wore or a suspect who wore a t-shirt with a distinctive or memorable slogan. Offenders might wear military, school, or work uniforms or safety gear, such as hard hats and reflective gear. A suspect might wear a religious or cultural garment, jewelry, or distinctive patches, badges, or pins.

Example clothing and accessories variables:

- Hat: color, style, logos, ornaments, how it is worn (bill forward, backward, to one side), (baseball cap, beanie, fedora, headscarf, hijab, sunhat)
- Coat: color, style, hood, buttons, fasteners, pockets (suit coat, jacket, topcoat, overcoat)
- Shirt/Sweatshirt/Blouse/Dress: color, design, pattern, sleeves, collar, buttons, fasteners, length
- Trousers/Pants/Slacks/Skirt: color, pattern, style, cuffs, buttons, fasteners, length
- Undergarments: undershirt, underwear, briefs, bra, panties
- Belts/Suspenders: color, buckles, style
- Leggings/Tights/Socks: note color, pattern, length
- Footwear: color, style, brand name for sneakers, laces, condition, (shoes, sneakers, boots, sandals, clogs, crocs)
- Accessories: sweater, vest, scarf, gloves, necktie, sunglasses, glasses, purse, bag, backpack, briefcase, fanny-pack
- Jewelry: rings (note what finger worn on), watch (note what arm worn on), bracelets, necklaces, ankle bracelet piercing jewelry, earrings, nose ring, pins
- Clothes General Appearance: neat or sloppy, clean or dirty, rips, tears, stains in clothing – note location, worn-out shoes/sneakers
- Oddities: clothing too large or too small, odd colors, patchwork, badges
- Layering of clothes
- Facial covering

Pets

If an offender had a pet with them at the scene, it could be a crucial detail. Noting the animal's type, breed, and color might be useful in linking crimes to the offender.

Crime Pattern Scenario

Serial ATM Robbery Pattern – "The Red Hat Robber"

Over a six-week period, seven ATM robberies in different neighborhoods shared remarkably consistent physical description elements that enabled quick pattern recognition. The suspect was consistently described as a Black male, approximately 5′8″ to 5′10″ tall, medium build, wearing a distinctive bright red baseball cap with a white logo. Across all incidents, witnesses noted he wore dark jeans, white sneakers, and kept his hands in a dark hoodie pocket throughout the approach. Most significantly, three separate witnesses mentioned he had a gold front tooth that was visible when he spoke, and two noted a small scar above his left eyebrow. The clothing consistency was striking: while the hoodie color varied (black, navy, dark gray), the red cap, white sneakers, and dark jeans remained constant. In the final robbery, a victim observed a tattoo on his wrist when he reached for money described as small black lettering. These consistent physical descriptors, particularly the distinctive red hat, gold tooth, and eyebrow scar, helped link all seven incidents definitively and focus surveillance efforts on individuals matching this specific profile in areas with high ATM density.

Example Cases

Police in Southfield, Michigan, identified a suspected serial robber through his TikTok videos after an anonymous tip directed investigators to the account. The suspect was observed wearing white Nike sneakers with red accents in his videos, the same shoes worn during four armed robberies between December 2021 and February 2022. Additional distinctive clues including pink/purple dyed hair visible under a mask and consistent clothing and backpack descriptions across incidents helped tie him to the crimes. Authorities obtained phone location records and surveillance confirming his presence at all robbery sites.[2]

Example query terms: pink hair, purple hair, white, Nike, red accent, sneakers, mask, backpack

In January 2016, Salt Lake City police investigated a series of three armed robberies committed by the same suspect. The incidents occurred on January 1 at a Jamba Juice, January 3 at a Starbucks, and January 8 at a State Farm Insurance office. In each case, the suspect brandished a weapon. He is described as a white male, approximately 6′2″ tall, with bright blue eyes, wearing all-black clothing including pants, boots, a bandana or balaclava, and gloves.[3]

Example query terms: blue eyes, unusual eyes, bright eyes, light eyes, gloves, bandana, balaclava

Exercises

1. Conduct an online search using the terms "serial robber" or "robbery series." Extract and catalog all suspect physical description variables from three different series of robberies. How detailed were the suspect descriptions? How significant might they be in linking the crimes?

2. Visit a busy public location (mall, transit station, or downtown area) and conduct a 30-minute observation exercise. Select five different people and write detailed physical descriptions as if you were a witness providing information to police. Include basic attributes (age, height, build, hair, clothing) and distinctive features (accessories, tattoos, scars, unique clothing items). After completing your descriptions, wait ten minutes and try to write the same descriptions from memory without looking at your notes. Compare the two sets of descriptions and note: Which details remained consistent? Which were forgotten or changed? Which distinctive features were easiest to remember? Finally, consider how factors like distance, lighting, your stress level, or the person's movement might have affected your observations. This exercise demonstrates both the value and limitations of eyewitness descriptions while highlighting which types of physical details tend to be most reliable for crime pattern linkage.

Critical Thinking Guidance

The reliability of eyewitness descriptions depends on the conditions under which the observation occurred and the potential for memory distortion. Examples of conditions that may affect memory:

- rapid or stressful incident conditions,
- lighting, weather, distance, or obstructions
- witness stress, intoxication, or fear
- multiple suspect or group crimes with conflicting accounts

It is essential for officers to be aware of implicit biases that can influence how suspect characteristics are perceived and reported. Bias awareness training supports more objective and complete data collection, which strengthens the overall integrity of pattern analysis.

Those conducting cross-case comparisons should also interpret both database coded and database narrative physical descriptions to identify possible links.

As facial-recognition technologies evolve, they impact how patterns based on physical description will be identified. Deepfakes are AI-generated images, videos, or audio that can mimic real people with alarming realism. In criminal investigations, they pose a risk to accurate suspect identification by fabricating appearances or falsely placing individuals at crime scenes. Analysts and investigators must verify all visual evidence through multiple sources when relevant and consider digital forensics to guard against deception.

Notes

1 The New Jersey Juvenile Justice Commission's Gang Awareness Guide "Recognize the Signs" has some examples of gang tattoos. www.nj.gov/lps/gang-signs-bro.pdf
2 Hudson and Rahbany (2022, February 25).
3 Gephardt Daily Staff (2016, January 22).

Bibliography

Gephardt Daily Staff. (2016, January 22). Salt Lake police seek help identifying serial robber. *Gephardt Daily*. https://gephardtdaily.com/local/salt-lake-police-seek-help-identifying-serial-robber/

Handler, A., & Frühholz, S. (2021). Eyewitness memory for person identification: Predicting mugbook recognition accuracy according to person description abilities and subjective confidence of witnesses. *Frontiers in Psychology*, *12*, 675956. https://doi.org/10.3389/fpsyg.2021.675956

Hudson, B., & Rahbany, C. (2022, February 25). Suspected robber found through TikTok; wore same shoes in TikTok videos during robberies. *FOX 2 Detroit*. www.fox2detroit.com/news/suspected-robber-found-through-tiktok-wore-same-shoes-during-robberies

National Institute of Justice. (1999). *Eyewitness evidence: A guide for law enforcement.* U.S. Department of Justice, Office of Justice Programs. www.ojp.gov/pdffiles1/nij/178240.pdf

Wells, G. L. (2018). Eyewitness identification. In E. Luna (Ed.), *Reforming criminal justice: Vol. 2. Policing* (pp. 259–278). Academy for Justice, Arizona State University.

Wells, G. L., Kovera, M. B., Douglass, A. B., Brewer, N., Meissner, C. A., & Wixted, J. T. (2020). Policy and procedure recommendations for the collection and preservation of eyewitness identification evidence. *Law and Human Behavior*, *44*(1), 3–36.

9 Offender Characteristics

Introduction

Offender characteristics beyond physical description elements can help connect crimes. Offender characteristics go beyond visible traits and into the realm of how a person moves, speaks, behaves, or interacts, sometimes leaving a strong impression on victims or witnesses. These elements, such as the way an offender walks, talks, smells, or carries themselves, are often overlooked in basic crime reports, yet they can be crucial to linking crimes. Analysts and investigators who examine these characteristics can uncover links that may otherwise remain hidden in a disconnected set of cases. This chapter encourages readers to think beyond checklists and pay attention to qualitative and sensory observations that provide a more comprehensive picture of the person committing the crime.

For example, victims and witnesses might notice if the offender was right-handed or left-handed, if they wore a certain cologne, if they seemed to limp, or if they seemed unusually polite.

Offender Example Characteristics Variables

Olfactory Traits (Smell/Odor)

Odors noticed at the time of the crime may reflect personal habits, substance use, environment, or occupation.

Examples: alcohol odor, alcohol on breath, smoke on breath, bad breath, body odor, cannabis odor, chemical odor, cleaning agent odor, cologne/perfume odor, gasoline odor, fuel odor, medicinal odor, smoke odor, unusual odor.

Gait (Walk/Mobility)

Walking patterns and movement behaviors can offer clues about physical health, age, injuries, or neurological conditions.

Examples: abnormal foot placement, average-paced, arms swinging freely, arms restricted when walking, confident, dragging feet, exaggerated swagger, fast, hunched, irregular rhythm in walking, leaned backward when walking, leaned forward when walking, limping, long stride, purposeful, short stride, shuffling, slouched, stomping, striding, stumbling, swagger, swaying, uses cane, uses mobility aid, uses walker, used wheelchair, varied rhythm in walking, walked heel to toe, walked toe to heel.

DOI: 10.4324/9781003728733-11

Speech/Voice Characteristics

Tone, pitch, fluency, speed, and diction can create distinct impressions and allow for later recognition or comparison.

Examples: did not speak, flat affect, foreign accent, high-pitched voice, lisp, loud, monotonous, mumbled, nasal, quiet, regional pronunciation or accent, slurred words, soft-spoken, sounded drunk, sounded high, sounded intoxicated, stuttered, talkative, talked quickly, talked slowly, whispered, used profanity, used quotable statement, used unique words, used unique phrases.

Verbal Demeanor

The offender's tone and intention in verbal exchanges provide insight into psychological state and behavior style.

Examples: apologetic, commanding, concerned, complimentary, demanding, derogatory, ego-satisfying, hostile, inquisitive, knowledgeable, negotiating, nervous, neutral, personal, polite, profane, reassuring, rude, self-demeaning, threatening.

Other Characteristics to Consider

Age: Offenders of different ages may have different crime patterns. For example, younger offenders might be more likely to engage in petty theft or vandalism, while older offenders might be more involved in white-collar crimes. Young offenders may lean toward opportunistic crimes; older ones may show specialization or sophistication.

Gender: Men and women can exhibit different crime patterns, in terms of both the types of crimes they commit and their methods of operation.

Socioeconomic Status: Individuals from different socioeconomic backgrounds may show different crime patterns. For instance, people facing economic hardship might be more likely to commit property crimes. Socioeconomic status may influence access to tools and vehicles.

Education Level: Education can influence the type of crime committed. Individuals with higher levels of education may commit more complex crimes, such as fraud or embezzlement.

Criminal History: Repeat offenders might show patterns in the type, location, and timing of their crimes. Prior offenses can help track behavioral patterns and MO consistency.

Substance Use: Substance use can contribute to crime patterns, particularly with crimes like theft, which may be committed to support a drug habit. Drug or alcohol involvement can show up in demeanor, speech, or target selection.[1]

Gang Affiliation: Gang members often show distinct crime patterns, including types of crimes committed, areas of operation, and use of symbols or signals.

Mental Health: Offenders with mental health issues may exhibit certain crime patterns, mainly if the crimes are related to their mental health condition. Offenders with mental illness may display behaviors tied to delusion, impulsivity, or lack of planning.

Crime Pattern Scenario

Serial Commercial Robbery Pattern – "The Polite Bandit"

A series of eight convenience store robberies over four months was linked primarily through distinctive offender characteristics rather than physical appearance. The suspect consistently displayed unusual verbal demeanor which included apologizing to clerks before demanding money, saying "please" and "thank you" during robberies, and expressing concern about not wanting to hurt anyone. Witnesses across different locations noted his soft-spoken, educated speech pattern with no regional accent, contrasting sharply with his criminal actions. Most significantly, five different victims mentioned he had a distinct limp favoring his left leg and walked with a measured, careful gait as if managing pain. His verbal patterns were remarkably consistent: he would approach the counter, apologize, quietly state "I need you to give me the money from the register, please," and thank clerks for their cooperation. In two instances, he asked if the clerk was "okay" before leaving. Despite varying physical disguises (different hats, glasses, facial hair), these behavioral characteristics provided a clear similarities that distinguished these robberies from other robberies in the area.

Example Case

Between 2009 and 2020, the FBI investigated a string of at least 16 bank and pharmacy robberies across Tennessee, North Carolina, and South Carolina committed by an unidentified suspect known as the "Too Tall Bandit." Witnesses consistently described the suspect as a white male standing between 6′0″ and 6′6″, weighing 210–250 pounds, with a noticeable limp on his right leg and a deep voice. The suspect wore a mask and gloves to conceal identity but used the same physical mannerisms and body type across incidents. These repeated characteristics enabled analysts and investigators to link geographically dispersed robberies.

Note that the physical description variables of height and weight are combined with the characteristics of limping and deep voice in this example.[2]

Example query terms: tall, limp, right leg, deep voice, low voice, mask, gloves, bank, pharmacy, drug store

Exercises

1. Choose one offender characteristic from this chapter and find a case online where an offender displayed the characteristic. Try the search terms "polite" and "robber." Try searching for the phrase "get down on the ground." Write about your findings.
2. Spend 45 minutes in a public setting where you can observe people interacting (coffee shop, retail store, public transportation). Focus on five different individuals and document their characteristics beyond physical appearance: How do they walk? What's their speech pattern or volume? Do they have any distinctive mannerisms, gestures, or behavioral traits? Note any sensory details you might observe (cologne, perfume, other odors). Pay attention to how they interact with others – are they polite, demanding, nervous, confident? After your observation period, consider: Which characteristics would be most memorable if you witnessed these individuals in a stressful situation like a crime? Which traits might be reliable enough to help link multiple incidents? Which details might be influenced by your own biases or assumptions? Finally, think about how stress, poor lighting, or time pressure might affect a victim's ability to recall these same characteristics accurately. This exercise demonstrates both the potential value and the limitations of using behavioral characteristics in crime pattern analysis.

Critical Thinking Guidance

Relying too heavily on subjective traits like gait, voice, or demeanor can lead to mistaken identification. Witnesses may forget, exaggerate, or misinterpret what they saw or heard, especially under stress. For example, several people may "walk with a limp" or "have a deep voice," but that doesn't mean they're the same person. These traits are useful clues but should always be backed up with physical evidence or corroborating details before drawing firm conclusions. Nevertheless, they can be significant in the early stages of linking crimes. The odor, gait, speech, voice, and verbal demeanor characteristics are used by crime analysts and investigators to link related cases, but there is little academic research on this as a practice in fieldwork. More research is needed.

Notes

1 Jones et al. (2017).
2 FBI Charlotte Field Office (2020, December 3).

Bibliography

FBI Charlotte Field Office. (2020, December 3). *Too Tall Bandit responsible for 16 bank robberies in a decade* [Press release]. Federal Bureau of Investigation. www.fbi.gov/contact-us/field-offices/charlotte/news/press-releases/too-tall-bandit-responsible-for-16-bank-robberies-in-a-decade

Jones, A. M., Hayhurst, K. P., Bird, S. M., Hickman, M., Seddon, T., Dunn, G., & Millar, T. M. (2017). Insights into the link between drug use and criminality: Lifetime offending of criminally-active opiate users. *Drug and Alcohol Dependence, 179*, 309–316. https://doi.org/10.1016/j.drugalcdep.2017.07.024

10 Victim Vulnerabilities

Introduction

In criminological and law enforcement contexts, victim vulnerability refers to the physical, psychological, environmental, or situational characteristics that increase a person's likelihood of being targeted by an offender.

Analysts, investigators, and officers can gain insights into offender targeting patterns by comparing these traits across victims. Understanding these vulnerabilities also supports preventive strategies and allows law enforcement to protect at-risk populations better. This chapter recognizes victim traits may not be simply background data but can be possible active elements in crime pattern dynamics.

Example Victim Vulnerabilities

Physical Vulnerabilities

- age (children, elderly individuals)
- physical disabilities or limitations
- size or physical stature
- health condition

Psychological Vulnerabilities

- mental health issues or disorders
- cognitive impairments
- substance abuse or addiction
- trauma or post-traumatic stress
- impulsivity or risk-taking behavior
- inability to assess danger or make sound judgments

Communication Vulnerabilities

- limited language skills or language barriers
- hearing or speech impairments
- communication disorders
- lack of access to communication devices or services

DOI: 10.4324/9781003728733-12

Socio-economic Vulnerabilities

- poverty
- unemployment
- homelessness
- lack of access to education or resources

Geographic Vulnerabilities

- high crime rate neighborhoods or areas
- remote, secluded, or isolated locations
- lack of security infrastructure (lighting, surveillance)

Home Vulnerabilities

- lack of home security measures
- absence from home (vacations, holidays, work, school)
- negligence in locking doors, windows

Social Vulnerabilities

- lack of social support or strong relationships
- social isolation
- membership in marginalized or stigmatized groups
- targeting based on social status or reputation
- peer pressure and influence
- discrimination or prejudice
- targeted on the basis of race, religion, sexual orientation, or other protected characteristics

Gender-Based Vulnerabilities

- targeting women for sexual crimes
- targeting homosexuals for crime
- gender-based violence and harassment
- sexual orientation-based violence and harassment
- domestic violence or intimate partner violence
- traditional gender roles and stereotypes

Technological Vulnerabilities

- lack of digital literacy
- weak online privacy and security practices
- cyberbullying or online harassment
- phishing scams and identity theft
- exploitation through social media or dating platforms
- over-sharing personal information online
- weak passwords
- revealing geotagged location details

Cultural Vulnerabilities

- language barriers
- limited knowledge of local customs or laws
- cultural or religious practices that may make individuals more susceptible to victimization
- targeting based on ethnic or cultural background
- unfamiliar with the local environment
- targeting in popular tourist destinations

Environmental Vulnerabilities

- natural disasters or emergencies
- lack of emergency preparedness
- poorly maintained infrastructure or public spaces
- exposure to environmental hazards (polluted areas, unsafe buildings)

Personal Lifestyle Vulnerabilities

- alcohol or drug use
- involvement in illegal activities
- reckless behavior (excessive partying, risky sexual behavior)
- inadequate personal safety precautions (not locking doors, walking alone at night)

Financial Vulnerabilities

- carrying large sums of cash
- lack of financial security measures
- falling victim to investment scams or fraud

Crime Pattern Scenario

Serial Purse Snatching Pattern – "The Purse-Snatching Stalker"

A series of seven purse snatchings over six weeks initially appeared random until analysts examined victim vulnerabilities as a pattern variable. All victims were women aged 55–78 who used mobility aids: four used walkers, two used canes, and one used a motorized wheelchair. The offender specifically targeted women exiting medical buildings between 2:00 and 4:00 PM on weekdays, timing that coincided with afternoon medical appointments when parking lots were busy but not crowded. Each victim displayed the same vulnerability cluster: visible mobility limitations that slowed their movement, hands occupied with mobility aids that prevented quick defensive responses, and predictable locations near orthopedic clinics, physical therapy centers, and dialysis facilities. Surveillance footage revealed the suspect conducted reconnaissance in medical building parking lots, observing which women struggled with balance while walking to their vehicles and noting those who set their purses in shopping cart seats or car trunks while maneuvering mobility equipment. The offender's approach exploited the victims' physical limitations through a consistent methodology: approaching from behind during the critical moment when victims were transitioning from walking aid to car door, grabbing purses when victims couldn't pursue or maintain balance, and escaping on foot while victims struggled to stabilize themselves or call for help. The vulnerability pattern (mobility impairments, predictable medical appointment timing, isolated parking lot locations, and physical inability to resist or pursue) enabled systematic targeting by the purse snatcher that averaged 45 seconds per incident. Recognition of this disability-focused targeting pattern led investigators to coordinate with medical facilities and deploy unmarked surveillance during peak afternoon appointment hours.

Example Case

Operating in London from the 1990s to 2009, Delroy Grant (known as "the Night Stalker") sexually assaulted dozens of elderly women and men after breaking into their homes at night, knowing victims were physically and cognitively unable to resist or report effectively. Grant's use of gloves and meticulous planning helped him evade detection. Investigators later criticized the delayed recognition of a serial pattern due to the advanced age and credibility issues surrounding his victims.[1]

> The suspect operates in a wide area of South London and identifies single elderly women living alone and on occasions, lone males. He breaks into properties during the early hours, often removing whole double-glazed units to gain entry. His Modus Operandi is one of meticulous preparation, pre and post offence. The telephone is disabled, either cut or pulled from sockets. The electricity is switched off at the mains or he removes fuses. Light bulbs are removed and curtains drawn. Tools to gain entry are often taken from nearby garden sheds. The suspect often wears a mask and gloves. Victims are awoken by shining a torch in their eyes. The offender spends considerable time with the victim, up to four hours in one instance. So far he has left his DNA at ten scenes with another eleven being linked on other forensic evidence. The ages of the victims range from between 68 to 93 years.
>
> The Metropolitan Police Authority[2]

Example query terms: elderly, early, morning, window, door, telephone, wire, cord, socket, electricity, switch, fuse, disable, curtain, drawn, garden, shed, mask, glove, torch, hours

Exercises

1. Using online resources, search for a case that exploited prostitution as a victim vulnerability. Summarize your findings.
2. Visit a public location where different types of people gather (shopping mall, public library, or transportation hub) and spend 30 minutes observing potential vulnerability indicators without focusing on any individual for more than a few seconds. Note general patterns you observe: Who appears to be struggling with technology (ATMs, ticket machines, smartphones)? Who seems socially isolated or confused about directions? Who displays visible signs of physical limitations or appears distracted by personal concerns? Create categories of potential vulnerabilities you observe (technological inexperience, physical limitations, social isolation, distraction, unfamiliarity with environment). After your observation, consider: Which vulnerability patterns might make someone an attractive target for different types of crimes (fraud, theft, assault)? How might environmental factors (lighting, crowd density, security presence) affect vulnerability levels? What ethical concerns arise when thinking about people in terms of their potential vulnerabilities? Finally, reflect on how your own biases might influence what you noticed or overlooked, and how stress or

criminal intent might change an offender's perception of the same vulnerabilities. This exercise demonstrates how vulnerability assessment works in practice while highlighting the importance of using such analysis responsibly and without contributing to discrimination or victim-blaming.

Critical Thinking Guidance

A significant obstacle to using victim vulnerabilities to link crimes is the inconsistent documentation of vulnerabilities in police reports and databases. Victims often do not disclose key details, such as drug use, sex work, or immigration status, due to stigma or fear, and law enforcement may overlook or inadequately record such factors. This leads to fragmented data which makes it difficult to establish patterns across cases. Additionally, many vulnerable groups (such as homeless individuals, elderly victims, undocumented migrants) are underrepresented in official reporting, further reducing visibility into recurring victimization.

Legal and ethical concerns also complicate the use of vulnerability-based profiling. Using characteristics like poverty, mental illness, or occupation as indicators in crime pattern recognition raises the risk of discriminatory policing or civil rights violations. Analytical errors can also occur when vulnerabilities are defined too broadly or when multiple overlapping factors such as race, substance dependency, and sex work make it hard to isolate which variable the offender exploited. Technology gaps, jurisdictional inconsistencies, and investigator biases compound the issue and can result in a missed or incomplete crime series identification.

Notes

1 Hill and Laville (2011, March 25).
2 Metropolitan Police Authority (2006, September 7).

Bibliography

Australian Institute of Criminology. (2002). *Crimes against business: A review of victimisation, predictors and prevention*. www.aic.gov.au/sites/default/files/2020-05/crimes-againts-business-a-review-of-victomisation-predictors-and-prevention.pdf

Bureau of Justice Statistics. (2022). *Criminal victimization, 2021*. U.S. Department of Justice, Office of Justice Programs. https://bjs.ojp.gov/library/publications/criminal-victimization-2021

Bureau of Justice Statistics. (n.d.). *National crime victimization survey data dashboard (N-DASH)*. U.S. Department of Justice, Office of Justice Programs. https://ncvs.bjs.ojp.gov/Home

Edwards, S. E., Cantor, D., Yan, T., Sun, H., & Giambo, P. (2023). *National Crime Victimization Survey redesign: The NCVS Crime Incident Report (CIR)*. Westat.

Fe, H., & Sanfelice, V. (2022). How bad is crime for business? Evidence from consumer behavior. *Journal of Urban Economics*, *129*, 103448. https://doi.org/10.1016/j.jue.2022.103448

Glensor, R. W., & Peak, K. J. (2004). *Crimes against tourists* (Problem-Specific Guide Series No. 26). U.S. Department of Justice, Office of Community Oriented Policing Services. https://popcenter.asu.edu/content/crimes-against-tourists-0

Hill, A., & Laville, S. (2011, March 25). 'Night Stalker' case: Police chief says sorry. *The Guardian*. www.theguardian.com/uk/2011/mar/25/night-stalker-case-police-sorry

Johnson, K. D. (2003). *Financial crimes against the elderly* (Problem-Specific Guide Series No. 20). U.S. Department of Justice, Office of Community Oriented Policing Services. https://popcenter.asu.edu/content/financial-crimes-against-elderly-0

Lee, M., Moir, E., & McKillop, N. (2025). A crime script analysis of court-adjudicated sexual offenses perpetrated against older adults. *Journal of Elder Abuse & Neglect*. Advance online publication, 1–32. https://doi.org/10.1080/08946566.2025.2550686

Metropolitan Police Authority. (2006, September 7). *The use of DNA in operation Minstead* (Report No. 060907/10). http://policeauthority.org/metropolitan/committees/x-eodb/2006/060907/10/index.html

Weisel, D. L. (2005). *Analyzing repeat victimization* (Problem-Solving Tools Guide No. 4). U.S. Department of Justice, Office of Community Oriented Policing Services. https://popcenter.asu.edu/content/analyzing-repeat-victimization

11 Victim-Offender Relationship

Introduction

The focus in crime pattern analysis is generally on stranger-on-stranger crimes, but there are crime patterns that involve other relationships. These relationships are part of the crime pattern. Understanding and documenting the type of relationship could help connect cases that might otherwise be overlooked.

The circumstances of victimization often play a role in the stranger-on-stranger crime pattern and may be considered a kind of relationship between the offender and victim. For example, two persons unknown to each other frequenting the same bar may provide a set up for violent crime after leaving the bar. The offender may then go on to commit the same type of crime with more victims.

Past research has shown that over half of the rapes, robberies, and assaults committed involved strangers.[1]

Relationship Examples

Stranger Crimes

Random Stranger: Neither the victim nor the offender has any prior knowledge of the other.
Non-Random Stranger: The offender targets a particular type of victim, for example, based on appearance, routine, or lifestyle, but has no personal connection to them.

Acquaintance Crimes

Casual Acquaintance: The victim and offender have met before but have a superficial relationship.
Known Acquaintance: The victim and offender have some level of familiarity with each other but are not close.
Friend or Neighbor: The victim and the offender are friends, colleagues, or neighbors, with a relatively established relationship.

Intimate Partner Crimes

Current Partner: The victim and offender are in a current romantic relationship.
Former Partner: The victim and offender were previously in a romantic relationship.

DOI: 10.4324/9781003728733-13

Familial Crimes

Parent-Child: The victim or offender is a parent or guardian of the other.
Sibling: The victim and offender are siblings.
Extended Family: The victim and offender are related but not part of the immediate family (cousins, uncles, aunts, etc.).

Professional Relationships

Employee-Employer: The victim and offender are connected through a work environment.
Client-Service Provider: The victim is a client of a service provided by the offender, or vice versa (such as doctor-patient).

Authority Relationships

Teacher-Student: The victim and offender are connected through an educational setting.
Law Enforcement-Civilian: The victim or offender is a law enforcement officer.

Online Relationships

Anonymous Online Interaction: Victim and offender have interacted only online and never met in person.
Known Online Interaction: The victim and offender have an online relationship and may have shared personal details but have not met in person.

Circumstances of Victimization

The circumstances of victimization often play a role in the stranger-on-stranger crime pattern.

Circumstances

- random victim (victim chosen without specific targeting)
- targeted victim (victim selected intentionally due to specific characteristics or circumstances)
- opportunistic victim (victim who becomes a target due to a crime opportunity arising)
- repeat victim (victim who has experienced multiple incidents of victimization)
- serial victim (victim targeted by a serial offender)

Non-Person Victims

NIBRS categorizes these victims in the following categories: business, financial institutions, government, religious organizations, and society/public. Offenders may have relationships with those entities. To apply this concept:

- Analyze crimes against the same business or institution across jurisdictions
- Link crimes using same MO, timeframe, or transportation access
- Maintain data on recurring non-person targets for prevention efforts

Relationship Information Aids Investigations

Investigators use information about an offender's family, friends, and associates to gather intelligence that can reveal routines, hideouts, resources, or accomplices. Relatives may provide insight into stressors or movements, while friends and acquaintances often identify vehicles, residences, or social settings linked to the offender. Even uncooperative contacts generate leads through surveillance, phone records, or social media connections. By mapping these ties, investigators can track offender behavior, uncover support networks, and exploit relational links to locate suspects and connect cases.

Crime Pattern Scenario

Serial Employment Fraud Pattern – "The Job Interview Scammer"

A series of 11 identity theft and fraud cases over five months initially appeared unrelated until investigators analyzed the victim-offender relationship patterns. All victims had recently applied for jobs through online platforms and participated in phone or video interviews with the same fraudulent "recruitment company." The relationship pattern was consistently professional but fabricated: the offender posed as an HR representative for legitimate companies, conducting convincing interviews that required victims to provide Social Security numbers, bank account information for "direct deposit setup," and personal details for "background checks." Each victim believed they were in a legitimate employer-applicant relationship, which the offender exploited to gain trust and access to sensitive information. The circumstances of victimization followed a consistent pattern: recently unemployed individuals aged 25–45 years who were actively job searching, had updated their resumes on job boards within the past month, and were desperate enough for employment to overlook red flags in the hiring process. The offender systematically searched job boards for fresh applicants, particularly targeting those who listed email addresses and phone numbers, then initiated contact within 24–48 hours of resume posting when applicants were most hopeful and least suspicious. The relationship exploitation was sophisticated: the offender used real company names, researched actual job openings, and even conducted multiple "interview rounds" to establish credibility before requesting sensitive information. Recognition of this professional relationship pattern – fake employer targeting desperate job seekers – led investigators to coordinate with job placement websites and develop warning systems for recently posted resumes showing vulnerability indicators.

Example Case

Rick Dugo, known as the "Neighborhood Serial Scammer," orchestrated numerous fraud schemes targeting acquaintances, friends, neighbors, and people he met in various social settings such as gyms. Over several years, he convinced victims to invest in fake business opportunities, including car washes, electronics resale, motorcycles, and more, with promises of high returns. Dugo routinely collected large sums for illegitimate investments, repeatedly returned to victims for more money, and never delivered on his promises. His scams devastated families and individuals, with losses in some cases reaching hundreds of thousands of dollars.[2],[3]

Example query terms: gym, friend, neighbor, acquaintance, scam, fake, phony, illegitimate, promise, car wash, electronics, motorcycle

Exercise

Research three different crime types online (fraud, stalking, domestic violence, workplace violence, or child abuse) and analyze how the victim-offender relationship influences the crime pattern in each case. For each crime type, identify:

1. How the specific relationship type provides access or opportunity for the offender,
2. How the relationship affects the victim's likelihood to report the crime, and
3. What relationship dynamics the offender exploits (trust, authority, dependency, isolation).

Create a comparison chart showing how the same offender behavior (threats, manipulation, financial exploitation) might manifest differently depending on the relationship context. After completing your research, consider: Which relationship types create the most vulnerability for victims? How might offenders strategically cultivate certain types of relationships to facilitate criminal activity? What challenges do different relationship types create for law enforcement in terms of evidence collection, victim cooperation, and pattern recognition?

Critical Thinking Guidance

Victim-offender relationships reveal key information about offender motives and access. Whether the tie is intimate, professional, casual, or purely situational, it shapes both opportunity and the victim's risk profile. Patterns such as neighbor frauds, employer assaults, or online grooming often emerge across jurisdictions when similar relationships are compared.

Not all relationships are obvious. Repeated chance encounters – like seeing the same person at a gym – or contact under multiple online identities can mask serial behavior. Offenders may take advantage of weak social ties, and their method of gaining trust becomes part of their modus operandi.

Relationship data must be evaluated carefully. Victims, offenders, investigators, or social media records can misrepresent ties, and each source carries bias. Complex cases may involve overlapping relationships – coworker, neighbor, and online contact – so avoid forcing them into a single category. Definitions of "family," "friend," or "authority" also vary across cultures.

Circumstances can create temporary trust structures, as with a rideshare driver and passenger. Such pseudo-relationships, common in the gig economy or online-to-offline interactions, can be exploited by offenders. Agencies should develop consistent ways to capture relationship data and integrate it into criminal databases, to facilitate spotting and linking patterns more effectively.

Notes

1 Riedel (1987).
2 Smith (2023, October 31).
3 Studio 847 (2023–present).

Bibliography

Harrell, E. (2012). *Violent victimization committed by strangers, 1993–2010 (NCJ No. 239424)* [Special report]. U.S. Department of Justice, Office of Justice Programs, Bureau of Justice Statistics. www.bjs.gov/content/pub/pdf/vvcs9310.pdf

Riedel, M. (1987). Stranger violence: Perspectives, issues, and problems. *The Journal of Criminal Law and Criminology*, *78*(2), 223–258. https://doi.org/10.2307/1143448

Smith, B. (2023, October 31). When your gym spotter turns out to be a scammer: Conman Rick Dugo targeted his victims in gyms until one man finally helped take him down. *Men's Health*. www.menshealth.com/trending-news/a45470868/scammer-rick-dugo/

Studio 847. (Producer). (2023–present). To catch a conman [Audio podcast]. *Studio 847*. https://podcasts.apple.com/us/podcast/to-catch-a-conman/id1710269532

12 Lifestyle and Employment

Introduction

Lifestyle and occupation may make someone a more likely victim of crime and often can tell us something useful to know about the offender in investigations. Victims may be targeted due to the visibility, location, or routine of their occupation or daily life. Similarly, an offender's lifestyle, including criminal habits, peer influences, addiction, or occupation, can explain their crime choices, locations, and methods.

Routine Activity Theory considers how lifestyle brings offenders and victims together in unguarded settings. Detailed modus operandi information is necessary in determining its application.

Recognizing how employment status, risk behaviors, or daily routines factor into a pattern helps law enforcement identify crime-prone environments, track suspect behaviors, and build stronger prevention strategies. This chapter highlights the importance of examining how people live and work, not just who they are, in understanding crime patterns.

Lifestyle

The way in which a person lives is their lifestyle.

Victim Lifestyle Aspects

- Routine Activities: Daily activities like commuting, shopping, or leisure activities can affect a person's likelihood of becoming a victim. Routine activities can also lead to hotspots of criminal activity.
- Residential Location: Areas with high poverty, low levels of social cohesion, or high population density can have higher rates of victimization.
- Occupation: Certain occupations may expose individuals to higher risks. For example, late-night workers or those in high-crime areas might be more susceptible.
- Social Circles: The people one associates with can influence the likelihood of becoming a victim.
- Risk Behavior: Engaging in risky behaviors like drug use, excessive alcohol consumption, or frequenting dangerous locations can increase victimization chances.
- Visibility: High public visibility or social media presence might make individuals attractive targets for certain types of crime, such as stalking or cyberbullying.
- Age and Gender: Different age groups and genders are susceptible to different types of crimes.

DOI: 10.4324/9781003728733-14

- Lack of Security Measures: Inadequate home or personal security measures can make individuals easier targets.
- Time and Place of Activities: Certain activities at specific times, like late-night outings, can make someone more susceptible.

Offender Lifestyle Aspects

- Criminal Opportunities: Offenders often choose areas where they believe crime can be committed with a lower risk of detection.
- Economic Status: Offenders from lower economic backgrounds may be more likely to engage in property crimes.
- Peer Influence: Criminal behavior is often influenced by an offender's social circle.
- Skill Level: The level of skill an offender has can influence the types of crimes they commit. For example, skilled hackers may engage in cybercrime, while unskilled offenders may stick to simpler forms of crime.
- Addiction: Substance abuse can drive crime, especially petty crimes, to sustain the addiction.
- Routine Activities: Just as with victims, the routine activities of offenders can influence where and when crimes are likely to be committed.
- Occupation: Some occupations provide greater opportunities for crimes like fraud or embezzlement.
- Motivation: The offender's underlying motivations can also dictate the types of crimes committed, ranging from thrill-seeking to economic necessity.
- Resource Availability: Having access to weapons, transportation, or technology can expand the types of crimes an offender might commit.

Example Lifestyle Variables

- alcohol abuser, alcoholic, bisexual, child, child molester, criminally active, crossdresser, drifter, drug addict, drug seller, drug user, elderly, gambler, habitual offender, heterosexual, hitchhiker, homeless person, homosexual, illegal alien, immigrant, loner, mentally disabled, mentally ill, physically disabled, panhandler, pedophile, pimp, promiscuous, prostitute, public figure, recluse, registered sex offender, retired, runaway, smuggler, street person, student, thief, trafficker, transgender, transient, transvestite, wealthy

Occupation

A person who lives a life of crime may have that lifestyle as their occupation. It may be their only work.

Occupation Examples

- Management: administrator, director, executive, manager
- Business and Financial Operation: accountant, agent, appraiser, event planner, loan officer, tax preparer
- Computer and Mathematical: computer programmer, database administrator, web developer, statistician, data scientist
- Architecture and Engineering: architect, drafter, engineer, surveyor, technologist
- Life, Physical, and Social Science: biologist, chemist, economist, physicist, psychologist, scientist

- Community and Social Service: case worker, clergy, counselor, human services worker, social worker, therapist
- Legal: judge, lawyer, magistrate, paralegal
- Educational Instruction and Library: curator, librarian, professor, teacher, teacher's aide, teaching assistant, tutor
- Arts, Design, Entertainment, Sports, and Media: actor, anchor person, artist, athlete, coach, dancer, designer, disc jockey, director, editor, entertainer, journalist, musician, producer, reporter, scout, writer
- Healthcare Practitioners and Technical: chiropractor, dentist, doctor, emergency medical technician, medical records specialist, nurse, paramedic, pharmacist, veterinarian
- Healthcare Support: massage therapist, nursing assistants, orderlies, occupational therapist, physical therapist
- Protective Service: correctional officer, firefighter, military member, police officer, security screener, security guard, game warden
- Food Preparation and Serving Related: cook, bartender, dishwasher, food preparation worker, food server, host/hostess, waiter/waitress
- Building and Grounds Cleaning and Maintenance: groundskeeper, housekeeper, janitor, landscaper, maid
- Personal Care and Service: animal caretaker, barber, coatroom attendant, fitness instructor, gambling dealer, hairdresser, nail technician, tour guide
- Sales and Related: cashier, clerk, door-to-door salesperson, model, sales representative, real estate agent, salesperson, street vendor
- Office and Administrative Support: administrative assistant, bank teller, bill collector, data entry worker, file clerk, mail carrier, secretary
- Farming, Fishing, and Forestry: agricultural worker, animal breeder, conservation worker, farm worker, logging worker, ranch worker
- Construction and Extraction: carpenter, electrician, highway maintenance worker, mining worker, oil drill operator, painter, plumber, roofer
- Installation, Maintenance, and Repair: locksmith, mechanic, service technician
- Production: baker, butcher, engraver, dry cleaner, laboratory technician, machine operator, production worker, tailor
- Transportation and Material Moving: bus driver, flight attendant, parking attendant, pilot, railroad worker, sailor, taxi driver, truck driver

Role or Status of Victim

Sometimes, the role or status of the victims has significance.

Role or Status

- bystander victim (victim unintentionally involved in a criminal incident)
- witness victim (victim who witnessed a crime and may be targeted as a result)
- whistleblower victim (victim targeted for exposing illegal activities)
- retaliation victim (victim targeted as retaliation for previous actions)
- high-profile victim (victim with public visibility, such as celebrities or politicians)
- vulnerable population victim (victim belonging to a group susceptible to victimization, such as children, the elderly, and homeless individuals)
- symbolic victim (victim whose case gains significant attention and represents a larger issue)
- community impact victim (victim whose victimization affects the community at large)
- accomplice victim (victim who is involved in criminal activities alongside the offender)

Life Pattern Analysis Versus Pattern of Life Analysis

Some software used in supporting criminal investigations and crime analysis integrate pattern of life analysis as used in the military, but in reality, in law enforcement's legal and ethical restrictions call for modifications of this technique. What we might think of as "life pattern analysis" used to link crimes is different than "pattern of life analysis" used by the military. As AI tools evolve and more and more technology is used by individuals that could track them (think of fitness/health apps and beyond), this subject will require more examination.

Life Pattern Analysis

- Definition: The study of an individual's long-term routines, habits, and behaviors (work schedules, travel routes, spending patterns, etc.).
- Purpose: Used in policing, intelligence, and criminology to identify consistencies that may help link crimes, assess risk, or prevent victimization.
- Data Sources: Lawful investigative records, interviews, surveillance conducted under warrant, open-source information, and victim/offender histories.
- Ethical/Legal Focus: Protecting privacy and civil liberties; requires compliance with criminal procedure, data protection laws, and proportionality standards.

Pattern of Life Analysis

Definition: A military and intelligence term referring to the observation of an individual or group's daily activities over shorter cycles (hours, days, weeks) to identify behaviors and predict future actions.

- Purpose: Often used in operational contexts to inform targeting, surveillance, or interdiction decisions.
- Data Sources: Signals intelligence, aerial surveillance, sensor data, and other intelligence streams.
- Ethical/Legal Focus: Raises questions about proportionality, collateral impact, and human rights in national security or combat environments.

Key Differences

- Life pattern analysis emphasizes lawful, long-term behavioral study within a policing or criminological framework.
- Pattern of life analysis emphasizes short-term operational observation in intelligence or military settings, where legal and ethical debates often focus on surveillance intensity and use of force.

Crime Pattern Scenario

Serial Vehicle Theft Pattern – "The Tow Truck Driver"

A series of 14 vehicle thefts over five months targeting luxury cars in shopping mall parking lots was linked through the offender's employment as a tow truck operator. The pattern emerged when investigators noticed all stolen vehicles were taken from locations along the offender's legitimate towing routes during his scheduled work hours. His employment provided systematic advantages: legitimate presence in parking lots without attracting suspicion, knowledge of which vehicles had mechanical problems or were likely to be abandoned temporarily, access to professional towing equipment that facilitated quick vehicle removal, and familiarity with impound lot procedures that helped him avoid detection when processing stolen vehicles. The lifestyle pattern showed methodical exploitation of his work territory: he identified high-value targets during legitimate service calls to shopping centers and office complexes, used his company radio to monitor police activity in areas where he planned to operate, and timed thefts during busy afternoon hours when his tow truck activity appeared routine. His occupational knowledge extended to victim selection – he targeted vehicles that appeared to have minor mechanical issues, reasoning that owners would initially assume their cars had been legitimately towed rather than stolen, buying him additional time before theft reports were filed. The employment pattern provided perfect cover: witnesses seeing a tow truck removing a vehicle assumed it was a legitimate repossession or breakdown service. Recognition of this occupation-based pattern led investigators to work with towing companies to identify the offender.

Example Case

Todd Kohlhepp, a licensed South Carolina realtor, exploited his profession to facilitate and conceal a series of murders over more than a decade. His role in real estate gave him access to isolated properties, allowed him to build trust with prospective victims through business transactions, and provided a pretext (such as job offers or property visits) to lure and ambush those he targeted. Kohlhepp used his professional credibility and access to remote land to abduct, kill, and dispose of victims discreetly, with several bodies buried on property he owned. His ability to leverage the occupational privileges of a realtor – mobility, access to vacant sites, and interactions with strangers – was central to both the execution and concealment of his serial crimes, illustrating the risk when offenders exploit positions of public trust for criminal purposes.[1]

Example query terms: real estate, property, lure, isolated, job offer, visit, remote, vacant

Exercise

Select a specific occupation (teacher, healthcare worker, delivery driver, security guard, or retail worker) and research online cases where someone in that profession either became a serial crime victim or committed serial crimes. Analyze how their lifestyle and employment factors influenced the crime pattern by identifying: (1) What aspects of their daily routine created vulnerability or opportunity, (2) How their work schedule, location, or professional relationships affected the crimes, and (3) What occupational access, skills, or credibility the person possessed that influenced the criminal activity. After completing your research, consider: How might employers in this field modify workplace policies or security measures to address these vulnerabilities? What warning signs might indicate when someone is exploiting their professional position for criminal purposes? How do different shift patterns, work locations, or job responsibilities create varying risk profiles? This exercise demonstrates how lifestyle and employment factors create both criminal opportunities and prevention possibilities while highlighting the intersection between legitimate activities and criminal behavior.

Critical Thinking Guidance

Think about how to gather reliable lifestyle and employment information and how that data can support linkage between cases. Consider multiple sources: interviews, criminal histories, employment records, social media activity, surveillance footage, and victimology reports. Routine activity data, such as where a victim or offender lives, works, or frequently travels, can be pieced together from cellphone records, transportation logs, service transactions, and witness accounts. These elements, when collected consistently, provide behavioral baselines that can reveal overlaps between victims and offenders across time and space.

Once this information is obtained, ask questions. Does the offender's job give them access to multiple jurisdictions, such as a long-haul trucker or utility worker? Have victims lived similar lifestyles that bring them into contact with the same areas or offender types, such as frequenting the same corridors, night-time zones, or homeless encampments? Do several crimes occur along a suspect's known delivery or patrol route? Linking cases through shared lifestyle factors, either among victims or via offender routines, can help establish geographic and temporal patterns, particularly when forensic evidence is limited.

Critical thinking means recognizing that not all patterns are immediately obvious. A series of seemingly unrelated assaults might be linked by a shared victim profile: late-night food service workers walking home from closing shifts in high-crime zones. An offender might choose targets based on opportunity created by their work schedule or territory. Look for these consistent intersections, places where the lifestyle of the victim overlaps with the accessibility or routines of the offender. This kind of pattern-based reasoning is key to linking crimes that might otherwise remain isolated on paper but are connected in the field.

Note

1 Associated Press (2016, November 12).

Bibliography

Associated Press. (2016, November 12). "Hair-on-fire kind of guy": Serial killer suspect hid secrets behind real estate success. *The Guardian*. www.theguardian.com/us-news/2016/nov/13/hair-on-fire-kind-of-guy-serial-killer-suspect-hid-secrets-behind-real-estate-success

Brignoni, H., & Edwards, T. (2020, February 24). Forensic pattern of life analysis. *Forensic Focus*. www.forensicfocus.com/articles/forensic-pattern-of-life-analysis/

Denley, J., Ariel, B., & Felson, M. (2024). Where can offenders be found when they are not committing crimes? A cross-sectional survey of British police officers on non-crime locations. *Heliyon*, *10*(1), e23385. https://doi.org/10.1016/j.heliyon.2023.e23385

Engström, A. (2020). Conceptualizing lifestyle and routine activities in the early 21st century: A systematic review of self-report measures in studies on direct-contact offenses in young populations. *Crime & Delinquency*, *67*(5), 737–782. https://doi.org/10.1177/0011128720937640

Hughes, S. E., Chaumont Menéndez, C. K., & Afanuh, S. E. (2023). *Reducing workplace violence in gasoline stations and convenience stores* (DHHS [NIOSH] Publication No. 2023–121). U.S. Department of Health and Human Services, Centers for Disease Control and Prevention, National Institute for Occupational Safety and Health. https://doi.org/10.26616/NIOSHPUB2023121

Lansing, J. (2018, September). *Patterns of life* (Report No. AD1061635). Space and Naval Warfare Systems Center Pacific, Distributed Common Ground System – Navy. Defense Technical Information Center. https://apps.dtic.mil/sti/trecms/pdf/AD1061635.pdf

Palazzolo, C. (2024, October 9). FBI crime analyst describes Highway Serial Killings Initiative [Video]. *YouTube*. www.youtube.com/watch?v=IX0is2ezYDY

Robinson, M. (1999). Lifestyles, routine activities, and residential burglary victimization. *Journal of Crime and Justice*, *22*(1), 27–56. https://doi.org/10.1080/0735648X.1999.9721081

U.S. Bureau of Labor Statistics. (2022, May). *Occupation profiles*. U.S. Department of Labor. www.bls.gov/oes/current/oes_stru.htm#00-0000

13 Vehicle Description

Introduction

Crimes are linked on the basis of descriptions of the vehicle or vehicles the offender used to commit crimes when vehicles are utilized. It is important to get detailed information from victims, witnesses, and CCTV cameras regarding any notable features of an offender's vehicle. Vehicles are used as transportation to and from crime scenes, as tools in the crime itself, or as concealment for stolen goods, weapons, or abducted victims. Whether a vehicle is repeatedly described in multiple offenses or has distinctive features, it can anchor disparate crimes into a coherent pattern. This chapter encourages law enforcement professionals to treat vehicle description with the same analytical importance as offender and victim details.

How Vehicle Descriptions Affect Investigations

Ignored accurate vehicle descriptions can lead to the delayed arrest of dangerous criminals, and the emphasizing the wrong vehicle description can prolong important investigations as illustrated in the following examples.

The Gilgo Beach serial murder cold case was solved because, in 2010, a victim's roommate reported the description of the vehicle he had seen the suspect drive, a first-generation Chevrolet Avalanche. Rex Heuermann, arrested in 2023, had been in the house fighting with the victim and the roommate, then left in the vehicle. A state investigator discovered the truck description after the launch of a new task force. A search of a vehicle records database led investigators to Heuermann.[1]

During the 2002 Beltway sniper investigation, law enforcement focused intensely on witness reports of a white box truck and a white van, believing these were the vehicles used by the shooters. That early misdirection consumed investigative resources and dominated media broadcasts. Meanwhile, numerous credible eyewitnesses had reported seeing an older-model, dark blue Chevrolet Caprice. These Caprice descriptions were largely ignored in the public alerts. Only after officials shifted their description did attention finally turn to the correct four-door sedan, with a modified trunk serving as a sniper's nest, leading to the discovery of John Allen Muhammad and Lee Boyd Malvo's vehicle and their eventual arrest. The initial focus on a white van is now seen as a significant investigative delay caused by tunnel vision and overreliance on the most repeated witness reports.[2]

Offender's Vehicle Example Variables

- General Descriptors
- Make (e.g., Ford, Toyota, Honda)

DOI: 10.4324/9781003728733-15

- Model (e.g., Mustang, Civic, F-150)
- Year or Estimated Age (e.g., 2000–2005, newer model, older model)

Color

- Standard Colors: Black, white, silver, red, blue, green, gray, yellow, brown, beige, maroon, purple, pink, orange
- Unusual or Descriptive Colors: Bronze, copper, gold, teal, taupe, ivory, cream, camouflage, multi-colored
- Shades: Light, dark, matte, metallic

License Plate Characteristics

- Characters: Full or partial alphanumeric sequence
- Jurisdiction: State, province, country
- Plate Type: Temporary, dealer, commercial, vanity (personalized)
- Condition: Dirty, obscured, damaged, altered, missing, covered
- Additional Clues: Unusual color, background design, expired tag

Vehicle Type

- Passenger Vehicles: Sedan, coupe, hatchback, station wagon, convertible, SUV, luxury car, sports car, classic or vintage car
- Commercial or Heavy Vehicles: Pickup truck, box truck, delivery truck, tractor trailer, bus
- Recreational or Other: Van, camper van, RV, motor home, jeep, off-road vehicle, motorcycle, moped, bicycle, electric bike, hybrid or electric car

Features and Modifications

- Exterior Modifications: Spoilers, body kits, lift kits, oversized tires, custom grilles
- Cosmetic Details: Custom paint, decals, bumper stickers, racing stripes, pinstriping
- Window and Roof Features: Tinted windows, sunroof, convertible top
- Accessories: Roof rack, ladder rack, aftermarket lights, unique mirrors or trim

Visible Damage

- Glass Damage: Cracked or broken windshield, rear window, side mirrors
- Body Damage: Dents, scratches, chipped paint, rust, corrosion
- Lighting Issues: Missing or broken headlight or taillight
- Missing Parts: Hubcaps, bumpers, mirrors, panels

Tires and Rims

- Condition: Flat tires, worn treads, snow chains
- Appearance: Custom rims, aftermarket or oversized wheels
- Brand: Recognizable tire brands or markings if observed

Unusual Noises

- Engine Sounds: Loud or modified exhaust, sputtering, backfiring
- Mechanical Issues: Rattling, dragging parts, scraping sounds

Vehicle Condition

- Clean
- Very clean (possibly newly washed)
- Dirty or covered in mud
- Neglected, heavily worn, or damaged

Note These Possibilities

- The offender(s) used multiple vehicles to commit crime(s).
- The offender(s) used a stolen vehicle to commit crime(s).

Crime Pattern Scenario

Serial Convenience Store Robbery Pattern – "The Silver Sedan Series"

A series of five armed robberies at gas station convenience stores over two months was linked through consistent vehicle descriptions provided by multiple witnesses and surveillance cameras. In each incident, the getaway vehicle was described as a silver four-door sedan, likely a Toyota Camry or Honda Accord from the mid-2000s, with a noticeable rust spot on the trunk and a missing front hubcap on the passenger side. The vehicle pattern became the primary linking factor when physical descriptions of the robber varied due to different hats and clothing worn during each incident. Store employees consistently noted the silver sedan idling in the parking lot for several minutes before each robbery, suggesting surveillance behavior. Security cameras from three different locations captured partial license plate sequences showing the same first three characters, and the distinctive rust damage on the trunk was clearly visible in footage from two stores. The vehicle's modest condition aligned with targeting pattern of smaller, independently owned gas stations rather than major chain stores with enhanced security. Traffic cameras near two robbery locations confirmed the same damaged silver sedan traveling consistent routes that avoided main highways, suggesting familiarity with back roads in the area. The timing pattern showed the vehicle arriving at target locations during evening shift changes when stores were typically staffed by single employees. Recognition of this vehicle-based pattern led investigators to canvass auto repair shops for silver sedans with trunk rust damage and ultimately identify the vehicle through a routine traffic stop where the officer noticed the distinctive damage described in the robbery bulletins.

Example Case

In March 2024, Asheville Police arrested a 19-year-old and two juveniles in connection with a spike of over 100 vehicle window smashings and thefts across the city. A key breakthrough came when officers located one stolen Kia bearing a unique bumper sticker, which led them to recover the vehicle, gather a receipt linked to a local restaurant, and ultimately identify and arrest Green. A detective in the investigation noted this distinctive sticker was instrumental in tracing the stolen Kia and bringing charges, which included dozens of felonies for breaking and entering, larceny, property damage, and conspiracy.[3]

Example query terms: window smashed, window smashing, Asheville, bumper sticker

Exercises

1. Describe how a vehicle feature, when recorded thoroughly, can serve as the connective tissue in a series of crimes. Use examples to support your position.
2. Research two real solved cases online where vehicle descriptions were crucial to identifying serial offenders (use search terms like "serial robbery vehicle description" or "serial crime solved vehicle"). For each case, document: (1) What specific vehicle details helped link the crimes, (2) How investigators used the vehicle information to identify suspects, and (3) What challenges or mistakes occurred with vehicle descriptions during the investigation. Create a comparison chart showing which types of vehicle features (damage, modifications, license plates, unusual characteristics) proved most reliable for case linkage versus which details were less helpful or led to false leads. After completing your research, consider: Why might some vehicle features be more memorable to witnesses than others? How do environmental factors (lighting, stress, observation time) affect the reliability of vehicle descriptions? What investigative techniques can verify or enhance witness vehicle descriptions? This exercise demonstrates the real-world importance of accurate vehicle documentation while highlighting both the potential and limitations of vehicle-based crime pattern analysis.

Critical Thinking Guidance

When vehicle descriptions appear in multiple incidents, investigators must think critically about what makes the vehicle data useful and how it can be applied to link crimes. A simple color or body type may be too common to draw strong conclusions, but when combined with unique features, such as a cracked taillight, personalized license plate, or bumper sticker, it can become a key linking element. Recognize the value of even partial or seemingly minor details, especially when they recur across different reports. For example, repeated witness mentions of a "loud, rusty red pickup with a missing hubcap" could help tie together geographically separated break-ins. Critical thinking also means verifying whether those descriptors are reliable and cross-referencing them with CCTV footage, license plate readers, and/or DMV records to confirm patterns rather than coincidences.

In addition, evaluate how the vehicle is used within the crime. Is it just transportation, or part of the offense itself, such as being used to ram a storefront, transport victims, or conceal weapons? Recognizing functional patterns in vehicle use can support offender profiling and crime linkage. Analysts should ask: Did the vehicle's role remain consistent across crimes? Is there evidence the offender switched vehicles, used stolen cars, or modified the same vehicle over time? As in the Gilgo Beach case, even a single well-documented vehicle description, when revisited or newly discovered, can break a case open years later. Applying critical thinking means treating vehicle details as dynamic, pattern-rich evidence, not just static descriptors in a report.

Notes

1 Offenhartz (2023, July 21).
2 Davenport (2002, November 17).
3 Thompson (2024, March 21).

Bibliography

Davenport, C. (2002, November 17). The white box truck that wasn't. *The Washington Post*. www.washingtonpost.com/archive/local/2002/11/18/the-white-box-truck-that-wasnt/bd5639ab-fc06-4312-99a2-12efe7ca6ddf

Offenhartz, J. (2023, July 21). He came face to face with Rex Heuermann; 12 years later, his tip helped crack the Gilgo case. *NBC New York*. www.nbcnewyork.com/news/local/he-came-face-to-face-with-the-alleged-gilgo-beach-killer-12-years-later-his-tip-helped-crack-the-case/4526677/

Thompson, T. (2024, March 21). Unique bumper sticker leads to arrests in Asheville vehicle vandalism spree. *WLOS*. https://wlos.com/news/local/unique-bumper-sticker-leads-to-arrests-in-asheville-vehicle-vandalism-spree-taysean-green-asheville-police-department

14 Deception

Introduction

Criminals who rely on deception demonstrate planning, confidence, and a willingness to manipulate victims or witnesses. Whether through a clever ruse, a lure, using a false identity, or actual physical disguise, because these methods are purposeful and often distinctive, they can link cases that share no other obvious similarities. Cataloguing details about the deception variable used in one incident helps analysts connect other geographically dispersed events, exclude look-alike crimes, and forecast offender escalation.

In recent years, deception has expanded beyond physical tactics into the digital realm. Offenders now exploit advanced technologies such as deepfakes and voice-cloning to impersonate trusted individuals, create false evidence, or manipulate communications in ways that are increasingly difficult to detect. Fraudulent video calls, synthetic audio messages, and AI-generated documents can be used to deceive victims, mislead investigators, or conceal criminal identities. These high-tech deception methods, while novel in form, share the same underlying purpose as traditional disguises: to manipulate perception and gain advantage. Tracking and categorizing these emerging techniques alongside conventional ruses ensure that investigators can recognize evolving deception patterns, distinguish between authentic and fabricated evidence, and anticipate offender adaptation.

The Anatomy of Deception

Deception preys on fundamental human psychology. Tactics succeed by exploiting cognitive biases, such as the tendency to trust authority figures (authority bias), the desire to help someone in perceived distress, or the response to a convincing pretext (social engineering). Understanding these principles is key to analyzing the offender's strategy and sophistication. Deceptive acts can be broken down into four core components: the ruse, the lure, the impersonation, and the disguise.

The Ruse (The Action)

A ruse is an action or contrived scenario intended to deceive a victim. It is the offender's "script" or ploy. For example, an offender might feign a traffic accident to compel a driver to exit their vehicle or pretend to be conducting a survey to enter a home. Other example ruses include the following:

- asking for/seeking directions
- being sent by someone

DOI: 10.4324/9781003728733-16

- going on a date
- lending assistance
- looking for a pet or person
- needing water, a bathroom, or a phone
- pretending to find money or other valuables
- pretending to want to make a purchase
- returning a purchase or stolen property

The Lure (The Bait)

A lure is the specific temptation used to persuade a victim to comply, come closer, or go somewhere. It is the "bait" that makes the ruse compelling. While the ruse is the action, the lure is the offer. Example lures offered by an offender include the following:

- Assistance: assistance with a vehicle, gas/oil/air for vehicle, carrying groceries, directions
- Goods: candy, treats, toys, cigarettes, drugs, a drink (alcohol, water, coffee, etc.)
- Opportunity: employment, a gift/prize, profit on an investment
- Services: transportation, use of a phone or toilet
- Social/Personal: information, amusement/game, fame, romance, sex

The Impersonation (The Role)

Impersonation involves pretending to be another person to deceive a victim. This role is chosen to gain access, inspire trust, or project authority. Below are example roles, grouped by category:

- Authority Figures: law enforcement/police, security guard, inspector (building, health, fire), emergency services/paramedic, firefighters
- Trusted Figures: doctor/nurse, minister/preacher, social worker, teacher
- Service and Utility Workers: delivery person, home contractor/repair person, utility worker (gas, electric, cable)
- Business Nexus: business professionals, businessperson/salesperson, journalist/reporter, model agent/photographer, insurance agent, customer, renter, renting agent
- Vulnerable Persons: lost person, stranded person, blind/deaf person, drunk/drugged/impaired, homeless person/panhandler, hurt/injured person, physically disabled/wheelchair-bound
- Other: deceased person, psychic, God/Satan

The Disguise (The Appearance)

> On January 26, 2020, an unknown subject entered the Goldy's Gas Station located in the 3300 block of North Arthur Ashe Boulevard in the City of Richmond, Virginia, pointed a semi-automatic handgun at the victim clerks and demanded money. At one point the subject pushed one of the clerks before moving behind the counter; and as the clerks complied with the demands, the subject flipped the register over and grabbed additional money underneath. The subject then fled the premises on foot. This robbery is the latest in a string of armed commercial robberies by a subject investigators have named the 'Scream Bandit'. The subject has been described as a black male, approximately 5′7″ to

5′10″, 160–180 pounds, and 20 to 30 years of age; wearing all black clothing, black or blue gloves, and a "scream" mask.[1]

Crimes, especially robbery, are sometimes committed by masked perpetrators[2] or those wearing some sort of disguise, serial crimes may be linked via these elements.

A disguise serves either to support an impersonation or to obscure identity. Note that these categories often overlap; a uniform is a disguise that also functions as a tool of impersonation. Example disguise elements include the following:

- Facial Obscurants: animal or Halloween mask, Anonymous/Guy Fawkes mask, balaclava/ski mask, bandana/scarf, burqa, gas mask, surgical mask, stocking, sunglasses
- Costumes and Uniforms: authority figure (police, security), delivery or maintenance worker, clown, construction worker, medical scrubs
- Identity Alterations: altered age appearance, ethnicity disguise, fake beard/mustache, prosthetics, wig, man disguised as woman, woman disguised as man

Emerging Deception Variables

Deepfakes (Video Manipulation)

AI-generated or altered video content used to impersonate someone, fabricate alibis, or create false evidence. Consistent technical markers in how deepfakes are produced (frame glitches, metadata anomalies, etc.) can help link cases.

Voice Cloning/Synthetic Audio

Digitally generated voice imitations deployed in scams, extortion calls, or impersonation of trusted individuals (e.g., a boss instructing an employee to transfer funds). The repeated use of certain cloned voices may connect dispersed incidents.

Synthetic Identities

Creation of hybrid identities blending real and fabricated data (e.g., stolen Social Security numbers combined with fake addresses). Used in fraud, organized theft, and cyber-enabled deception. Similar identity construction methods may indicate a serial offender or network.

AI-Generated Text or Images

Use of large language models or image generators to craft fraudulent documents, social media accounts, or fake online personas. Stylometric patterns or reuse of generated materials may reveal offender consistency.

Augmented Reality (AR)/Virtual Reality Deception

Use of immersive technologies to manipulate victims during fraud or luring scenarios (e.g., false environments in virtual meetups). Offenders may reuse the same avatars, environments, or scripts.

Digital Spoofing (Caller ID, Email, GPS)

Manipulation of communication systems to disguise origins – such as spoofed phone numbers, GPS locations, or email headers. Recurring spoofing techniques can link incidents to the same operator.

Social Engineering With AI Assistance

Use of AI chatbots or automated scripts to enhance phishing, romance scams, or recruitment pitches. Language style, targeting strategy, or interaction patterns can reveal common offenders.

Virtual Camouflage

Deliberate alteration of online presence to conceal true identity – such as using "face filters" or voice-changing apps in livestream crimes. Repeated use of the same filters or software tools may create a distinctive offender signature.

Digital Evidence Manipulation

Tampering with surveillance footage, photographs, or forensic records using editing software or AI tools. Shared methods or software artifacts can connect seemingly isolated cases.

Crime Pattern Scenario

Serial Home Invasion Pattern – "The Utility Worker Ruse"

A series of six home invasions over three months targeting elderly residents was linked by analysts through the offender's consistent impersonation and deception tactics. In each incident, the offender approached victims' homes during weekday afternoons wearing a reflective safety vest, hard hat, and carrying a clipboard with utility company logos. His ruse remained identical: claiming to be conducting mandatory gas leak inspections following neighborhood reports and stating that immediate entry was required for safety. The lure was safety-focused – warning victims of potential gas explosions if the inspection wasn't completed immediately. His impersonation as a utility worker was reinforced by a van with magnetic signs reading "Metro Gas Services" and authentic-looking work orders on official letterhead. The disguise included safety equipment that made him appear legitimate to both victims and neighbors who might observe him. Once inside, he abandoned the utility worker pretense, revealing his true intent to commit robbery. The timing pattern showed he targeted homes where only elderly residents were present, often following up on houses where he had observed daily routines during previous "route surveys." His method remained consistent: gaining entry through authority and urgency, then zip-tying victims while searching for cash, jewelry, and prescription medications. Recognition of this utility worker impersonation pattern led investigators to coordinate with actual utility companies, verify that no legitimate inspections were scheduled in affected neighborhoods, and ultimately identify the offender through identification of his parked van.

Example Case

In Denver, between 2018 and 2022, John Pastor-Mendoza posed as a rideshare driver in order to abduct at least 12 women, many of whom were intoxicated and waiting outside bars or clubs. Using deceptive tactics such as rideshare signage and apps to gain victims' trust, he lured them into his vehicle, where he is believed to have drugged some before sexually assaulting them. Several victims awoke in unfamiliar locations without memory of how they got there, and investigators later recovered their cell phones, IDs, and controlled substances, including tranquilizers, from his home. His modus operandi involved exploiting intoxicated individuals, impersonating legitimate transportation services, and using chemical restraint to facilitate sexual violence, ultimately leading to his conviction on 30 counts and a 290-year prison sentence.[3]

Example query terms: rideshare, Uber, Lyft, taxi, unconscious, unfamiliar, woke up, drugged, lost memory, memory loss

Exercises

1. Search online for five robberies involving suspects who wore a "scream mask" and report your findings.
2. Compare deception methods in cybercrime versus street crime. What are the similarities and what are the differences? Discuss.
3. Research online for three different serial crime cases where deception was a key element (search terms like "serial impersonator," "fake police officer crimes," or "fraud series disguise"). What specific deception tactics were used (ruse, lure, impersonation, disguise). How the deception methods evolved or remained consistent across incidents? What ultimately led to the offender's identification and arrest? Create a comparison chart showing traditional deception methods versus emerging technological deception (deepfakes, voice cloning, digital spoofing) used in recent cases. This exercise demonstrates the evolution of deceptive tactics while highlighting the importance of documenting specific deception details for pattern recognition and prevention strategies.

Critical Thinking Guidance

Deception-based crimes, including impersonation, cons, lures, and disguises, require precise documentation for meaningful pattern analysis. Capture details like the ruse and lure types, impersonated role, verbal script, and disguise in structured, searchable fields, when possible, but in narrative fields when the structured fields are inadequate. These variables often become the linking factors across cases that may otherwise appear unrelated, especially when geographic or temporal connections are unclear.

Impersonation tactics can escalate over time, from non-violent fraud to abduction or sexual assault. Offenders like John Pastor-Mendoza, who posed as a rideshare driver, show how deception can be used to gain access to vulnerable victims and commit more serious crimes. Analysts should track changes in method, risk level, and victim targeting to detect escalation early.

Corroborate victim statements through surveillance footage, digital purchase records, and physical evidence like uniforms, props, or chemical agents. Field officers must be trained to note not just the suspect's claim, but the specifics: badge details, uniforms, tools, language, and behavior. Civilians should be taught simple verification steps when approached by anyone claiming official authority.

Because impersonators are often mobile and opportunistic, agencies should issue bulletins across jurisdictions and partner with regulatory bodies such as licensing boards and utility companies. Analysts can enhance detection by using keyword searches for impersonation terms and mapping disguise-based incidents for clustering. Comparing street-level deception to online fraud may also reveal common manipulative strategies that cut across crime types.

When examining deception in modern crime patterns, investigators must expand their perspective beyond physical disguises and traditional ruses. Technological tools such as deepfakes, voice-cloning, and synthetic identities present new challenges because they can be convincingly realistic while leaving little immediate trace of fabrication. Analysts and officers should approach suspicious communications, digital evidence, and online personas with skepticism, verifying authenticity through independent sources, metadata analysis, and technical forensics. A key consideration is that offenders may combine both old and new deception methods, for example, pairing a physical disguise with AI-manipulated documents or spoofed phone calls. Identifying these hybrid strategies requires asking whether elements of the deception appear repeated across cases, whether technical artifacts point to specific software or methods, and whether the deception could indicate preparation for escalation into more serious crimes. By treating technological deception not as an outlier but as part of a continuum with traditional methods, law enforcement can better connect dispersed incidents and anticipate offender innovation.

Notes

1 FBI Richmond (2020, February 4).
2 Manley et al. (2022).
3 Williams (2025, March 8).

Bibliography

Clare, J., & Townsley, M. (2018). Preventing impersonation-based crime: A situational approach. *Security Journal, 31*(4), 935–955. https://doi.org/10.1057/s41284-016-0071-7

Europol Innovation Lab. (2022). *Facing reality? Law enforcement and the challenge of deepfakes.* Publications Office of the European Union. www.europol.europa.eu/cms/sites/default/files/documents/Europol_Innovation_Lab_Facing_Reality_Law_Enforcement_And_The_Challenge_Of_Deepfakes.pdf

FBI Richmond. (2020, February 4). *Update: Crime spree continues for "Scream Bandit"; $10,000 reward offered* [Press release]. Federal Bureau of Investigation. www.fbi.gov/contact-us/field-offices/richmond/news/press-releases/update-crime-spree-contnues-for-scream-bandit-10000-reward-offered

Manley, K. D., Chan, J. Y., & Wells, G. L. (2022). Improving face identification of mask-wearing individuals. *Cognitive Research: Principles and Implications, 7*(1), 1–15. https://doi.org/10.1186/s41235-022-00369-7

Turvey, B. (2020). *Criminal profiling: An introduction to behavioral evidence analysis* (5th ed., Ch. 17, Con-artists and Confidence Games). Academic Press.

U.S. Department of Justice, Office of Community Oriented Policing Services. (2013). *False police impersonation incidents (Problem-Specific Guides for Police).* https://cops.usdoj.gov/RIC/Publications/cops-p278-pub.pdf

Williams, T. (2025, March 8). Colorado man gets 290 years for kidnapping and assaulting women while posing as rideshare driver. *The New York Times.*

Verdoliva, L. (2020). Media forensics and deepfakes: An overview. *IEEE Journal of Selected Topics in Signal Processing, 14*(5), 910–932. https://cybersecurity.uniroma1.it/sites/default/files/Media%20Forensics%20and%20Deepfakes%20-%20An%20overview.pdf

15 Approach and Escape

Introduction

Law enforcement practitioners can link crimes by analyzing how offenders approach victims and escape crime scenes, particularly in crimes like murder, assault, sexual assault, robbery, kidnapping, and human trafficking. Examining these behaviors can offer a framework for identifying these harmful crime patterns. This chapter describes approach and escape methods.

The ways offenders approach victims and escape from crime scenes are valuable elements in understanding criminal behavior and linking cases. These behaviors often reflect planning, intent, environmental awareness, and adaptability, and they are especially significant in violent crimes such as homicide, assault, sexual assault, robbery, kidnapping, and human trafficking. By examining approach and escape methods, it is possible to uncover offender routines, assess risk levels, and develop leads that strengthen pattern recognition.

Approach Methods

Offender approach techniques typically reflect their intent, familiarity with the environment, and degree of planning. Example methods include the following.

Manipulative or Deceptive Approaches

- following or observing individuals
- concealment in vehicles or buildings
- using intermediaries to lure or access victims
- initiating contact via telephone, social media, or email
- administering incapacitating substances
- ongoing stalking or surveillance

Surprise or Sudden Attacks

- ambushing or startling the victim
- rapid, forceful entry followed by immediate confrontation
- lying in wait, both indoors and outdoors
- use of threats or display of weapons

DOI: 10.4324/9781003728733-17

Blitz Attacks

- swift, overwhelming physical assault using hands, fists, blunt objects, or weapons
- actions such as stabbing, shooting, or choking executed with little or no warning

Escape Methods

Analyzing how offenders depart from crime scenes is integral to understanding their capabilities and intent. Key variables include the following:

Means of Escape

- fleeing on foot, often exploiting crowds or terrain
- departing by vehicle, possibly planned or involving stolen/borrowed/unregistered cars
- utilizing public transportation, especially in dense urban areas
- switching modes of travel to evade pursuit or hinder investigation

Route Selection

- pre-planned routes suggest forethought and area knowledge, possibly with contingencies
- random or opportunistic routes may indicate impulsive decision-making

Geographic and Environmental Factors

- urban environments provide numerous exits and observers; rural settings limit options but reduce surveillance
- physical features such as rivers, highways, and train tracks can facilitate or obstruct escape

Temporal Aspects

- offenses occurring at night offer concealment but reduced visibility; daylight brings more witnesses
- weekdays, weekends, and holidays affect crowd size, traffic, and routine activities

Counter-Surveillance and Evidence Management

- efforts to change appearance, use disguises, or destroy/discard tools and evidence
- employing technology such as police scanners or burner phones

Role of Accomplices

- lookouts, getaway drivers, and coordinated diversions can complicate investigations

Psychological Dynamics

- stress can prompt mistakes or deviations from plans; overconfidence may reinforce risky, patterned behavior – look for changes in escape strategy under pressure (such as sloppier exits, abandoned tools)

Crime Pattern Scenario

Serial Sexual Assault Pattern – "The Campus Stalker"

A series of four sexual assaults over six months on a university campus was linked through consistent approach and escape behaviors that revealed sophisticated planning and environmental knowledge. The offender's approach method remained identical across incidents: he conducted surveillance of female students leaving the library between 9 and 11 PM, followed victims at a distance along dimly lit campus pathways, then used a blitz attack from behind near secluded areas like construction zones or parking lot edges. His approach timing exploited predictable student routines during finals periods when the library stayed open late, and pathways were less populated. The escape pattern showed intimate knowledge of campus geography: he consistently fled through maintenance areas behind academic buildings, used service roads accessible only to university vehicles, and disappeared into a network of steam tunnels that connected multiple buildings across campus. Cameras captured him approaching from the same direction in two incidents – emerging from the engineering building's rear exit – suggesting he used this location as a staging area. His escape routes avoided main campus walkways and student gathering areas, instead utilizing infrastructure known primarily to maintenance staff or long-term students. His knowledge of security camera blind spots and maintenance schedules suggested either current or former connection to the university. Recognition of this campus-specific approach and escape pattern directed focus on individuals with institutional knowledge, cross-reference maintenance staff and former students, and ultimately identify the offender through keycard access records showing unauthorized use of maintenance areas during the timeframe of the assaults.

Example Case

John Duffy and David Mulcahy, known as the "railway rapists," terrorized London in the 1980s. The offenders meticulously selected victims along railway lines, exploiting the discrete environments provided by train stations and isolated walkways for both approach and getaway. After each attack, Duffy and Mulcahy used the rail system's extensive, interconnected routes not only to access multiple crime scenes but also to disappear quickly, avoiding populated areas and decreasing the chance of witness encounters. This tactical use of trains and rail corridors as escape routes complicated police efforts to predict or intercept them, providing a crucial example of how transportation infrastructure can be leveraged in serial crime patterns.[1]

Example query terms: train, corridor, walkway, railroad, track, station, rail system, escape

Exercises

1. Choose a familiar location (school, workplace, shopping center). Imagine a hypothetical robbery there. Sketch or list at least three possible escape routes an offender might use. Note environmental features (roads, alleys, rivers, train stations) that help or hinder escape.
2. Research how the serial murderer Ted Bundy approached his victims and document your findings.
3. Research three different serial crime cases online where approach and escape methods were crucial to identifying the offender (use search terms like "serial attacker escape route" or

"crime pattern approach method"). For each case, document: (1) The specific approach tactics used by the offender, (2) How escape routes revealed offender knowledge or planning, and (3) How law enforcement used approach/escape patterns to predict or intercept future crimes. Create a comparison chart showing how different types of crimes (sexual assault, robbery, burglary) typically involve different approach and escape strategies. After completing your research, consider: How do environmental factors (urban vs. rural, transportation hubs, geographic features) influence offender tactics? What role does timing play in approach and escape success? How might offenders modify their methods when they realize law enforcement is tracking their patterns? This exercise demonstrates how approach and escape behaviors provide insight into offender psychology, planning capabilities, and local knowledge while highlighting the importance of analyzing these elements for crime pattern recognition and prevention.

Critical Thinking Guidance

Critical thinking about offender approach and escape goes beyond labeling tactics. Ask what these behaviors reveal about planning, intent, and local knowledge. Did the offender exploit predictable routines, transportation schedules, or terrain that allow both easy access and quick exit?

Approach methods signal intent: manipulative or deceptive tactics suggest planning and comfort with victim interaction, while blitz attacks often indicate impulsivity or a need for rapid control. Shifts in approach or escape – such as switching from on-foot getaways to public transit – may show learning or reaction to police pressure.

Escape choices often reveal geography and timing awareness. Pre-planned routes, use of secondary roads, or counter-surveillance efforts (disguises, burner phones, discarded clothing) can demonstrate reconnaissance. Stress or overconfidence can lead to mistakes like inconsistent routes or abandoned tools.

Approach and escape are often linked: a secluded access point may be chosen because it lies near a hidden exit. Environmental and temporal factors, for example, alley networks, time of day, weather, or holidays, can shape both strategies.

Accomplices and diversions can mask patterns, so coordination with other agencies and sharing surveillance or behavioral data is essential. Finally, question whether similarities across cases reflect a single offender or simply common opportunities.

Note

1 Campbell (1999, March 25).

Bibliography

Campbell, D. (1999, March 25). How the police caught the railway rapists. *The Guardian*. www.theguardian.com/uk/1999/mar/25/duncancampbell

Federal Bureau of Investigation. (2022). *ViCAP case submission form*. U.S. Department of Justice. https://omb.report/icr/202205-1110-002/doc/123643900

16 Entry, Search, and Exit

Introduction

In burglary and other unlawful entry crimes, how the offender enters, searches, and exits a property can reveal consistent behavior that links cases into a recognizable pattern. Offenders make choices based on access, speed, concealment, and familiarity with security systems or architectural features. When physical descriptions are unavailable and property taken varies, these behavioral elements often become the key linkage points. This chapter emphasizes the value of detailed documentation of the entry method, search behavior, and exit route, especially for pattern detection in residential and commercial burglaries, home invasion robberies, and sexually motivated break-ins.

Example Variables

Point of Entry and/or Exit

- adjacent building, back door, balcony door, balcony window, basement door, basement window, basement window well, chimney, cellar door, concealed in building, exterior garage door, fire escape, first-floor window, floor, front door, garage door, interior garage door, loading dock, elevator shaft, roof, side door, service entrance, shutters, skylight, sliding door, underground service tunnel, underground utility tunnel, unsecured doors, unsecured windows, wall, ventilation shaft, window

Means of Entry (and Related Behaviors)

- bodily force, broke door panel, broke glass, broke lock, broke skylight, broke through wall, broke window, climbed a pole, climbed a tree, climbed on object to assist entry, climbed to higher floor, climbed to higher level, cut lock, cut through wall, entered through roof, forced door, exploited a gap or hole in a fence or perimeter, gap in structure that facilitated entry, hacking/digital tool, hid in building, jimmied lock, kicked door in, manual force, no force, opened window, picked lock, pried lock, pushed door in, reached in an unlatched, reached in and unlocked, removed air conditioner, removed door, removed door panel, removed fan, removed jalousie, removed window, scaled wall, similar key, smash and grab, smashed glass, stolen key, stood on trash cans, tunneled, used key, used pass key, used passcode, used plastic card, used roof hatch, used security credentials, used scaffolding platform, used stolen vehicle to ram door/wall/window, used vehicle to ram door/wall/window, went through open window

DOI: 10.4324/9781003728733-18

Detection Avoidance Measures

- disabled alarm, disabled security devices, hacked a digital lock or security system, tampered with security cameras, tampered with sensors, wore a disguise, wore gloves

Search Type

- gratuitous mess, messy, neat tidy, unnoticeable, untidy

Extent of Search

- contents dumped, contents tipped out, cupboards opened, drawers opened, extensive – multiple rooms, limited to one room

Post-offense Behavior

- behaviors such as quickly selling stolen goods or returning to the scene of the crime.

Presence of Victim

- absent for a short period, asleep at home, at funeral, at home but unaware of the burglary, at work, away for an extended period, on premises, on vacation

Property Security

- alarm – audible, alarm – inoperative, alarm – silent, bars, biometric (fingerprints, retinal scan, etc.), security, card-key access system, CCTV system, code entry, community watch, concierge, deadbolt locks, digital password entry, dog on premises, fenced perimeter, guard dog, home security system, listening device, locks, motion detector, neighborhood watch, no security, private security, security guard, security patrol, surveillance system, unlocked

Crime Pattern Scenario

Serial Residential Burglary Pattern – "The Basement Window Burglar"

A series of 11 residential burglaries over five months was linked through highly consistent entry, search, and exit behaviors that revealed specialized knowledge and methodical planning. The offender's entry method remained identical across all incidents: he targeted single-family homes with basement windows facing rear yards, used a small pry bar to remove window frames rather than breaking glass, and entered through basement laundry rooms where motion detectors were rarely installed. His search pattern was distinctive – he avoided basement areas entirely after entry, proceeded directly to main floor kitchens to disable landline phones, then conducted systematic searches of master bedrooms focusing exclusively on jewelry boxes, dresser drawers, and closet safes. The search type was notably neat and organized: he left rooms appearing undisturbed except for slightly opened drawers and moved jewelry boxes, suggesting experience in avoiding detection by residents returning home. His exit strategy showed consistent planning: he departed through the same basement window after resetting the frame to appear undamaged from outside, and timing analysis revealed he completed each burglary within a brief timeframe during weekday afternoons when neighborhoods were least populated. The property security pattern showed he specifically avoided homes with visible alarm company stickers, dogs, or security cameras, but targeted houses with privacy fencing that concealed basement windows from neighbor observation. Recognition of this basement window entry pattern led to coordinatization with alarm companies to identify recent basement sensor installations, canvass neighborhoods for residents who had discovered slightly disturbed jewelry boxes. They found the offender through a probation officer who recognized the modus operandi and identified the suspect.

Example Case

In 2017, Tulsa police investigated a series of commercial burglaries committed by a suspect who gained entry through rooftop air vents. The offender removed air conditioning units and entered businesses through the ventilation system, effectively bypassing traditional alarm systems. This method was used in at least five confirmed burglaries, including a case where approximately $100,000 in jewelry and coins were stolen. Similar break-ins occurred at nearby businesses, such as a cell phone store and a beauty salon, all involving rooftop access through vents. Police recovered large amounts of stolen property following the suspect's arrest and urged business owners to reinforce rooftop units and enhance surveillance to prevent similar intrusions.[1]

Example query terms: roof, rooftop, ventilation, vent, air conditioning, unit, jewelry, coins, cell phone, mobile phone, phone, beauty salon, hairdresser, barber

Exercises

1. Review three burglary news articles. List the point of entry (door, window, roof, tunnel, etc.). Note whether force was used, and if so, how (lock picked, glass broken, door kicked).
2. Visit a public building (library, mall, office building) and spend 20 minutes observing entry and exit points. Document: (1) How many different ways someone could enter or exit the building, (2) Which entry/exit points have security measures (cameras, card readers, alarms), and (3) Which routes would be most/least visible to security staff or other people. After your observation, research two real burglary cases online where unusual entry methods were used (roof access, tunnels, adjacent buildings, etc.). For each case, analyze how the entry method affected the investigation and what security improvements could have prevented the crime. Consider: How do different types of buildings (residential vs. commercial) present different entry opportunities and challenges? What role does timing play in entry method selection? How might an experienced burglar's approach differ from an opportunistic offender? This exercise demonstrates how environmental factors shape offender decision-making while highlighting the importance of comprehensive security planning and detailed documentation of entry/exit behaviors for crime pattern analysis.

Critical Thinking Guidance

Linking crimes through offender entry, search, and exit behaviors requires careful consideration of both consistency and variation. While certain methods, such as forced entry through doors or windows, are common, small details (like the choice of tool, level of force, or the extent of a search) can distinguish one offender from another. Avoid assuming that similar entry points automatically indicate the same offender, as environmental factors such as weak security or poor lighting can shape method selection. Instead, patterns should be evaluated alongside contextual variables, including the presence or absence of victims, property security measures, and whether the search was methodical or reckless. Critical analysis also involves questioning whether changes in technique reflect offender adaptation, experimentation, or pressure from increased law enforcement attention.

Note

1 Slanchik (2017, July 28).

Bibliography

Jewelers' Security Alliance. (2020, January 22). JSA issues warning after spate of rooftop burglaries. *National Jeweler*. https://nationaljeweler.com/articles/3283-jsa-issues-warning-after-spate-of-rooftop-burglaries

Justia. (n.d.). *Uniform crime reporting handbook: Burglary*. Retrieved August 6, 2025, from www.justia.com/criminal/docs/uniform-crime-reporting-handbook/burglary/

Slanchik, A. (2017, July 28). Serial 'rooftop burglar' may have targeted more than 20 businesses, TPD says. *News On 6*. www.newson6.com/story/5e35f4422f69d76f62028f78/serial-rooftop-burglar-may-have-targeted-more-than-20-businesses-tpd-says

17 Tools and Equipment

Introduction

The type of tools and equipment used to commit crimes can help investigators identify commonalities across different incidents. In some cases, offenders repeatedly use the same tools, leave distinctive tool marks, or carry specialized equipment that can be linked across crime scenes. These choices may also reflect the offender's skill level, occupational knowledge, access to resources, and level of premeditation. Whether analyzing burglary, arson, cybercrime, or vehicle theft, tools and equipment are essential variables to document and analyze for potential linkage. If an offender uses unusual or unique tools or always uses the same tools, crimes might be linked. This chapter describes tools and equipment used in patterned crimes.

Tool Variable Examples

- bolt cutter, bump key, car lock bypass tool, chain, coat hanger, crowbar, drill, gardening tool, glass breaking tool, gas torch, glass cutter, hammer, ignition punch, "jaws of life" tool, jiggle key, key, knife, laser cutter, lock de-icer, lock pick, lock-picking kit, lock puller, lock snap gun, pliers, master key, pry bar, pry tool, rake, rope, saw, screwdriver, shimming tool, shovel, siphon, sledgehammer, slim jim, tape, tension wrench, vice grips, wire, wire cutter, wrench

Equipment Variable Examples

- back pack/bag, baggies/packaging materials, binoculars, body armor, bugs, bulletproof vest, burner phones, cords, counterfeit currency, cutting agent (diluents, fillers), demand letter, disposable phones, drone, drug extraction equipment, drug manufacturing equipment (lab, chemicals), drug paraphernalia (pipe, syringe, bong), duct tape, electrical tape, fake identification document, gloves, GPS tracking device, handcuffs, hidden camera, holographic foils and ribbons, listening device, makeup, mask, metal detectors, night vision goggles, notes, packaging material (bags, wraps), pill presses, RFID signal blocker, scales/weighing equipment, scanner/printer, signal jammer, specialized inks and papers, spy camera, telescope, tow-truck/trailer for stealing vehicles, uniform, watermark replication tools, wig, wiretapping tool, zip ties

Note that offenders may have the tools and/or equipment needed to commit a crime, but at times they find them nearby or at the crime site.

DOI: 10.4324/9781003728733-19

Crime-Specific Tools/Equipment

Arson

- used matches to start/spread the fire, used lighter to start/spread the fire, used an accelerant to start/spread the fire, used a torch to start/spread fire, used a tool to start/spread the fire, used debris to start/spread the fire, used wood for fuel, used paper for fuel, used gasoline for fuel, used kerosene for fuel, used propane for fuel, used alcohol for fuel, used benzene for fuel, used petroleum ether for fuel, used naphtha for fuel, used turpentine for fuel, used chemicals for fuel, used flammable gas for fuel, used a time-delayed device, used candles as a time-delayed device, used electrical equipment to set fire, used explosive device, used improvised incendiary device, used Molotov cocktail

Burglary

Instruments

- bolt cutter, brick, chopping tool, crowbars, cutting tool, cutting torch, drill, hammer, incendiary, key, knife, lock pick, mallet, pliers, prying tool, rock, saw, screwdriver, sledgehammer, stone

Equipment

- climbing equipment, camera, gloves, ladder, rappelling gear, rope, special clothes, tape

Cybercrime

- anonymous browsing tool (VPN, proxy), card skimmer (ATM or point of sale device), credit card/other card, electronic device, exploit kit, hacking software, hardware device, keylogger, keystroke logger, laptop, malware, network scanning tool, password cracking software, phishing kits, skimming device, SIM card cloning equipment, smartphone, Wi-Fi cracking software

Vehicle Theft

- coat hangers, flashlights, glass cutters, gloves, lock picks, pliers, screwdrivers, Slim Jim, spark plugs, window punches

Crime Pattern Scenario

Serial Auto Theft Pattern – "The Spark Plug Burglar"

A series of 14 vehicle thefts over three months targeting Honda Civics and Toyota Corollas was linked by analysts through the offender's consistent use of an unusual tool combination and distinctive entry method. In each incident, the offender used ceramic pieces from spark plugs to quietly break passenger-side windows – a technique known as "ninja rocks" that creates minimal noise compared to traditional glass-breaking tools. Subsequent investigation revealed that tool kit remained consistent: ceramic spark plug fragments carried in a small cloth bag, a modified coat hanger for door manipulation, and a USB-powered programming device for bypassing ignition systems. The equipment pattern showed sophisticated preparation: he wore latex gloves, carried a small LED penlight for precision work, and used a portable jump starter to ensure vehicles would start immediately. His tool selection demonstrated specialized knowledge of automotive security systems and suggested either mechanic experience or extensive research into vehicle theft techniques. Video footage from two locations showed the same methodical approach: positioning himself to shield the breaking glass from view, completing window entry within 30 seconds, and using the programming device to start vehicles without traditional hotwiring. The consistency of this specialized tool combination distinguished these thefts from opportunistic vehicle crimes and suggested a skilled offender with access to automotive equipment.

Example Case

The Los Angeles Police Department issued a community alert following a marked increase in residential burglaries across upscale neighborhoods in West Los Angeles – areas such as Bel Air, Brentwood, Pacific Palisades, Beverlywood, and others – where an organized crew of two to four masked individuals targeted unoccupied single-family homes for high-value items like jewelry, luxury handbags, safes, and cash. A key investigative detail is the recurring use of ladders – and alternative elevation aids like outdoor furniture and drainpipes – to access second-story master bedrooms, a modus operandi that could help link separate burglaries to the same perpetrators.[1]

Example query terms: ladder, drainpipes, furniture, climbed, jewelry, handbag, purse, luxury, safe, cash, mask, master bedroom, second story, second floor

Exercises

1. Collect short news articles describing multiple burglary or arson cases. Highlight repeated use of the same tools (such as crowbars, ladders, Molotov cocktails). Discuss whether the tool use is common (many offenders would use it) or distinctive (could point to a specific offender or crew).
2. Research two different types of crime cases online (burglary, fraud, cybercrime, arson, or vehicle theft) where specific tools or equipment were crucial to identifying the offender. For each case, document: (1) What tools/equipment were used and how they were distinctive, (2) Whether the tools required specialized knowledge or access, and (3) How investigators traced the tools to identify suspects. Create a comparison chart showing common versus specialized tools used in each crime type. After completing your research, consider: Which types of tools leave the most reliable forensic evidence? How might tool availability affect crime patterns in different geographic areas? What role does occupational knowledge play in tool selection? How can law enforcement monitor tool procurement without infringing on legitimate uses? This exercise demonstrates how tool analysis provides insight into offender capabilities and planning while highlighting the investigative value of documenting specific implements used in crime patterns.

Critical Thinking Guidance

Intelligence sharing between agencies is essential for identifying regional offenders who employ similar methods, such as the repeated use of distinctive tools. Law enforcement can also collaborate with retailers to monitor purchases of suspicious items, including accelerants, lock kits, or other specialized equipment, which may provide early indicators of criminal activity. From an investigative and analytical standpoint, specific tools often leave identifiable marks, such as pry tool damage to windowsills or lock impression marks, which can be compared by forensic technicians to link incidents. Tools requiring specialized or occupational access, such as locksmith tools or pill presses, can help narrow the suspect pool. Consistent use of the same tools or tool combinations, such as gloves, a pry bar, and rope, may point to the same offender or crew operating repeatedly. Additionally, recovered tools should be examined for biological or trace evidence, as they may retain DNA, fingerprints, or material transfers. Tracking the source of tools can also reveal broader patterns, potentially connecting multiple crimes or offenders through shared procurement channels.

Note

1 Santa Monica Mirror Staff (2024, August 25).

Bibliography

Fullár, A., Kutnyánszky, V., & Leiner, N. (2020). Identification of burglars using foil impressioning based on tool marks and DNA evidence. *Forensic Science International*, *316*, 110524. https://doi.org/10.1016/j.forsciint.2020.110524

Kumar, S., Singh, D., Kumar, A., & Kumar, A. (2021). Forensic analysis and interpretation of tool marks. In *Forensic analysis – Scientific and medical techniques and evidence under the microscope* (Ch. 7). IntechOpen. https://doi.org/10.5772/intechopen.98251

Rai, A. (2023, June 4). Tool marks examination. *Forensic's Blog*. https://forensicfield.blog/tool-marks-examination/

Santa Monica Mirror Staff. (2024, August 25). LAPD issues community alert amid surge in upscale West LA neighborhood burglaries. *Santa Monica Mirror*.

18 Signature Behaviors

Introduction

In crime pattern analysis, signature behavior refers not to the inner psychology of the offender, but to distinctive, observable actions or strategies that repeat across a series of crimes. These behaviors can provide investigators with powerful linkage indicators, details that may not be necessary to complete the crime but that show consistency and uniqueness. Signature elements are often overlooked in traditional data collection because they may fall outside core offense variables. However, when recorded systematically, they can reveal connections between crimes, particularly in serial cases.

Rather than interpreting signature as a psychological footprint, this chapter focuses on the operational behavior patterns that may be functionally unnecessary but diagnostically useful – those repeated features that persist over time, even as circumstances or targets change.

Signature behavior often refers to an act or acts the offender commits at a crime scene that remains consistent throughout the crime series, but research suggests that signature behaviors may evolve or vary more than traditionally assumed. Use critical thinking when using this element of a crime series. Question assumptions.

Rather than focus on the psychology of the offender, which is a common interpretation of the concept of signature behavior, look for the elements (behaviors, actions, or strategies) of the crime that are distinctive and suggest that the same offender may be responsible.

Example of Signature Behaviors

Method of Entry

- specific techniques or tools used to gain unauthorized access, such as lock picking, forced entry, or bypassing security systems
- preferred points of entry, such as windows, doors, or roof access

Specific Target Selection

- consistent choice of specific victim profiles, such as age, gender, occupation, or physical characteristics
- preference for specific types of locations or settings, such as residential areas, schools, or parks

DOI: 10.4324/9781003728733-20

Selected Time Frames

- consistent timing or frequency of criminal activities, such as specific days of the week, specific times of day, or significant dates
- offender's adherence to a particular pattern or cycle related to their criminal behavior

Signature Prowling or Surveillance

- consistent patterns of surveillance or stalking behavior leading up to the crime
- use of specific techniques or tools for monitoring victims or potential targets

Signature Weapons or Tools

- consistent use of specific weapons or tools in the commission of the crime
- customized or modified weapons or tools used by the offender

Means of Subduing or Controlling Victims

- use of physical force, restraints, or incapacitating substances to control or immobilize victims
- specific weapons or tools employed to intimidate or subdue victims, such as firearms, knives, or stun guns

Ritualistic Elements

- specific rituals or patterns consistently observed during the commission of the crime, such as arranging objects in a particular manner or leaving symbolic messages
- symbolic acts or gestures that have personal meaning to the offender

Signature Items or Objects

- use or placement of specific objects or items at the crime scene that hold personal significance to the offender, such as specific clothing, tokens, or personal belongings
- purposeful leaving of unique or distinct physical evidence, such as a calling card or distinctive markings

Ritualistic Actions

- specific actions or behaviors repeated in a consistent manner during the crime, such as specific verbal phrases, acts of mutilation, or posing of victims
- observed patterns of behavior, such as meticulous cleaning or arranging of the crime scene

Symbolism

- use of symbolic elements or messages at the crime scene, such as religious symbols, markings, or cryptic messages
- incorporation of specific symbols or motifs related to the offender's beliefs, ideologies, or obsessions

Signature Sexual Acts

- specific sexual behaviors or acts consistently exhibited in the commission of sexual crimes
- ritualistic or distinctive actions related to sexual acts, such as specific restraints or use of props

Signature Staging

- deliberate alteration or manipulation of the crime scene to mislead investigators or send a specific message
- arrangement of objects or positioning of victims to create a specific scene or narrative
- Post-Crime Behavior: specific actions or behaviors observed by the offender after the commission of the crime, such as returning to the crime scene, revisiting victims, or engaging in post-offense rituals
- communication or taunting behaviors directed toward victims, law enforcement, or the media

Crime Pattern Scenario

Serial Gas Station Robbery Pattern – "The Receipt Collector"

A series of six armed robberies at gas stations over two months was linked through minimal but distinctive signature behaviors that extended beyond the functional requirements of robbery. The offender's modus operandi was straightforward: entering stations during evening shifts, displaying a handgun, demanding cash from registers, and departing on foot. However, two specific signature behaviors distinguished these robberies from others in the area. First, the offender consistently took receipt paper rolls from behind the counter after collecting cash – not for their monetary value, but apparently as a compulsive behavior since the rolls were found discarded in nearby parking lots after each incident. Second, he performed a specific ritual of tapping the counter three times with his knuckles before leaving, captured on security cameras in four of the six robberies. Unlike cases with elaborate staging or complex rituals, these signature elements were subtle: the unnecessary collection of worthless receipt paper and the brief knocking gesture. The receipt-taking behavior had no functional purpose – the paper rolls had no resale value and were immediately abandoned – making it a true signature element that persisted even when other aspects of the crimes varied. The three-tap ritual was equally distinctive and served no operational function for the robbery. Recognition of these simple but consistent signature behaviors – receipt paper theft and counter tapping – enabled exclusion of copycat robberies and focus on incidents with these specific unnecessary elements, ultimately leading to the offender's identification through fingerprints found on discarded receipt rolls. This example shows how signature behaviors don't need to be complex or numerous – even simple, repetitive actions that serve no functional purpose can effectively link crimes in a pattern.

Example Case

A man committed two unusual burglaries in Monmouthshire, Wales, where instead of stealing valuables, he engaged in domestic behaviors such as hanging out laundry, preparing food, organizing the kitchen, replacing toothbrush heads, and leaving handwritten notes. In a second incident, he showered, used a hot tub, and consumed food and drink at another property. His actions reflected a consistent and distinctive signature behavior, a psychological imprint not necessary for the crime itself, but indicative of personal gratification or compulsion. Such behavior, which included cleaning, organizing, and leaving messages, suggests a possible need for control, familiarity, or delusional caretaking, distinguishing his actions from typical burglary patterns.[1]

Example query terms: laundry, clothesline, hanging out, clothes, food, drink, ate, drank, cleaned, organized, kitchen, toothbrush, note, handwritten, shower, hot tub

Exercises

1. Select two or more well-documented serial offenders (examples: Zodiac Killer, Jack the Ripper, Golden State Killer, or Jeffrey Dahmer). Research their crimes using academic articles, case summaries, or reputable media sources. For each offender, identify:

    - Modus Operandi (MO): the functional methods used to commit the crime (such as forced entry, choice of weapon, victim access)
    - Signature Behaviors: distinctive, unnecessary actions or patterns repeated across crimes (such as binding rituals, staging of victims, symbolic messages, unusual post-offense actions)

    Compare the offenders by addressing the following: How did their MO evolve over time, and did their signature behaviors remain stable or change? Which signature behaviors would be most useful for linking cases if the offender were unknown? How did investigators or researchers use signature elements to understand or connect their crimes? Conclude by discussing why it is was important to identify signature in these serial crime patterns.
2. Visit a location where you can observe people engaging in routine activities (coffee shop, library, waiting area, or cafeteria) and spend 20 minutes documenting individual behavioral patterns that go beyond the functional requirements of their tasks. Note actions that seem unnecessary but consistent for specific individuals: Does someone always arrange their items in a particular way? Tap their pen in a specific pattern? Check their phone at regular intervals in a distinctive manner? Organize their workspace in an unusual way? After your observation, consider: Which behaviors would be most distinctive if you encountered the same person in a different location? Which actions seemed compulsive rather than purposeful? How might stress or time pressure affect these behavioral patterns? Next, apply this thinking to crime scene documentation by creating a checklist of questions investigators should ask when reviewing unusual crime scene details: "Was this action necessary to complete the crime?" "Does this behavior serve any functional purpose?" "What environmental factors might influence this behavior?" "How might this action be documented for future comparison?" This exercise demonstrates how behavioral observation skills can improve recognition of signature elements while highlighting the difference between functional actions and distinctive personal patterns that persist across different situations.

Critical Thinking Guidance

When reviewing incident report narratives or related data, flag any rare or unusual elements that may appear, as these could indicate signature behaviors, actions that go beyond the necessities of committing the crime and are often repeated, distinctive, and potentially unconscious or expressive in nature. Unlike modus operandi (MO), which pertains to the method used to accomplish the crime, signature behaviors are consistent actions that can serve as high-value indicators for linking otherwise unconnected crimes across different times, locations, or methods. Document these atypical behaviors even if they initially seem irrelevant, as they may later prove critical to pattern recognition. To aid in this, consider building query structures or coding schemes that allow for efficient detection and comparison of such behaviors across databases. Avoid psychological interpretation unless supported by clear behavioral evidence; the focus should remain on what was done, not why it may have been done. Behaviors that are "odd" or "unnecessary" in a crime scene may indicate a serial crime pattern.

Note

1 BBC News (2024, October 3).

Bibliography

BBC News. (2024, October 3). Burglar hung out washing and cooked meal for victim. *BBC News*. www.bbc.com/news/articles/czeg6xk6rkko

Federal Bureau of Investigation. (2019). *ViCAP case submission form* (Form FD-676; OMB No. 1110–0011). U.S. Department of Justice. https://omb.report/icr/201904-1110-003/doc/92517501.pdf

Schlesinger, L. B., Kassen, M., Mesa, V., & Pinizzotto, A. J. (2010). Ritual and signature in serial sexual homicide. *Journal of the American Academy of Psychiatry and the Law*, *38*(2), 239–246.

19 Weapons

Introduction

When part of a crime series, weapons are not only tools of offense but also key forensic markers that can link otherwise distinct criminal events. Various types of weapons, ranging from handguns, rifles, and knives to improvised tools, possess unique physical and forensic characteristics. These details, such as toolmarks, ballistic signatures, or the specific make or modification of a weapon, can provide critical evidence for connecting cases across time and jurisdictions. Crimes can be linked by the weapons used, most reliably through forensics ballistics information.

But in many crimes, there are only descriptions of weapons used at threats, and it is important to know those descriptions can be used to link crimes

Be conscious that offenders can and sometimes do change the weapons they use to commit crimes. This chapter explores the variables of the crime pattern element "weapons."

Weapon Variable Examples

Firearms/Guns (including non-lethal)

Types

- airsoft gun, antique gun, assault rifle, bb-gun, flare gun, fictitious gun, ghost gun, handgun, machine gun, paintball gun, pistol, rifle, shotgun, sniper rifle, stun gun, submachine gun, taser.

Features/Qualities

- automatic, black, blue, bolt action, bump stock, caliber, cartridge, chrome, direction of twist, domestic, double barrel, extended magazine, flashlight, foreign, gauge, grip, iron sight, laser sight, lever action, magazine capacity, manufacturer, the number of grooves/lands, pellet size, revolver, sawed-off, silencer, single barrel, stainless barrel, stainless steel, telescopic sight.

Knives/Cutting Instruments

- axe, balisong knife, bayonet, boxcutter, broken glass, butterfly knife, ceramic knife, combat knife, corkscrew, dagger, drill, flick knife, hatchet, hunting knife, karambit knife, kitchen

DOI: 10.4324/9781003728733-21

knife, knife, kukri knife, machete, makeshift knife, pocketknife, saw, scalpel, screwdriver, scythe, shank, shiv, skewer, straight razor, stiletto, switchblade, sword, tanto knife, throwing knife, utility knife.

Blunt Instruments

- baseball bat, baton, billiard cue, blackjack, blunt end of screwdriver, blunt end of tool, brass knuckle, brick/stone fragment, cane/walking stick, candlestick, chain, club, cricket bat, crowbar, dumbbell/barbell, fire extinguisher, fireplace tool, frying pan, glass bottle/can, golf club, hammer, hockey stick, mallet, metal pipe/rod, nightstick, pot/pan, rock, rolling pin, sac, shovel, slapper, sledgehammer, tire iron, tire jack, wood stick, wooden plank/board.

Explosives/Flammables

- accelerants, binary explosives, bomb-making materials, butane, diesel fuel, dynamite, firecrackers/fireworks, flash grenade/flashbang, gasoline, grenade, gunpowder, ignition device/timer, improvised explosive device (IED), incendiary device, incendiary rounds/ammo, kerosene, lighter, lighter fluid, match, missile, Molotov cocktail, napalm, pipe bomb, pressure cooker bomb, rocket, smoke grenade, thermite, torpedo, turpentine.

Poisonous Substances

- abrin, aconite, ammonia, antifreeze, arsenic, belladonna, bleach, botulinum toxin, carbon monoxide, chloroform, cyanide, digitalis, fentanyl, hemlock, hydrofluoric acid, insecticides, lead, mercury, oleander, pesticide, poisonous mushrooms, polonium-210, potassium chloride, rat poison, ricin, spider/snake venom, strychnine, thallium

Chemical Weapons

- acid, chemical spray, chlorine gas, hydrogen cyanide gas, mace, mustard gas, Novichok nerve agent, pepper spray (capsaicin), phosgene gas, sarin gas, sodium cyanide, soman gas, tabun gas, tear gas, VX nerve agent, white phosphorous[1]

Vehicles Used as a Weapon

- ATV, airplane (9/11 attacks), bicycle, boat, car, construction/heavy machinery (forklift, bulldozer, etc.), motorcycle, taxi/cab, train, truck, van

Miscellaneous Weapons

- slingshot, crossbow

Questions to Consider

- Did the offender use more than one weapon?
- Was the weapon held in the right hand or the left hand?
- Was the weapon shown to the victim?
- Was the weapon pointed at the victim?

- Was the weapon racked or cocked?
- Was the weapon kept concealed in a pocket or visible in a belt?
- Was the weapon covered with a coat, jacket, newspaper, or something else?
- Was the weapon wrapped in a bag, hankie, bandana, or another item?
- Was the weapon taken from a bag or box or another item?
- Was the weapon placed on a counter?
- Did the offender bring the weapon to the crime event?
- Did the offender use a weapon from the crime site?
- Did the offender use the victim's weapon?
- Did the offender improvise a weapon?

Specific Pattern Example Scenario

Serial Gas Station Robbery Pattern – "The Small Caliber Robber"

A series of six armed robberies at gas stations over four months was linked through consistent firearm descriptions and handling patterns documented by witnesses and security cameras. In each incident, the offender displayed what appeared to be a small, dark-colored semi-automatic pistol, which witnesses consistently described as "smaller than most handguns" and "like a .22 or .25 caliber." His weapon presentation was distinctive: he kept the gun low and close to his body, never fully extending his arm, and held it with both hands in what appeared to be a proper shooting stance despite making no threats to fire. Security footage from three locations showed the same compact firearm profile and the offender's consistent two-handed grip. Witnesses noted he always kept his finger off the trigger and pointed the gun downward toward the counter rather than directly at employees, suggesting some firearms training or safety awareness. The weapon appeared to be matte black or dark blue, and clerks from two different stores mentioned it looked "well-maintained" rather than scratched or damaged. His verbal demands were always calm and quiet, contrasting with the weapon display, and he never racked the slide or made aggressive gestures with the firearm. One store employee trained in robbery response noted his unusual "professional" handling of the weapon compared to other robberies they had experienced. Recognition of this small-caliber firearm description, combined with the distinctive two-handed grip and low-carry position, helped distinguish these robberies from others involving different firearms or handling techniques and focus on suspects with possible military or law enforcement training. This example uses realistic witness observations of firearm details that would be noticeable and memorable without requiring specialized ballistic evidence.

Example Case

A man was suspected in a series of at least six robberies at several drug stores across the Houston area. In most of the incidents, the suspect would approach an employee at the counter, brandish a knife, and demand money. In at least one instance, he used a rifle. In one instance he was shirtless. The suspect was described as a man between 40 and 45 years old, with a heavy build and a limp. He was seen driving a white Hyundai SUV.[2]

Example query terms: drug store, pharmacy, knife, rifle, weapon, robbed, robbery, counter, employee, brandish, heavy, limp, shirtless, white car, SUV, Hyundai[3]

Exercises

1. Using online resources, research and then compare two separate cases that were solved through use of the National Integrated Ballistic Information Network (NIBIN). Note what other crime pattern elements and variables were mentioned in those cases and discuss whether or not they would have been useful in finding other linked cases.
2. Choose two different types of crimes (robbery, assault, burglary, domestic violence, or gang violence) and research online how weapon choice typically varies within each crime type. For each crime category, document: (1) What weapons are most commonly used and why, (2) How weapon availability in different geographic regions affects crime patterns, and (3) Whether offenders in that crime type tend to use consistent weapons or switch between different types. Create a comparison chart showing how weapon preferences might reflect factors like offender experience, crime planning level, victim targeting, and environmental constraints. After completing your research, analyze: Which weapon characteristics would be most reliable for linking crimes within each category? How might weapon availability (legal restrictions, black market access, improvised options) influence crime patterns differently across jurisdictions? What role does weapon familiarity versus intimidation factor play in offender selection?

Critical Thinking Guidance

When evaluating crimes for potential linkage via weapon description and/or evidence, approach each case by asking: What specific features of the weapon, such as type, caliber, manufacturer, or marks, might connect it to other offenses? Is there a repeated use of a particular weapon or switching between weapon types, and what does that indicate about offender access or intent? How does the weapon's method of concealment, deployment, or disposal compare across incidents? Be mindful that offenders sometimes improvise or switch weapons, which may complicate linkage analysis. For this reason, weapon variables should not be viewed in isolation but compared alongside other elements such as offender description, location, and timing. Systematic documentation of both forensic evidence and witness-reported details increases the likelihood that weapon-related patterns can be recognized across cases.

Notes

1 Biological agents such as anthrax and ricin, as well as radiation can be weaponized.
2 Man wanted in Houston drug store robberies arrested. (2022, September 2).
3 In this case the suspect used a rifle once and a knife five times. He also had characteristics such as a limp that could help link crimes through searching report narratives. The vehicle description could also help link his crimes.

Bibliography

Bureau of Alcohol, Tobacco, Firearms and Explosives. (2025, June). *National Integrated Ballistic Information Network (NIBIN): Fact sheet.* U.S. Department of Justice. www.atf.gov/resource-center/fact-sheet/2024-national-integrated-ballistic-information-network

Lopez, B. E., McGrath, J. G., & Taylor, V. G. (2020, October 21). Using forensic intelligence to combat serial and organized violent crimes. *NIJ Journal*, (282). National Institute of Justice. https://nij.ojp.gov/topics/articles/using-forensic-intelligence-combat-serial-and-organized-violent-crimes

Man wanted in Houston drug store robberies arrested. (2022, September 2). KHOU 11. www.khou.com/article/news/crime/drug-store-robberies-houston/285-a4e6b69d-6fcf-46de-bef1-9d886552cd0a

United Nations Office on Drugs and Crime. (2018). Firearms as evidence. In *Education for justice: Firearms module 8, key issues*. United Nations. www.unodc.org/e4j/en/firearms/module-8/key-issues/firearms-as-evidence.html

Zawitz, M. W. (1995, July). *Guns used in crime* (BJS Publication No. NCJ-148201). U.S. Department of Justice, Bureau of Justice Statistics. https://bjs.ojp.gov/content/pub/pdf/GUIC.PDF

20 Force and Physical Trauma

Introduction

Patterns in the level and type of force used during violent crimes can serve as critical indicators when determining whether multiple offenses are linked. Consistencies across incidents (such as the nature of injuries, the degree of violence, or methods of applying force) may reveal a serial offender's behavioral signature. However, force is not always static; some offenders begin with lower levels of violence or less sophisticated methods, escalating to more extreme or lethal force over time. These changes may reflect increased confidence, desensitization, or a shifting motive. Alternatively, an offender might deliberately alter their use of force to avoid detection or to adapt to situational factors, such as a victim's resistance. This chapter describes levels of force and variables of physical trauma.

Force

The level of force used in a crime can vary widely and often provides insight into the offender's intent, emotional state, or level of control. Categorizing force consistently helps in case comparison and in evaluating whether a pattern exists. The following are common examples of escalating force levels, ranging from minimal to lethal:

No Physical Force: Intimidation, presence, verbal threats only
Threat of Violence: Threatening with a weapon or implying harm
Coercive Force: Forcing movement, forcing compliance, or using physical restraint
Physical Aggression: Hitting, slapping, punching, kicking
Use of Weapon: Displaying or using a weapon to inflict harm
Lethal Force: Actions intended or likely to cause death: stabbing, shooting, strangulation

Variations in force can occur between incidents or within a single crime event. These should be documented precisely, as they may reflect offender escalation, de-escalation, or adaptations to victim behavior or situational dynamics.

Physical Trauma

Physical trauma resulting from a violent offense can reveal critical details about offender intent, method of attack, and victim vulnerability. Identifying the specific type and severity of trauma assists in distinguishing among cases and can contribute to offender profiling and linkage analysis. Common trauma types include the following:

DOI: 10.4324/9781003728733-22

Airway Obstruction and Asphyxiation: Choking, Smothering, Suffocation

Blunt Force Trauma: minimal, moderate, excessive, or brutal force causing injury by impact
Sharp Force Trauma: cutting, incised wounds, stab wounds
Compressive Injuries: crushing trauma, compressive asphyxia
Burns: Thermal (fire), chemical, or electrical
Explosive Trauma: injuries from blast force or shrapnel
Gunshot Wounds: distant, intermediate, close-range, or contact wounds
Strangulation: manual, ligature, or undetermined type
Environmental Trauma: drowning, smoke inhalation, malnutrition, dehydration, hypothermia
Chemical or Biological Causes: drug injection or overdose, poisoning
Documenting the nature and context of injuries (such as defensive wounds, restraint marks, or postmortem trauma) further supports assessments of offender intent and consistency across events.

Victim Self-Protection Behaviors

The victim's response to an offender can directly influence the type and extent of force used. Offenders may increase or reduce the level of violence based on perceived resistance or cooperation. Understanding the nature of victim self-protection behaviors helps contextualize the crime and can support linkage efforts. Types of victim resistance include the following:

Armed Physical Resistance

- attacked offender with a firearm or other weapon
- fired weapon during the attack
- threatened offender with a weapon

Unarmed Physical Resistance

- hit, kicked, struggled, or otherwise used physical force
- attempted to hold, restrain, or chase the offender

Verbal or Psychological Resistance

- yelled, screamed, threatened to call police
- pleaded, reasoned, argued, or bargained

Defensive or Evasive Actions

- blocked blows, ducked, held onto property
- hid, locked doors, attempted escape by running or driving away

Deceptive Compliance

- pretended to cooperate to delay or prevent harm
- seeking help or drawing attention
- called police or security, cried out for help
- alerted others

The presence or absence of resistance can alter the dynamics of an encounter. In some cases, a victim may prevent a more serious crime through resistance, even if physical harm still occurs. These details can help in establishing offender behavior patterns and discerning escalation.

Crime Pattern Scenario

Serial Sexual Assault Pattern – "The Minimal Force Attacker"

A series of four sexual assaults over six months was linked through consistently low force levels and similar trauma patterns documented by medical examiners and victim statements. In each incident, the offender used verbal threats and minimal physical restraint rather than significant violence, resulting in nearly identical injury patterns: minor bruising on wrists consistent with being held, no facial trauma, and minimal defensive wounds. Medical reports showed consistent findings across cases: superficial bruising at restraint points, no internal injuries requiring medical intervention, and psychological trauma disproportionate to physical injuries. The force pattern remained stable – the offender relied primarily on intimidation, surprise, and brief physical control rather than escalating violence. Victim statements consistently described similar experiences: initial verbal threats, brief physical restraint of hands or arms, and immediate cessation of physical force after compliance. The absence of significant trauma distinguished these cases from more violent sexual assaults in the area. Crime scene evidence showed no signs of struggle beyond minor displacement of personal items, and victims consistently reported the encounters lasted only minutes. The pattern of minimal physical force combined with significant psychological impact helped investigators recognize these incidents as linked while excluding more violent cases from the series. This consistent low-force signature proved valuable for linking cases where the primary evidence was behavioral rather than physical trauma.

Example Case

In Aurora, Colorado, a serial robber targeted Spanish-speaking victims. Over at least 13 separate robberies, the suspect's acts escalated: while he initially displayed a weapon to threaten compliance, investigators documented an incident in which he actually fired a round during the robbery. This use of actual gunfire represented a significant escalation in violence and risk, causing police to express concern that the suspect's behavior was becoming "more violent" as his crime series progressed.[1]

Example query terms: robbery, gun, threatened to shoot, displayed gun, menaced with gun, gunfire, shot

Exercises

1. Choose one violent crime case (news or court report). Identify what resistance, if any, the victim displayed (armed, unarmed, verbal, evasive). Discuss how this resistance might have shaped the offender's level of violence.
2. Research how three different professional fields document and categorize force: law enforcement use-of-force reports, emergency medical services trauma documentation, and domestic violence advocacy organizations' injury classification systems. For each field, identify what terminology they use to describe force levels, how they categorize injury

severity, what details they prioritize in documentation, and how they track escalation over time. Create a comparison chart showing similarities and differences in their approaches to documenting violence and trauma, then consider which documentation methods would be most useful for crime pattern analysis and how different professional perspectives on the same incident might provide complementary information. Finally, design a brief training checklist for investigators that incorporates the most effective documentation practices from all three fields while remaining practical for crime scene use. This exercise demonstrates how systematic force documentation varies across professions while highlighting opportunities to improve consistency and completeness in crime pattern analysis.

Critical Thinking Guidance

Practitioners should avoid making assumptions based solely on the apparent level or type of force used; instead, they should systematically consider all variables, such as changes in offender behavior, escalation or de-escalation of violence, and the victim's resistance tactics. Compare each case for consistencies and anomalies in the use of force, recognizing, for example, when blunt force is minimal versus excessive or when weapon use shifts over time. Evaluate whether these patterns reflect an offender adapting methods to avoid detection or respond to victim behaviors.

Evaluate evidence sources critically, since injury documentation from medical, law enforcement, or advocacy records may use different terms and carry biases. Cross-referencing these perspectives strengthens linkage analysis and reduces misinterpretation. Identify consistencies that define an offender's "signature," such as distinctive injury patterns, weapons, or methods of restraint, but question whether similarities truly indicate one offender or simply reflect common opportunities. Systematic comparison of force, trauma type, and victim resistance across victims and jurisdictions can improve pattern recognition and helps investigators anticipate escalation or strategic change.

Note

1 Werthmann (2024, October 16).

Bibliography

Bennett, S., Gilmour, J., Carr, K., Helton, K., & Anderson, K. (2025). Evaluating the impact of victim-centric, trauma-informed training on sexual violence case outcomes: A quasi-experimental study of a program for police investigators. *Cambridge Journal of Evidence-Based Policing*, *9*(3). https://doi.org/10.1007/s41887-025-00098-z

Britt, C. L. (2000). *Correlates of specialization and escalation in the criminal career: Summary report* (Report No. 182217). U.S. Department of Justice, National Institute of Justice. www.ojp.gov/pdffiles1/nij/grants/182217.pdf

Federal Bureau of Investigation. (2013, August 13). *New information released in serial killer case*. www.fbi.gov/news/stories/new-information-released-in-serial-killer-case

Federal Bureau of Investigation. (2019). *ViCAP case submission form* (Form FD-676) (OMB No. 1110–0011). U.S. Department of Justice. https://omb.report/icr/201904-1110-003/doc/92517501.pdf

Lantz, B. (2021). The consequences of crime in company: Co-offending, victim-offender relationship, and quality of violence. *Journal of Interpersonal Violence*, *36*(7–8), NP4363–NP4388. https://doi.org/10.1177/0886260518786497

Petreca, V. G., Tzani-Pepelasis, K., Ioannou, M., Siggery, A., McBride, L., Barros, E., & Burgess, A. W. (2025). The grip of crime: Analyzing strangulation and asphyxiation typologies in homicide cases. *Journal of Forensic Sciences*, *70*(3), 1094–1104. https://doi.org/10.1111/1556-4029.70021

Werthmann, K. (2024, October 16). Aurora police search for serial robber targeting Spanish-speaking victims in Colorado. *CBS Colorado*. www.cbsnews.com/colorado/news/aurora-police-search-serial-robber-targeting-spanish-speaking-victims-colorado/

21 Knowledge and Skills

Introduction

Most offenders do not need special knowledge or skills to commit their crimes. Nevertheless, many do exhibit some skills that could help in linking crimes. Some crimes demand specialization or expert knowledge. A crime pattern might be identified when unusual or specific knowledge or skills are involved. This chapter provides examples of knowledge and skills variables.

While many crimes can be carried out with little or no specialized ability, certain offenses require distinct knowledge or skills that can serve as important indicators in linking crime patterns. Offenders may demonstrate technical expertise, physical ability, organizational capacity, or social manipulation that distinguishes their methods from opportunistic or unsophisticated crime. These abilities may be acquired through formal education, professional training, prior military or law enforcement service, or criminal apprenticeship. When unusual or advanced skills appear consistently across incidents, they can provide valuable linkage points, narrowing suspect pools and highlighting offender backgrounds.

Knowledge and Skill Variables

Technical Skills

- Cybercrime: Knowledge of computer systems, networks, coding, encryption, malware development, and hacking techniques
- Financial Fraud: Understanding of banking systems, financial instruments, accounting practices, and money laundering techniques
- Vehicle Theft: Skills in locksmithing, hotwiring, and mechanical knowledge related to vehicles

Physical Abilities

- Burglary/Robbery: Skills in lock picking, climbing, stealth, and evasion
- Assault: Hand-to-hand combat or martial arts skills, weapon handling abilities

Social Engineering Skills

- Fraud/Scams: Proficiency in manipulation, persuasion, impersonation, and exploiting human psychology
- Espionage/Insider Trading: Abilities in covert information gathering, networking, and intelligence analysis

DOI: 10.4324/9781003728733-23

Organizational Abilities

- Drug Trafficking/Organized Crime: Knowledge in logistics, operations, management, and understanding of legal loopholes to navigate complex criminal enterprises
- Terrorism: Political and ideological indoctrination, recruitment, planning, coordination, and execution of large-scale illegal activities

Legal Knowledge

- White-Collar Crime: Understanding of corporate law, regulations, loopholes, and exploitation of legal structures

Artistic Abilities

- Art Forgery/Counterfeiting: Skills in painting, sculpture, graphics design, or other artistic mediums to create forgeries of art or counterfeit money

Scientific Knowledge

- Environmental Crime: Understanding of environmental regulations, toxic substances, waste disposal, and illegal trade in endangered species
- Drug Manufacturing: Knowledge in chemistry, biology, or pharmaceutical practices to create or distribute illicit drugs

Geographical and Cultural Understanding

- Human Trafficking/Smuggling: Knowledge of international borders, local cultures, languages, and customs to facilitate illegal migration or trafficking
- Tools and Equipment Handling
- Weaponry: Knowledge of firearms, explosives, and other weaponry
- Surveillance: Skills in using surveillance equipment, anti-surveillance techniques, and intelligence gathering

Psychological Abilities

- Manipulation and Control: Abilities to manipulate or control others, particularly in cases involving human trafficking, grooming, or gang leadership

Examples of Crimes Requiring Specialized Training or Education

Cybercrime and Digital Offenses

- Offenders carrying out cybercrimes (such as hacking, identity theft, complex financial scams, or ransomware attacks) typically have substantial training or self-taught skills in computer programming, network security, and digital forensics. These offenses require in-depth knowledge of software, systems, and sometimes social engineering tactics.

White-Collar and Financial Crimes

- Fraud schemes, embezzlement, insider trading, and money laundering schemes often involve offenders with backgrounds in finance, accounting, or law. The perpetrators understand banking systems, regulatory loopholes, and financial instruments, allowing them to design schemes that are difficult to detect or trace.

Skilled Burglary and High-Value Theft

- Some serial burglars – such as those specializing in safes, art, or jewelry – acquire expertise in areas like alarm bypassing, lock picking, safecracking, tunneling, or even construction. This "criminal expertise" can be developed through both hands-on experience and the acquisition of technical knowledge (sometimes via legitimate work in trades).

Organized Crime and Specialized Enterprises

- Members of organized crime groups may receive various forms of training, often informally, in areas like document forgery, weapons handling, logistics, or even smuggling. These skills can be enhanced through shadowing experienced criminals or prior military training.

Crime Pattern Scenario

Serial Safecracking Pattern – "The Master Locksmith"

A series of seven high-end jewelry store burglaries over four months was linked through sophisticated safecracking skills that required professional-level expertise. In each incident, the offender bypassed alarm systems and opened vintage safes using manipulation techniques rather than drilling or explosives, leaving no damage to the safe mechanisms. Security footage from two locations captured the same methodical approach: using a stethoscope to listen for lock mechanism sounds, employing precise finger movements consistent with professional locksmith training, and completing the safe opening within 10–15 minutes, a timeframe that suggested extensive practice or formal education. Investigation revealed the offender specifically avoided newer electronic safes, focusing only on older mechanical models that required traditional manipulation skills. The precision of his work distinguished these burglaries from typical smash-and-grab operations and suggested someone with legitimate access to locksmith training materials and practice safes. The knowledge pattern extended to timing: he consistently worked during early morning hours when his lengthy safe manipulation process wouldn't be interrupted, indicating understanding of both the technical requirements and operational security needed for this specialized skill. Recognition of this professional-level safecracking expertise led investigators to examine licensed locksmiths and safe technicians.

Example Case

Theodore Kaczynski's actions as the Unabomber were based on a combination of his academic training and self-taught practical skills. His background as a mathematician with a PhD from the University of Michigan provided a foundation in logic and analytical thought. He used this background to design and construct mail bombs from scrap materials, often incorporating handcrafted wooden components to impede forensic analysis. His methodical approach allowed him to operate with caution, which contributed to his evasion of a 17-year manhunt by the FBI. Kaczynski's academic background was also reflected in his 35,000-word manifesto, a lengthy text that articulated the ideology behind his actions and contained the linguistic patterns that ultimately led to his identification.[1]

Example query terms: designed, constructed, mail, bomb, handcrafted, wooden, component, scrap, materials

Exercises

1. Consider the following: a series of fraud cases involving complex accounting schemes and a series of cybercrimes involving sophisticated technical skills. For each, hypothesize what kinds of legitimate occupational or educational backgrounds investigators should examine.
2. Examine three crime scenarios to practice identifying specialized knowledge as a linkage variable. First, consider a series of ATM skimming devices that capture card data without triggering bank security alerts – what electronic engineering, programming, and banking system knowledge would this require, and what legitimate occupations might provide such expertise? Second, analyze multiple thefts of rare orchids from botanical gardens where specimens remain undamaged – what botanical knowledge, handling techniques, and transportation methods suggest formal horticultural training versus amateur collecting? Third, evaluate sequential contamination of competitors' pharmaceutical production lines causing recalls – what understanding of manufacturing processes, quality control systems, and chemical interactions points to insider knowledge versus external sabotage? For each scenario, identify the technical skills needed, consider possible legitimate backgrounds that would provide these abilities, and describe how investigators could use skill requirements to narrow suspect pools. This analysis helps develop pattern recognition skills by focusing on how specialized knowledge creates traceable behavioral signatures in serial crimes, remembering that expertise often leaves evidence in both the execution and targeting decisions of criminal acts.

Critical Thinking Guidance

Certain types of criminals, especially those involved in complex, high-reward, or technical crimes, often require specialized education or training to successfully execute their offenses. This is particularly evident in crimes that demand advanced planning, technical ability, or knowledge beyond what most people possess.

Identifying the skills or backgrounds necessary to commit certain crimes can be crucial for both suspect profiling and crime pattern analysis. For example, successfully linking a series of digital frauds to individuals with IT backgrounds, or a series of complex burglaries to workers in related trades becomes much more likely with awareness of these variables.

When analyzing knowledge and skills as linkage variables, consider that expertise often leaves multiple traces beyond the crime itself. Offenders with specialized training frequently exhibit "signature competencies" – unnecessary displays of skill that serve no practical purpose but demonstrate mastery. These behavioral artifacts can be as identifying as physical evidence. Additionally, consider the learning curve: early crimes in a series may show developing skills while later ones demonstrate refinement, helping establish chronology and potentially identifying practice attempts or failed crimes that weren't initially linked to the series.

Note

1 Federal Bureau of Investigation. (n.d.).

Bibliography

Federal Bureau of Investigation. (n.d.). *The Unabomber*. www.fbi.gov/history/famous-cases/unabomber

22 Group Affiliation

Introduction

The offender(s) responsible for crimes in a pattern may have group affiliations that offer clues regarding modus operandi, background, and location. Group affiliation can be broken down into two categories: non-criminal and criminal. Those lines may blur when, for example, an offender is in a family group that also, as a family, engages in criminal behavior.

While we most often think in terms of group affiliation when trying to understand, investigate, and apprehend the offender, it is also useful to think of the victim's group affiliations in order to understand why they might be targeted by an offender.

Social network analysis of criminal group affiliation can reveal more offenders involved in the patterned criminal activity and provide clues to their roles. This chapter provides descriptions of group affiliation variables.

Non-Criminal Group Affiliation

Employment/Occupational Groups: Includes workplaces and groups related to professions and occupations (such as unions) – knowing where an offender works offers clues into their schedule, skill set, and possibly co-offenders. Victims may be selected because of occupation, such as realtors showing homes while alone being targeted for violent crimes.

Educational Institutions: Includes schools, colleges, vocational training centers, alumni networks, enrollment status, and attendance – knowing an offender's schedule based on classes they attend can be helpful in an investigation. Victims may be selected for harassment because they attended a certain school and a disgruntled former classmate stalks them. Fraternities or sororities may be of interest.

Religious Organizations: Be careful not to stereotype based on religion, but consider how an offender's connection to a religious group may inform their actions. Victims are sometimes targeted for hate crimes based on religion.

Social Clubs and Recreational Groups: Includes sports clubs, hobby groups, and meetup groups – offenders may meet other co-offenders or target victims in such groups.

Family Groups: Includes family ties, family circles, extended families – these relationships may offer insights into domestic or organized crime.

Geographic Communities: Includes neighborhood area and housing complexes and the contexts – offenders may also be victims in high-crime areas.

Online Communities: Includes online forums and social media groups – offender participation may reveal ideologies, planning, and criminal contacts. Victims may be selected through the relative anonymity offered to offenders online.

DOI: 10.4324/9781003728733-24

Political or Activist Groups: These are usually non-criminal but may engage in illegal activities as a form of protest or expression. Victims may be targeted because of their affiliations with these groups.

Military or Paramilitary Groups: Veterans and active duty personnel may have particular sets of skills or experiences that could be relevant to certain types of offenses.

Healthcare or Therapeutic Groups: Includes addiction or recovery groups, healthcare programs, and therapy sessions – participation in such groups may provide insight into the offender's motivations or capabilities.

Cultural Organizations: Includes cultural or ethnic clubs, societies, or groups – may offer context for better understanding an offender or victim.

Volunteer Organizations: Includes volunteer groups and charitable organizations – may provide an understanding of the offender's or victim's life.

Criminal Group Affiliation

Different types of criminal groups vary in their scale of operation – local, national, or global – as well as in their methods, aims, and structures. An offender's affiliation in a criminal group provides insight into possible activities within a specific crime pattern.

Street Gangs

- Scale: local
- Activities: drug distribution, robbery, assault, turf wars
- Identification Methods: tattoos, graffiti, clothing, hand signs, language, known associates, hangout areas, territories, informants, specific criminal behavior

Drug Cartels

- Scale: global
- Activities: production, transportation, and distribution of illegal drugs
- Identification Methods: financial investigations, surveillance, wiretapping, undercover operations

Human Trafficking Rings

- Scale: global
- Activities: forced labor, sex trafficking, organ trafficking
- Identification Methods: financial investigations, surveillance, wiretapping, undercover operations

Mafia or Mob

- Scale: national to global
- Activities: drug trafficking, extortion, gambling, money laundering
- Identification Methods: financial investigations, surveillance, wiretapping, undercover operations

Triads

- Scale: global
- Activities: drug trafficking, extortion, human trafficking, illegal gambling

- Identification Methods: financial investigations, surveillance, wiretapping, undercover operations

Syndicates

- Scale: global
- Activities: drug trafficking, human smuggling, arms smuggling, fraud
- Identification Methods: financial investigations, surveillance, wiretapping, undercover operations

Counterfeit Networks

- Scale: global
- Activities: production and distribution of counterfeit goods
- Identification Methods: financial investigations, surveillance, wiretapping, undercover operations

Terrorist Organizations

- Scale: global
- Activities: acts of terror, bombings, assassinations
- Identification Methods: intelligence agencies, online communications monitoring, financial transactions, travel patterns, international law enforcement collaboration, public tips

Extremist Ideological Groups

- Scale: national
- Activities: promotion of extremist beliefs, sometimes violent
- Identification Methods: informants, online activity, social media, rallies, extremist literature, open expression of beliefs

Financial Crime Networks

- Scale: global
- Activities: fraud, money laundering, insider trading, cybercrime
- Identification Methods: forensic accounting, business records, insider reports, whistleblowers, regulatory agencies, financial transactions

Organized Cybercrime Groups

- Scale: global
- Activities: hacking, identity theft, ransomware, data breaches
- Identification Methods: cyber forensic tools, online forums, digital footprints, dark web surveillance, digital forensics, IP tracking, technology company collaboration, international collaboration

Outlaw Motorcycle Clubs

- Scale: national
- Activities: drug trafficking, weapons smuggling, extortion, violence

- Identification Methods: monitoring meetings, traffic stops, known associates, specific activities, undercover operations, community informants, insignias, patches, bike styles, gathering locations

Prison Gangs

- Scale: local to national
- Activities: various, often continue after incarceration
- Identification Methods: prison behavior, tattoos, hand signals, surveillance, communication monitoring, interviews, correctional officer collaboration, informants

Organized Theft Rings

- Scale: national to global
- Activities: large-scale thefts targeting valuable assets
- Identification Methods: surveillance, informants, specialized expertise within the group

Criminal groups can be local, national, or global. It is important to learn what types of organized crime groups might be operating in your jurisdiction.

Offender Group Affiliation Example Variables

- cartel, cybercrime network, drug trafficking organization, gang, hate group, human trafficking network, Italian Mafia, military, militia group, motorcycle gang, organized crime group, prison gang, professional group, Russian Mafia, school, street gang, team, terrorist group, trade union, Triad, weapons trafficking group, white-collar crime group, white supremacist group, Yakuza

Question to Ask

Use the following questions to evaluate the role of group affiliation when analyzing a crime pattern:

Influence: Did the group's culture or hierarchy drive the offender's actions?
Support: What resources or skills came from the group?
Victim Link: Was the victim chosen due to their group ties?
Network Impact: Did group connections sustain or hide the activity?
Disruption Point: Where could intervention have stopped the pattern?

Crime Pattern Scenario

Over several months, packages begin disappearing from porches in the same mid-size apartment complex, almost always during weekday mornings when most residents are at work. Security camera footage eventually shows a pair of uniformed delivery drivers entering the building's locked mailroom. Investigators learn the offenders are part-time employees of the contracted parcel-delivery company who also live in the complex and belong to the tenants' association. Their role in the association gave them access to resident directories and knowledge of which apartments regularly receive high-value shipments. They used their legitimate work uniforms and building access codes, obtained through association communications, to move freely without raising suspicion. The thefts cluster around units known to receive frequent online orders, demonstrating how a routine neighborhood organization can unintentionally provide both the information and the access that sustain a repeated theft pattern.

Example Case

Gérald Gallant was a Canadian contract killer who carried out at least 28 murders and 12 attempted murders from 1978 to 2003, often in public settings with targeted gunshots to the head, neck, or chest – his consistent modus operandi. Gallant was affiliated with the Rock Machine outlaw motorcycle gang (OMG) during the Quebec Biker War (1994–2002), a violent conflict between the Rock Machine and the Hells Angels over control of drug trafficking in Quebec. Acting on orders from Rock Machine leaders and allied organized crime figures, Gallant carried out 28 murders and over a dozen attempted murders, primarily targeting Hells Angels members, their puppet clubs, and other rivals. His crimes were tightly linked to group affiliation, as victim selection, timing, and methods were shaped by the ongoing gang conflict. The killings followed predictable retaliatory cycles and reinforced the group's strategic objectives, making his role a key example of how organized criminal networks direct violence to maintain power and territory.[12]

Example query terms: motorcycle, gang, OMG, Rock Machine, Hells Angel, patch, targeted, contract

Exercises

1. Identify and research a historical or contemporary case where group affiliation played a role in criminal behavior and explain the influence of the group on the criminal activity.
2. Select a criminal organization and map out, in words or diagrams, how different members or roles (leaders, enforcers, financiers, recruiters) support group activity. Discuss how understanding these connections could help disrupt crime patterns.
3. Analyze how group affiliation influences criminal patterns by examining a well-documented case from your region or historical records. Research the offender's connections to either criminal organizations (gangs, cartels, organized crime families) or non-criminal groups (employment, religious organizations, social clubs) that facilitated their crimes. Consider how the group provided resources such as weapons, vehicles, or safe houses; knowledge including target selection, security vulnerabilities, or operational methods; social support through alibis, intimidation of witnesses, or recruitment of accomplices; and ideological justification that normalized or encouraged the criminal behavior. Document your findings in a brief analysis that demonstrates how group affiliation serves as a critical linkage variable in some serial crime patterns.

Critical Thinking Guidance

When assessing the role of group affiliation in a crime pattern, look beyond merely identifying the existence of a group connection. Evaluate the operational, logistical, and motivational influence the affiliation exerts on the offender or victim. Consider how the group's structure, culture, and resources shape behavior, such as whether the group provides criminal know-how, physical resources, or an ideological framework that encourages or justifies the offense. Likewise, group affiliation may dictate methods of recruitment, define target selection, or enable concealment of criminal activities through established networks. Weigh both the formal and informal ties within the group, examine how membership intersects with other affiliations, and determine whether the group's norms reinforce or restrain offending behavior. Such analysis aids in distinguishing between incidental associations and relationships that actively facilitate or sustain the crime pattern.

Group affiliation analysis requires distinguishing between correlation and causation – not everyone affiliated with a group participates in its criminal activities, and not all crimes by group members are group-directed. Consider the hierarchy of influence: some affiliations provide only passive benefits (like insider knowledge), while others actively direct criminal behavior through formal orders or informal pressure. Examine temporal patterns – did criminal activity increase after joining the group, or did the offender seek group membership to facilitate existing criminal intentions? Understanding these distinctions helps investigators avoid confirmation bias while recognizing genuine group-facilitated crime patterns. Additionally, consider how multiple overlapping affiliations create unique criminal opportunities that wouldn't exist within single group membership alone.

Notes

1 Séguin and Thibault (2014, November 8).
2 Associated Press (2009, March 31).

Bibliography

Associated Press. (2009, March 31). Canadian man pleads guilty to killing 27 people. *The Guardian*. www.theguardian.com

Denley, J., Ariel, B., & Assaraf, N. (2025). Police-led interventions for deterring organized crime: A UK cluster randomized trial targeting criminal network recruiting and its vicarious effects on co-offenders. *Justice Quarterly*, *42*(5), 767–798. https://doi.org/10.1080/07418825.2025.2473720

Global Initiative Against Transnational Organized Crime. (2021). *Global organized crime index 2021*. https://ocindex.net/assets/downloads/global-ocindex-report.pdf

Global Investigative Journalism Network. (n.d.). *Reporter's guide to investigating organized crime*. https://gijn.org/reporters-guide-to-investigating-organized-crime/

Le, V. (2012). Organised crime typologies: Structure, activities and conditions. *International Journal of Criminology and Sociology*, *1*, 121–131. https://doi.org/10.6000/1929-4409.2012.01.12

Ratcliffe, J. H., Strang, S. J., & Taylor, R. B. (2014). Assessing the success factors of organized crime groups. *Policing: An International Journal of Police Strategies & Management*, *37*(1), 206–227. https://doi.org/10.1108/pijpsm-03-2012-0095

Séguin, F., & Thibault, É. (2014, November 8). *Gerald Gallant: Confessions of Canada's most prolific hit man*. Niagara Falls Review (QMI Agency). Internet Archive. https://web.archive.org/web/20170421195003/www.niagarafallsreview.ca/2014/11/07/gerald-gallant-confessions-of-canadas-most-prolific-hit-man

United Nations Office on Drugs and Crime. (2002). *Results of a pilot survey of forty selected organized criminal groups in sixteen countries*. www.unodc.org/pdf/crime/publications/Pilot_survey.pdf

23 Travel

Introduction

How the offender travels can provide information to link crimes based on similarities and preferences of the offender. This information may not be available at first. If the offender is the starting point of crime linkage efforts, meaning that they are known by law enforcement as a suspect, this type of information can be quite useful for further investigations. The time it takes to travel by specific means reveals whether or not a possible offender could have committed a crime. Knowledge of an offender's routine travel patterns allows law enforcement to intercept the offender. Knowledge of routine travel patterns by victims of a crime pattern allows law enforcement to warn other potential victims. This chapter provides travel variables to consider when linking and investigating crime patterns.

Example Travel Variables

Mode of Transportation

- walking
- running
- personal vehicle (car, truck, motorcycle, bicycle)
- public transportation (bus, subway, train, ferry, airplane)
- rental vehicle
- stolen vehicle
- taxi or ride-sharing service
- boat or watercraft
- private air travel
- commercial air travel

Distance Traveled to Commit Crime

- local crime committed within a specific area or neighborhood
- crimes committed across different neighborhoods or jurisdictions
- regional or cross-country travel for specific criminal activities
- international travel to commit crimes
- cybercrime needing no travel
- proximity of the offender's residence to the crime scene
- travel within a specific radius or geographic area
- long-distance travel for specific types of crimes such as smuggling

DOI: 10.4324/9781003728733-25

Times of Travel to Commit Crime

- daytime
- nighttime
- during rush hour or high-traffic periods
- during off-peak hours or low-visibility times
- travel based on public transportation schedules

Travel Routes Taken

- direct routes to target locations
- circuitous or roundabout routes to avoid suspicion or detection
- use of specific highways, roads, or shortcuts
- alternate routes to evade law enforcement or surveillance

Travel Patterns

- regular travel routines and patterns
- travel to familiar or known areas
- random or opportunistic travel without a fixed pattern
- travel to specific locations associated with criminal activity

Frequency of Travel

- one-time travel for a specific crime
- serial travel to commit multiple crimes in the same area
- serial travel to commit multiple crimes in different locations
- regular travel to maintain criminal operations or connections
- seasonal or periodic travel for specific criminal activities

Travel Companions

- solo travel
- travel with a partner or accomplice
- travel with a group or gang
- coordinated travel with other criminals or criminal organizations

Travel Motivation

- travel for the purpose of committing crimes of opportunity, such as burglaries in affluent neighborhoods or pickpocketing in crowded tourist areas
- travel for the purpose of reconnaissance or surveillance
- travel at a certain time of day to maximize opportunity, such as daylight for visibility and nighttime for cover
- targeted travel for specific types of crimes, such as human trafficking or smuggling drugs
- travel to escape or evade law enforcement or prosecution
- travel to establish an alibi

Travel Accessories

- carrying forged or stolen identification documents
- possession of multiple passports and/or travel documents
- travel tickets, itineraries, or receipts as evidence of travel patterns
- disguised or changed appearance with items such as clothing, makeup, wigs, glasses
- weapons, tools, or equipment related to the crime
- bags or backpacks
- communication devices such as cell phones, radios

Travel Behavior

- speed of travel (fast, slow, erratic)
- traffic violations or patterns such as running red lights and speeding
- use of alternative or less-traveled routes to avoid detection
- avoidance of high-traffic or surveillance cameras

Travel History

- previous travel patterns and/or history of criminal activity in specific locations
- travel to known criminal hotspots or areas of interest
- known associates or contacts in various locations
- travel to specific jurisdictions with favorable conditions for criminal activity

Travel Support

- use of rental or stolen vehicles from criminal activities
- access to safe houses or temporary accommodations during travel
- support from accomplices or criminal networks in different locations
- utilization of transportation networks or smuggling routes for illicit activities
- financial resources to support travel expenses such as gas and tolls

Travel Interactions With Witnesses or Bystanders

- encounters with witnesses or bystanders (pedestrians, motorists, law enforcement, etc.) during travel
- use of distractions or diversionary tactics to divert attention away from criminal activity during travel
- strategies employed to avoid suspicion or interaction with potential witnesses

Use of Technology or Communication Tools and Devices

- use of GPS navigation systems or mapping applications for travel directions
- use of cell phones or radios for coordination of criminal activities or real-time information
- use of social media platforms or online tools to plan or gather information about targets during travel

Investigators use a variety of tools to study an offender's travel patterns, including mapping crime locations and routes, and traffic and CCTV cameras for real-time monitoring. Other resources include cell phone data triangulation, GPS and ANPR (Automatic Number Plate Recognition) systems for vehicle tracking, and public transit records. Interviews, eyewitness accounts, and statistical models can also contribute to a comprehensive analysis of an offender's movements.

Crime Pattern Scenario

Serial Prescription Fraud Pattern – "The Pharmacy Hopper"

A series of 21 fraudulent prescription fills across three cities over four months was linked through the offender's systematic exploitation of pharmacy systems. The offender, a former medical office assistant, drove between pharmacies in neighboring cities using stolen prescription pads and DEA numbers she had memorized from her previous employment. Her travel pattern was deliberate but unremarkable: driving her personal vehicle 15–30 miles between cities during weekday afternoons, targeting chain pharmacies near medical complexes where prescription traffic was high, and spacing visits to the same pharmacy chains at least three weeks apart to avoid recognition. Her travel routine minimized suspicion: wearing scrubs suggesting she was picking up prescriptions for a medical office, parking in busy retail plaza lots where her vehicle wouldn't be noticed and paying cash to avoid credit card records. The fraud pattern evolved as she learned pharmacy procedures: initially targeting independent pharmacies with less sophisticated verification systems, later moving to chain stores during known shift changes when new pharmacists wouldn't recognize her from previous visits, and eventually recruiting others to fill prescriptions while she waited in the car. Recognition of this pattern began when a pharmacist noticed the same handwriting on prescriptions from different doctors, prescription monitoring programs flagged multiple fills for the same patients at different locations, and security footage showed the same woman in scrubs at various pharmacies, ultimately leading to her arrest when a suspicious pharmacist called to verify a prescription while she waited.

Example Case

The Felony Lane Gang is a South Florida – based traveling theft-and-fraud crew that dispatches teams from the Fort Lauderdale area to operate across multiple states, typically moving in rental cars, staying in hotels, and working a locality for days or weeks before shifting to the next jurisdiction or returning later after law-enforcement scrutiny fades. Their modus operandi targets parked, often unattended vehicles at daycares, gyms, parks, and recreation areas for "smash-and-grab" thefts of purses, checkbooks, and IDs. Stolen identity documents are then used to cash checks at bank drive-throughs, especially the farthest lane ("felony lane"), offenders disguised by wigs and glasses to impersonate victims. Widespread interstate travel to exploits unfamiliarity and bank procedures.[1]

Example query terms: Felony Lane Gang, smash and grab, parked, identification, ID, impersonate, wig, glasses, drive-through, lane, far lane, purses, wallets, credit card, debit card, parking lot, checkbooks, checks, counterfeit checks, daycare, pre-school, school, gym, fitness, park, recreation, out-of-state license plate, rental car

Exercises

1. Research a case for a specific Felony Lane Gang arrest and describe the findings. Explain the role of travel in this criminal case.

2. Investigate the phenomenon of organized retail crime (ORC) rings that travel between states to conduct large-scale shoplifting operations. Research a specific case by searching for terms like "organized retail crime ring arrest," "interstate shoplifting ring," or "retail theft crew" combined with terms like "multi-state" or "traveling." Analyze how these groups use travel strategically: mapping their routes between major retail centers and outlet malls, timing their movements to coincide with seasonal sales when stores are crowded and security is stretched thin, and selecting cities based on differences in felony theft thresholds that determine prosecution severity. Examine their travel logistics which may include use of rental vans with false compartments for stolen merchandise, recruitment of local accomplices through social media before arriving in new cities, and establishment of temporary housing in extended-stay hotels near interstate highways. Consider how they exploit travel to complicate investigations: hitting multiple stores across several jurisdictions in a single day to fragment law enforcement response, using counter-surveillance techniques learned from studying police patrol patterns, and shipping stolen goods to different states to separate theft from resale locations. Document how investigators overcame these travel-related challenges through responses such as multi-jurisdictional task forces, analysis of license plate reader data along common trafficking routes, and coordination with loss prevention teams who recognized repeat offenders across different stores. Your analysis should demonstrate how criminal groups weaponize mobility to maximize profit while minimizing arrest risk, and how law enforcement adapts to these traveling criminal enterprises.

Critical Thinking Guidance

Critical thinking requires going beyond simply noting the offender's mode of transportation or route. Consider how travel variables interact with opportunity, victim routines, and offender decision-making. Ask whether the travel pattern is habitual or adaptive, whether it reflects logistical needs (such as access to certain targets) or strategic concealment, and whether it suggests prior knowledge of the area or insider information. Comparisons across incidents may reveal consistencies – such as favored highways, rental vehicle use, or timing tied to public transit schedules – that can narrow suspect pools or predict future offenses. Think about the inverse: how offender travel patterns might overlap with victim travel patterns, and how those intersections create risk. Apply this mindset to both offender and victim movements to identify proactive intervention points, potential linkages between cases, and strategies to disrupt ongoing criminal activity.

Note

1 U.S. Immigration and Customs Enforcement (2014, March 19).

Bibliography

Andresen, M. A., & Shen, J.-L. (2019). *Journey to crime: How far does the criminal travel?* Final report. Office of Crime Reduction and Gang Outreach. www.crimrxiv.com/pub/slkb1v54

eFraud Prevention. (n.d.). *Felony lane awareness.* https://efraudprevention.com/security/Felony_Lane_Awareness.html

Levine, N. (2013). *Case studies in crime travel demand modeling I: Travel patterns of Chicago robbery offenders* (CrimeStat IV Technical Report No. NCJ 242991). National Institute of Justice. https://nij.ojp.gov/library/publications/case-studies-crime-travel-demand-modeling-i-travel-patterns-chicago-robbery

U.S. Immigration and Customs Enforcement. (2014, March 19). Leader of Florida's million dollar 'Felony Lane Gang' sentenced to more than 15 years in prison. *ICE News Release*. www.ice.gov/news/releases/leader-floridas-million-dollar-felony-lane-gang-sentenced-more-15-years-prison

Woodhams, J., Davies, K., Galambos, S., Andrew, S., & Hicks, J. (2021). A descriptive analysis of the temporal and geographical proximities seen within UK series of sex offenses. *Journal of Police and Criminal Psychology*, *36*(4), 706–715. https://doi.org/10.1007/s11896-021-09473-8

24 Communication

Introduction

Like travel elements, linking crimes through variables in types of communication usually depends on linking crimes of known offender(s). Sometimes, this information is provided by the victim or a witness. Communication records can be very important in criminal investigations. Analysis of cell phone records, emails, and social media posts help investigators and analysts uncover connections between offenders.

Investigators employ a range of tools to analyze an offender's communication patterns. These include lawful wiretaps for monitoring phone conversations, email and social media monitoring with legal approval, and cell phone forensics to recover messages and call logs. Additional methods encompass Internet Service Provider (ISP) records, pen registers, and trap and trace devices to track calls, as well as specialized software for analyzing text and voice data. Cryptanalysis tools may be used for encrypted messages, while human intelligence sources like informants and undercover agents offer qualitative insights. Facial and voice recognition technologies and sting operations may also be used to understand the offender's communication habits.

Examples of Types of Communication and Their Variables

Direct Communication

- in-person conversations between individuals involved in criminal activities
- verbal communication during the commission of a crime (such as issuing commands or threats)
- meetings or exchanges between criminals to plan or coordinate criminal acts
- verbal communication between offenders during the planning or execution of a crime
- face-to-face conversations or instructions exchanged between individuals involved in criminal activities
- direct communication with victims or witnesses during the commission of a crime

Phone/Electronic Communication

- traditional phone calls made using landline or mobile phones
- use of burner phones or prepaid cell phones to avoid detection
- text messages or SMS communication between criminals
- voicemail messages or voice recordings left by the offender

DOI: 10.4324/9781003728733-26

- phone calls made or received by the offender before, during, or after the crime
- text messages exchanged between offenders, victims, or accomplices
- emails or instant messaging conversations related to the planning or coordination of criminal activities
- communication via social media platforms or private messaging applications

Internet-Based Communication

- email communication between criminals or with accomplices
- instant messaging platforms (e.g., WhatsApp, telegram, signal) for covert conversations
- communication via social media platforms (e.g., Facebook, twitter, X, Instagram) for coordination or sharing information
- use of encrypted communication tools or secure messaging apps for covert communication
- use of internet forums, chat rooms, or social media platforms to discuss or plan criminal activities
- posting or sharing of content related to crimes, including threats or incriminating information
- creation or participation in dark web or encrypted communication channels for illegal purposes
- use of anonymous or pseudonymous online identities to hide one's true identity

Online Forums and Message Boards

- participation in online forums or discussion boards related to criminal activities
- exchange of information, tips, or plans on specialized platforms or websites
- use of coded language or cryptic messages to communicate covertly

Dark Web Communication

- use of the dark web for anonymous communication and coordination of criminal activities
- utilization of encrypted communication channels, such as tor or encrypted messaging platforms on the dark web
- accessing hidden online marketplaces for the exchange of illegal goods or services

Postal Communication

- use of traditional mail services to exchange messages, documents, or illicit goods
- sending anonymous letters or packages as part of criminal activities
- use of false identities or aliases on envelopes or packages to avoid detection

Graffiti and Street Art

- use of graffiti tags or symbols to communicate with other criminals or mark territories
- street art or murals used to convey messages or intimidate rivals
- codes or symbols hidden within graffiti as a form of secret communication

Symbols and Codes

- utilization of specific symbols or codes to communicate covertly
- markings or symbols left at crime scenes to indicate the involvement of a particular criminal group or individual

- use of coded language or jargon within conversations or written messages to conceal the true meaning
- use of specific symbols, marks, or graffiti to convey messages or claim responsibility for crimes
- selection of specific objects or items left at crime scenes to communicate a particular meaning or intention
- displaying or arranging objects in a symbolic manner to send a message or establish an identity

Written Communication

- handwritten or typed notes left at crime scenes as a form of communication or intimidation
- anonymous letters sent to victims, law enforcement, or media to claim responsibility or issue threats
- correspondence between criminals or with accomplices through written letters or notes
- handwritten notes or letters used to convey messages or threats
- graffiti or symbols left at crime scenes as a form of communication or identification
- posters, flyers, or other printed materials used for criminal purposes or to send a message
- messages or markings left on victims or objects as a signature or form of communication

Encryption and Cryptography

- use of encryption techniques to secure digital communication and protect sensitive information
- employment of cryptographic algorithms or software for secure messaging or data transfer
- development or use of custom encryption methods or protocols to avoid detection
- use of encryption techniques or secret codes to communicate covertly
- creation or utilization of specific symbols or patterns with hidden meanings
- utilization of known code systems or the development of custom codes for communication

Non-verbal, Covert Signals, and Body Language

- non-verbal communication signals used between criminals during criminal activities
- hand gestures, facial expressions, or body language employed to convey messages or coordinate actions
- use of prearranged signals or cues to indicate danger, escape routes, or other tactical information
- use of hand signals or gestures to coordinate actions or convey messages
- visual cues or body language used by offenders to communicate instructions or warnings
- specific clothing, attire, or colors used as identifiers or means of communication within criminal networks

Audio and Video Recordings

- use of audio recordings to issue threats, demands, or instructions
- video recordings made by criminals to document or share evidence of their criminal activities
- live-streaming criminal acts or broadcasting messages online for public consumption
- covert audio or video recordings made by offenders to document criminal activities

- surveillance footage capturing interactions, communication, or actions related to crimes
- creation or dissemination of audiovisual materials online for criminal purposes or to intimidate others

Misdirection and Deceptive Communication

- deliberate misleading or deceptive communication to misdirect investigators or confuse witnesses
- false or misleading information shared with the intention to divert attention or suspicion from the offender
- manipulation of communication channels or technology to create false alibis or establish alternative narratives

Communicating Through Intermediaries

- use of intermediaries or messengers to convey messages or instructions related to criminal activities
- communication through third parties to avoid direct involvement or detection by law enforcement
- utilization of coded or covert language when communicating through intermediaries to maintain secrecy
- Dead Drops or Secret Locations
- physical locations where information or items are exchanged or hidden
- secret compartments or hiding spots used for leaving or retrieving messages or items
- covert exchange points known only to the involved parties

Database Queries

Many cases involving communication links will rely on intelligence (such as searching social media posts or interviewing informants) or analyzing by legally obtained communication records of known suspects.

In linking crimes by searching databases proactively, begin with a finding that seems relevant. For example, if a burglar left a note at the scene, query note, message, letter, paper – whatever seems relevant to check if other related cases may be found.

Crime Pattern Scenario

Serial Extortion Pattern – "The Instagram Blackmailer"

A series of 14 extortion cases targeting young professionals across one metropolitan area over nine months was linked through consistent digital communication patterns. The offender initiated contact through Instagram direct messages using fake profiles of attractive individuals, engaged victims in romantic conversations over several weeks, then solicited compromising photographs before demanding payment to prevent their release. The communication methodology showed systematic exploitation: creating profiles using stolen photographs from foreign modeling sites that wouldn't trigger reverse image searches, crafting initial messages referencing specific details from victims' public posts to establish credibility, and transitioning conversations to encrypted WhatsApp within days to avoid Instagram's monitoring systems. The linguistic pattern was consistent across cases: using British spelling despite targeting

American victims, employing similar phrases like "just between us" and "you can trust me completely," and structuring extortion demands with identical formatting including Bitcoin wallet addresses and 72-hour deadlines. His technical communication showed sophistication: using VPNs to mask IP addresses, creating new Bitcoin wallets for each victim to complicate financial tracking, and sending follow-up threats through anonymous email services with victims' photographs attached as proof of possession. The escalation pattern in communications was predictable: romantic messages for two weeks, photograph requests by week three, extortion demands by week four, and increasingly aggressive threats if payment wasn't received. Recognition of this communication pattern emerged when victims began reporting to police rather than paying, linguistic analysis software identified similar writing patterns across different cases, and metadata from shared photographs revealed the same phone model despite different account names, ultimately leading to the offender's identification through a single VPN connection error that exposed his real IP address during a threat transmission.

Example Case

From 1974 to 1991, an individual known as the "BTK Killer" was responsible for a series of murders in Wichita, Kansas. The perpetrator, who created the "BTK" moniker (an abbreviation for "Bind, Torture, Kill") himself, also sent multiple communications to law enforcement and media outlets. After a lengthy period of no contact, communications from the individual resumed in 2004.

A critical turning point in the investigation occurred when the perpetrator sent a floppy disk to a local news station. Previously, he had inquired in a letter if police could trace information from a floppy disk, and police had responded via a newspaper ad that it would be safe. Forensic specialists analyzed metadata embedded in a deleted document on the disk. This analysis uncovered the name "Dennis" and identified the Christ Lutheran Church, where Dennis Rader served as president of the church council. This digital evidence led investigators to identify Rader as the primary suspect, resulting in his arrest and the resolution of the case.[1]

(Note that law enforcement database queries would not have been useful in uncovering the communication pattern because it was unique/unprecedented.)

Exercises

1. Locate five social media posts and identify what they reveal about the individuals' who made the posts. Describe how this information hypothetically could be used in an investigation of linked crimes.
2. Research the MS-13 (Mara Salvatrucha) gang and their graffiti. Identify how these symbols function as communication. Consider how repeated use of tags, symbols, or colors could help link crimes across jurisdictions.
3. Analyze a real case involving criminal communication by researching the "Craigslist Killer" (Philip Markoff) and examining how digital communications enabled both his crimes and ultimate identification. Focus on how Markoff used online classified advertisements to identify and contact victims, the digital trail left by his email communications with victims before meetings, and how his attempt to use anonymous communication methods ultimately failed. Consider the specific communication variables that linked his crimes: consistent language patterns in his email responses to ads, use of disposable email addresses that still contained traceable IP data, text message exchanges that placed him at crime scenes, and hotel surveillance footage that corroborated digital communication timestamps.

Critical Thinking Guidance

Linking serial cases through communication patterns is a critical strategy for investigators aiming to uncover offender connections and recognize broader crime series. When reviewing multiple incidents, practitioners should systematically analyze how repeated or unique modes of communication – such as calls from burner phones, encrypted emails, or recurring social media handles – may signal coordinated criminal activity. By cross-referencing communication records, such as call logs or email exchanges, across various cases, analysts can identify consistent contacts, similar linguistic patterns, or logistical arrangements that point to the same offender or group. Lawful analysis through wiretaps, ISP records, pen registers, and advanced software, combined with informant testimony and covert surveillance, enables investigators to track evolving strategies, evasions, and collaboration efforts that characterize serial offending. Integrating findings from both direct (face-to-face interactions) and electronic exchanges provides critical corroboration, amplifies detection of serial patterns, and strengthens the evidentiary foundation needed to tie together seemingly disparate offenses.

Note

1 Forensics Colleges (2025, April 18).

Bibliography

Forensics Colleges. (2025, April 18). How digital forensics caught the BTK strangler. *ForensicsColleges.com*. www.forensicscolleges.com/blog/forensics-casefile-btk-strangler?utm_source=chatgpt.com

Kikerpill, K. (2023). The crime-as-communication approach: Challenging the idea of online routine activities by taking communication seriously. *Journal of Economic Criminology*, *3*, 100035. https://doi.org/10.1016/j.jeconc.2023.100035

Kulm, A. (2023, March 11). *Solving crime through digital evidence*. Dakota Digital Review. North Dakota University System.

25 Location

Introduction

Before there were computers, officers put maps up on a wall and used pins to show where crimes occurred. Now most law enforcement agencies use sophisticated Geographic Information Systems (GIS) to map the "where" of crime, and often that information includes the "when." While these technological advances have revolutionized crime analysis, they primarily show us dots on a map – the geographic coordinates of where crimes happened.

This chapter takes a fundamentally different approach to understanding location in crime pattern analysis. Rather than focusing on mapping coordinates and hotspot clustering, it examines the qualitative, descriptive characteristics of crime locations that cannot be captured by a simple dot on a map. A GIS system can tell us that five burglaries occurred within a six-block radius, but it cannot tell us that all five targeted corner houses with alley access, mature hedges blocking sight lines, and detached garages – details that might be crucial for linking these crimes and identifying future targets.

Consider the difference: a crime map shows that multiple thefts occurred at "123 Main Street" which is a shopping center. The qualitative location analysis reveals these thefts specifically targeted vehicles parked in the northwest corner of the lot, furthest from security cameras, during the 2–4 PM shift change when security patrol patterns left this area unmonitored for exactly 12 minutes. This descriptive information about the location's characteristics, vulnerabilities, and temporal patterns provides the crucial details needed for crime linkage that no amount of mapping alone can reveal.

Geographic hotspots of crime ARE crime patterns of a general type, but the relatedness of the crimes can only be fully understood by drilling down to discover the MO details embedded in location characteristics. While mapping remains essential for identifying spatial patterns and clusters, this chapter focuses on extracting and analyzing the descriptive location variables that explain why certain places are repeatedly targeted and how offenders exploit specific environmental features across their crime series.

Location Variables

Residential Locations

- houses, apartments, and condominiums
- gated communities or housing complexes
- low-income neighborhoods or public housing projects

DOI: 10.4324/9781003728733-27

Examples of Crime at Residential Locations

- burglaries targeting residential properties
- vehicle theft or break-ins in residential driveways or parking areas
- domestic violence incidents occurring within households
- drug-related activities and sales in residential neighborhoods
- robberies targeting individuals in (home invasion) or near their residences

Detailed Descriptors of Residential Locations

- apartment, assisted living facility, barracks, basement, boat, bungalow, condominium, convalescent home, cottage, dormitory, duplex, tri-plex, garage/carport, hotel, houseboat, mansion, military housing, mobile home, motel, multi-family dwelling (apartment), nursing home, ranch (one story), rest home, single family, temporary quarters, tent, three + floors, townhouse, trailer, transient quarters, treehouse, two-story, vacant, vessel, yurt

Condition of Residential Location

- cover present (fences/bushes), displays signs of wealth, dog present, door unlocked, driveway, fenced yard, garage door(s) open, poor lighting, previously burgled, vacant

Context of Residential Location

- no one home (funeral, work hours), time of day (nighttime, daytime, early morning, middle of the night)

Commercial Locations

- shopping centers and malls
- retail stores and shops
- restaurants and bars
- banks and financial institutions
- office buildings and business parks
- gas stations and convenience stores

Examples of Crime at Commercial Locations

- shoplifting or theft from retail stores
- robberies targeting businesses or financial institutions
- fraudulent activities, such as credit card scams or counterfeit currency, in commercial establishments
- vandalism or property damage to commercial properties
- illegal sale or distribution of controlled substances near or within businesses

Detailed Descriptors of Business-Type Locations

- airport, arcade, bank/ATM/credit union, bar/tavern/nightclub/lounge, business office, cargo container, casino, catering truck, church/synagogue/temple/religious building, coin shop, commercial building, clothing/shoe store, coffee shop/café, construction site, convenience store, convention facility, day laborer site, daycare facility, dental office, entertainment center, fast food restaurant, gas/service station, grocery store/market, hair/nail/tan salon, hotel/motel, industrial complex, jail/prison, jewelry store, laundromat, liquor store, lounge, manufacturing, market, medical office/veterinarian, mini-mart, motel/hotel, movie theater, nursing facility, offender's workplace, office, pawn shop, pet store, pharmacy, racetrack, restaurant, retail business, service station, shopping mall/center/retail store, sports complex, storage facility, thrift store, victim's workplace, warehouse

Recreational and Entertainment Venues

- parks and playgrounds
- sports stadiums and arenas
- theaters and cinemas
- concert venues and music halls
- amusement parks and arcades
- casinos and gambling establishments

Examples of Crimes at Recreational and Entertainment Venues

- assaults or fights occurring at bars, nightclubs, or entertainment venues
- theft from parked vehicles near recreational areas or stadiums
- drug-related activities at music festivals or concerts
- vandalism or property damage in parks or public recreational areas
- sexual assaults or harassment at tourist destinations or entertainment venues

Educational Institutions

- schools (elementary, middle, high schools)
- colleges and universities
- vocational or technical schools
- libraries and research facilities

Examples of Crimes at Educational Institutions

- theft of personal belongings or electronics from lockers or classrooms
- bullying or harassment incidents among students
- drug-related activities on school grounds or nearby
- vandalism or property damage to school property
- assaults or fights among students or involving staff members

Transportation Hubs

- airports and train stations
- bus terminals and stops
- seaports and docks
- taxi stands and ride-sharing pick-up points

Examples of Crimes at Transportation Hubs

- theft or pickpocketing in crowded transit stations or buses
- assaults or harassment on public transportation
- drug-related activities in or around transportation hubs
- robberies targeting commuters carrying valuable items
- vandalism or property damage to transit infrastructure

Healthcare Facilities

- hospitals and medical centers
- clinics and doctor's offices
- nursing homes and assisted living facilities
- pharmacies and drugstores

Examples of Crimes at Healthcare Facilities

- theft of medication or medical equipment from hospitals or pharmacies
- assaults on healthcare workers or patients
- illegal drug diversion or prescription fraud
- vandalism or property damage to healthcare facilities
- trespassing or unauthorized access to restricted areas within healthcare facilities

Government and Public Facilities

- police stations and law enforcement agencies
- courthouses and legal institutions
- government offices and administrative buildings
- prisons and correctional facilities
- public parks and squares

Examples of Crimes at Government and Public Facilities: Vandalism or Graffiti in Public Parks or Government Buildings

- protests, demonstrations, or civil unrest near government offices or public spaces
- theft or damage to public property or infrastructure
- assaults or disturbances at courthouses or government hearings
- disorderly conduct or public intoxication in public spaces

Detailed Descriptors of Government and Public Facilities

- abandoned building, aquarium, art gallery, athletic field, barn, bus, bus station, carnival, church, circus, college campus, concert hall, elementary school, fair, golf course, government building, high school, hospital, house, library, locker room, mall, market, military installation, movie theatre, museum, office building, outdoor concert, outdoor market, parking lot, parking lot structure, private school, public building, public restroom, public school, public transportation stations, racetrack, religious building, reservation, shed, shopping mall, sidewalk, storeroom, synagogue, temple, theatre, tourist area, vacant building, zoo

Industrial and Manufacturing Facilities

- factories and production plants
- warehouses and distribution centers
- construction sites and building projects
- power plants and utilities

Examples of Crimes at Industrial and Manufacturing Facilities

- theft of raw materials or finished goods from warehouses or factories
- vandalism or property damage to industrial facilities
- occupational health and safety violations leading to accidents or injuries
- illegal dumping or pollution in industrial zones
- unauthorized access or trespassing in restricted areas

Tourist Destinations

- tourist attractions and landmarks
- hotels and resorts
- museums and art galleries
- beaches and waterfronts
- historical sites and monuments

Examples of Crimes at Tourist Destinations

- theft or pickpocketing targeting tourists in crowded areas
- scams or fraudulent activities aimed at tourists
- assaults or harassment of tourists in popular tourist spots
- vandalism or property damage to tourist attractions
- identity theft or credit card fraud targeting tourists

Rural and Natural Areas

- farms and agricultural areas
- forests and national parks
- camping sites and hiking trails
- lakes, rivers, and bodies of water

Examples of Crimes in Rural and Natural Locations

- poaching or illegal hunting activities
- theft or vandalism of farm equipment or livestock in rural areas
- illicit drug production or cultivation in remote locations
- burglaries or thefts targeting isolated rural properties
- environmental crimes, such as illegal dumping or wildlife trafficking

Detailed Descriptors of Outdoors Areas

- alley, beach, bay, bayou, boat, bridge, camp, camping area, canal, cave, cemetery, creek, culvert, desert, dirt, ditch, dock, driveway, embankment, farm, field, foothills, forest, freeway, garage, gravel, harbor, highway, hills, isolated, lake, landfill, mine, mountain area, mountains, ocean, open field, orchard, overpass, park, parking lot, path, pond, pool, quarry, ramp, rest stop, river, road, rural area, shoreline, sidewalk, storm drain, stream, swamp, swimming pool, trail, vacant lot, waterway, wooded area, woods

Religious Institutions

- churches, mosques, temples, and synagogues
- religious community centers and meeting places
- religious schools and training facilities

Examples of Crimes at Religious Institutions

- vandalism, arson, or property damage to religious buildings
- hate crimes targeting religious communities
- theft or burglaries in religious institutions
- trespassing or unauthorized access to religious premises
- harassment or intimidation of individuals based on religious affiliation

Underground and Subterranean Locations

- tunnels and underground passages
- sewers and drainage systems
- caves and underground storage facilities

Examples of Crimes at Underground and Subterranean Locations

- drug-related activities or illicit gatherings in underground spaces
- vandalism or graffiti in subway tunnels or underground passages
- assaults or robberies in poorly lit or secluded underground areas
- trespassing or unauthorized access to restricted underground locations
- illegal activities, such as gambling or drug trade, in hidden subterranean spaces

Vacant or Abandoned Locations

- abandoned buildings and properties
- vacant lots and construction sites
- derelict structures or infrastructure

Examples of Crimes at Vacant or Abandoned Locations

- squatting or unauthorized occupation of vacant buildings or lots
- vandalism, arson, or property damage to abandoned properties
- illegal drug use or drug dealing in vacant buildings
- trespassing or loitering in abandoned areas
- illegal dumping or disposal of waste in vacant or abandoned lots

Border Areas and Crossings

- border checkpoints and crossings
- ports and border terminals
- immigration detention centers

Examples of Crimes at Border Areas and Crossings

- smuggling of contraband goods, such as drugs, weapons, or illegal immigrants
- border-related fraud, such as document forgery or human trafficking
- robberies or assaults targeting individuals crossing the border
- illegal trade or trafficking in border regions
- vandalism or property damage to border infrastructure

Online and Cyber Spaces

- social media platforms and online forums
- e-commerce websites and online marketplaces
- dark web marketplaces and illicit online forums

Examples of Crimes Online and in Cyberspace

- cyber fraud, including phishing scams, identity theft, or financial fraud
- online harassment, cyberbullying, or stalking
- unauthorized access to computer systems or hacking activities
- online scams or fraudulent schemes targeting individuals or businesses
- distribution or consumption of illegal content, such as child pornography or pirated material, in online spaces

Specific Locations

The specificities of a location can help connect crimes. For example, a burglar might target only the bedrooms in a house for ransacking, or a rapist may grab and rape his targets in driveways.

Detailed Example Descriptors of Specific Locations

- adjacent open field, alley, attic, backyard bedroom, break room, closet, corner, cul-de-sac, dining room, driveway, elevator, family room, garage, hallway, kitchen, laundry room, living room, locker room, mailbox, middle of the block, office, parking area, parking lot, patio, porch, restroom, room, safe/box, stables, stables tack room, storage area, storage shed, sunroom

Geographic Profiling Locations

In geographic profiling, "location types" refer to the key spatial points in a crime series that help investigators identify and prioritize the probable area where an offender lives or bases operations. They are included in this chapter because they provide concepts to consider in linking crimes by variables as well. If you can narrow down the qualitative information, you can search for it in databases in an effort to link crimes.

Primary Location Types in Geographic Profiling

- Crime Location: The actual site where the criminal act occurred; includes the victim's location during the offense.
- Encounter Location: Where the offender first came into contact with the victim or target.
- Attack Location: The place where the offender initiated the criminal act against the victim.

- Crime Scene (Primary): The main area where the majority of the criminal activity took place.
- Crime Scene (Secondary): Any location related to the crime that is separate from the primary scene, such as where evidence is deposited.
- Body Recovery Site: The location where a victim's body is found, which may differ from where the killing occurred.
- Dump Site: A location chosen by the offender to dispose of a body or other evidence.
- Offender's Anchor Point: A habitual location that the offender uses as a base, such as a residence, workplace, or favorite hangout.
- Target Backcloth: the geographic area within which an offender searches for or encounters potential targets.
- Buffer Zone: An area around the offender's anchor point where crimes are less likely to occur due to increased risk of recognition.
- Activity Space: The set of locations that the offender routinely travels between in daily life, which shapes their awareness of potential crime sites.
- Journey-to-Crime Path: The route taken from the offender's anchor point to the crime location.[1]

Challenges With Addresses

When an officer completes a crime report, the location he or she writes is an address. When the address is mapped, latitude/longitude is used. Geocoding, the process of converting addresses or descriptions into geographic coordinates for computer mapping, has challenges. Errors in geocoding can lead to inaccuracies in crime location mapping and subsequent pattern analysis. In some cases, addresses to be geocoded are imprecise, lacking specific details such as building numbers or street names. Therefore, all addresses cannot be mapped. Then qualitative data found in the reports becomes even more valuable for linking crimes.

If an investigator of cybercrime creates a report, the location field might contain an IP address. An IP address can sometimes be used to trace a criminal's location. Each device connected to the internet is assigned an IP address, and this address can sometimes be traced back to a specific geographical location. However, criminals often use techniques like VPNs (Virtual Private Networks), proxies, or TOR (The Onion Router) to mask their true IP addresses. Internet Service Providers (ISPs) can provide information about the owner of an IP address, but this generally requires a court order or other legal processes. Qualitative details about the crime helps link one crime to others.

Crime series can and do transcend jurisdictional boundaries, making it difficult to pinpoint specific locations. Location data is unavailable if another agency has it in their separate databases. Crimes occur in border areas, overlapping jurisdictions, or transitional zones, requiring coordination and data sharing among multiple agencies. This is a real challenge. Human interactions about qualitative information in reports serve to link crimes when nothing else can. An officer or analyst can call up another jurisdiction and ask whether they had a robbery targeting a fast-food chain or read about it in the news and call the other agency for information.

Crime Pattern Scenario

Serial Church Burglary Pattern – "The Donation Box Thief"

A series of 22 burglaries targeting religious institutions across three counties over six months was linked through consistent location-specific behaviors. The offender exclusively targeted older churches with traditional architecture featuring multiple entry points, poor lighting in rear parking areas, and minimal security systems. His location methodology showed systematic reconnaissance: choosing churches located on corner lots with alley access for multiple escape routes, targeting buildings with dense landscaping that provided concealment from street view, and selecting locations at least one mile from police stations to maximize response time. The pattern revealed specific architectural preferences: churches with basement windows accessible from ground level, older wooden doors with outdated locks rather than modern steel security doors, and buildings with attached fellowship halls that created blind spots from the main sanctuary. His timing exploited location-based routines: striking between Tuesday and Thursday when churches had minimal activity, avoiding locations with attached schools or daycare facilities that increased foot traffic, and targeting churches that held only Sunday services rather than daily programs. The entry pattern was location-dependent: always accessing through rear or side doors facing away from residential areas, exploiting original stained-glass windows that couldn't accommodate modern security film, and focusing on donation boxes located in vestibules rather than secured offices. Physical evidence at locations showed knowledge of church layouts: direct paths to administrative offices suggested familiarity with typical church floor plans, avoidance of sanctuaries with motion-activated lighting indicated prior observation, and selection of churches without rectories or caretaker residences demonstrated understanding of occupancy patterns. Recognition of this location-specific pattern emerged when analysts mapped targeted churches and identified common architectural features and analyzed why certain churches in the same areas remained untouched. Investigators discovered the offender was a former church maintenance contractor familiar with multiple denominations' building standards, leading to his arrest when surveillance was established at churches matching his target profile.

Example Case

Between February 21 and early March 2021, burglars targeted several veterinary clinics in the Idaho Falls area, including Sunnyside Veterinary Clinic, Countryside Veterinary Clinic, and Willowcreek Animal Hospital. Suspects broke into the buildings to steal controlled substances and cash, with some attempts resulting in theft and others causing property damage. The incidents occurred within a short time span and in multiple locations, prompting responses from both the Idaho Falls Police Department and the Bonneville County Sheriff's Office. Authorities advised veterinary clinics in the region to enhance security, safeguard medications in compliance with regulations, and monitor for suspicious activity.[2]

Example query terms: veterinarian, vet, animal hospital, veterinary clinic

Exercises

1. Select a location variable then conduct an online search to find a related crime series. Report on your findings and include the query terms you used (e.g., burglaries at schools or robberies at banks).
2. Search online and locate then compare two different crime series: one targeting commercial sites (and one targeting residential sites. Identify how location factors shaped offender methods in each. Reflect on which descriptors (access, concealment, routine victim activity) would be most useful for linkage.
3. Analyze how specific location characteristics enable serial crimes by researching pharmacy burglaries in your region over the past five years. Search news archives and crime reports for patterns in how offenders select and exploit pharmacy locations, paying attention to both

successful and attempted burglaries. Examine location-specific factors including whether targeted pharmacies were standalone buildings or located within larger stores, proximity to major roads or highways for escape routes, presence or absence of drive-through windows that might indicate 24-hour operations, and whether locations had neighboring businesses that were closed during overnight hours.

Critical Thinking Guidance

Critical thinking about location in crime pattern recognition and identification requires moving beyond simply plotting incidents on a map to examining specific location variables that can directly link cases. Factors such as type of facility, physical layout, lighting conditions, access points, and surrounding land use can reveal whether different crimes share a common environmental quality.

For example, burglaries at older homes with alley-facing garages, poor lighting, and fences that conceal activity may indicate a single offender exploiting the same vulnerabilities across multiple targets. When investigators consistently capture these detailed descriptors – such as "second-floor apartment, rear entrance, minimal street visibility" – patterns can emerge even when the incidents occur in different jurisdictions.

These variables not only help connect crimes but also clarify offender knowledge and preferences. An arsonist repeatedly targeting vacant structures on dead-end streets, or a robber who consistently strikes convenience stores located near freeway on-ramps, is revealing both behavioral consistencies and geographic familiarity. Record and compare such details, noting any recurring environmental factors or situational contexts. The more precise the location descriptors, the greater the potential to identify cross-case similarities, prioritize suspects with known familiarity to those environments, and develop prevention measures tailored to the specific settings.

Location analysis becomes most powerful when investigators move beyond administrative boundaries to examine the experiential qualities of crime sites. Consider how offenders perceive and navigate spaces differently than law-abiding citizens – what appears as a bustling shopping center to customers might represent a target-rich environment with predictable security gaps to criminals. Examine the temporal dimension of locations: a school parking lot transforms from a supervised educational space during day hours to an isolated meeting spot at night. Understanding these dual natures helps explain why certain locations repeatedly host different crime types at different times.

Notes

1 Rossmo (2000).
2 Grossarth (2021, March 8).

Bibliography

Bowen, D. A., Anthony, K. M., & Sumner, S. A. (2022). Business and property types experiencing excess violent crime: A micro-spatial analysis. *Journal of Injury and Violence Research*, *14*(1), 1–10. https://doi.org/10.5249/jivr.v14i1.1566

Clarke, R. V., & Eck, J. E. (2007). *Understanding risky facilities* (Problem-Solving Tools Series No. 6, Problem-Oriented Guides for Police Series). U.S. Department of Justice, Office of Community Oriented Policing Services. https://popcenter.asu.edu/content/understanding-risky-facilities

Curtis-Ham, S., & Bernasco, W. (2025). Prioritising suspects using their activity locations. *CrimRxiv*. https://doi.org/10.21428/cb6ab371.394f4952

Curtis-Ham, S., Bernasco, W., Medvedev, O. N., & Polaschek, D. L. L. (2020). A framework for estimating crime location choice based on awareness space. *Crime Science*, *9*(1), 1–13. https://doi.org/10.1186/s40163-020-00132-7

Curtis-Ham, S., Bernasco, W., Medvedev, O. N., & Polaschek, D. L. L. (2023). Relationships between offenders' crime locations and different prior activity locations as recorded in police data. *Journal of Police and Criminal Psychology*, *38*(2), 172–185. https://doi.org/10.1007/s11896-022-09540-8

Grossarth, E. (2021, March 8). Burglars targeting vet clinics for drugs and cash. *East Idaho News*. www.eastidahonews.com/2021/03/burglars-targeting-vet-clinics-for-drugs-and-cash/

Harries, K. (1999). *Mapping crime: Principle and practice*. U.S. Department of Justice, National Institute of Justice, Office of Justice Programs. www.ojp.gov/pdffiles1/nij/178919.pdf

Rossmo, D. K. (2000). *Geographic profiling*. CRC Press.

Shane, J. M. (2012). *Abandoned buildings and lots* (Problem-Specific Guide Series No. 64, Problem-Oriented Guides for Police Series). U.S. Department of Justice, Office of Community Oriented Policing Services. https://popcenter.asu.edu/content/abandoned-buildings-and-lots-0

Weisburd, D. L. (2008, January). *Place-based policing* (Ideas in American Policing No. 9). Police Foundation.

Zahm, D. (2007). *Using crime prevention through environmental design in problem solving* (Problem-Solving Tools Series No. 8, Problem-Oriented Guides for Police Series). U.S. Department of Justice, Office of Community Oriented Policing Services.

26 Time and Conditions

Introduction

Linking crimes relies heavily on analyzing time variables to uncover the underlying patterns that distinguish a series from unrelated incidents. Specific temporal (time) consistencies, such as crimes occurring on the same day of the week, at particular times of day, or at regular intervals can indicate offender routines. A burglar who strikes every Friday morning or a robber who targets convenience stores just before closing time on weekends demonstrates temporal regularity that supports linking these offenses as part of a serial pattern. The short time gaps between certain events, or the clustering of offenses around holidays, major events, or specific seasons, serve as additional anchors that strengthen associations between incidents and help distinguish serial offending from random occurrence.

Temporal escalation or de-escalation, where the gap between offenses shortens or lengthens, may reflect changes in offender confidence, law enforcement presence, time away from the area, or situational opportunity, offering further insight for linking cases. Identifying cyclic patterns, such as crimes aligning with paydays or local events, also helps identify offender links to crimes.

Conditions such as weather, lighting, or special circumstances can shape both an offender's decision to act and the likelihood of series formation. For example, a pattern of assaults that only occur during periods of heavy rainfall, or burglaries clustered on foggy nights, signal that specific environmental factors may influence offender behavior. Similarly, the presence or absence of daylight, school vacations, or local events like parades or sports games can serve as temporal "triggers" that conditionally frame when and how offenses are committed. Consider condition alongside time variables when looking for links in crimes.

Examples of Time Variables

Day of the Week

- weekdays
- weekends
- specific weekdays

Time of Day

- specific time
- morning

DOI: 10.4324/9781003728733-28

- midday
- afternoon
- evening
- nighttime
- late night
- specific time range
- daylight hours
- darkness
- dawn or dusk

Day of Month

- specific days of the month
- beginning or end of the month paycheck distribution
- specific days of the month paycheck distribution
- moon phases (full moon, new moon, etc.)

Time Duration of Criminal Activity

- brief incidents (snatch-and-grab thefts)
- extended incidents (burglaries, hostage situations)
- patterns of repeated incidents over time (serial crimes)
- patterns when one cannot pinpoint the exact time

Seasonal/Periodic Patterns

- winter
- spring
- summer
- fall/autumn
- holidays and special occasions
- travel seasons
- school calendar
- tax season
- inventory periods for businesses

Yearly Time Patterns

- significant dates or anniversaries criminals choose to commit crimes
- long-term trends in specific types of crimes
- comparisons of crime rates over time

School-Related Time

- before school hours
- during school hours
- after school hours
- school breaks and holidays

Travel/Traffic Times

- morning rush hour
- evening rush hour
- holiday travel peaks
- public transportation schedules

Shift Work/Shift Changes

- day shift
- evening shift
- night shift
- rotating or irregular shifts
- workplace shift changes
- law enforcement shift changes
- security guard shift changes

Events and Gatherings

- festivals and parades
- sporting events and matches
- concerts and performances
- political rallies or demonstrations
- significant events for specific cultures or religions
- peak tourist seasons in specific areas

Seasonal or Weather-Related Factors

- daylight saving time changes
- temperature extremes (very hot or very cold weather)
- severe weather conditions (storms, heavy rain)
- basic weather descriptions: clear skies, rainy, snowy, foggy, windy, hot, cold
- long-term changes in climate leading to social and economic disruptions
- longer lasting effects of natural disasters, such as displacement and increased vulnerability

Time of Scheduled Deliveries

- postal or courier services
- freight deliveries
- online shopping deliveries

Opening and Closing Hours

- retail store opening or closing times
- bar and restaurant opening or closing times
- office building opening or closing times

Time of Routine Activities

- school drop-off or pick-up times
- commuting hours
- peak hours for bars, clubs, and restaurants

- opening and closing times
- ATM cash replenishment times

Time of Critical Infrastructure Maintenance

- power outage or maintenance schedules
- road or transportation network maintenance schedules

Time-Based Vulnerabilities

- walking alone at night
- when security measures are lax
- when emergency services cannot access an area
- strikes, changes in public transport routes/times, or major infrastructure projects
- periods of economic instability
- pandemics and public health crises

Absence in Time From Place

- patterns of no criminal activity when a prolific offender is incarcerated
- crime pattern activity ceased because offender moved away or was away for a span of time

Examples of Temporal Crime Patterns

Spike in residential burglaries during weekdays when homes are typically unoccupied due to work or school.[1]

- Spike in commercial burglaries on weekends when businesses are closed and areas around them are deserted.
- Rise in thefts from vehicles during warm summer months when people leave windows open or belongings unattended
- Spike in vehicle thefts during cold winter mornings when owners warm up their cars and leave them unattended.
- Surge in assault incidents around closing time at bars and nightclubs.
- Increase in incidents of public disorder, including fights or disturbances, during major sporting events or festivals.
- Rise in bicycle thefts during summer when more people are out cycling.
- Surge in retail thefts during the holiday season, particularly in the weeks leading up to major gift-giving holidays.

Trends

It can be helpful to link crimes in a series if current crime trends are understood. Look for particular offenders responsible for linked crimes that fall under the umbrella of a particular trend. A trend is a change over time – in these examples, an increase in types of crimes.

Examples of Trend Crime Patterns

- the trend of iPhone thefts decreased when better security features (the Apple Activation Lock) made them less appealing to steal[2]
- as the price of copper increased in 2008, thefts of copper surged enough that the FBI warned that the trend was a threat to the critical infrastructure[3]

Reporting and Recording Issues to Consider

Police reports may only include one field to record the time of a crime, but all crimes occur in a period, even if it is merely seconds from the time the criminal event started to the time it ended. Even if a "start" and "end" time is on a crime report, it may not accurately reflect the time. If a summer cottage was burglarized sometime in the off-season, the actual time and duration (how long it took to commit the crime) are unknown whether there are no witnesses or video. If someone is robbed by force, they are more likely to be able to provide a beginning and end time to the robbery, and it is possible then to calculate the duration of the crime.[4]

Significant Dates or Anniversaries Examples

It is uncommon for significant dates of anniversaries to be part of linking crimes but be aware that some offenders act based on these variables.

April 20th: This is Adolf Hitler's birthday and has been used by white supremacist groups and other far-right extremists as a day of significance.

April 19th: This date marks the anniversary of the 1995 Oklahoma City bombing and the end of the Waco siege in 1993. Some anti-government or extremist groups may view this date as significant.

June 17th: On this date in 2015, a white supremacist killed nine African Americans in a church in Charleston, South Carolina. This date may hold significance for those motivated by racial hatred.

July 22nd: On this date in 2011, a far-right extremist in Norway killed 77 people in a bombing and mass shooting. This date may hold significance for far-right extremists.

August 12th: This date marks the anniversary of the 2017 "Unite the Right" rally in Charlottesville, Virginia, where a white supremacist drove his car into a crowd of counter-protestors, killing one.

September 11th: Known primarily for the 2001 attacks on the World Trade Center and the Pentagon, this date may hold significance for various extremist groups.

Dates Associated With Religious Holidays or Observances: Perpetrators may choose dates that are significant to the religion of the group they are targeting. This could include Christian holidays like Christmas or Easter, Jewish holidays like Passover or Yom Kippur, Islamic holidays like Eid al-Fitr or Eid al-Adha, or any other religious observances.

Dates Associated With Cultural or National Holidays: This could include days like Martin Luther King Jr. Day in the United States, which may be targeted by those motivated by racial hatred, or LGBTQ+ Pride Month in June, which could be targeted by those motivated by anti-LGBTQ+ bias.

Crime Pattern Scenario

Serial Package Theft Pattern – "The School Run Thief"

A series of 17 package thefts across two suburban neighborhoods over five months was linked through temporal patterns aligned with elementary school schedules. The offender struck exclusively between 8:45 and 9:15 AM on weekdays, the 30-minute window after parents returned from morning school drop-off but before they typically checked their doorsteps. Her temporal methodology showed careful observation: targeting only Tuesday through Thursday when delivery volumes peaked, avoiding Mondays when residents worked from home more frequently, and skipping Fridays when many retrieved packages immediately for weekend projects. Weather conditions influenced her activity: operating only on dry days when packages wouldn't be damaged and homeowners were less likely to immediately retrieve deliveries, increasing thefts during overcast conditions that reduced doorbell camera clarity, and avoiding extremely cold days when residents stayed home. The pattern showed seasonal adaptation: shifting from 8:45 AM starts in September to 9:00 AM in November as school start times adjusted for darkness, exploiting the week before Christmas when package volumes overwhelmed porches, and ceasing operations during school breaks when the parent drop-off pattern disappeared. Her victim selection was temporally specific: targeting homes where cars left and returned within the school-run timeframe, focusing on addresses receiving multiple deliveries suggesting regular online shopping habits, and avoiding houses where retirees retrieved mail promptly each morning. Recognition of this temporal pattern emerged when victims compared theft times and realized all occurred during the brief post-school-run window, doorbell cameras showed the same woman walking a small dog as cover for her presence, and thefts stopped completely during school vacation weeks, leading to her identification as a neighborhood resident whose walking route perfectly timed with package delivery patterns.

Example Case

Between June 16 and July 6, 2025, a group of armed robbers targeted intoxicated bar-hoppers in Chicago's River North neighborhood during the early morning hours as venues were closing. The assailants befriended persons who appeared drunk, then physically assaulted them, held a gun to their heads and demanded access to their phones, specifically passcodes and Cash App credentials, rather than cash.[5]

Example query terms: group, bar, tavern, last call, bar closing, hopping, early morning, intoxicated, drunk, gun, passcode, CashApp

Exercises

1. Search online for a terrorism case where investigators created a timeline, for example, the Oklahoma City bombing or 9/11 hijackers investigations. Summarize how the timeline clarified offender movements and/or activities over time.
2. Locate a study or news case that connects crime to weather conditions (such as assaults during heat waves, burglaries during storms). Describe how conditions influenced when offenders acted and how investigators could use this to anticipate risk.
3. Track how time patterns reveal criminal behavior by documenting bicycle thefts in your community for one month (or longer) using local police reports, campus security alerts, or neighborhood social media posts. Note the specific times thefts occur, whether patterns emerge around certain days of the week, and any connection to local conditions like weather, events, or business hours. For example, do more bikes disappear during morning commute hours when owners quickly lock them and rush to work, during evening hours when fewer witnesses are present, or during special events when parking areas overflow? Document whether thefts cluster around specific locations at predictable times, such as gym parking lots during peak workout hours or transit stations during rush hour. Consider seasonal factors like whether thefts increase during good weather when more people cycle, or if patterns shift when schools are in session versus summer break. Your simple tracking

exercise should reveal how even property crimes follow temporal patterns that could help owners adjust their security habits and help police allocate resources during high-risk time windows.

Critical Thinking Guidance

Linking serial crimes effectively means analyzing time and place together to spot patterns that suggest the same offender or group. Breaking incidents into precise time units, such as specific hours, days of the week, or seasons, can reveal consistent offending windows that match an offender's routine or opportunities. Look for recurring locations or nearby areas with similar conditions, like lighting, crowd levels, or business hours, and compare these with known suspect movements. Time-stamped evidence from CCTV, GPS, phone records, or transactions can confirm whether the same individual was present at multiple scenes. Consider broader cycles, like holidays, paydays, or major events, to further explain when the offender chooses to act.

In crimes that have steps that take place over a non-consecutive time period, calculating the time of the crime is more complex. For example, making counterfeit money involves getting the materials and equipment, making the money, and then distributing the money. This may have days or months between steps. Prepare timelines when investigating cases with various steps. A timeline visually represents significant events in the order in which they occurred. It displays events in chronological order for investigations and crime pattern analysis.

Temporal analysis becomes most powerful when investigators recognize that time operates at multiple scales simultaneously. A crime occurring at "2:15 AM on a Tuesday" exists within hourly patterns (bar closing time), daily patterns (overnight vulnerability window), weekly patterns (lowest staffing on Tuesday nights), monthly patterns (rent due dates), seasonal patterns (summer vacation), and even multi-year patterns (economic recession). Each temporal layer may offer different insights into offender decision-making. Additionally, consider "temporal displacement" – when prevention efforts successfully reduce crimes at one time, offenders may simply shift to different hours rather than cease offending. This displacement can actually help identify serial patterns by showing consistent offender adaptation to changing conditions. Remember that absence of crimes during specific periods (when an offender is incarcerated, hospitalized, or traveling) can be as revealing as presence of crimes in establishing patterns.

Notes

1 van Sleeuwen et al. (2021).
2 Etherington (2015, February 11).
3 FBI Criminal Intelligence Section (2008, September 15).
4 Ratcliffe (2002).
5 Sabes (2025, August 4).

Bibliography

Etherington, D. (2015, February 11). Apple's activation lock leads to big drops in smartphone theft worldwide. *TechCrunch*. https://techcrunch.com/2015/02/11/apples-activation-lock-leads-to-big-drops-in-smartphone-theft-worldwide

FBI Criminal Intelligence Section. (2008, September 15). *Intelligence assessment: Copper thefts*. Federal Bureau of Investigation. www.fbi.gov/stats-services/publications/copper-thefts

Kim, Y. (2021). *Weather and crime: New York State* [Master's thesis, John Jay College of Criminal Justice, City University of New York]. CUNY Academic Works. https://academicworks.cuny.edu/cgi/viewcontent.cgi?article=1197&context=jj_etds

Newton, A., & Felson, M. (2015). Editorial: Crime patterns in time and space: The dynamics of crime opportunities in urban areas. *Crime Science*, *4*(1), Article 11. https://doi.org/10.1186/s40163-015-0025-6

Ratcliffe, J. H. (2002). Aoristic signatures and the temporal analysis of high volume crime patterns. *Journal of Quantitative Criminology*, *18*(1), 23–43. https://doi.org/10.1023/A:1013240828820

Sabes, A. (2025, August 4). Armed robbers target bar hoppers in ritzy blue city neighborhood: 'Held the gun to my head'. *Fox News Digital*. www.foxnews.com (also distributed via AOL)

van Sleeuwen, S., Ruiter, S., & Steenbeek, W. (2021). Right place, right time? Making crime pattern theory time-specific. *Crime Science*, *10*, Article 10. https://doi.org/10.1186/s40163-021-00139-8

27 Opportunity

Introduction

Opportunity is often the unifying thread that links separate incidents to a single offender or group. Even when motives vary, repeat offenders often exploit the same types of vulnerabilities, operating in familiar environments or under similar situational conditions that minimize their risk and maximize their success. These opportunities can be rooted in physical factors, such as poor lighting, lack of surveillance, or easy access points, or in predictable human behaviors and routines, such as unsecured valuables, consistent staff schedules, or lapses in oversight. By identifying recurring opportunity conditions across incidents, it is possible to detect hidden links between cases that might not otherwise appear connected. Recognizing opportunity patterns can aid in case linkage.

Opportunities in the Physical Environment

Poor Lighting Conditions

- dimly lit streets, alleys, and parking lots
- insufficient lighting in residential areas and public spaces
- lack of streetlights in secluded or high-crime areas
- Inadequate lighting in building entrances, stairwells, and corridors

Absence of Surveillance

- lack of video surveillance cameras in public spaces and high-crime areas
- insufficient CCTV coverage in residential complexes, parking lots, and businesses
- absence of security personnel or patrolling officers in vulnerable locations
- inadequate monitoring of critical infrastructure and transportation hubs

Poorly Maintained or Abandoned Buildings

- vacant or abandoned buildings prone to vandalism, squatting, and criminal activities
- buildings with broken windows, damaged doors, and easy access points
- neglected properties with overgrown vegetation, providing hiding spots for criminals
- unsecured construction sites with valuable materials and equipment

DOI: 10.4324/9781003728733-29

Inadequate Access Control

- buildings with faulty or easily bypassed access control systems
- unsecured entrances or exits in residential complexes, schools, and commercial premises
- lack of controlled entry points in public spaces and transportation facilities
- insufficient barriers or gates to restrict unauthorized access to restricted areas

Insufficient Natural Surveillance

- poorly designed urban layouts with limited visibility and sightlines
- overgrown shrubbery or trees obstructing views of public spaces
- absence of windows or balconies overlooking streets and parks
- lack of pedestrian-friendly environments with active street life and natural surveillance
- lack of alarm systems and burglar-proof measures in residential and commercial properties
- insufficient security patrols or guards in high-crime areas or vulnerable locations
- absence of security protocols in schools, hospitals, and other public facilities
- failure to secure valuable assets and resources in public and private spaces

Lack of Territoriality and Ownership

- disrepair and neglect of public spaces, signaling a lack of community ownership
- poorly maintained parks, playgrounds, and recreational areas with limited community engagement
- neglected neighborhoods with abandoned properties and unattended public infrastructure
- absence of clear property boundaries and territorial markers, allowing for encroachment and criminal activities

Limited Surveillance Opportunities for Witnesses

- lack of public transportation or transportation hubs, limiting witness presence
- absence of public gathering spaces with adequate lighting and visibility
- insufficient seating and waiting areas with limited surveillance capabilities
- poorly designed public restrooms or remote facilities with low visibility and safety concerns

Vulnerable Public Transportation

- inadequate security measures on buses, trains, and subway systems
- poorly lit and unsafe stations or stops with limited surveillance
- absence of security personnel or emergency communication systems on public transportation
- lack of secure bike parking facilities or safeguards for personal belongings

Insecure Public Infrastructure

- insufficient fencing or barriers around critical infrastructure and utilities
- poorly secured manholes, sewer access points, and underground tunnels
- lack of protective measures for bridges, overpasses, and tunnels
- absence of proper lighting and surveillance in public infrastructure areas

Environmental Design Issues

- lack of natural surveillance in public spaces due to inadequate design
- poorly maintained sidewalks that make it difficult for pedestrians to navigate safely
- absence of proper signage and wayfinding, leading to confusion and potential criminal opportunities
- insufficient public amenities, such as seating, rest areas, and public toilets, causing discomfort and reducing surveillance

Opportunity Based on Crime Type

Opportunities for crime arise based on victims' behavior and on the physical environment. Specific crimes occur because of specific opportunities. Examples follow in this section.

Residential Burglary

- unlocked doors or windows
- absence of occupants
- lack of security systems or alarms
- poorly lit areas around the property
- visible valuable items from outside

Vehicle Theft

- unlocked vehicles
- keys left inside the vehicle
- poorly lit parking areas
- lack of visible security devices (steering wheel locks, alarms)
- valuables left in plain sight inside the vehicle

Pickpocketing/Purse Snatching

- crowded public spaces
- distracted individuals
- easy access to bags or pockets
- lack of awareness of surroundings
- unsecured bags or wallets

Shoplifting/Retail Theft

- inattentive or overwhelmed store staff
- poorly monitored store aisles or blind spots
- absence of security devices (such as cameras, electronic article surveillance)
- inadequate customer bag checks
- large crowds or distractions in the store

Robbery

- isolated or dimly lit areas
- lack of security personnel or surveillance
- cash-heavy businesses or individuals

- inadequate security measures (panic buttons, security barriers)
- predictable routines of potential victims

Fraud

- unsolicited phone calls or emails
- lack of proper identification verification
- weak or easily guessed passwords
- unsecured online transactions
- lack of employee training on fraud prevention

Cybercrime

- outdated or unpatched software systems
- weak or easily guessed passwords
- phishing emails or malicious attachments
- unsecured Wi-Fi networks
- lack of cybersecurity awareness or training

Identity Theft

- unsecured personal information (such as discarded documents and unprotected online accounts)
- public Wi-Fi networks
- stolen or lost identification documents
- data leaks

Sexual Assault

- vulnerable individuals (such as intoxicated, incapacitated)
- dimly lit or secluded areas
- lack of bystander intervention
- lack of consent education and awareness

Drug Dealing/Trafficking

- high drug demand areas
- poorly monitored borders or transportation hubs
- accessible drug supply chains
- lack of community awareness or involvement

Graffiti/Vandalism

- poorly secured public or private property
- absence of surveillance cameras or alarms
- limited community engagement in property maintenance
- lack of immediate removal or cleanup efforts

Financial Crimes

- lack of financial transaction monitoring
- inadequate anti-money laundering measures

Hate Crimes

- lack of community education and tolerance
- inflammatory rhetoric
- weak reporting mechanisms or fear of reprisals

Organized Crime

- corrupt individuals in positions of power
- illegal drug markets
- human trafficking networks
- money laundering opportunities

Environmental Crimes

- improper waste disposal practices
- pollution from industrial facilities
- illegal dumping of hazardous materials

Child Exploitation

- lack of parental supervision or awareness
- vulnerable children in unstable environments

Terrorism

- public events or gatherings
- soft targets with minimal security measures
- accessibility to weapons or explosive materials

Illegal Firearms Possession/Trafficking

- weak border control or smuggling routes
- gang activity and territorial disputes
- availability of unregistered firearms
- abilities to produce ghost guns

Crime Pattern Scenario

Serial Parking Meter Theft Pattern – "The Early Bird Collector"

A series of 34 parking meter thefts over nine months was linked through systematic targeting of municipal collection schedule vulnerabilities. The offender chose to steal from meters in downtown districts on Wednesday mornings between 5:30 and 6:30 AM, the gap between overnight security patrols ending and morning commuters arriving. His opportunity assessment was precise: focusing on older mechanical meters along streets with broken streetlights, selecting blocks where nearby businesses had no external cameras, and targeting meters that showed visible wear suggesting delayed maintenance. The pattern revealed understanding of city operations: striking the day before official Thursday collections when meters held maximum coins, avoiding smart meters with real-time monitoring, and focusing on streets scheduled for later collection routes. Environmental opportunities guided his selection: choosing meters near construction sites where noise covered his drilling, operating during garbage collection when truck sounds masked his activity, and selecting locations where parked delivery vehicles provided visual barriers. His method evolved to maximize opportunity: initially using crude prying techniques on single meters, later bringing professional drilling equipment to hit multiple meters quickly, and eventually recruiting lookouts to extend his operating window. Recognition of this pattern occurred when parking enforcement noticed collection revenues dropping on specific routes, maintenance crews found similar drill patterns across jurisdictions, and a traffic camera captured his vehicle at multiple theft locations, leading to arrest when GPS tracking of city collection routes predicted his next target area.

Example Case

Between December 2023 and January 2024, Radnor Township police investigated six incidents of professional pickpocketing at St. David's Shopping Center (specifically at HomeGoods and Homesense), where a coordinated three-person team took advantage of crowded store settings by distracting shoppers. One woman engaged the victim in conversation while an accomplice lifted items from purses and bags, and the third person acted as a lookout; the stolen payment cards were immediately used at high-end retailers in the King of Prussia area.[1]

Example query terms: HomeGoods, Homesense, shopping, purse, bag, pickpocket, credit card, debit card, three, team, conversation, distracted

Exercises

1. Opportunity Audit (CPTED[2] Walkthrough): Select a public place such as a shopping center or transit stop. Document fixed and temporary opportunity factors (lighting, sightlines, access points, crowding patterns, closing times). Propose three feasible opportunity-reducing changes.
2. Visit a local coffee shop during different times over a week and observe how opportunity factors change throughout the day. Without photographing or making obvious notes, mentally catalog vulnerability patterns such as when laptops are left unattended while customers get refills, peak times when the register area becomes chaotic with orders, and whether staff can see all seating areas from their work stations. Notice behavioral patterns like customers leaving purses on chairs while ordering, the predictable timing of cash register drawer changes, and how long mobile orders sit unattended on pickup shelves. Document environmental factors including blind spots created by furniture arrangement, whether bathroom locations require leaving belongings unattended, and if outdoor seating areas are visible from inside. After your observations, identify the specific time windows when theft would be easiest and suggest three low-cost changes that could reduce opportunities, such as rearranging furniture to eliminate blind spots, installing mirrors to increase visibility, or implementing a claim ticket system for mobile orders.

Critical Thinking Guidance

Consider a methodical approach to examine the element of opportunity in suspected crime patterns. List the specific environmental, security, and behavioral factors that allow each potentially relevant crime to occur and then compare these lists. Look for consistent conditions: repeated use of poorly lit access points, targeting of similar businesses during predictable quiet periods, or exploitation of the same procedural weaknesses. Consider whether these opportunities are fixed (unchanging features like an abandoned property or unmonitored alley) or temporary (event schedules, seasonal changes, shift patterns) and whether they align with known or suspected offender routines. Use time and location data to see if the offender is revisiting the same types of places at similar times which might indicate both familiarity and preference. Integrate multiple data sources such as CCTV footage, license plate hits, phone and transaction records, and witness statements, to confirm that recurring opportunity factors are not coincidental. Once the opportunity pattern is described, identify other locations or situations with the same conditions and treat them as potential future targets.

Notes

1 Bennett (2024, February 14).
2 CPTED stands for Crime Prevention Through Environmental Design.
It is a crime-prevention approach that uses the design, management, and use of the built environment to reduce opportunities for crime and increase natural surveillance, territoriality, and access control.

Bibliography

Bennett, M. (2024, February 14). Six pickpocketing incidents reported at Radnor Shopping Center. *Patch.* https://patch.com/pennsylvania/radnor/pickpocketers-hitting-shoppers-radnor-shopping-center-report

Clarke, R. V. (2012). Opportunity makes the thief. Really? And so what? *Crime Science*, *1*(1), Article 3. https://doi.org/10.1186/2193-7680-1-3

Cornish, D. B. (1994). The procedural analysis of offending and its relevance for situational prevention. In R. V. Clarke (Ed.), *Crime prevention studies* (Vol. 3). Criminal Justice Press. www.popcenter.org/sites/default/files/library/crimeprevention/volume_03/06_cornish-2.pdf

Felson, M., & Clarke, R. V. (1998). *Opportunity makes the thief: Practical theory for crime prevention* (Police Research Series, Paper 98). Policing and Reducing Crime Unit, Home Office. https://popcenter.asu.edu/sites/default/files/opportunity_makes_the_thief.pdf

Zahm, D. (2007). *Using crime prevention through environmental design in problem solving* (Problem-Solving Tools Series No. 8, Problem-Oriented Guides for Police Series). U.S. Department of Justice, Office of Community Oriented Policing Services.

28 Property

Introduction

The term property in this chapter refers to the things stolen, damaged, or destroyed in a criminal act.

Property plays a critical role in connecting seemingly unrelated criminal incidents. Whether stolen, damaged, or destroyed, property can carry unique characteristics that facilitate identifying patterns across cases. The type of property targeted, the method of theft or destruction, and the manner in which it is recovered or disposed of can all provide insight into an offender's modus operandi. Specific items appear repeatedly in related crimes for various reasons – because of their cash value, because they are in high demand in illicit markets, serve as tools for further offenses, or hold value to the offender. Track property details across incidents to link offenses across jurisdictions, to reveal organized criminal activity, and to uncover networks of offenders and facilitators. By systematically analyzing property data, including theft location, time, value, recovery method, and disposal channel, helps connect cases, narrow suspect pools, and identify broader crime trends that might otherwise go undetected.

Property Information

The property lists in this book were adapted from the 2021.1 National Incident-Based Reporting User's Manual.[1]

The author added some variables to the categories; these follow the word additions in the sections where they were added. The NIBRS User's Manual also includes buildings as property, because in arson and vandalism, they are property targets.

Targeted Structure Types Variable Examples

- single dwelling residence, other residence, commercial structure, industrial structure, public structure, storage structure, farm/agricultural building, transportation structures (vehicles, trains/ships), targeted inhabited building, targeted vacant building, targeted specific business type

While the NIBRS categories included for readers of this book already exist, the users of this information usually are the workers who are tasked with the administrative chore of coding reports to comply with statistical reporting requirements. Those collecting, analyzing, and investigating do not use this NIBRS list to consider crime patterns identification or as a starting point for searching for property crime patterns.

DOI: 10.4324/9781003728733-30

The NIBRS manual requests law enforcement agencies document the outcome of property crimes. These elements can be helpful for crime pattern recognition and identification: none (no outcome), burned (includes damage caused in fighting the fire), counterfeited/forged, destroyed/damaged/vandalized, recovered (to impound property that was previously stolen), seized (to impound property that was not previously stolen), stolen/etc. (includes bribed, defrauded, embezzled, extorted, ransomed, robbed, etc.), unknown

Property Types

Financial/Valuables-Related Property

Money: any circulating medium of exchange, legal tender, currency; coins, paper money, demand deposits, etc.; counterfeited currency, cryptocurrency

Purses/Handbags/Wallets: bags or pouches used for carrying articles such as money, credit/debit cards, keys, photographs, and other miscellaneous items; briefcases, fanny packs, and backpacks when used as a purse or wallet

Credit/Debit Cards: cards and/or the account number associated with the cards that function like a check and through which payments or credit for purchases or services are made electronically to the bank accounts of participating establishments directly from the cardholders' accounts; automated teller machine (ATM) cards, electronic benefit transfer (EBT) card, gift cards (included here but not by FBI)

Negotiable Instruments: documents, other than currency, that are payable without restriction; an unconditional promise or order of payment to a holder upon issue, possession, on demand, or at a specific time; endorsed checks (including forged checks that have been endorsed), endorsed money orders, endorsed traveler's checks, bearer checks, and bearer bonds

Non-Negotiable Instruments: documents requiring further action to become negotiable; unendorsed checks, money orders, traveler's checks, stocks, bonds, blank checks, etc.

Jewelry/Precious Metals/Gems: articles made of gold, silver, precious stones, etc. used for personal adornment; bracelets, necklaces, rings, watches, platinum, loose gems, etc. Luxury watches such as Rolex.

Collections/Collectibles: objects that are collected because they arouse interest due to being novel, rare, bizarre, or valuable; fine art objects, stamp/baseball/comic book collection

Transportation-Related Property

Aircraft: machines or devices capable of atmospheric flight; airplanes, helicopters, dirigibles, gliders, ultra-lights, hot air balloons, blimps, etc.

Aircraft Parts/Accessories: parts or accessories of an aircraft, whether inside or outside (does not include aircrafts that are intact or model/toy planes)

Automobiles: any passenger vehicles designed for operation on ordinary roads and typically having four wheels and a motor with the primary purpose of transporting people other than public transportation; sedans, taxicabs, minivans, sport-utility vehicles, limousines, and other similar motor vehicles. Luxury vehicles such as Ferrari, Lamborghini.

Trucks: motor vehicles which are specifically designed, but not necessarily used, to transport cargo on a commercial basis, or vehicles designed for transporting loads

Buses: motor vehicles specifically designed, but not necessarily used, to transport groups of people on a commercial basis; trolleys, school/coach/tourist/double-decker buses, commercial vans, etc.

Other Motor Vehicles: motorized vehicles that do not fit the definition of automobile, bus, truck, or recreational vehicle; motorcycles, motor scooters, trail bikes, mopeds, snowmobiles, motorized golf carts, motorized wheelchairs, all-terrain vehicles, go-carts, etc.

Recreational Vehicles: motor vehicles that are specifically designed, but not necessarily used, to transport people and provide them temporary lodging for recreational purposes; motor homes

Trailers: transportation devices designed to be hauled by a motor vehicle; truck trailers, semi-trailers, utility trailers, farm trailers, etc.

Watercraft: vehicles used in the water, propelled by a motor, paddle, or sail; motorboats, sailboats, canoes, fishing boats, jet skis, etc.

Watercraft Equipment/Parts/Accessories: watercraft equipment or accessories that are used for the crafts' maintenance or operation; buoys, life preservers, paddles, sails

Vehicle Parts/Accessories: items attached to the inside or outside of a vehicle; motor vehicle batteries, engines, transmissions, heaters, hubcaps, tires, radios, CD/DVD players, automotive global positioning system (GPS) navigation systems, Radar Device, etc.

Bicycles: vehicles usually propelled by pedals, connected to the wheel by a chain, and have handlebars for steering and a saddle-like seat; tandem bicycles, unicycles, and tricycles

Resource Property

Fuel: products used to produce energy; coal, gasoline, diesel, biodiesel, natural gas, oil, etc.

Chemicals: substances with distinct molecular compositions that are produced by or used in chemical processes; herbicides, paint thinner, insecticides, industrial or household products, solvents, fertilizers, lime, mineral oil, antifreeze, etc.

Metals, Non-Precious: base metals or alloys possessing luster, malleability, ductility, and conductivity of electricity and heat; ferrous and non-ferrous metals such as iron, steel, tin, aluminum, copper, brass, copper wire, copper pipe, etc.

Weapons and Law Enforcement Property

Firearms: weapons that fire a projectile by force of an explosion; handguns, rifles, shotguns, assault rifles, semiautomatics, homemade guns, flare guns, etc.

Weapons – Other: weapons not classified under other categories; knives, swords, nunchakus, brass knuckles, crossbows, bows and arrows, pepper spray, Tasers, sling shots, "BB" guns, pellet guns, gas-powered guns, paintball guns, etc.

Explosives: devices that explode or cause an explosion; bombs, dynamite, Molotov cocktails, fireworks, ammunition, etc.

Firearm Accessories: items used in conjunction with a firearm to improve ease of use or maintenance; gun belts, cases, cleaning tools/equipment, targets, aftermarket stocks, laser sights, rifle/spotting/handgun scopes

Law Enforcement Equipment: anything specifically used by LE personnel during the performance of their official duties; vests, uniforms, handcuffs, flashlights, nightsticks, badges, etc.; canines (K-9s), horses, Tasers, etc.

Farm Property

Farm Equipment: any kind of machinery used on a farm to conduct farming; tractors, combines, etc.

Livestock: domesticated animals raised for home use or profit; cattle, chickens, hogs, horses, sheep, bees, household pets such as dogs and cats if commercially raised for profit; animals raised and/or used for illegal gambling, for example, dogs, roosters, etc. Purebred dogs, exotic pets (parrots, reptiles), show animals such as horses/racehorses.

Crops: cultivated plants or agricultural produce grown for commercial, human, or livestock consumption and use that is usually sold in bulk; grains, fruits, vegetables, tobacco, cotton (not illegal crops)

Goods

Household Goods: items normally used to furnish a residence; furniture, appliances, utensils, air conditioning/heating equipment, mailboxes, household lighting, etc.
Consumable Goods: expendable items used by humans for nutrition, enjoyment, or hygiene; food, non-alcoholic beverages, grooming products, cigarettes, firewood, etc.
Clothes/Furs: garments for the body, articles of dress, wearing apparel for human use; accessories such as belts, shoes, scarves, ties, etc.; eyewear/glasses, hearing aids, etc.
Additions: Luxury Goods: designer clothing and accessories

Building and Equipment Property

Lawn/Yard/Garden Equipment: equipment used for maintaining and decorating lawns and yards; mowers, line trimmers, tools, tillers, etc.
Office-type Equipment: items normally used in an office or business setting; calculators, cash registers, copying machines, facsimile machines, shredders, etc.
Heavy Construction/Industrial Equipment: large-scale equipment used in the construction of buildings, roads, etc.; cranes, bulldozers, steamrollers, oil-drilling rigs, backhoes, excavators, etc.
Logging Equipment: equipment specifically used by logging industry personnel during the performance of their duties; choker cables, binders, blocks, etc.
Medical/Medical Lab Equipment: equipment specifically used in the medical field; X-ray machines, testing equipment, MRI (magnetic resonance imaging) machines, ultrasound machines, wheelchairs, stethoscopes, etc.
Building Materials: items used to construct buildings; lumber, concrete, gravel, drywall, bricks, plumbing supplies, uninstalled windows, uninstalled doors, etc.
Tools: hand-held implements that are used in accomplishing work; hand and power tools

Documents and Identity

Documents/Personal or Business includes affidavits, applications, certificates, credit card documents, savings account books, titles, deposit slips, pawn shop slips, patents, blueprints, bids, proposals, personal files, and US mail
Identity Documents: formal documents and/or their numbers that provide proof pertaining to a specific individual's identity; passports, visas, driver's licenses, Social Security cards, alien registration cards, voter registration cards, etc.
Identity – Intangible: sets of characteristics or behavioral or personal traits by which an entity or person is recognized or known; damaged reputation, disclosed confidential information, etc.

Electrical/Technology Property

Computer Hardware/Software: electrical components making up a computer system, written programs/procedures/rules/associated documentation pertaining to the operation of a computer system stored in read/write memory; computers, laptops, printers, storage media, video games, software packages, video consoles such as Wii®, PlayStation®, and Xbox®

Photographic/Optical Equipment: equipment used to take photographs and/or relating to the science of optics or optical equipment; cameras, camcorders, telescopes, lenses, prisms, optical scanners, binoculars, monoculars, etc. (does not include camera phones)

Portable Electronic Communications: electronic devices used to communicate audible or visual messages; cell phones, camera phones, pagers, tablets, e-readers, portable game devices

Radios/TVs/VCRs/DVD Players: items used to transmit audible signals and visual images of moving and stationary objects; high fidelity and stereo equipment, CD players, MP3 players, cable boxes, etc. (does not include radios/stereos installed in vehicles)

Recordings – Audio/Visual: phonograph records or blank or recorded tapes or discs upon which the user records sound and/or visual images; compact discs (CDs), digital video discs (DVDs), cassettes, VHS tapes, etc.

Recreation Property

Artistic Supplies/Accessories: items or equipment used to create or maintain paintings, sculptures, crafts, etc.; frames, oil paints, clay

Camping/Hunting/Fishing Equipment/Supplies: items, tools, or objects used for recreational camping, hunting, or fishing; tents, camp stoves, fishing poles, sleeping bags, etc.

Musical Instruments: instruments relating to or capable of producing music; percussion, brass, woodwind, and string instruments, etc.; guitar strings, picks, drumsticks, etc.

Pets: animals kept for pleasure or companionship, other than livestock; cats, dogs, household birds, fish, rodents, reptiles, and exotic animals raised as pets and not for profit

Recreational/Sports Equipment: equipment and materials used for recreational purposes, or during sports activities; skis, balls, gloves, weights, nets, bats, rackets, team uniforms, accessories for water sports, etc.

Alcohol, Drugs, and Gambling Property

Alcohol: any intoxicating liquors containing alcohol used for human consumption; alcoholic beverages, that is, beer, wine, and liquor

Drugs/Narcotics: substances such as narcotics or hallucinogens that affect the central nervous system causing changes in behavior and often addiction; prescription, over-the-counter, legal, and illegal drugs

Drug/Narcotic Equipment: unlawful articles, items, products, etc. used to prepare and consume drugs or narcotics; glass pipes, bongs, pop cans, methamphetamine (meth) labs, etc.

Gambling Equipment: any equipment or devices used to produce, manufacture, or perpetrate gambling; slot machines, keno, card tables, poker chips, bingo, raffles, lottery tickets, etc.

Additions

Intellectual Property: trade secrets, confidential business information, research and development data, software code and algorithms

Historical and Cultural Artifacts: archaeological artifacts, ancient manuscripts, historical memorabilia, tribal and indigenous artwork

Environmental Resources: timber and wood products, endangered plants and animals, fisheries, and marine resources

Type of Stolen Property

Stolen property plays a multifaceted role in identifying serial crime patterns and types of stolen property can indicate specific crime problems.

High-Value Items: Theft of high-value items like electronics, jewelry, or automobiles may indicate a more organized or experienced criminal element.

Low-Value Items: Petty thefts or burglaries involving low-value items can point to opportunistic criminals or those with less planning.

Specific Items: The theft of unique or specific items may indicate a specialized type of criminal activity, like art theft, which can be easier to trace.

Contraband: Stolen items like firearms or drugs can signify more severe criminal enterprises and may correlate with other types of criminal activity.

Disposal of Stolen Property

Fencing Operations: Tracing stolen goods to a fencing operation can reveal larger criminal networks.

Online Sales: Some criminals use online platforms to quickly sell stolen goods, which can sometimes be traced.

Direct Use: In some cases, criminals keep stolen property for personal use, which, if recovered, can serve as direct evidence.

Serial Numbers and Identifiers

Tracking: Items with serial numbers or unique identifiers can be tracked and may lead to the identification of criminals.

Database Cross-Referencing: Law enforcement agencies often use databases to cross-reference stolen property recovered in different jurisdictions to identify patterns.

Importance for Law Enforcement

Linking Cases: Similar types of stolen property across various cases can indicate the work of a serial offender.

Resource Allocation: Identification of patterns can guide law enforcement in allocating resources more effectively for prevention and investigation.

Community Alert: Recognizing patterns can facilitate more effective community warnings about specific types of property being targeted.

Probable Cause: Recovery of stolen property can sometimes provide the probable cause needed to secure search or arrest warrants.

Legal Prosecution: Evidence related to stolen property can strengthen the legal case against the accused.

Crime Pattern Scenario

Serial Power Tool Theft Pattern – "The Home Improvement Bandit"

A series of 29 commercial burglaries targeting home improvement stores over eight months was linked through consistent theft of specific DeWalt and Milwaukee brand cordless tool sets.

The offender entered stores during overnight hours through loading dock doors, bypassed alarm systems by cutting phone lines, and went directly to tool aisles, suggesting inside knowledge. Property selection was precise: only taking 20V MAX and M18 FUEL product lines worth $300–500 per unit, avoiding cheaper brands despite easier access, and focusing on combo kits rather than individual tools. The disposal pattern showed sophistication: tools appeared on Facebook Marketplace and Craigslist 2–3 days post-theft in cities 75–150 miles away, listed at 60% retail price with stock photographs rather than actual items, and sellers insisted on cash-only parking lot transactions. Recovery efforts revealed serial number removal using a Dremel tool in consistent patterns, original packaging discarded but batteries retained, and tools sold in mixed brand lots to obscure their origin. Recognition emerged when loss prevention teams identified the brand-specific targeting pattern, online marketplace monitoring detected similar listing language across multiple accounts, and a buyer's tip about suspiciously cheap tools led to a controlled purchase operation capturing the seller.

Example Case

Between 2008 and 2015, a multi-county theft ring transported stolen construction machinery, which included skid-steer loaders, backhoes, a mini excavator, all-terrain vehicles, a compact tractor with implements, a large excavator, and multiple trailers, into Shelby County from seven other counties in Indiana. Over time, law enforcement executed arrests connected to the theft ring and were able to recover the stolen equipment.[2]

Example query terms: skid-steer, loader, backhoe, excavator, mini, all-terrain, ATV, tractor, compact, implements, constriction, machinery

Exercises

1. Conduct an online search for a crime series involving theft of copper and describe your findings.
2. Locate two publicly reported theft investigations (e.g., from police press releases or credible news sources) that involve different categories of stolen property – for example, heavy construction equipment and luxury jewelry. Create a side-by-side table noting property type, value, theft method, recovery status, and disposal method. Identify at least two analytical questions that investigators could pursue to determine whether the incidents might be linked to broader patterns.
3. Spend 30 minutes browsing Facebook Marketplace, Craigslist, or OfferUp in your area, focusing on one category such as bicycles, power tools, or electronics. Document suspicious patterns that might indicate stolen property: listings with stock photographs instead of actual items, sellers insisting on immediate cash-only sales, prices significantly below market value, or multiple high-value items from different brands in single posts. Compare asking prices to retail values to identify which items maintain resale value (making them attractive theft targets) versus those that depreciate quickly. Create a brief summary identifying three red flags that might indicate stolen property and explain how legitimate sellers could better differentiate themselves from potential criminals in online marketplaces.

Critical Thinking Guidance

When property crimes appear linked, begin by asking why a particular type of property attracts the offender and whether theft or damage serves a functional, financial, or symbolic purpose. Examine the full range of property variables together – type, brand, value, method of acquisition, and recovery location – because patterns often emerge only when these factors are analyzed in combination. Consider how the property fits into a larger opportunity structure: is it easily converted to cash through pawn shops, scrap dealers, or online markets; does it require specialized skills or insider access to obtain; or does it provide materials or tools for further crimes? Evaluate how offender knowledge of security measures, storage practices, or supply chains might influence the timing and method of the offense.

Critical thinking also requires questioning initial assumptions. A low-value item stolen repeatedly in different jurisdictions might appear to be a series of minor opportunistic thefts, yet it could reveal an organized resale scheme once disposal routes or fencing operations are mapped. Compare recovery sites and disposal methods to identify common marketplaces, geographic corridors, or repeat intermediaries that indicate coordinated activity. By weighing economic incentives, logistical challenges, and behavioral cues together, investigators can distinguish isolated incidents from property crimes that signal serial or organized offending, improving both investigative strategies and long-term crime prevention efforts.

Notes

1 FBI Criminal Justice Information Services Division (2021).
2 National Insurance Crime Bureau (n.d.).

Bibliography

Bowers, K. J., & Johnson, S. D. (2013). *Understanding theft of hot products* (Problem-Solving Tools Series No. 12). U.S. Department of Justice, Office of Community Oriented Policing Services.

FBI Criminal Justice Information Services Division. (2021). *National Incident-Based Reporting System user manual, 2021.1* (pp. 96–107). U.S. Department of Justice.

National Insurance Crime Bureau. (n.d.). *Multiple arrests made in theft of construction equipment.* www.nicb.org/news/blog/multiple-arrests-made-theft-construction-equipment

29 Commodity Flow and Markets

Introduction

Commodity flow refers to the movement of goods, currency, or services through legitimate or illicit supply chains. When applied to criminal activity, the examination of these flows can reveal recurring patterns, interconnections between incidents, and the operational hierarchy of criminal groups.

By comparing commodity flow characteristics across multiple incidents, investigators can uncover signature elements of a specific offender's operations. For example:

- repeated use of a particular freight company or shipping route.
- consistent concealment methods (e.g., drugs hidden inside specific vehicle parts).
- identical counterfeit labeling or product markings.
- matching financial transfer patterns or laundering techniques.

When these patterns are documented and cross-referenced, they can link seemingly unrelated crimes to the same individual, crew, or network. This not only strengthens individual cases but also builds a larger picture of a criminal operation's scope, participants, and hierarchy, allowing law enforcement to disrupt the entire supply chain rather than just individual transactions.

Commodity Flow Examples

Illicit Trafficking: Commodity flow analysis can reveal patterns in the illegal trade of goods such as drugs, wildlife, stolen artworks, and human trafficking. Understanding these flows can help law enforcement to identify sources, routes, and destinations and develop strategies to combat these crimes.

Economic Crimes: The flow of legal commodities can be manipulated for criminal gains, such as tax evasion, fraud, and money laundering. Analyzing commodity flows can uncover inconsistencies that point to these activities.

Supply Chain Security: Criminal organizations might exploit vulnerabilities in legitimate commodity flows to smuggle illegal goods. This includes using legal shipments to hide contraband or illegally diverting legal shipments.

Relationship with Organized Crime: Organized crime groups often control or influence legal and illegal commodity flows. Understanding these flows can provide insights into the structure and operations of these groups.

DOI: 10.4324/9781003728733-31

Environmental Crimes: Commodity flows can reveal patterns in illegal dumping, pollution, or other environmental crimes related to the production, transportation, and disposal of goods.

Counterfeit Products: Analyzing the flow of commodities can help identify sources of counterfeit or substandard goods, which is essential for consumer protection and industry regulation.

Terrorism Financing: Illicit commodity flows may be used to finance terrorist activities. Tracking these flows can help in identifying and stopping such financial sources.

Fencing Operations as Flow Intermediaries

Fencing operations represent crucial intermediary points in illicit commodity flows, transforming stolen goods from criminal liability into liquid assets. These operations serve as the bridge between theft and legitimate markets, making them essential targets for disrupting entire commodity chains. Investigators can identify fencing operations within commodity flows by recognizing these indicators:

Suspicious Pricing: Goods being sold at significantly lower prices compared to their market value or legitimate sources.

Cash Transactions: Frequent use of cash for transactions, as it is harder to trace compared to electronic payment methods.

Large Quantities: Selling or buying items in bulk quantities, especially when combined with unusually low prices.

Frequent Inventory Turnover: Rapid turnover of merchandise, indicating a high volume of sales and potential involvement in illegal activities.

Frequent Sales of High-End or Luxury Items: Consistent sales of high-value or luxury goods at suspiciously low prices could be indicative of a fencing operation. These items may include electronics, jewelry, designer clothing, or high-end appliances.

Incomplete or Altered Documentation: Inability or reluctance to provide receipts, invoices, or other legitimate documentation for the merchandise being sold, missing or altered serial numbers, removed security tags, or modified invoices to conceal the items' origins.

Altered or Removed Serial Numbers: Merchandise with altered or removed serial numbers, making it difficult to trace the origin or ownership.

Discreet Locations: Sales occurring in non-public or unconventional settings, such as private residences, storage units, or parking lots, rather than legitimate business establishments.

Limited or No Advertising: Minimal or no advertising of goods for sale, relying mainly on word-of-mouth or connections within criminal networks.

Suspicious Customer Profiles: Buyers showing little concern for the origin or legality of the goods, focusing solely on low prices and quick transactions.

Connections to Known Criminals: Fences having relationships with known criminals or being associated with illicit activities in the past.

Unusual Working Hours: Operating during unconventional hours or remaining open outside regular business hours to avoid detection.

Unlicensed or Illegal Business Operations: Fences lacking proper licenses or permits for conducting business or operating in restricted areas.

Crime Pattern Scenario

Serial Prescription Drug Diversion Pattern – "The Clinic Circuit"

A series of 23 cases of prescription opioid diversion over seven months was linked through tracking the flow of pills from legitimate prescriptions to street-level distribution. The pattern began with "patients" visiting multiple pain clinics using variations of the same complaints, receiving prescriptions for oxycodone and fentanyl patches from doctors later found to be over-prescribing. The commodity flow showed systematic organization: pills moved from pharmacies to a central aggregator within 24 hours of filling, sorted by strength and brand at a suburban house, repackaged in smaller quantities for street distribution, and sold through a network of dealers at predetermined locations. Transportation methods were consistent: legitimate-appearing elderly "patients" filled prescriptions to avoid suspicion, pills transferred during seemingly casual meetings at grocery store parking lots, bulk supplies moved in hidden compartments of food delivery vehicles, and street-level distribution occurred via bicycle couriers to avoid vehicle stops. The financial flow revealed layered transactions: patients paid $100 per doctor visit plus $50 per prescription filled, the aggregator paid patients $5–10 per pill depending on strength, street dealers purchased at $15–20 per pill for resale at $30–40, and profits laundered through small cash businesses. Market indicators included consistent pricing across the network, branded packaging using specific-colored bags to indicate pill strength, and customer loyalty programs offering quantity discounts. Recognition emerged when prescription monitoring programs flagged multiple patients with identical addresses, surveillance showed the same individuals at different pharmacies, and overdose victims possessed pills in the signature packaging, leading to identification of the distribution chain.

Example Case

In Philadelphia, law enforcement uncovered a large-scale theft ring in which thieves, known as "cutters," removed converters from vehicles and sold them to intermediaries. One central buyer, TDI Towing, allegedly purchased thousands of stolen converters, about 175 per week at the operation's peak, and then funneled them to recyclers. The appeal for criminals lies in the ease of theft, high resale value, and minimal traceability, enabling stolen parts to move quickly through underground networks before entering legitimate recycling channels. Once in the hands of recyclers, the converters are dismantled to extract and sell their metal content, effectively laundering stolen goods into the legal commodities market. Prosecutors noted that the Philadelphia ring moved an estimated $8.2 million worth of stolen converters over several years.[1]

Example query terms: catalytic converter, metal

Note: This theft-to-recycling pipeline underscores the role of unscrupulous buyers as critical links between street-level theft and industrial recycling operations.

Exercises

1. Identify a recent publicly reported case of smuggling, large-scale theft, or counterfeit distribution (e.g., wildlife trafficking or counterfeit electronics). Create a simple flow diagram tracing the commodity from point of origin through transportation, intermediaries, and final market. Label at least three investigative "choke points" where law enforcement could intervene.
2. Select a commonly stolen item category in your area (bicycles, catalytic converters, or power tools) and spend an hour researching its illicit market flow using public sources. Start by checking local police reports or news articles for recent thefts, noting any patterns in what's stolen. Then browse online marketplaces to see whether similar items appear for sale shortly after reported thefts. Document the typical price difference between retail and resale values, which indicates the profit margin driving theft. Look for patterns in how sellers describe items ("no papers needed," "cash only," "must go today") that might

indicate stolen goods. Create a simple flow chart showing: theft location → transportation method → storage/processing → sales venue → final buyer. Identify at least two points in this flow where law enforcement or businesses could intervene to disrupt the market, such as requiring documentation at scrap yards or creating safe exchange zones for online sales.

Critical Thinking Guidance

Investigating illicit commodity flows begins with clearly identifying the type of contraband involved, whether it be drugs, stolen goods, firearms, counterfeit products, illicit currency transfers, or other prohibited items. Map the commodity's movement through the supply chain. Document the route from its point of origin, such as manufacturing sites or theft locations, through smuggling routes, storage facilities, intermediaries, and ultimately to retail-level distribution. Track repeated use of the same suppliers, transportation methods, concealment techniques, or distribution markets to link the involvement of the same individuals or organized networks over time. Locate the end markets for illicit goods, such as fencing operations, underground trading hubs, or black-market platforms when possible. Similarities in packaging, shipment timing, transaction methods, or the profiles of recipients can indicate coordination by a single offender or group.

Because illicit commodities frequently cross-national borders, successful enforcement often depends on international cooperation, including intelligence sharing, coordinated surveillance, and joint enforcement efforts. This approach is particularly critical for transnational crimes like drug trafficking, arms smuggling, and large-scale financial fraud. Monitoring the flow of commodities also plays a regulatory role, allowing authorities to detect non-compliance with trade, transport, and customs regulations. Such non-compliance, whether intentional, such as concealing contraband, or unintentional, can provide valuable investigative leads.

Note

1 New York Times (2023, June 29).

Bibliography

Johns, T., & Hayes, R. (2003). Behind the fence: Buying and selling stolen merchandise. *Security Journal, 16*(1), 29–44. https://doi.org/10.1057/palgrave.sj.8340144

New York Times. (2023, June 29). $8 million catalytic converter theft ring operated out of Philadelphia towing company, prosecutors say. *The New York Times*. www.nytimes.com/2023/06/29/us/philadelphia-catalytic-converter-theft.html

Sutton, M. (2010). *Stolen goods markets* (Problem-Specific Guide Series No. 57, Problem-Oriented Guides for Police Series). U.S. Department of Justice, Office of Community Oriented Policing Services. https://popcenter.asu.edu/content/stolen-goods-markets-0

30 Concealment Methods

Introduction

Concealment methods allow offenders to transport, store, or disguise illicit goods, activities, and profits while evading detection. These methods range from simple concealment on a person's body to highly sophisticated, multi-layered schemes involving specialized engineering, digital obfuscation, or complex financial networks. Identifying similarities in concealment techniques across incidents can provide a vital link between seemingly unrelated cases. For example, a unique compartment design, a recurring packaging method, or a distinct use of forged documentation may signal the work of the same offender or criminal group. Recognizing these patterns is critical for disrupting illicit supply chains, anticipating offender adaptations, and building stronger cases that stand up in court. Because concealment strategies often evolve in response to enforcement measures, remain alert to both established methods and emerging innovations.

From US Customs and Border Protection

> Criminals use various ploys to smuggle their drugs across the border and into the U.S. They hide their drugs in false compartments on cars, taped to their body, in spare tires, and other creative schemes; U.S. Customs and Border Protection (CBP) has seen these strategies before. While those initiatives happen at the border, smugglers are also using the mailing system to conceal and ship their narcotics. However, CBP officers at the Port of Louisville are also aware of these tactics and are stopping shipments dead in their tracks. In the past week, officers have seized shipments containing items that were laced or concealed drugs. Officers saw packages with wood wind trumpets laced with cocaine, Chromebooks packed with two pounds of methamphetamine, and seven pounds of Methamphetamine-soaked Nerf children's toys.[1]

Concealment Variable Examples

Physical Concealment in Transportation

- Hidden Compartments: Criminals may build secret compartments in vehicles, shipping containers, or luggage to hide illicit goods. Examples: Building compartments within vehicle fuel tanks to smuggle drugs, using false bottoms in suitcases for carrying illegal cash.

DOI: 10.4324/9781003728733-32

- Mixing With Legitimate Goods: Illicit items can be hidden within legal shipments. Examples: Concealing illegal firearms within shipments of toys, hiding contraband inside commercial food products.
- Person Concealment: Individuals may hide items on their bodies or inside their clothing. Examples: using prosthetic devices to hide small amounts of narcotics, sewing illicit substances inside the lining of jackets.

Digital Concealment

- Encryption: Criminals may use encryption to hide the contents of digital communication related to illegal activities. Examples: Utilizing end-to-end encryption apps for coordinating illegal activities, encrypting hard drives containing evidence of fraud.
- Anonymizing Technologies: Tools like Tor can be used to conceal the origin of digital communications. Examples: using Tor for anonymous access to illegal marketplaces, utilizing VPNs to conceal hacking activities.

Document Concealment

- Forgery and False Documentation: Creating fraudulent documents to mask the true nature or origin of goods. Examples: Counterfeiting driver's licenses, forging export documentation to evade taxes.
- Multiple Layers of Documentation: Using a complex web of documents to confuse and hide the real transaction. Examples: Creating a chain of fictitious companies to disguise illegal financial transactions, using multiple fake identities to obscure the perpetrator.

Architectural Concealment

- Hidden Rooms and Spaces: Buildings may be designed with concealed areas for hiding illegal goods or activities. Examples: Constructing underground tunnels for drug trafficking, building false walls in homes to conceal stolen property.
- Camouflaged Facilities: Structures or areas used for illegal activities may be disguised to blend in with the surroundings. Examples: Converting ordinary-looking trailers into mobile meth labs, using seemingly abandoned buildings for illegal gambling.

Financial Concealment

- Money Laundering: Criminals may use complex financial transactions to hide the origin of illicit funds. Examples: Breaking down large amounts of illicit money into smaller transactions to avoid detection, investing in art to disguise the origin of funds.
- Shell Companies and Offshore Accounts: Utilizing legal structures to conceal the ownership and control of illegal assets. Examples: Setting up shell companies in multiple countries to conceal the flow of illegal revenue, using offshore accounts to hide bribery money.

Behavioral and Social Concealment

- Front Organizations: Legal businesses may be used to mask illegal operations. Examples: Operating a pawn shop as a front for selling stolen goods, using a charity organization to launder money.
- Utilizing Insider Assistance: Collaborating with individuals within legal entities to aid in concealment. Examples: Bribing airport security staff to bypass customs checks, collaborating with bank employees to facilitate fraud.

Concealment Through Complexity

- Using Multiple Intermediaries: Criminals might use a series of middlemen to obscure the origin and destination of illegal goods. Examples: Arranging multiple brokers in different countries to facilitate human trafficking, employing a series of agents to obscure the path of stolen intellectual property.
- Multiple Jurisdictions: Operating across various countries to complicate law enforcement tracing efforts. Examples: Conducting cybercrimes from various countries to hinder investigation, moving illegal goods through multiple borders to confuse tracing.

Natural Concealment

- Using Natural Features: Terrain, vegetation, or underwater locations might be used to hide illegal activities or goods. Examples: Burying contraband in remote desert locations, using underwater caves to store smuggled items, utilizing dense jungle terrain to hide illegal logging activities.

Product Alteration and Disguise

- Changing Appearance: Illicit goods may be altered to appear as something else. Examples: Converting stolen cars' appearances through repainting and altering VIN numbers, disguising illegal alcohol in legitimate beverage containers.
- Dissolving or Mixing: Substances may be dissolved or mixed with others to hide their true nature. Examples: Mixing narcotics with legitimate pharmaceuticals to disguise them, melting stolen precious metals to create new items, thereby erasing their original form.

Crime Pattern Scenario

Serial Retail Return Fraud Pattern – "The Receipt Collector"

A series of 38 fraudulent returns across major retail chains over five months was linked through a consistent concealment method involving legitimate receipts and repackaging techniques. The offender systematically collected discarded receipts from store parking lots and trash bins, purchased identical items from the same stores using stolen credit cards, then returned the stolen merchandise using the legitimate receipts for cash refunds. The concealment methodology showed retail knowledge: targeting stores with liberal return policies and minimal verification, selecting high-value items commonly purchased with cash like small electronics and tools, and timing returns during busy periods when staff scrutiny decreased. The repackaging concealment was meticulous: items professionally rewrapped using commercial shrink-wrap machines, security tags reattached with legitimate-looking fasteners, and serial number stickers carefully transferred from receipt-matching items. The documentation pattern revealed planning: receipts collected from multiple stores to avoid pattern recognition, returns spread across different locations within the same chain, and careful matching of receipt dates to fall within return policy windows. Physical concealment supported the fraud: wearing different clothing styles for each return, using reading glasses and different hairstyles to alter appearance, and carrying shopping bags from other stores to appear as a legitimate shopper. The operation evolved to reduce detection: initially returning items to the purchase location, later crossing stores within the chain, and eventually recruiting accomplices to conduct returns while the offender remained outside. Recognition of this pattern emerged when loss prevention noticed unusual return patterns for cash-purchased items, security footage showed the same individual's gait despite appearance changes, and credit card fraud investigators linked stolen cards to initial purchases matching returned items, leading to arrest when stores coordinated to flag suspicious returns matching the pattern.

Example Case

A former elite car stereo installer, became known for crafting highly sophisticated hidden compartments, called "traps," inside vehicles. These compartments were designed with hydraulic systems and secret electronic triggers, allowing them to be opened only by pressing a precise sequence of switches. Drug trafficking groups repeatedly used his creations to conceal and transport large quantities of cocaine, methamphetamine, and cash between Southern California and Kansas City. He claimed he was unaware of the compartments' illegal purpose, but DEA investigators documented a clear pattern: the same concealment design appeared in multiple seizures tied to the same trafficking network. The consistency, technical sophistication, and operational reuse of the offender's traps served as a forensic signature, ultimately linking him to the conspiracy and leading to his conviction.[2]

Example query terms: hidden, compartment, trap, hydraulic, trigger, sequence, switch, cocaine, methamphetamine, cash

Note: Because the crimes covered multiple states and law enforcement agencies, database searches would not be enough to link these crimes. Formal and informal intelligence sharing between law enforcement entities is crucial in these types of cases.

Exercises

1. Choose one real or fictional criminal case involving a concealment method. In one to two paragraphs, describe the concealment in detail, explain how it helped the offender avoid detection, and discuss how similarities in the method could link it to other crimes. Include any investigative challenges the concealment created.
2. During your regular travels over a week, observe and mentally note potential concealment locations in vehicles you encounter (your own car, buses, rideshares) without conducting any searches or suspicious behavior. Consider factory-designed storage spaces that could be modified: spare tire wells, air filter housings, seat cushions, door panels, or dashboard vents. Think about how someone might create hidden compartments using existing vehicle architecture. Notice aftermarket modifications that seem unusual: non-functional speakers, oversized center consoles, or custom panels that don't match factory specifications. Document your observations focusing on three aspects: accessibility (how quickly could items be retrieved), capacity (approximate volume of potential hiding spots), and detectability (how obvious would modifications be to casual inspection). This exercise helps you understand how criminals evaluate vehicles for smuggling while recognizing that most vehicle modifications are legitimate and lawful.

Critical Thinking Guidance

When evaluating concealment methods, it is not enough to simply note what was hidden and where it was found. Ask why this method was chosen, how it compares to methods in similar cases, and what it reveals about offender resources, experience, and network connections. Consider the level of sophistication, the materials or technologies required, and the likelihood that the method has been used before by the same individual or group. Weigh the possibility of copycat methods or industry-specific concealment trends. In serial or organized crime contexts, recurring concealment methods can function as a "signature" that helps link multiple incidents, but they may also indicate the influence of shared training, supply sources, or criminal alliances. Move beyond the obvious and exploring the operational context, such as whether the concealment was designed for long-term storage, rapid movement across borders, or protection against environmental damage, and think about how these factors could inform future interdiction strategies.

Notes

1 U.S. Customs and Border Protection (2022, May 18).
2 Greenberg. (2013, March 7).

Bibliography

Greenberg, A. (2013, March 7). The secret compartments of the dope world. *Wired*. www.wired.com/2013/03/alfred-anaya/

U.S. Customs and Border Protection. (2022, May 18). *Louisville CBP identifies concealment methods used to smuggle narcotics* [Press release]. U.S. Department of Homeland Security. www.cbp.gov/newsroom/local-media-release/louisville-cbp-identifies-concealment-methods-used-smuggle-narcotics

Part III

Crime Elements

31 Murder

Introduction

Murder is the killing of one human being by another. It is often examined as a single event. While patterns of murder often refer to serial crimes, murder can be patterned in places, such as gang territories, and by specific groups, such as contract killing by organized crime entities. These types of crimes may be considered serial if committed by the same person.

Linking murders committed by the same person requires examining specific elements and variables within crime patterns. Analyze how an offender selects victims, plans attack, chooses methods, and behaves after crimes, to identify consistent patterns that connect seemingly separate cases. The variables outlined in this chapter, from weapon choice and victim selection to signature behaviors and geographic patterns, serve as building blocks for establishing these connections. When multiple murders share similar combinations of these elements, they likely represent crimes committed by the same individual, allowing investigators to recognize serial behavior and predict future actions.

Patterns in motive, method, and victimology can assist investigators in identifying, preventing, or solving cases. Patterns also emerge geographically or situationally and offer insights that help forecast future behavior and allocate resources.

Note that individuals are murdered by terrorists, active shooters, kidnappers, robbers, rapists, and by criminals while they are committing other crimes, such as rape and robbery. See those chapters for more details on those specific crime-type elements.

Serial Versus Spree Versus Mass Murder

Serial murderers commit a series of murders with cooling-off periods in between crimes, spree murderers commit multiple murders at two or more locations with no cooling-off period, and mass murderers commit multiple murders at one location in one continuous period.

Murder MO Variables

Objectives

- Motive: Underlying reasons can range from desire for power or personal animosity to financial gain and can be ideological (hate crimes, terrorism).

DOI: 10.4324/9781003728733-34

Planning and Target Selection

- Victim Selection: Some murderers select victims based on specific criteria such as appearance, affiliation, or vulnerability.
- Location Scouting: Locations for carrying out the act and disposing of evidence may be pre-selected.
- Timing: The perpetrator often chooses a time when they are least likely to be caught, such as late at night or when the victim is alone.

Location

- In serial murder: Crime sites might be victim encounter location, point of first attack, murder scene, body dump site, vehicle dump site, or property dump site. These sites may be the same location in some murders but are differentiated when using an investigative tool like geographic profiling.[1]

Tools and Equipment

- Weapon Choice: Anything from firearms and knives to poisoning or strangulation. The choice often depends on the murderer's expertise, the availability of the weapon, or the desired impact on the victim or public.
- Disguise and Deception: Some murderers use disguises, fraudulent identification, or deceptive tactics to approach the victim without raising suspicion.

Execution

- Method: The actual killing may be premeditated and executed according to plan or more spontaneous.
- Signature: Some murderers leave behind evidence or indicators of a "signature" – a specific act or ritual unique to them. These include staging the scene, posing the body, leaving "calling cards," or sadistic acts.[2]
- Control Measures: Restraints, sedatives, or other methods may be used to subdue the victim before the murder.

Evasion

- Escape Route: Planned or impromptu paths may be used to leave the crime scene.
- Evidence Disposal: Perpetrators may make efforts to clean the crime scene, dispose of the weapon, and remove any traces of their presence.
- Alibi Creation: Some go to great lengths to create a believable alibi that places them far from the crime scene.

Aftermath

- Media Monitoring: Some perpetrators keep track of media coverage related to their crimes, which may influence future actions.
- Contact with Law Enforcement: Murderers may contact law enforcement or media to taunt authorities or provide clues.

Adaptation and Variation

- Evolution of MO: Murderers may adapt methods based on past experiences, close calls, or new information.
- Copycat Elements: Some murderers incorporate elements they've seen in media, read about, or observed in other crimes.

Murder Method Example Variables[3]

Murder Methods

- airway compressive (crushing), airway occlusion (choking), asphyxiation, axed, blunt force, bombing, burns (chemical), burns (fire), crushing injury, cutting or incised wound(s), drowning, drug injection/overdose, excessive brutal force, explosive trauma, exposure, firearm, gunshot wound(s), hanging, malnutrition/dehydration, pushed to fall, run over, smoke inhalation, smothering/suffocation, stab wounds, stabbing, strangulation (ligature), strangulation (manual)

Location of Human Bite Marks on or Body Parts Removed From Body

- abdomen, ankle, anus, arm(s), back, breast(s), buttock(s), chest, ear(s), eye(s), face, finger(s), foot/feet, genitalia, groin, hand(s), head, leg(s), lip(s), neck/throat, nipple(s), nose, shoulder(s), thigh(s), tongue

Dismemberment Method

- bitten, cut/sawed, disarticulated, hacked/chopped, ripped/torn

Unusual Assault/Trauma/Torture

- beat sexual areas with hands/fists/objects, body cavities or genitalia mutilated, body cavities or wounds explored/probed, body set on fire, burns (cigarette, iron, branding), cannibalism, carving on victim, douche/enema given to victim, evisceration, hair cut/shaved/pulled – head or pubic, hanged/suspended, kicked/stomped, offender urinated/defecated at scene or on victim, patterned injury, pierced body parts, pinched with device or hands, postmortem sexual or other assault, shocked with stun gun/taser or other electrical shock, skinned, vampirism, dragged by/thrown from/pushed from/run over by vehicle, whipped/paddled

Writing Tool at Crime Scene

- blood, computer, crayon, knife/sharp instrument, lipstick, marker, paint/spray paint, pen/pencil, typewriter

Rarity of Serial Murder

The 2005 report "Serial Murder: Multi-Disciplinary Perspectives for Investigators," edited by Robert J. Morton, was the resulting conclusions of the Serial Murder Symposium, a gathering of serial murder experts including the FBI Behavioral Analysis Unit-2. Despite its widespread portrayal in movies, films, and other media, serial murder is a relatively rare event, estimated to comprise less than 1% of all murders committed each year, according to the findings of the serial murder symposium of experts.

The report stresses that there are many common myths and misconceptions about serial killers, which are important to note when looking for patterns in such crimes.

Belief: Serial killers are all dysfunctional loners. Reality: Many serial killers appear to be normal, functioning members of the community.

Belief: Serial killers are all white males. Reality: The racial diversification of serial killers reflects that of the overall US population.

Belief: Serial killers are only motivated by sex. Reality: Some serial murderers are motivated by emotional or financial reasons.

Belief: All serial murderers travel and operate interstate. Reality: Most serial killers have defined geographic areas of operation within their comfort zone.

Belief: Serial killers cannot stop killing. Reality: Some serial killers stop murdering due to a variety of events or circumstances in their lives.

Belief: Serial killers are seriously mentally ill or brilliant. Reality: Serial killers are not often deemed insane under the law, and their intelligence is comparable to the levels in the general population.[4]

Crime Pattern Scenario

Over six months, an offender committed four murders following a consistent pattern. He selected elderly women living alone in ground-floor apartments, observed each victim for three days from a nearby coffee shop, and entered through unlocked patio doors during evening news broadcasts. He used manual strangulation with a cloth belt, arranged victims face-down on living room floors with hands folded, removed only wedding rings while leaving other valuables, and exited through front doors after wiping down surfaces with kitchen towels. Between murders, he mailed newspaper clippings about the crimes to the police with identical blue ink pens. Each crime occurred within two miles of a bus route he used for work, showing geographic consistency tied to his daily routine.

Note: Remember that while popular on television and movie screens, serial murder is rare. Note that this scenario does not speculate on the psychology of the murderer, yet it provides behavioral data that can link cases and thus aid investigations.

Exercises

1. Choose one common myth about serial murder highlighted in this chapter. In a brief paragraph, explain why this belief persists in popular culture and how it can mislead investigators or the public if left unchallenged.
2. Watch a movie about a serial murderer and use their crimes in this assignment. Using the MO variables from this chapter, analyze the patterns in victim selection, planning methods, execution behaviors, and post-crime actions. Include at least one signature element and one adaptive change across the series. Write a brief one-page summary explaining which behavioral elements you think would most strongly link these crimes.

- Research three unsolved murders in your region from the past five years using public news sources and identify any potential patterns without speculation about suspects. Focus on factual elements: victim demographics (age, gender, occupation, lifestyle), location types (residential, commercial, outdoor), time patterns (day of week, time of day, season), and method of killing if reported. Create a simple comparison chart noting similarities and differences across these cases. Consider whether any share enough common elements to suggest possible linkage: similar victim types, geographic clustering, matching weapons or methods, or comparable crime scene behaviors.

Critical Thinking Guidance

Forensic evidence is the most reliable way to link serial murders. In the absence of that or limitations in such evidence, look at victim selection patterns, pre-crime preparation, murder methods, signature behaviors, and post-crime actions as possibly connected decisions. Notice unnecessary behaviors that serve no practical purpose. Consider how an offender's routine life influences crime location patterns and timing choices. Look into cross-jurisdictional behavior patterns that can reveal linked crimes. This requires inter-agency cooperation. Consider submitting any murders committed by unknown offenders into the FBI's Violent Criminal Apprehension Program (ViCAP) database (or similar database in other countries besides the USA).

Notes

1 Rossmo (2000).
2 Douglas and Munn (1992, February).
3 Federal Bureau of Investigation (2022).
4 Morton (2005).

Bibliography

Aamodt, M. G. (2016, September 4). *Serial killer statistics*. Radford University Serial Killer Information Center. http://maamodt.asp.radford.edu/serial%20killer%20information%20center/project%20description.htm

Douglas, J. E., Burgess, A. W., Burgess, A. E., & Ressler, R. K. (2013). *Crime classification manual: A standard system for investigating and classifying violent crime* (3rd ed.). Wiley.

Douglas, J. E., & Munn, C. (1992, February). *Violent crime scene analysis: Modus operandi, signature, and staging. FBI Law Enforcement Bulletin*, *61*(2), 1–10.

Federal Bureau of Investigation. (2022). *ViCAP case submission form*. https://omb.report/icr/202205-1110-002/doc/123643900

Federal Bureau of Investigation. (n.d.). *Serial murder: Pathways for investigations*. Behavioral Analysis Unit 4, National Center for the Analysis of Violent Crime. www.fbi.gov/file-repository/serialmurder-pathwaysforinvestigations.pdf/view

Hood, B., White, P., & Bunner, J. (2022). Method of identification: Catching serial killers. *Forensic Science International*, *337*, 111377. https://doi.org/10.1016/j.forsciint.2022.111377

Morton, J. (Ed.). (2005). *Serial murder: Multi-disciplinary perspectives for investigators: The serial murder symposium*. Federal Bureau of Investigation, Behavioral Analysis Unit-2, National Center for the Analysis of Violent Crime, Critical Incident Response Group. www.ojp.gov/ncjrs/virtual-library/abstracts/serial-murder-multi-disciplinary-perspectives-investigators

Rossmo, D. K. (1995). Place, space, and police investigations: Hunting serial violent criminals. In J. E. Eck & D. Weisburd (Eds.), *Crime and place* (Vol. 4, pp. 217–235). Criminal Justice Press.

Rossmo, D. K. (2000). *Geographic profiling* (p. 128). CRC Press.

Salfati, C., & Bateman, A. (2005). Serial homicide: An investigation of behavioral consistency. *Journal of Investigative Psychology and Offender Profiling*, *2*(2), 121–144. https://doi.org/10.1002/jip.27

United Nations Office on Drugs and Crime. (2019). *Global study on homicide: Understanding homicide: Typologies, demographic factors, mechanisms, and contributors*. United Nations. www.unodc.org/documents/data-and-analysis/gsh/Booklet_3.pdf

Wellford, C., & Cronin, J. (1999). *Analysis of variables affecting the clearance of homicides: A multisite study* (NIJ Research Report). National Institute of Justice, Justice Research and Statistics Association. www.ojp.gov/ncjrs/virtual-library/abstracts/analysis-variables-affecting-clearance-homicides-multisite-study
White, J., Lester, D., Gentile, M., & Rosenbleeth, J. (2011). The utilization of forensic science and criminal profiling for capturing serial killers. *Forensic Science International*, *209*(1–3), 160–165.

32 Sexual Assault

Introduction

Sexual assault crimes include rape, attempted rape, fondling or unwanted touching, or forcing a victim to perform sexual acts.

Beyond forensic evidence, linking sexual assaults by the same person involves examining behavioral patterns that repeat across crimes. This means looking at how an offender chooses victims, approaches them, uses force, commits the assault, and acts afterward. The variables in this chapter, including victim selection, approach methods, and force patterns, help identify these connections.

One study found that almost 40% of sexual assaults were committed by repeat offenders, which only included those crimes that were reported and had a sexual assault kit (SAK) tested.[1] Thus, sexual assault is a significant serial crime problem and investigating it by connecting related crimes is crucial.

Repeat offenders may display behavioral patterns that, when identified through data analysis, allow law enforcement to arrest them or prevent crimes through preventative measures.

Sexual Assault MO Variables

Objectives

- Motive: The underlying motivation may range from the desire for power and control to specific fetishes or retaliatory actions.

Planning and Target Selection

- Victim Selection: Often based on vulnerability or opportunity, sometimes involving stalking behavior or preliminary interaction to gauge the victim's susceptibility.
- Attempts that failed and/or pre-execution surveillance by the offender may be a significant part of this pattern type (reports of assaults or suspicious person/vehicles).

Location

- The location may be pre-chosen for its isolation, convenience, or symbolic significance to the perpetrator. Locations often include homes, cars, or secluded public places.
- Tools and Equipment:

DOI: 10.4324/9781003728733-35

- Weapons: May involve firearms, knives, or makeshift weapons to intimidate the victim. Sometimes, no weapon is used, relying instead on physical strength or threat of weapon.
- Restraints: Some perpetrators use ropes, cuffs, or drugs to incapacitate the victim.

Execution

- Approach: The perpetrator may use force, surprise, or manipulation to control the victim. Sometimes, the victim is known to the perpetrator, which allows for manipulative tactics like grooming.
- Level of Force: The amount of force used may vary, including anything from verbal threats to physical violence.

Evasion

- Escape Planning: A planned or impromptu escape route from the crime scene may be used.
- Evidence Elimination: Efforts to clean the crime scene or instruct the victim to wash to remove DNA evidence.
- Disguise or Change of Appearance: Some perpetrators change clothes or appearance to evade capture post-offense.

Aftermath

- Follow-Up: In some cases, perpetrators may continue to harass or stalk the victim post-assault, either to intimidate them into not reporting the crime or for continued manipulation and control.
- Media and Social Media Monitoring: Some perpetrators may monitor media coverage of their crimes or stalk victims online post-assault.

Adaptation and Variation

- Changing MO: A perpetrator's methods may evolve over time, either to elude capture or because of changing psychological needs.
- Multiple MOs: Some sexual assault perpetrators may have more than one MO, particularly if they commit other types of crimes as well.

Sexual Assault Method Example Variables[2]

Force Before/During/After Sexual Assault

Example Variables of Types of Force in Sexual Assault: bit, blindfolded, brutally assaulted, burned, choked, covered victim's eyes/face, covered victim's mouth, cut, drugged victim, forced into auto, forced into small enclosure, forced to floor, forced victim into vehicle, forced victim to another location, forced victim to disrobe, forced victim to enter restroom, forced victim to ground/lie down, gagged, handcuffed, held down, hit after act, hit during act, hit prior to act, humiliated, intimidated, kicked, kidnapped, pulled victim's hair, taped up, threatened victim's family, tied, tied to object such as bed, tore clothes off victim, tore phone out of wall, tortured, twisted arm, used of restraints, used threats, whipped without hands, whipped with hands

Sexual Actions: anal intercourse, cunnilingus, ejaculation on victim, fellatio, fondling, foreign objects inserted into the victim (vaginal/anal), masturbation, penetration with fingers, vaginal intercourse

Sex-related paraphernalia/devices: belts/leathers, condoms/contraceptive devices, handcuffs, lubricants/lotions, masks/costumes/clothing, rape kit/crime kit, sexual bondage items, sexual devices/toys, torture devices

Related Example Variables

Sex-related collections: sex-related collections (erotica, pornography) possessed by offender

Sexual practices and preferences: bestiality, bondage, exhibitionism, group sex, incest, masochism, necrophilia, sadism, voyeurism

Crime Pattern Scenario

A college town has experienced three unsolved sexual assaults over six months. All occurred late at night on weekends, within a few blocks of each other. Victims reported being approached from behind and forced into nearby alleys. The attacker used verbal threats and force but left few physical injuries. Two victims noted a distinct cologne and described the assailant's voice as calm. The assaults stopped during winter break and resumed when classes restarted, suggesting possible connection to the academic calendar.

Exercises

1. Using the MO variables from this chapter, create a standardized checklist that investigators could use to compare sexual assault cases for potential linkage. Your checklist should include the five main behavioral categories (victim selection, approach method, force used, assault conduct, post-assault behavior) with specific yes/no questions under each category. Write a brief assessment explaining which behavioral elements from your checklist would be most reliable for linking cases and which might produce false connections due to coincidental similarities. Refer to elements and variables from Part Two of this book for additional details to use in your checklist.
2. Develop a comprehensive list of 20 search terms investigators might use when querying databases for potentially linked sexual assault cases. Organize terms into categories: approach methods, force indicators, location descriptors, temporal patterns, and unique behaviors. For each term, provide two variations or synonyms that might capture the same behavior described differently across reports.

Critical Thinking Guidance

Forensic evidence from sexual assault kits (SAKs) provides the strongest foundation for linking cases, but behavioral analysis is crucial for identifying patterns before DNA results are available and for connecting cases where evidence collection was incomplete. Remember that many sexual assaults go unreported, meaning a series may include unknown crimes between documented cases. Examine calls for service about suspicious persons, attempted assaults, or "peeping tom" incidents in areas where sexual assaults occurred, as these may represent failed attempts or surveillance by the same offender. Focus on behavioral choices that repeat across crimes: consistent victim selection criteria, specific approach tactics, distinctive use of force, and unique post-assault behaviors. Pay attention to timing patterns and geographic clusters that might indicate an offender's routine or comfort zone. Consider that offenders may escalate from less serious offenses or change jurisdictions to avoid detection, making cross-jurisdictional communication essential for recognizing linked behavior patterns. Consider submitting any sexual assaults committed by unknown offenders into the FBI's Violent Criminal Apprehension Program (ViCAP) database (or similar database in other countries besides the USA).

Notes

1 Campbell et al. (2019).
2 Adapted from FBI (2022).

Bibliography

Beauregard, E., Chopin, J., & Andresen, M. (2022). Modus operandi in sexual assaults of female strangers does not change over time. *Sexual Abuse: A Journal of Research and Treatment*. Advance online publication. https://doi.org/10.1177/10790632221139174

Beauregard, E., Proulx, J., Rossmo, D. K., Leclerc, B., & Allaire, J. (2007). Script analysis of the hunting process of serial sex offenders. *Criminal Justice and Behavior*, *34*(8), 1069–1084. https://doi.org/10.1177/0093854807300851

Campbell, R., Pierce, S. J., Sharma, D., Feeney, H., Goodman-Williams, R., & Ma, W. (2019). *Serial sexual assaults: A longitudinal examination of offending patterns using DNA evidence* (Report No. 252707). National Institute of Justice, U.S. Department of Justice. www.ojp.gov/pdffiles1/nij/grants/252707.pdf

Dedel, K. (2011). *Sexual assault of women by strangers* (Problem-Specific Guide Series No. 62). U.S. Department of Justice, Office of Community Oriented Policing Services. https://popcenter.asu.edu/content/sexual-assault-women-strangers-0

Federal Bureau of Investigation. (2022). *ViCAP case submission form*. https://omb.report/icr/202205-1110-002/doc/123643900

Sorochinski, M. (2015). *Assumptions underlying behavioral linkage revisited: A multidimensional approach*. U.S. Department of Justice, National Institute of Justice. www.ojp.gov/library/publications/assumptions-underlying-behavioral-linkage-revisited-multidimensional-approach

Verde, A., & Nurra, A. (2009). Criminal profiling as a plotting activity based on abductive processes. *International Journal of Offender Therapy and Comparative Criminology*, *54*(5), 829–849. https://doi.org/10.1177/0306624X09339175

33 Assault

Introduction

Assault involves the intentional infliction or threat of physical harm against another person and encompasses a wide range of behaviors, from unarmed fights to attacks with weapons. Unlike burglary or larceny, which often display repeatable methods, assaults are frequently spontaneous and fueled by alcohol, drugs, interpersonal disputes, or gang dynamics, making them more difficult to link into a pattern. Nonetheless, assaults can form part of broader serial crime activity, such as gang initiation rituals, retaliation cycles, intimidation tactics, or systematic attacks on targeted groups like delivery drivers or transit workers.

While many assaults appear isolated, systematic tracking of victim types, locations, offender approaches, and methods of violence may reveal linkages that might otherwise be overlooked. Forensic evidence plays an especially important role in assaults involving firearms, where ballistic comparisons, fingerprints, DNA, and weapon identifiers (make, model, caliber, manufacturer, serial number)[1] can connect cases. Recognizing consistent clusters of variables such as time of day, geographic proximity, and type of weapon used, enables law enforcement to distinguish opportunistic disputes from recurring assault patterns.

Active shooter incidents, though often considered single large-scale events rather than serial crimes, also display patterns that are critical to recognize. These incidents typically occur in populated areas such as schools, malls, workplaces, or houses of worship and involve one or more individuals actively attempting to kill or injure multiple people. Examining common variables, such as offender preparation, choice of location, weapon type, and behavioral warning signs, can help law enforcement prepare for and possibly prevent future attacks. By including active shooter events within the broader scope of assault analysis, investigators can understand how these high-impact incidents fit into patterns of violent behavior and incorporate lessons learned into prevention and response strategies.

Examples of Assault Crime Patterns

- A gang that requires new members to assault rival gang members as a form of initiation
- A person who frequents a certain neighborhood to randomly attack pedestrians at night
- A serial offender who targets delivery drivers from a particular company or service

DOI: 10.4324/9781003728733-36

Assault MO Variables

Objectives

- Motive: The underlying reasons for assault can range from random acts of violence to targeted attacks due to interpersonal conflict, business disputes, or hate crimes.

Planning and Target Selection

- Victim Selection: May be opportunistic or targeted, depending on the motive. Sometimes involves stalking or surveillance of the victim.
- Location: Chosen for convenience, isolation, or even symbolic reasons. It could be a public space, private residence, or somewhere secluded.

Tools and Equipment

- Weapons: Use of firearms, blunt objects, knives, or bodily force like fists or feet. The choice often depends on the perpetrator's comfort and skill level with the weapon, as well as the intended level of harm.
- Protection: Some perpetrators might wear gloves to avoid leaving fingerprints or masks to conceal their identity.

Execution

- Approach Method: May vary from a surprise attack to a confrontational approach. Sometimes involves cornering the victim or blocking escape routes.
- Level of Force: Depends on the intent, ranging from enough to incapacitate the victim temporarily to causing severe harm or life-threatening injuries.

Evasion

- Escape Route: Preplanned or spontaneous. Sometimes involves a getaway vehicle or accomplice.
- Evidence Elimination: Measures to remove traces like wiping fingerprints, discarding weapons, or changing clothes.

Aftermath

- Behavior Post-Assault: Some perpetrators engage in taunting or further threats, either directly to the victim or indirectly, like through social media.
- Monitoring: Some may keep tabs on police investigations or news reports about the assault, adapting their future MO accordingly.

Adaptation and Variation

- MO Evolution: Methods may change over time to evade law enforcement or adapt to new opportunities or technologies.
- Multi-faceted MO: The perpetrator might engage in different types of assault or crimes, each with its MO.

While most assault patterns involve repeated incidents by the same offender or group, active shooter events represent a distinct category that requires separate consideration. Though typically single incidents rather than serial crimes, active shooters share behavioral patterns, planning methods, and target selection processes that parallel other assault patterns. Understanding these commonalities helps investigators recognize warning signs, assess threats, and apply lessons from one incident to prevent others. Furthermore, some active shooters have histories of lesser assaults that escalate to mass violence, making it critical to examine these events within the broader context of assault pattern analysis.

Active Shooter Incidents

Active shooter situations are typically not considered serial events in the conventional sense since they often involve a single, isolated event rather than a recurring pattern by the same individual. However, active shooter events can display patterns in terms of tactics, locations, and motivations that may help law enforcement understand, prepare for, and possibly even prevent future incidents.[2]

Active Shooter Definition: One or more individuals actively engaged in killing or attempting to kill people in a populated area.

Active Shooter Pattern Variables

Pre-Attack Indicators

- Behavioral Changes: sleep disruption, increased aggression, impulsive actions, social withdrawal, obsession with previous attacks, collection of weapons, surveillance of targets
- Communications: manifestos, threats, grievance statements, online posts glorifying violence, direct or veiled warnings to associates
- Preparatory Actions: weapons acquisition, tactical training, site reconnaissance, timeline development, acquiring tactical gear

Target Selection Patterns

- Symbolic Targets: government buildings, religious sites, educational institutions representing perceived grievances
- Opportunistic Targets: crowded public spaces, venues with limited security, locations with constrained exits
- Personal Connection Sites: current or former workplaces, schools attended, locations tied to specific grievances

Attack Methodology

- Weapon Preferences: specific firearm types, multiple weapons, explosive devices, vehicles as weapons
- Tactical Approaches: mobile shooting, barricaded positions, ambush tactics, coordinated team attacks
- Timing Patterns: significant dates, shift changes, maximum occupancy periods, symbolic anniversaries

Environmental Exploitation

- Security Gaps: unsecured entrances, predictable security routines, emergency exit locations
- Crowd Dynamics: bottleneck areas, limited escape routes, confusion points
- Response Delays: remote locations, complex layouts, communication dead zones

Post-Incident Patterns

- Escape Planning: predetermined routes, vehicle placement, disguise preparations
- Surrender Behaviors: planned suicide, suicide-by-cop, negotiated surrender
- Documentation: livestreaming, pre-recorded videos, timed message releases

Crime Pattern Scenario

In a mid-sized city, police respond to a series of assaults outside late-night bars over a two-month period. Victims, primarily young men, report being struck with bottles or fists during unprovoked altercations as they left the establishments. The incidents occur between midnight and 3 a.m., often in poorly lit areas near parking lots and alleyways. Several victims describe the offender as acting intoxicated and aggressive, sometimes accompanied by others who encouraged the violence but did not directly participate. No weapons beyond improvised objects have been recovered, but the repetition in timing, victim type, and location suggests a recurring pattern that may be linked to a single offender or group frequenting the nightlife district.

Exercise

1. A manufacturing district has experienced a series of assaults on delivery drivers over the past six weeks. In each case, the driver reported being approached by two or more individuals after making a delivery. The assaults occurred in the late afternoon as drivers returned to their vehicles, and the offenders used fists, blunt objects, or in one case a knife, to intimidate the victim before stealing packages or personal items. Several incidents occurred within a half-mile radius of each other. Answer these questions: What variables would you prioritize to determine whether these incidents form a linked series (time, victim type, offender method, location)? How could intelligence from package thefts, local gangs, or fencing networks help clarify the connection between these assaults? What environmental or security factors might make delivery drivers particularly vulnerable in this setting? If you were building a crime prevention strategy, what partners (delivery companies, unions, business associations) would you include in your approach?
2. Research general patterns in gang initiation assaults using academic sources or law enforcement publications (not specific cases). Document five common characteristics such as victim selection criteria, the number of participants, duration of attack, symbolic elements, and geographic boundaries. Create a checklist investigators could use to distinguish gang initiation assaults from other group violence. Explain how recognizing these patterns could inform both investigation and prevention strategies.

Critical Thinking Guidance

Linking assault and shooting cases into discernible patterns is challenging because many incidents are impulsive, fueled by alcohol, drugs, or immediate disputes, while others are tied to gangs, organized crime, or opportunistic violence. Unlike burglary or larceny, which often show repeat methods and target preferences, assaults and shootings can lack consistent offender behaviors, clear motives, or reliable suspect descriptions. Many occur quickly in public spaces, with vague witness accounts and broad time ranges rather than precise timelines.

To identify true serial patterns, focus on clusters of variables like consistent victim types (such as delivery drivers, gang members, or bar patrons), recurring locations (nightlife districts, transit hubs, or gang territories), offender methods (group attacks, drive-bys, or use of improvised weapons), and time patterns (nighttime, weekends, or event-related). Forensic evidence is especially valuable: ballistic matches, fingerprints, DNA, or shell casings can link otherwise disconnected incidents.

It is also important to separate one-off disputes from recurring series. For example, gang initiation rituals, retaliatory shootings, or repeated assaults on certain worker groups may appear random without intelligence integration. Combine assault and shooting data with information from gang, robbery, or narcotics investigations to uncover overlaps in offenders, motives, and victims. Careful separation of datasets, such as distinguishing confirmed shootings from "shots fired" calls, is essential to avoid confusing signals.

A systematic approach that emphasizes motive, victim, location, method, and forensic evidence, while accounting for offender adaptation, helps distinguish isolated incidents from serial activity.

Notes

1 UNODC (n.d.).
2 FBI and ALERRT Center (2023).

Bibliography

Blair, J. P., Martaindale, M. H., & Tanksley, P. T. (2025). Active attacks with motor vehicles: A short report and case study of the 2025 new year's day attack in New Orleans, LA. *American Journal of Criminal Justice*. Advance online publication. https://doi.org/10.1007/s12103-025-09806-x

Blair, J. P., & Schweit, K. W. (2014). *A study of active shooter incidents, 2000–2013*. Texas State University and Federal Bureau of Investigation, U.S. Department of Justice. www.fbi.gov/file-repository/active-shooter-study-2000-2013-1.pdf/view

Bureau of Alcohol, Tobacco, Firearms and Explosives. (2021). *Firearms trace data – 2021*. U.S. Department of Justice. www.atf.gov/resource-center/firearms-trace-data-2021

City of Chicago. (2020). *Our city, our safety: A comprehensive plan to reduce violence in Chicago 2020*. www.chicago.gov/content/dam/city/sites/public-safety-and-violenc-reduction/pdfs/OurCity-OurSafety.pdf

Dedel, K. (2007). *Drive-by shootings* (Problem-Specific Guide Series No. 47, Problem-Oriented Guides for Police Series). U.S. Department of Justice, Office of Community Oriented Policing Services. https://popcenter.asu.edu/content/drive-shootings-0

Federal Bureau of Investigation & Advanced Law Enforcement Rapid Response Training (ALERRT) Center. (2023). *Active shooter incidents in the United States in 2022*. www.fbi.gov/file-repository/active-shooter-incidents-in-the-us-2022-042623.pdf/view

Kena, G., & Truman, J. L. (2022). *Trends and patterns in firearm violence, 1993–2018*. U.S. Department of Justice, Office of Justice Programs, Bureau of Justice Statistics. https://bjs.ojp.gov/library/publications/trends-and-patterns-firearm-violence-1993-2018

Police Executive Research Forum. (2017). *The "crime gun intelligence center" model: Case studies of the Denver, Milwaukee, and Chicago approaches to investigating gun crime*. www.policeforum.org/assets/crimegunintelligencecenter.pdf

Silver, J., Simons, A., & Craun, S. (2018). *A study of the pre-attack behaviors of active shooters in the United States between 2000 and 2013*. Federal Bureau of Investigation, U.S. Department of Justice. www.fbi.gov/file-repository/pre-attack-behaviors-of-active-shooters-in-us-2000-2013.pdf/view

United Nations Office on Drugs and Crime. (n.d.). *Firearms as evidence*. www.unodc.org/e4j/en/firearms/module-8/key-issues/firearms-as-evidence.html

34 Robbery

Introduction

Robbery is the unlawful taking of property from another person through force, violence, or intimidation. It occupies a distinctive place among violent crimes because it merges elements of both property and personal offenses. Unlike burglary or theft, robbery involves direct confrontation with victims, creating immediate risk of physical harm and producing valuable investigative information. Victims, and often witnesses, can typically describe the offender's appearance, verbal demands, and actions. They may also provide details on weapons displayed, the exact time and location of the offense, and even the type of property stolen. These firsthand accounts, when combined with forensic evidence and surveillance footage, give investigators a strong starting point for identifying commonalities and linking related incidents.

Robbery patterns are often easier to detect than those of many other crimes because of this abundance of reliable data. While property crimes may be discovered hours after the event with no witnesses, robberies are almost always reported quickly and leave behind a trail of descriptive and sometimes physical evidence. The presence of a live victim means law enforcement can collect immediate statements regarding the offender's clothing, physical features, and mannerisms and often secure evidence such as fingerprints, shell casings, or DNA from discarded items. Video surveillance, common in banks, convenience stores, and commercial settings, further strengthens the capacity to identify serial offenders and compare incidents across jurisdictions. Recognizing both consistencies and changes in offender behavior is essential to distinguishing an actual series from unrelated but superficially similar incidents.

Robbery MO Variables

Objectives

- Financial Gain: The most common motive is the immediate acquisition of money or valuable goods.
- Resource Funding: In organized crime or terrorist activities, robbery can serve as a way to fund other operations.
- Intimidation or Power: Some robbers are motivated by the psychological gain involved in risking and confrontation.

DOI: 10.4324/9781003728733-37

Planning and Organization

- Target Selection: Whether targeting an individual, a residence, or a commercial establishment, robbers may scout locations for vulnerabilities.
- Timing: Robberies often happen when victims are most vulnerable – early mornings, late nights, or during particular events.
- Accomplices: More organized robberies might involve multiple individuals with defined roles such as lookouts, drivers, and the primary robber.

Technical Framework

- Weapons: The use of weapons, like guns or knives, is common to intimidate victims into compliance.
- Disguise: Masks, fake uniforms, or other disguises may be employed to conceal identity.
- Communication: In-group communication may involve untraceable phones, coded language, or hand signals.

Execution

- Approach Method: This may vary from a stealthy, surprise attack to a confrontational approach.
- Escape Plan: A well-thought-out escape route or vehicle may be arranged in advance.
- Diversion Tactics: Distractions or other diversions may be used.

Intermediaries

- Fencing Operations: Stolen goods are often quickly sold or traded through intermediaries.
- Financiers: In some cases, particularly in organized crime, a financier may back the operation in return for a cut of the proceeds.

Legal Evasion

- Changing MO: To avoid detection, a robber may change their methods or targets periodically.
- Alibis: False alibis may be prepared in advance to deflect suspicion.
- Counter-Surveillance: Measures might be taken to detect and avoid police or security presence.

Aftermath

- Laundering: Cash or valuable items may be laundered through various means to make them difficult to trace.
- Relocation: Perpetrators might leave the area or even the country to avoid capture, especially after high-stakes robberies.

Serial Robbery Type Examples

ATM Robberies: These involve targeting individuals withdrawing money from ATMs. It can be done opportunistically or by carefully observing a target. Serial offenders might choose the same type of location (isolated, poorly lit) and time (usually late at night) for their crimes. Series of these crimes usually follow a pattern based on the types and locations of targeted ATMs.

Bank Robberies: These include robberies of credit unions, location is often in a commercial or shopping district, mostly male offenders who target branch offices at the counter, offender often presents a note to the bank teller that demands money and implies or explicitly states that the robber is armed, may exploit knowledge of bank procedures and layouts.[1]

Carjacking: This is stealing a person's vehicle while they're in it, most often one person in the car, offender most often has a weapon, may target specific models of cars, locations, or times of day, more likely to occur at or near person's home, males, and females equally targeted.[2]

Cash-in-Transit Robberies: Offenders target vehicles moving cash or other valuables between locations, may use force and/or weapons to overpower the drivers, possibly organized crime group.

Convenience Store Robberies: These may involve one or two individuals who rob small retail stores during late-night hours when fewer witnesses are around, may use firearms or other weapons, and typically target cash registers or safe boxes. May have a repeat offense pattern of location, time, and modus operandi, often armed robberies, due to the late operating hours and often minimal security measures, may work quickly, threatening staff, and take cash from registers or safes

Delivery Person: Delivery persons are often alone and may be more susceptible when carrying goods or cash. The offender intercepts the delivery person at the delivery point, or earlier, sometimes posing as a customer.

Delivery Truck Robberies/Hijackings: This form of robbery involves the interception and robbery of delivery trucks; criminals often operate in teams and have inside information about delivery routes and schedules.

Gas Station Robberies: Criminals often target gas stations due to the consistent cash flow and often minimal security. Serial robbers might target stations along specific highways or regions, and usually, act quickly, often armed. Serial robbers frequently target gas stations because they're often open late and staffed by a single clerk.

Home Invasions: This involves breaking into houses when they are occupied, often threatening and sometimes assaulting residents and stealing valuables. The serial home invader may prefer a specific neighborhood or type of home and often develops a consistent method of entry and escape. They may use a ruse to gain entry.

Liquor Store Robberies: Like convenience store robberies, these target small liquor stores. These crimes might follow patterns concerning time (often after dark), location (isolated areas), and method (quick, sometimes violent).

Pharmacy Robberies: Criminals might target pharmacies for prescription drugs to use or sell. Serial pharmacy robbers may have a consistent strategy, such as presenting fraudulent prescriptions before resorting to threats or violence and may target chains in similar locations. They may also use disguises or wear hats and sunglasses to avoid being recognized by CCTV cameras.

Purse Snatching: This involves stealing women's purses directly from their persons. Serial purse snatchers might target specific locations (like shopping malls or parking lots) and use consistent methods. Commonalities in approach method can help link crimes.

Restaurant Robberies: These occur in restaurants, especially fast-food restaurants, often at closing time when the day's earnings are still on the premises. Serial restaurant robbers might target the same chain or similar types of establishments, often with a consistent strategy.

Retail Store: These involve robbers who specialize in specific types of retail stores, such as electronics or jewelry stores, where stolen items may be resold easily in the black markets.

Street Robberies: This involves robbing individuals in public spaces, typically involving a threat of violence. Serial muggers might target specific types of victims (tourists, older individuals) or certain locations, often late at night.

Taxi Driver Robberies: Taxi drivers are targeted because they have contact with many strangers or people they do not know well, often work in high-crime areas, may carry cash with them in an unsecured manner and handle money as payment, usually work alone, often go to, or through, isolated locations, often work late at night or early in the morning. With ride-share alternatives available, taxi driver robberies may be less likely; ride share drivers are also targeted for robbery. Offenders can create fake profiles to use their services and target them.[3]

Crime Pattern Scenario

A small city experiences a string of late-night robberies at fast-food restaurants located near highway off-ramps. In each case, a single masked individual brandishing a pistol demands cash, threatens staff, and escapes before police arrive. Surveillance video shows a similar stature and getaway car in several cases. Police are unsure if it's one individual or a small group.

Exercises

1. Conduct online research to identify two well-documented serial robbery cases – one involving a commercial target such as a bank or convenience store and another involving a person-focused crime such as a series of carjackings or street robberies. Summarize the key details of each case, including the offenders' motives, planning, weapons, and escape strategies. Compare and contrast the modus operandi and discuss which investigative techniques (forensic evidence, witness statements, surveillance footage, or financial tracking) proved most effective in linking the incidents. Reflect on how differences in target type influenced both the offenders' strategies and the police response.
2. Using publicly available crime mapping or police department open-data portals, locate a city or region with multiple reported robberies over a defined time frame. Examine whether the incidents cluster geographically near transportation routes, commercial districts, or other high-traffic areas. Identify any repeated features such as time of day, type of establishment, or weapon use. In a brief summary, explain how geographic information systems (GIS) or simple spatial analysis can help identify robbery hot spots and support proactive policing strategies.
3. Research how technology has changed robbery patterns over the past decade. Consider the impact of cashless transactions, surveillance improvements, GPS tracking, social media, and ride-sharing apps. Document three ways technology has made certain robbery types more difficult and three new vulnerabilities it has created. Propose how investigators should adapt their pattern recognition methods to account for these technological shifts.

Critical Thinking Guidance

When analyzing robbery cases, critically evaluate both the consistencies and deviations across incidents. Consider whether similarities in offender descriptions, approach methods, timing, or target types are strong enough to suggest a series but recognize that offenders may deliberately change elements of their modus operandi to evade detection. Distinguish between coincidental similarities and meaningful patterns by weighing the reliability of victim and witness accounts, corroborating them with physical evidence, surveillance footage, and geographic or temporal clustering. Critical thinking requires asking what information might be missing or underreported, how offender behavior could adapt over time, and whether environmental conditions (such as lighting, accessibility, or security presence) are influencing both target selection and victim vulnerability.

Notes

1 FBI (2021).
2 Harrell (2022).
3 Smith (2005).

Bibliography

Altizio, A., & York, D. (2007). *Robbery of convenience stores* (Problem-Specific Guide Series No. 48, Problem-Oriented Guides for Police Series). U.S. Department of Justice, Office of Community Oriented Policing Services. https://popcenter.asu.edu/content/robbery-convenience-stores-0

Dunn, C. (1976). *Patterns of robbery characteristics and their occurrence among social areas* (Analytic Report No. 15). Utilization of Criminal Justice Statistics Project, Criminal Justice Research Center.

Federal Bureau of Investigation. (2021). *Bank crime statistics report, 2021*. U.S. Department of Justice. www.fbi.gov/file-repository/bank-crime-statistics-2021.pdf/view

Harrell, E. (2022). *Carjacking victimization, 1995–2021*. Bureau of Justice Statistics, Office of Justice Programs, U.S. Department of Justice. https://bjs.ojp.gov/carjacking-victimization-1995-2021

Heinonen, J. A., & Eck, J. E. (2012). *Home invasion robbery* (Problem-Specific Guide Series No. 70, Problem-Oriented Guides for Police Series). U.S. Department of Justice, Office of Community Oriented Policing Services. https://popcenter.asu.edu/content/home-invasion-robbery-0

Jiang, S., Felson, M., Scott, M. S., & Tapp, K. (2023). *Carjacking* (Problem-Specific Guide Series No. 75, Problem-Oriented Guides for Police Series). U.S. Department of Justice, Office of Community Oriented Policing Services. https://popcenter.asu.edu/content/carjacking

Lancashire Police, DNAS. (2011). *Robbery prevention initiative: Cash and valuables in transit* (Herman Goldstein Award Submission, 2011). https://popcenter.asu.edu/sites/default/files/library/awards/goldstein/2011/11-45.pdf

La Vigne, N., & Wartell, J. (2016). *Robberies of pharmacies* (Problem-Specific Guide Series No. 73, Problem-Oriented Guides for Police Series). U.S. Department of Justice, Office of Community Oriented Policing Services. https://popcenter.asu.edu/content/robbery-pharmacies

Monk, K. M., Heinonen, J. A., & Eck, J. E. (2010). *Street robberies* (Problem-Specific Guide Series No. 59, Problem-Oriented Guides for Police Series). U.S. Department of Justice, Office of Community Oriented Policing Services. https://popcenter.asu.edu/content/street-robbery-0

Scott, M. S. (2001). *Robbery at automated-teller machines* (Problem-Specific Guide Series No. 8, Problem-Oriented Guides for Police Series). U.S. Department of Justice, Office of Community Oriented Policing Services. https://popcenter.asu.edu/content/robbery-automated-teller-machines-0

Smith, M. (2005). *Robbery of taxi drivers* (Problem-Specific Guide Series No. 34, Problem-Oriented Guides for Police Series). U.S. Department of Justice, Office of Community Oriented Policing Services. https://popcenter.asu.edu/content/robbery-taxi-drivers-0

Weisel, D. L. (2007). *Bank robbery* (Problem-Specific Guide Series No. 48, Problem-Oriented Guides for Police Series). U.S. Department of Justice, Office of Community Oriented Policing Services. https://popcenter.asu.edu/content/bank-robbery-0

35 Burglary

Introduction

Burglary, defined as the unlawful entry into a building or structure with the intent to commit theft, vandalism, or another felony, represents a crime where physical evidence often substitutes for eyewitness accounts. Because most burglaries occur when no one is present, investigators frequently lack immediate suspect descriptions or precise timelines. Instead, successful linkage of serial burglaries depends on recognizing consistent behavioral and environmental indicators. These include the method of entry, the typical time of day or day of the week the crime occurs, and the types of property targeted. Patterns in these variables can reveal a series even when individual incidents appear unrelated.

Geographic analysis is a critical component of burglary investigations. Offenders often select areas familiar from their daily routines resulting in spatial clustering that helps narrow investigative focus. Similarities in offender travel routes, preferred concealment strategies, and methods for disposing of stolen goods, such as fencing through pawnshops or online marketplaces, can further strengthen links among cases. Forensic evidence, along with video surveillance or vehicle sightings, provides additional opportunities to connect incidents.

Burglary methods range from opportunistic entry through unlocked doors or windows to sophisticated commercial crimes involving safe-cracking, roof entry, or the disabling of alarm systems. Offenders may also adapt over time, changing targets, timing, or techniques to avoid capture. Investigators must therefore balance attention to recurring features with awareness of these potential variations.

The principle of distance decay suggests burglars typically operate within a limited radius of anchor points such as their residence, workplace, or other routine activity locations. Research indicates most residential burglars travel less than two miles from their home base, creating identifiable geographic patterns when multiple incidents are mapped. This clustering often follows transportation routes – bus lines, major streets, or walking paths – that connect the offender's familiar territory. Investigators can use this principle to prioritize suspects living within the cluster zone and predict future targets along established travel corridors.

See the chapters Entry, Search, and Exit and Tools and Equipment in this book for important variables to consider in burglary pattern identification.

DOI: 10.4324/9781003728733-38

Burglary MO Variables

Objectives

- Financial Gain: Often, the primary motive is to steal money or valuables.
- Thrill-Seeking: Some burglars may be motivated by the thrill of breaking and entering without detection.
- Resource Gathering: Acquiring goods for resale or for use in other illegal activities.

Planning and Target Selection

- Reconnaissance: Scouting neighborhoods, businesses, or residences to identify vulnerable targets, which may involve observing routines, checking for security measures, and so on.
- Timing: Choosing an opportune time for the burglary, often when occupants are away, or the area is less frequented. (It is often difficult to pinpoint the exact timing of a burglary because no one is present.)
- Information Gathering: Utilizing online platforms, like social media or property records, to gather information about the target.

Tools and Equipment

- Breaking and Entering Tools: Such as crowbars, lock picks, and screwdrivers.
- Transport: A vehicle for getting to and from the scene, as well as for transporting stolen items.
- Communication Devices: Prepaid mobile phones or radios to communicate with accomplices, if any.

Execution

- Entry Method: Breaking a window, picking a lock, or entering through an unlocked door or window.
- Movement Inside: Often fast and directed towards areas likely to contain valuables like bedrooms or offices.
- Containment: Use of bags, pillowcases, or other items to gather and contain stolen goods.
- Signature Behaviors: Eating food, defecating, watching TV, or leaving graffiti on a wall are some examples.

Evasion and Exit

- Quick Exit: Efficient routes preplanned for leaving the scene quickly.
- Disguise or Change of Appearance: To avoid identification by witnesses or security cameras.
- Destruction of Evidence: Disposing of tools, clothing, or stolen items packaging to leave no trace.

Intermediaries and Aftermath

- Fencing: Selling stolen goods quickly, often through pawn shops, online marketplaces, or known associates.
- Laundering Proceeds: Through various means, such as cryptocurrencies, cash businesses, or gambling.
- Cooling-Off Period: A period of low activity to reduce the chances of detection, especially if the burglary attracts significant media or police attention.

Adaptation

- Changing MO: Adapting techniques, targeting different areas, or changing appearance to avoid capture or identification.

Vulnerable Residential Burglary Targets

- Located near burglarized homes, on the outskirts of neighborhoods, previously burglarized, routinely vacant during the day, unoccupied for periods, vacant for extended periods
- Proximity to athletic venues, drug markets, major thoroughfares, parks, pawnshops, schools, stores, transit centers, treatment centers
- Qualities: careless about security, concealing architectural designs, covered (trees and dense shrubs), displays of wealth, easily entered through side or back doors or windows, few security devices, new to neighborhood, next to alleys, no dogs, no security devices, on a corner, poor lighting, secluded, weakened entry points

Example Types of Burglary

Opportunistic Burglaries: This is the most common type of residential burglary, where a burglar takes advantage of an opportunity such as an open or unlocked door or window.

Forced Entry Burglaries: The burglar forcibly gains entry to the home by breaking a window, picking a lock, or kicking in a door.

Unlawful Entry Without Force: The burglar gains entry to a home without using force, such as through an unlocked door or window.

Sneak-in Burglaries: These occur when a burglar enters a home while the residents are present, often while they are distracted or in a different part of the house.

Distraction Burglaries: In these cases, one burglar distracts the resident (often an elderly or vulnerable person) while another burglar enters the property to steal.

Ruse Entry Burglaries: The burglar poses as a utility worker, delivery person, or another trusted individual to gain access to the home.

Second-Story Burglaries: The burglar gains entry to a home through a second-story window, balcony, or other access point.

Garage Burglaries: The burglar gains entry through an attached garage, often by stealing or duplicating a garage door opener.

Unoccupied Residential Burglaries: These are burglaries that occur when the residents are away from home, such as during work hours, vacation, or an extended absence. Burglars may watch a home for signs of absence before striking.

Loft or Apartment Burglaries: These are burglaries in shared residential buildings. Burglars may exploit lax security in common areas or take advantage of close proximity to other residences.

Rural Burglaries: These occur in less densely populated areas, where homes may be more isolated and thus seen as easier targets.

Non-Residential Burglary

Serial non-residential burglaries refer to a series of burglaries carried out by the same person or group of people, often using similar methods, or targeting similar types of non-residential premises, such as schools or businesses. Here are some common types:

Smash and Grab: This is the most common type of commercial burglary. In this case, the burglars usually break the store's glass windows or doors (hence the name "smash") and quickly take as much as they can before leaving the scene ("grab"). This method is fast and requires little skill.

Lock Manipulation: In these types of burglaries, the criminals manipulate or pick the locks to enter the premises. This often requires a higher level of skill and equipment, but it can be less detectable as it may not cause immediate visible damage.

Safe Cracking: These types of burglars target businesses with safes. They either force the safe open or manipulate the locking mechanism to access the contents. This requires more skill and time, but the rewards can also be higher.

Roof Entry: Some burglars will access commercial buildings via the roof, often by cutting through it. This can allow them to bypass security measures at the main entrances and go undetected until after they have left.

Rear or Side Entry: Many commercial burglaries involve entering the building through a back or side door, where there's often less visibility and less security than at the front.

Utility Access: In some cases, burglars might gain access to the premises through utility entrances, such as air vents or sewer systems. This requires a good knowledge of building layouts and systems.

Sophisticated Burglaries: These are burglaries where advanced technology or equipment is used. This could include jamming alarm systems, using cloned key cards or hacking into security systems.

Crime Pattern Scenario

Over the span of three weeks, a downtown business district experienced a string of burglaries targeting high-end electronics stores. Each incident occurred between midnight and 3 a.m. Security footage showed masked offenders smashing the front glass with sledgehammers, grabbing items within two minutes, and escaping in stolen vehicles. The same type of duffel bags were used to carry stolen merchandise. Pawn shops in the area later reported attempts to sell identical models of electronics with serial numbers removed. Investigators began linking the cases through the method of entry, time of attack, stolen property type, and disposal strategy.

Exercises

1. Research recent developments in forensic or investigative technology – such as DNA sampling protocols, toolmark analysis, or smart-home security integrations – that have aided in solving serial burglary cases. Select at least two real-world examples and describe how these tools contributed to case linkage or offender identification. Evaluate their advantages and limitations for future investigations.
2. Walk through your own home or apartment and identify three potential burglary vulnerabilities (unlocked windows, hidden spare keys, valuable items visible from outside). Write a paragraph explaining how recognizing these vulnerabilities helps understand burglar target selection. Think about your daily routine and identify when your home is typically empty. Write a paragraph explaining how burglars might identify these patterns (mail piling up, no cars in driveway, lights always off during certain hours) and suggest two simple changes to disrupt predictable absence patterns.

Critical Thinking Guidance

Efforts find links between serial burglaries often involves limited or incomplete information. Unlike crimes where victims or witnesses are present, burglaries frequently occur when no one is home, meaning there is often no suspect description available. Similarly, reports usually provide only a time range, such as "between 10:00 a.m. and 3:00 p.m.," rather than a specific time of occurrence, making it harder to establish precise temporal patterns. Because of these gaps, effective linkage involves comparing other variables across cases, such as consistent entry methods, types of property stolen, and geographic proximity. Weigh these recurring behaviors collectively and be cautious not to overstate common burglary practices that could occur in unrelated cases.

Bibliography

Bennell, C., & Canter, D. V. (2002). Linking commercial burglaries by modus operandi: Tests using regression and ROC analysis. *Science & Justice*, *42*(3), 153–164. https://doi.org/10.1016/s1355-0306(02)71820-0

Boba, R., & Santos, R. (2006). *Burglary at single-family house construction sites* (Problem-Specific Guide Series No. 43, Problem-Oriented Guides for Police Series). U.S. Department of Justice, Office of Community Oriented Policing Services. https://popcenter.asu.edu/content/burglary-single-family-house-construction-sites-0

Butler, G. (2005). Commercial burglary: What offenders say. In M. Gill (Ed.), *Crime at work* (pp. 39–55). Palgrave Macmillan. https://doi.org/10.1007/978-1-349-23551-3_3

Clarke, R. V. (2002). *Burglary of retail establishments* (Problem-Specific Guide Series No. 15, Problem-Oriented Guides for Police Series). U.S. Department of Justice, Office of Community Oriented Policing Services. https://popcenter.asu.edu/content/burglary-retail-establishments-0

Erwood, N. J. (2000). *How non-residential burglaries are solved: The effectiveness of police operations* [Doctoral dissertation, University of Birmingham]. University of Birmingham Institutional Repository. https://etheses.bham.ac.uk/id/eprint/4768/1/Erwood02PhD.pdf

Keller, K., & McKeown, M. (n.d.). *Breaking and entering: A profile of 100 burglars.* Crime Strategies Unit, Santa Clara County District Attorney's Office. https://countyda.sccgov.org/sites/g/files/exjcpb1121/files/CSU%20Report%20-%20100%20Burglars.pdf

Nee, C., van Gelder, J., Otte, M., Vernham, Z., & Meenaghan, A. (2019). Learning on the job: Studying expertise in residential burglars using virtual environments. *Criminology*, *57*(3), 481–511. https://doi.org/10.1111/1745-9125.12210

Prenzler, T. (2009). *Preventing burglary in commercial and institutional settings: A place management and partnerships approach* (CRISP Report). ASIS Foundation Research Council.

Tièche, C. C., & Dubach, M. (2021). Efficient DNA sampling in burglary investigations. *Genes*, *13*(1), 26. https://doi.org/10.3390/genes13010026

Weeks, M. J. (2017). *Behavioural case linkage: Linking residential burglary offences in New Zealand* [Master's thesis, Massey University]. Massey Research Online. https://mro.massey.ac.nz/bitstream/handle/10179/11812/02_whole.pdf

Weisel, D. L. (2002). *Burglary of single-family houses* (Problem-Specific Guide Series No. 18, Problem-Oriented Guides for Police Series). U.S. Department of Justice, Office of Community Oriented Policing Services. https://popcenter.asu.edu/content/burglary-single-family-houses-0

36 Larceny/Theft

Introduction

Larceny refers to the unlawful taking of another person's property without the use of force, threat, or unlawful entry. Unlike burglary, which involves breaking into a structure, or robbery, which involves direct confrontation with a victim, larceny typically occurs in public or semi-public spaces and relies on stealth, deception, or opportunity. Common examples include shoplifting, pickpocketing, bicycle theft, theft from motor vehicles, and stealing unattended property such as purses, phones, or packages. Larceny is a term used interchangeably with theft.

Because larceny offenses often appear opportunistic, identifying crime patterns requires close attention to MO variables such as the offender's method of approach (such as distraction, stealth, speed), the specific types of property targeted, concealment or carrying techniques, and the times and locations where incidents occur. For instance, repeated thefts of high-value electronics from the same retail chain, or a series of purse thefts in transit hubs during commuting hours, may signal a pattern involving a prolific offender or group. Analyzing these behaviors systematically enables law enforcement to distinguish between isolated thefts and linked series.

Theft MO Variables

Objectives

- Financial Gain: The primary motive is usually to obtain money or items that can be resold.
- Opportunism: Many acts of larceny occur when the perpetrator sees an unguarded item.
- Resource Gathering: Stealing items for personal use or as resources for other illegal activities.

Planning and Target Selection

- Target Identification: Identifying easy targets, such as unattended belongings, shop items, or even livestock.
- Low Risk: Choosing targets with the lowest risk of getting caught, such as isolated areas or busy stores with limited surveillance.
- Information Gathering: May use casual observation, social interactions, or even online platforms to determine the location and availability of items to steal.

DOI: 10.4324/9781003728733-39

Tools and Equipment

- Concealment Tools: Items like bags, clothing with hidden compartments, or tools to remove security tags in shops.
- Lookout Tools: Use of mirrors, periscopes, or accomplices to serve as lookouts.

Execution

- Stealth and Speed: Quick and unnoticeable actions are employed to take possession of the item.
- Distraction: Creating a diversion or using social engineering techniques to distract the victim or store personnel.
- Concealment: Quickly concealing the stolen item on their person, in a bag, or transferring it to an accomplice.

Evasion

- Quick Exit: Leaving the scene as quickly as possible once the item is secured.
- Blending In: Acting naturally or blending into the crowd to avoid arousing suspicion.
- Alternate Routes: Using different routes to evade any pursuers or surveillance cameras.

Aftermath

- Fencing: Selling the stolen goods through various channels like pawnshops, online marketplaces, or directly to known associates.
- Destruction of Evidence: Removing any identifiable markings, tags, or other forms of identification from the stolen items.

Adaptation and Variation

- Changing MO: Perpetrators may adapt or change their MO to avoid detection, especially if they become aware of increased scrutiny or security measures.

Example Larceny Crime Patterns

Automobile Parts Theft: Stealing car parts from cars, such as tires, mirrors, or radios.
Bicycle Theft: Stealing a bicycle that is locked up or unattended.
Cell Phone Theft: Stealing mobile devices from individuals or stores.
Construction Site Theft: Stealing tools, materials, or equipment from construction sites.
Fuel Theft: Stealing gasoline or diesel fuel, often directly from vehicles.
Garden Equipment Theft: Stealing equipment from residential or commercial gardens, such as lawnmowers or power tools.
Jewelry Theft: Stealing jewelry from individuals or retail establishments.
Mail Theft: Stealing mail from personal mailboxes or postal service boxes.
Metal Theft: Stealing metals, often from industrial sites, to sell as scrap.
Package Theft: Stealing delivered packages from someone's property.
Petty Theft: The theft of items of relatively low value.
Pickpocketing: Stealing from someone's person without their noticing.
Purse Snatching: The act of stealing a purse from a person without force.

Retail Employee Theft: Stealing from an employer, often merchandise or cash from a register.
Shoplifting: The theft of merchandise from a retail establishment.
Charity Box Theft: Stealing donations intended for charity.
Coin-Operated Machines Theft: Stealing cash from vending machines, laundromats, or arcade games.
Gym or Locker Room Theft: Stealing personal belongings from lockers or other areas in gyms, schools, or workplaces.
Hotel/Motel Room Theft: Stealing property from hotel or motel rooms.
Unattended Bag Theft: Stealing items from bags left unattended in public places.
Theft from Vehicles: Stealing items from inside a parked vehicle.
Baby Formula Theft: Stealing baby formula from retail stores, often to resell it.
Electronic Device Theft: Stealing devices like laptops, tablets, or gaming systems.
Office Equipment Theft: Stealing items like computers, printers, or office supplies from workplaces.
Personal Care Item Theft: Stealing items like makeup, perfumes, or skincare products from retail stores.
Power Tool Theft: Stealing power tools from construction sites, garages, or retail stores.
Prescription Drug Theft: The act of stealing prescription medications, often directly from individuals, pharmacies, or medical facilities.
Vehicle Accessories Theft: Stealing items like GPS devices, stereos, or custom accessories from vehicles.

Emerging Crime Patterns in Larceny/Theft

Recent theft patterns show a shift from purely opportunistic acts to more technologically enabled and organized forms of larceny. Offenders are increasingly exploiting digital tools such as RFID skimmers, QR code payment fraud, and online coordination platforms to facilitate and conceal thefts. At the same time, the rise of mobility-related thefts (including catalytic converters, electric scooter and bike parts, and entire EV batteries) reflects how criminals adapt to changes in consumer technology. Organized "flash mob" retail thefts coordinated through social media highlight how groups overwhelm security through speed and numbers. Package theft, long a familiar pattern, is also evolving with offenders using drones and surveillance tools to identify vulnerable deliveries. These trends indicate that larceny is expanding beyond traditional shoplifting or pickpocketing into a broader ecosystem of digitally driven and highly adaptive crimes, requiring tracking both technological enablers and offender collaboration methods to detect emerging serial patterns.[1]

Flash mob thefts represent a significant evolution in organized retail crime, where groups of 20–80 individuals coordinate through encrypted messaging apps to simultaneously overwhelm a store's security, grab merchandise, and disperse within minutes. These incidents blur the line between individual larceny and organized crime, requiring new investigative approaches that focus on digital coordination patterns and social network analysis rather than traditional offender identification.

Crime Pattern Scenario

A downtown shopping district has experienced a wave of shoplifting incidents over the past three weeks. Security reports show that small groups of offenders, usually two or three working together, are targeting high-value cosmetics and designer accessories from multiple retail stores. In several cases, offenders use distraction tactics: one engages staff in conversation while others conceal items in bags modified with foil lining to bypass electronic sensors. Most thefts occur in the afternoon and early evening, coinciding with peak shopping hours. Surveillance video suggests the same group is responsible for at least five incidents, and several of the stolen items were later recovered at a nearby pawn shop. The consistency in target type, concealment methods, and fencing location suggests an organized retail theft pattern rather than isolated opportunistic shoplifting.

Exercises

1. Review the following list of common larceny targets: bicycles, cell phones, purses, garden equipment, packages, and vehicle accessories. Rank these targets from easiest to hardest to protect based on opportunity, offender access, and typical victim behavior. For the two easiest targets, propose a practical community prevention strategy (such as awareness campaigns, environmental design, or partnerships with businesses). Explain how consistent targeting of these items in your jurisdiction might reveal a prolific offender or theft ring.
2. Identify two real-world larceny or theft series reported in reliable online sources – for example, a flash-mob retail theft ring and a catalytic converter theft spree. For each case, summarize the offenders' methods, targeted property, and strategies for evasion or resale. Compare the MO variables across the two cases and explain how investigators were able to connect the incidents despite limited eyewitness evidence.
3. Research one emerging theft method mentioned in the chapter (RFID skimming, drone surveillance for packages, or flash mob coordination). Write a paragraph explaining how this technology changes traditional theft patterns and what new investigative approaches might be needed to address it.

Critical Thinking Guidance

Larceny investigations often involve incomplete or ambiguous data. Unlike robbery or burglary, larceny is frequently unwitnessed, and victims may not realize the theft occurred until much later. This results in vague time frames and limited suspect descriptions, making single-variable linkages unreliable. Therefore, compare clusters of factors such as recurring times of day, property types, concealment methods, and geographic proximity to distinguish opportunistic one-off thefts from a series committed by the same offender. Particular attention should be given to whether an offender adapts over time (changing methods or locations) while still displaying consistent underlying preferences, such as targeting electronics or preying on transit users. Recognizing these consistencies despite missing data is critical to building sound case linkages and directing proactive prevention efforts.

Note

1 U.S. House Committee on Homeland Security (2023, December 12).

Bibliography

Clarke, R. V., & Petrossian, G. (2012). *Shoplifting* (2nd ed., Problem-Specific Guide Series No. 11, Problem-Oriented Guides for Police Series). U.S. Department of Justice, Office of Community Oriented Policing Services. https://popcenter.asu.edu/content/shoplifting-2nd-ed

Johnson, S. D., Bowers, K. J., Gamman, L., Mamerow, L., & Warne, W. (2010). *Theft of customers' personal property in cafés and bars* (Problem-Specific Guide Series No. 60, Problem-Oriented Guides for

Police Series). U.S. Department of Justice, Office of Community Oriented Policing Services. https://popcenter.asu.edu/content/theft-customers-personal-property-caf%C3%A9s-and-bars
Johnson, S. D., Sidebottom, A., & Thorpe, A. (2008). *Bicycle theft* (Problem-Specific Guide Series No. 52, Problem-Oriented Guides for Police Series). U.S. Department of Justice, Office of Community Oriented Policing Services. https://popcenter.asu.edu/content/bicycle-theft-0
Kooi, B. R. (2010). *Theft of scrap metal* (Problem-Specific Guide Series No. 58). Problem-Oriented Guides for Police Series). U.S. Department of Justice, Office of Community Oriented Policing Services. https://popcenter.asu.edu/content/theft-scrap-metal-0
Marcius, C. R. (2022, May 26). Shoplifting ring swept stores for luxury goods, prosecutors say. *The New York Times*. www.nytimes.com
Meini, B., & Clarke, R. V. (2012). *Gasoline drive-offs* (Problem-Specific Guide Series No. 67). Problem-Oriented Guides for Police Series). U.S. Department of Justice, Office of Community Oriented Policing Services. https://popcenter.asu.edu/content/gasoline-drive-offs
U.S. House Committee on Homeland Security. (2023, December 12). *Statement on organized retail crime during house hearing on combating organized retail crime act (H.R. 895)* [Testimony]. https://homeland.house.gov/wp-content/uploads/2023/12/2023-12-12-CTI-HRG-Testimony.pdf

37 Theft of and From Vehicles

Introduction

Theft of and from vehicles includes two related but distinct crimes: the unlawful taking of a vehicle itself (commonly referred to as auto theft) and the theft of property from inside a vehicle (often called theft from vehicle or, in some jurisdictions, auto burglary). Both crimes are widespread and costly, but they differ in offender motives, methods, and investigative approaches. Stolen vehicles may be used for transportation, resold whole, dismantled for parts, or exported as part of organized criminal activity. By contrast, thefts from vehicles are often opportunistic, targeting visible valuables such as purses, electronics, or tools left inside. Although federal crime reporting classifies thefts from vehicles under larceny, they are examined together here because they frequently overlap in offender type, victimization patterns, and prevention strategies. Offenders who begin by stealing items from inside vehicles may escalate to stealing the vehicles themselves, while organized theft rings may commit both crimes depending on opportunity and demand. Understanding the modus operandi variables in both theft of and from vehicles, including target selection, entry methods, tools used, and disposal channels, is essential for recognizing serial activity, disrupting organized theft networks, and developing effective prevention strategies at the community level.

Stolen Vehicles MO Variables

Objectives

- Financial Gain: The primary motive is often to resell the vehicle or its parts.
- Transport: Some steal vehicles to use as transportation for themselves or for committing other crimes.
- Resource Gathering: Stolen vehicles might be used in other illegal activities such as drug trafficking or human smuggling.

Planning and Target Selection

- Vehicle Type: Certain makes and models are targeted due to their resale value, demand for parts, or ease of theft.
- Location Scouting: Parking lots, driveways, and streets are surveyed to identify potential targets.
- Vulnerability Assessment: Perpetrators look for vehicles with visible vulnerabilities such as unlocked doors, open windows, or keys left inside.

DOI: 10.4324/9781003728733-40

Tools and Equipment

- Lock Picking Tools: Various tools may be used to unlock vehicle doors or disable security systems.
- Ignition Bypass Tools: Devices or knowledge to bypass ignition systems, hot-wiring the car.
- Electronic Hacking Equipment: Advanced thieves might use electronic devices to hack keyless entry systems.

Execution

- Quick Operation: The actual act of stealing the vehicle is often executed as quickly as possible to minimize the risk of detection.
- Minimal Noise and Attention: Efforts are made to operate quietly and without drawing attention.
- Vehicle ID Alteration: In some cases, Vehicle Identification Numbers (VIN) are altered on-the-spot before moving the vehicle.

Evasion

- Immediate Exit: Perpetrators quickly drive the stolen vehicle away from the crime scene.
- Route Planning: Pre-planned or spontaneous routes are used to evade law enforcement.
- Abandonment: In some cases, the stolen vehicle is left at a predetermined location for later retrieval.

Aftermath

- Chop Shops: Vehicles may be taken apart for parts that are then sold individually.
- Resale: Stolen vehicles might be resold, often with falsified documents and altered VINs.
- Export: In some instances, stolen vehicles are smuggled out of the country for resale in foreign markets.

Adaptation and Variation

- Changing Tactics: Perpetrators adapt their MO based on successful and unsuccessful attempts, media coverage, or changes in law enforcement strategies.

Example Methods

Offenders employ various methods for stealing vehicles, often relying on their knowledge, expertise, and tools to bypass security measures. Here are some common methods used by steal vehicles:

Key Theft: Criminals may steal the vehicle owner's keys through various means, such as pickpocketing, burglary, or even robbery. They may target homes, workplaces, or public spaces where keys are left unattended. Criminals can steal a vehicle by stealing the key or using a duplicate key.

Hot-wiring: This method involves bypassing the ignition system and starting the vehicle without using the key. Skilled thieves can manipulate the wiring system to start the engine, especially in older models that lack advanced security features.

Relay Theft: This technique is primarily used for vehicles equipped with keyless entry and start systems. Criminals use relay devices to amplify the signal from the owner's key fob, tricking the vehicle into unlocking and starting. This method is particularly effective when the key fob is within close proximity to the vehicle, even inside the owner's home.

Electronic Hacking: Advanced criminals may use electronic hacking tools or devices to gain access to a vehicle's electronic control units (ECUs) and manipulate the security system. By exploiting vulnerabilities in keyless entry systems or the vehicle's network, they can unlock doors, start the engine, or disable security features.

Theft of Documentation: Criminals may target individuals' personal belongings to steal vehicle registration documents, title certificates, or other ownership-related paperwork. With these documents in hand, they can sell or transfer the stolen vehicle more easily.

Tow Truck Theft: In some cases, criminals may use stolen or fraudulent tow trucks to seize parked vehicles. They exploit the assumption that a tow truck is legitimately removing the vehicle, making it less suspicious.

Carjacking: This method involves forcefully stealing a vehicle from its owner or occupant. Carjackers may threaten the driver with weapons, use physical force, or take advantage of vulnerable situations, such as stopping at traffic lights or parking lots.

Vehicle Cloning: Criminals sometimes create counterfeit or cloned vehicle identification numbers (VINs) to disguise a stolen vehicle's true identity. They replace the original VIN with a legitimate one from a similar make and model, making it difficult to trace the stolen vehicle back to its original owner.

Illegal Acquisition of Keys: Some criminals may resort to illicit means to obtain duplicate keys for the targeted vehicle. This can involve corrupting dealership employees or locksmiths or using unauthorized methods to duplicate keys.

Opportunistic Theft: In many cases, vehicle theft occurs due to opportunities presented by owners who leave their vehicles unlocked or with keys inside. Criminals look for easy targets and take advantage of carelessness or negligence on the part of vehicle owners.

Tow Truck Theft: Criminals can use a tow truck to steal a vehicle by towing it away from its location. This method is commonly used when the vehicle is parked in a public place or on the street.

Valet Key Theft: Some vehicles come with a valet key that can be used to start the vehicle but does not provide access to the trunk or glove compartment. Criminals can steal the valet key and use it to start the vehicle.

Electronic Hacking: Criminals can use electronic hacking tools to bypass the vehicle's security system and gain access to the vehicle's computer system, allowing them to start the vehicle remotely.

Example Locations of Vehicle Theft

Urban Areas With High Crime Rates: Cities and urban areas with higher crime rates tend to have a higher incidence of car theft. This can be due to factors such as a larger population, higher demand for stolen vehicles, and more opportunities for thieves.

Parking Lots and Public Areas: Car thefts commonly occur in parking lots, including shopping centers, airports, train stations, and residential complexes. Thieves may target these areas due to the presence of unattended vehicles and a higher likelihood of finding valuable items inside.

Residential Neighborhoods: Thieves may target residential areas, especially those with inadequate security measures, as they offer opportunities for theft with less visibility and potential witnesses. Vehicles parked on the street or in driveways are often vulnerable.

Locations Near Borders or Major Transportation Routes: Areas near international borders or major highways can be attractive to car thieves due to the potential for quick escapes and easier transportation of stolen vehicles across borders or to other locations.

Auto Dealerships and Repair Shops: Car thefts can also occur at auto dealerships or repair shops where vehicles are temporarily stored. Thieves may take advantage of lax security measures or inside knowledge to steal cars from these locations.

Public Streets and Roadways: Cars parked on public streets are not immune to theft. Thieves may quickly break into parked vehicles, hot-wire them, or use other techniques to steal them.

Specific Location Examples

Specific Location Variables for Where Cars Are Stolen: airports, auto dealerships, car wash facilities, construction sites, gas stations, hotels and motels, parking lots (shopping centers, malls, movie theaters, etc.), public transportation stations (train stations, bus stops, etc.), rental car lots, residential driveways, restaurants and bars, schools and university campuses, sporting event venues (stadiums, arenas, etc.), street parking, workplaces (office complexes, industrial areas, etc.)

Stolen Vehicle Indicators

Altered or Missing Vehicle Identification Number (VIN): The VIN plate on the dashboard or door jamb may be tampered with, missing, or appear altered. Mismatched vehicle identification number (VIN): If the VIN plate on the dashboard or door jamb appears to be tampered with, or if the VIN number on the registration, title, or insurance documents does not match the one on the car, this could be a sign that the car is stolen.

Inconsistent or Missing Documentation: The car's registration, title, or other important documents may be missing, forged, or inconsistent with the vehicle's details.

Broken Ignition or Steering Column: Evidence of a broken or damaged ignition or steering column can indicate forced entry or hot-wiring, which could suggest a stolen vehicle.

Modified or Removed Key Locks: If the key locks have been changed or damaged, or if there are signs of tampering, it may indicate unauthorized access to the vehicle.

Unauthorized License Plates: The car may have license plates from a different state or mismatched plates that do not correspond to the vehicle's make and model.

Fresh Paint or Repairs: Recently applied paint, mismatched paint colors, or signs of repair work that don't match the vehicle's history could be an indicator of attempts to conceal the car's identity.

Altered or Removed VIN Tags: The VIN tags on major parts of the vehicle, such as the engine or frame, may be missing, altered, or scratched off.

Stolen Parts or Accessories: If the car contains stolen parts, such as a stereo system, airbags, or tires, or if valuable accessories are missing, it could suggest the vehicle has been stolen.

Stolen Vehicle Reports: Checking databases or contacting the local authorities to see whether the vehicle has been reported as stolen is an important step.

No License Plates or Altered License Plates: A car without any license plates or with altered plates is a potential sign that the car has been stolen.

Keys That Don't Fit: If the keys that come with the car don't work, or if the ignition or door locks have been tampered with, this could indicate that the car has been stolen

Low Price: If the price of the car is significantly lower than its market value, this could be a red flag that the car is stolen.

Out-of-State Plates: If the car has out-of-state license plates or temporary plates that have been on the car for an extended period, this could be an indication that the car is stolen or has been taken across state lines to avoid detection.

Signs of Forced Entry: If there are signs of forced entry, such as a broken window or a damaged lock, this could indicate that the car has been stolen.

Inability to Access the Trunk: If the trunk cannot be opened or if the lock has been tampered with, this could be a sign that the car is stolen and that the thief is trying to hide something in the trunk.

Thefts From Vehicles

Offender Characteristics

- Motive: Financial gain, opportunistic theft, thrill-seeking, or necessity (such as stealing a GPS for re-sale vs. grabbing loose change).
- Skill Level: Experienced thieves may be adept at quickly bypassing locks or disabling alarms, while amateurs might only target unlocked cars.
- Criminal History: Offenders with a past criminal record may use more sophisticated methods.
- Risk Tolerance: Willingness to commit the crime in high-surveillance areas or during peak hours.
- Local Knowledge: Familiarity with the area can impact the choice of location and timing for the theft.
- Addiction: many offenders have addiction problems and commit this crime to fuel their addiction.

Situational Factors

- Vehicle Type: Some vehicles may be targeted more frequently due to the perceived value of their contents.
- Visibility of Valuables: The presence of visible items like electronics, bags, or loose change can make a vehicle more attractive to thieves.
- Vehicle Condition: Older or poorly maintained vehicles might be perceived as easier targets.
- Time of Day: Thefts commonly occur during the night or when the vehicle is expected to be unattended for an extended period.
- Entry Method: Whether the vehicle was unlocked, or if forced entry was used (such as smashing windows, jimmying locks).
- Presence of Security Measures: Car alarms, steering wheel locks, or surveillance cameras can act as deterrents.

Environmental Considerations

- Location: High-crime areas, secluded spots, and locations far from police stations may be preferred by offenders.
- Surveillance: Areas with low visibility or lack of CCTV can provide thieves more opportunities.
- Social Cohesion: Neighborhoods with low social interaction may have fewer natural "eyes on the street," making it easier for thieves to operate without being noticed.
- Police Presence: The frequency of patrolling can serve as a deterrent.
- Lighting: Poorly lit areas may offer offenders more cover.

Examples of Items Stolen From Vehicles

Stolen From Vehicles: airbags, automotive tools, backpacks, bags, bicycles, car audio systems, car batteries, car speakers, car stereos, cash, catalytic converters, clothing, construction tools, credit cards, debit cards, driver's license, fishing gear, garage door opener, golf clubs, GPS device, jewelry, ladders, loose change, luggage, laptop, passport, personal documents, personal identification, portable DVD player, portable music player, power tools, prescription medications, purse, rims, shopping bags, smartphone, social security card, sporting goods, tablet, tires, toolboxes, tools, watch, wallet

Emerging Crime Pattern

In the UK, relay theft, where criminals use electronic devices to intercept and relay signals from keyless vehicle key fobs, has become an increasingly pervasive challenge. According to the Crime Survey for England and Wales (2022–2023), approximately 40% of all vehicle thefts involved manipulation of remote locking signals using devices like repeaters or amplifiers. In response, the UK government is preparing to ban the possession and distribution of such devices – signaling a shift toward stricter regulation as part of a broader strategy to curb technologically enabled auto crime. This marks a crucial policy-level response to the evolving methods of vehicle theft.[1]

Crime Pattern Scenario

In a border city, police noticed an uptick in stolen pickup trucks and SUVs parked at hotels and highway rest stops. Surveillance footage showed offenders using tow trucks with falsified business logos to remove vehicles without drawing attention. Within weeks, several of the stolen trucks were intercepted at a nearby port, prepared for shipment overseas. Investigators concluded that a transnational theft ring was specifically targeting vehicles with high resale value in foreign markets, using professional methods to disguise theft as legitimate towing.

Exercises

1. A series of thefts from vehicles in a suburban shopping mall parking lot. Items stolen include purses, laptops, and backpacks, usually visible inside the cars. Most thefts occur between 6 p.m. and 9 p.m. during peak shopping hours. Which situational and environmental factors (lighting, patrols, surveillance) might contribute to the repeated thefts? How could analysts use victim data (such as repeat targeting of certain types of vehicles) to refine their understanding of the pattern? What partnerships (mall security, retail management, neighborhood watch groups) would be most effective in preventing further incidents? Who else could be contacted to see if this is part of a larger crime series?
2. Observe a parking lot for 15 minutes and note behaviors that increase theft risk (valuables visible, windows cracked, parking in isolated spots). Without identifying specific vehicles or people, create a risk ranking of the five most common vulnerabilities you observed. Propose one simple behavior change that would eliminate the highest risk factor.

Critical Thinking Guidance

Vehicle theft and theft from vehicles are often opportunistic, but many offenders operate with a high degree of planning and adaptation. Avoid treating each report as an isolated event and instead look for recurring clusters of variables such as target vehicle make/model, method of entry, time window, and geographic concentration. For example, catalytic converter thefts, keyless-entry relay attacks, or smash-and-grab thefts from vehicles each carry distinctive patterns that can be tracked over time.

A key challenge is distinguishing between casual offenders who exploit visible opportunities (unlocked cars, valuables left in plain sight) and organized groups who adapt techniques, use advanced technology, or feed stolen vehicles and parts into larger criminal networks, including transnational smuggling operations. Integrating intelligence from multiple sources (police reports, pawn shop and scrap metal transactions, customs and border alerts, and electronic surveillance) provides a more complete picture of offender activity.

Consider environmental and situational variables, such as parking facilities, lighting, neighborhood cohesion, and police patrol presence, that influence offender decision-making as much as vehicle vulnerabilities do. Systematic data collection and separation of subtypes (auto theft, theft from vehicles, parts theft) are essential, as these crime types overlap but differ in offender motive, skill, and linkage potential.

Note

1 Home Office and Johnson (2025, February 24).

Bibliography

Clarke, R. V. (2001). *Thefts of and from cars in parking facilities* (Problem-Specific Guide Series No. 10, Problem-Oriented Guides for Police Series). U.S. Department of Justice, Office of Community Oriented Policing Services. https://popcenter.asu.edu/content/thefts-and-cars-parking-facilities-0

Dallas Police Department. (n.d.). *Auto related crimes.* https://dallaspolice.net/communitys/autoRelatedCrimes

Home Office, & Johnson, D. (2025, February 24). Vehicle theft equipment to be banned under new government law. *Gov.UK, U.K. Government.* www.gov.uk/government/news/vehicle-theft-equipment-to-be-banned-under-new-government-law?utm_source=chatgpt.com

Keister, T. (2007). *Thefts of and from cars on residential streets and driveways* (Problem-Specific Guide Series No. 46, Problem-Oriented Guides for Police Series). U.S. Department of Justice, Office of Community Oriented Policing Services. https://popcenter.asu.edu/content/thefts-and-cars-residential-streets-driveways-0

U.S. Customs and Border Protection. (2020, February 10). *Stolen vehicle epidemic* [Local media release]. U.S. Department of Homeland Security. www.cbp.gov/newsroom/local-media-release/stolen-vehicle-epidemic-0

38 Arson

Introduction

Arson is the deliberate setting of fire to property such as buildings, vehicles, wildlands, or other structures, with the intent to cause damage, conceal another crime, or achieve personal, financial, or ideological goals. Offender motives range from insurance fraud and revenge to intimidation, thrill-seeking, or political violence. Some arsonists act impulsively, while others carefully plan their crimes, conducting surveillance, selecting ignition points, and even disabling safety systems to maximize destruction.

Identifying serial arson patterns requires close attention to MO variables, including the use of accelerants, ignition devices, points of origin, and timing of incidents. The contents destroyed (such as vehicles, records, valuables, or symbolic structures) provide insight into offender motive and can help link cases. Forensic evidence (accelerant traces, burn patterns, toolmarks) and behavioral indicators (returning to the scene, fascination with fire, symbolic targeting) are central to distinguishing isolated acts from serial arson.

Arson MO Variables

Objectives

- Financial Gain: Insurance fraud is where the perpetrator sets fire to property to collect insurance money.
- Revenge or Emotional Release: Personal grievances or emotional disturbances can drive the act.
- Terrorism or Political Goals: Ideologically motivated arson aimed at creating fear or advancing political objectives.
- Destruction of Evidence: Used as a means to destroy evidence of another crime.

Planning and Organization

- Target Selection: The choice of target may be random or well-planned, based on ease of access, likelihood of total destruction, and potential for evading detection.
- Timing: Off-peak hours or when the building is unoccupied are often chosen to minimize witnesses and maximize damage.
- Reconnaissance: Surveillance of the target to understand its vulnerabilities may be involved in more organized forms of arson.

DOI: 10.4324/9781003728733-41

Technical Framework

- Accelerants: The use of flammable liquids or substances to hasten the fire.
- Ignition Devices: Simple matches, electrical devices, or more sophisticated timers may be used.
- Placement: Where the fire is started in the building or property can indicate the arsonist's level of knowledge and objectives.

Execution

- Incendiary Method: The specific way the fire is set, such as pouring gasoline in a pattern, using a Molotov cocktail, or rigging an electrical fire.
- Exit Strategy: Quick escape routes are often pre-identified to evade immediate capture.

Intermediaries

- Accomplices: Sometimes multiple individuals are involved in planning and execution.
- Informants: In organized criminal networks, third parties may provide key information about targets.

Legal Evasion

- Disguise or Concealment: Perpetrators may try to make the arson look accidental or like an electrical fire.
- Alibis: Constructing solid alibis for the time of the arson to mislead investigators.
- Avoidance of Surveillance: Evading CCTV cameras or witnesses during both the planning and execution stages.

Aftermath

- Resale of Property: In cases of insurance fraud, once the insurance money is collected, the property may be rebuilt and sold.
- Pattern Avoidance: Serial arsonists may alter their MO to avoid detection and apprehension.

Scene of Arson Evidence Examples

Set distinctly separate fires, trailers/streamers of combustibles used to spread fire, consistent point of origin, consistent burn pattern, ignited fire in trash can, ignited fire in building, ignited fire in vehicle, indicators of professional arsonist, indicators of amateur arsonist, unidentifiable point of origin of fire, blocked/obstructed entry/exit, disabled sprinklers/alarms, covered or blocked windows, broken windows/doors, multiple items fired, altering natural gas flow, altering electrical system, forcible entry, multiple ignition points

Tools and Equipment Variable Examples

- used matches to start/spread the fire, used lighter to start/spread the fire, used an accelerant to start/spread the fire, used a torch to start/spread fire, used a tool to start/spread the fire, used debris to start/spread the fire, used wood for fuel, used paper for fuel, used gasoline for fuel, used kerosene for fuel, used propane for fuel, used alcohol for fuel, used benzene for fuel, used petroleum ether for fuel, used naphtha for fuel, used turpentine for fuel, used chemicals for fuel, used flammable gas for fuel, used a time-delayed device, used candles as a time-delayed device, used electrical equipment to set fire, used explosive device, used improvised incendiary device, used Molotov cocktail

Tactics/Behaviors/Motives Examples

- seeks out locations with limited surveillance or visibility
- conducts arson during specific weather conditions (high wind, low humidity)
- targets locations based on specific religious, ethnic, or cultural identities
- used distraction tactics (setting a smaller fire elsewhere to draw attention away from main target)
- used remote/digital methods to trigger the fire (such as hacked IoT devices)
- consistent time of arson occurrence (time of day, day of the week)
- used smoking materials to start the fire (cigarettes, cigars)

Other Offender MO Example Variables

- appeared to surveil target
- appeared to cover up arson
- appeared to conceal another crime
- entered/exited/escaped through window
- entered/exited/escaped through door
- entered/exited/escaped through roof
- possible return to the scene
- removal of valuables/pets before fire was set
- disguising a burglary
- disguising a vehicle theft
- theft from premises
- suspicious questioning prior to arson
- suspicious or unattended items prior to arson,
- communication/claims made by the arsonist
- suspicious social media messages prior to arson,
- suspicious or unattended items prior to arson
- appeared to divert attention from another crime
- non-local or transient offender
- the arsonist with a recognizable modus operandi
- the arsonist that leaves symbolic or message-based evidence at the crime scene

Offender Characteristics and Behavioral Patterns

Offender Typologies

Serial arsonists who set multiple fires over time following consistent patterns; firefighter arsonists who set fires to appear heroic or alleviate boredom; financially motivated adults seeking insurance fraud or eliminating business competition; gang-affiliated firesetters using arson for intimidation or retaliation; juvenile groups setting fires for excitement or peer acceptance; and organized crime-related arsonists destroying evidence or sending warnings.

Behavioral Indicators

Observable patterns include returning to watch fires or monitoring emergency response, showing unusual interest in media coverage of fires, demonstrating extensive knowledge about fire behavior and investigation techniques, conducting surveillance of targets before setting fires, removing valuables or pets before ignition, using consistent methods or signatures across multiple fires, and displaying fascination with fire-related topics in conversation or online activity.

Background Characteristics

Common background factors encompass employment history in fire services, construction, or related fields providing knowledge of buildings and fire behavior; criminal records for vandalism, threats, or property crimes that may escalate to arson; family instability or childhood trauma including abuse or neglect; recent significant losses such as job termination, relationship breakdown, or financial crisis; residence patterns showing transient lifestyle or proximity to fire locations; and educational or military background providing technical knowledge about accelerants or timing devices.

Psychological and Emotional Factors

Psychological elements include antisocial personality traits showing disregard for others' safety and property; signs of personal crisis or extreme stress preceding fire-setting behavior; learned behavior patterns from childhood fire-setting or family modeling; revenge motivation stemming from perceived wrongs or grievances; thrill-seeking tendencies using fire for excitement or power; and ideological extremism targeting symbols of opposed beliefs or groups.

Post-Incident Response Patterns

After fires, offenders may exhibit denial or minimization of involvement despite evidence, blame-shifting to others or circumstances, expressions of remorse that may be genuine or manipulative, detailed knowledge about fires they claim not to have set, nervous or excited behavior when discussing the incidents, attempts to insert themselves into investigations as witnesses or helpers, and social media activity revealing knowledge or satisfaction about fires.

Crime Pattern Scenario

Over the course of two months, a small city experiences a series of late-night vehicle fires in residential neighborhoods. The vehicles are all older sedans parked on the street, and each shows evidence of accelerant use. No suspects have been identified, but neighbors reported seeing the same individual on a bicycle in the area shortly before several of the fires. Investigators suspect a serial arsonist motivated by thrill-seeking or revenge against the community, given the consistency in target type, timing, and method.

Exercises

1. A warehouse district reports a suspicious fire that destroyed stored business records along with the structure itself. Investigators are uncertain whether the fire was set intentionally to conceal evidence of financial crime. What variables should be examined to distinguish

between an accidental fire and deliberate arson? How might the destruction of certain contents point to motive? What partnerships (insurance investigators, financial crime units, fire marshals) could strengthen the investigation? How should analysts and investigators compare this incident to other arsons in the area to determine whether it belongs to a series?

2. Given three hypothetical fires (all involving accelerants, occurring at night, targeting similar structures), identify five additional variables investigators should examine to determine whether they're linked. Explain which variables would provide the strongest linkage (same accelerant type, geographic clustering, similar ignition devices) versus those that might be coincidental.

Critical Thinking Guidance

Linking serial arson cases requires separation of accidents from intentional fires and looking beyond surface similarities. Fires can appear opportunistic, but clusters of similar variables (accelerant use, ignition devices, multiple points of origin, or the removal of valuables before ignition) provide stronger evidence of intentional and possibly serial behavior. Weigh motive indicators tied to contents destroyed: vehicles linked to concealment, business records tied to fraud, or symbolic sites tied to ideology. Because arson often overlaps with other crimes such as burglary or insurance fraud, integrating data from fire investigators, police, and financial crime units is essential.

Bibliography

Bureau of Alcohol, Tobacco, Firearms and Explosives. (2020). *Arson incident report (AIR)*. U.S. Department of Justice. www.atf.gov/file/155146/download

Canter, D., & Fritzon, K. (1998). Differentiating arsonists: A model of firesetting actions and characteristics. *Legal and Criminological Psychology*, *3*(1), 73–96. https://doi.org/10.1111/j.2044-8333.1998.tb00352.x

Rider, A. O. (1980, July). The firesetter: A psychological profile, part II. *FBI Law Enforcement Bulletin*. U.S. Department of Justice. www.ojp.gov/pdffiles1/Digitization/76361NCJRS.pdf

39 Fraud

Introduction

Fraud is the deliberate use of deception to obtain money, property, services, or other benefits to which the offender is not entitled. Unlike theft, which often relies on stealth or force, fraud depends on manipulation, misrepresentation, or abuse of trust. Fraudsters may operate as individuals or in organized networks, exploiting vulnerabilities in people, businesses, and institutions. Common variables in fraud patterns include the method of deception (false documents, impersonation, digital phishing), the target population (elderly, investors, businesses), and the channels used (phone, email, online platforms, or face-to-face). Understanding these recurring behaviors allows law enforcement and analysts to identify fraud series, track offender strategies, and implement effective prevention and intervention.

Fraud MO Variables

Objectives and Motivation

- Financial Gain: The primary motive is almost always monetary. Fraudsters aim to secure money, goods, or services through deception.
- Non-Monetary Benefits: Sometimes, the objective may not be direct financial gain but other advantages, such as obtaining sensitive information or gaining unauthorized access.

Planning and Target Selection

- Victim Profiling: Criminals often select targets based on vulnerability, such as the elderly, or based on the likelihood of success.
- Information Gathering: Collecting details about the target, which may include personal, financial, or business-related information.

Types of Schemes

- Advance Fee Schemes: Requiring payment upfront with the promise of larger financial returns.
- Ponzi Schemes: Using capital from new investors to pay off earlier investors.
- False Representation: Providing misleading or incorrect information to deceive targets.
- Impersonation: Posing as a trustworthy entity or person to gain confidence.

DOI: 10.4324/9781003728733-42

Tools and Techniques

- Document Forgery: Creating or modifying documents to support fraudulent claims.
- Technology-Aided Techniques: Use of phishing emails, malware, or hacking to aid in the fraud.
- Communication Channels: Utilizing phone calls, mail, emails, or face-to-face meetings for deceit.

Execution

- Illegal Transactions: Carrying out transactions that result in the transfer of funds or assets from the victim to the fraudster.
- Deception and Manipulation: Employing psychological tactics to manipulate the victim into performing certain actions beneficial to the criminal.

Intermediaries

- Money Mules: Individuals used for transferring money acquired through illegal means, knowingly or unknowingly.
- Accomplices: Other participants who may aid in various capacities, such as information gathering or asset transfer.

Evasion Techniques

- Altering Digital Trails: Deleting or modifying digital records to avoid detection.
- Use of Shell Companies: Employing legal entities to mask the true nature and ownership of fraudulent activities.
- Jurisdiction Hopping: Operating across multiple jurisdictions to make legal pursuit more difficult.

Post-Offense Activities

- Money Laundering: Attempting to legitimize the illegally obtained money through various transactions.
- Cover-Up and Exit Strategies: Taking steps to wind down the fraudulent operation while minimizing the risk of detection or capture.

Example Fraud Types

Identity and Impersonation Frauds

These frauds involve assuming another's identity or creating false identities to deceive victims. Types include identity theft using personal information to access accounts or benefits; account takeover fraud where criminals gain control of existing accounts; child identity theft exploiting minors' SSNs that won't be checked for years; medical identity theft specifically for healthcare services; government identity fraud for obtaining official documents or services; impersonation fraud where offenders pose as trusted entities like IRS agents, utility companies, or law enforcement; business email compromise (BEC) where criminals impersonate executives to authorize transfers; and synthetic identity fraud combining real and fake information to create new identities. Deepfake technology increasingly enables sophisticated impersonation through manipulated audio and video, while biometric bypass techniques evolve to defeat fingerprint and facial recognition systems.

Investment and Financial Frauds

These schemes promise financial returns or involve manipulation of financial systems. Common types include Ponzi and pyramid schemes that use new investor funds to pay earlier participants; securities fraud involving stock manipulation, insider trading, or pump-and-dump schemes; investment fraud offering fake or worthless opportunities; forex trading scams exploiting foreign exchange markets; precious metals and coins fraud selling overpriced or counterfeit collectibles; loan fraud through falsified applications or predatory lending; mortgage and real estate fraud including property flipping schemes and foreclosure scams; timeshare and timeshare resale fraud; cryptocurrency fraud exploiting digital currency platforms through fake ICOs or wallet theft; and NFT fraud involving fake or stolen digital assets.

Retail and Commerce Frauds

These target businesses and consumers in commercial transactions. Types include return fraud through wardrobing, receipt manipulation, or returning stolen goods; invoice fraud sending fake bills to businesses; auction fraud on online platforms; counterfeit goods and coupons; credit card fraud through stolen numbers or skimming devices; check fraud including forgery and kiting; bait-and-switch tactics; organized retail theft rings; reshipping fraud using victims as unwitting package forwarders; triangulation fraud where sellers use stolen cards to fulfill orders; gift card fraud through tampering or social engineering; and various forms of warranty and refund fraud exploiting return policies.

Healthcare and Insurance Frauds

These exploit medical and insurance systems for illegal gain. Common schemes include healthcare provider fraud through billing for services not rendered or upcoding procedures; patient fraud filing false insurance claims; prescription fraud via doctor shopping, forgery, or illegal online pharmacies; Medicare and Medicaid fraud targeting government programs; disability fraud through false claims; medical equipment fraud billing for unnecessary devices; dental and vision fraud; workers' compensation fraud by employees or employers; and insurance fraud across auto, home, life, and other policies through staged accidents, arson, or inflated claims.

Government Benefit and Tax Frauds

These involve illegally obtaining government funds or avoiding obligations. Types include tax fraud through false returns, unreported income, or fake deductions; benefit fraud illegally claiming unemployment, welfare, or social security; disaster relief fraud exploiting emergency assistance programs; pandemic relief fraud including PPP and EIDL schemes; veterans benefits fraud through false service claims; grant fraud misusing research or program funds; contractor fraud overcharging or providing substandard services to government agencies; immigration fraud including marriage, visa, and asylum fraud; and education fraud involving financial aid or fake institutions.

Technology-Enabled Frauds

These leverage digital platforms and tools as primary vehicles for deception. Common types include phishing and email scams; tech support fraud claiming computer problems; click fraud manipulating online advertising; mobile payment app fraud; ATM skimming using devices to capture card data; SIM swapping to bypass two-factor authentication; ransomware and malware attacks; online dating and romance scams through fake profiles; social media fraud including fake crowdfunding campaigns; synthetic media fraud using AI-generated documents or media; wire fraud through electronic communications; and various forms of digital marketplace fraud.

Relationship-Based Frauds

These exploit personal relationships and emotional connections. Types include romance scams developing fake romantic relationships for money; elder fraud targeting vulnerable seniors often by building trust; caregiver fraud by those providing home care or family members; charity fraud exploiting compassion through fake causes; adoption fraud involving illegal practices in adoption processes; funeral fraud taking advantage of grieving families; wedding vendor scams; contractor and home repair fraud especially after disasters; affinity fraud targeting members of specific communities, religious groups, or social circles; lottery and sweepstakes fraud claiming fake winnings; and advance fee fraud promising large returns for upfront payments.

Emerging Crime Pattern: Deepfakes and Identity Theft

Deepfakes are AI-generated audio, video, or images that realistically impersonate real people and are becoming a powerful tool in identity theft schemes. While a deepfake alone is not identity theft, criminals can use them to commit fraud or gain unauthorized access to sensitive information. For example, deepfake videos have been used to impersonate executives during virtual meetings to authorize fraudulent wire transfers, and manipulated images have been deployed to bypass facial recognition security. These techniques blur the line between traditional identity theft and digital deception, creating new challenges for law enforcement, financial institutions, and victims alike. As biometric verification systems become more common, deepfake-enabled identity theft is expected to grow as an emerging crime pattern.

Crime Pattern Scenario

Over six months, multiple small businesses in a metropolitan area report receiving invoices from a supposed office supply company. Each invoice looks legitimate and lists products the businesses commonly use, such as printer toner. Many businesses pay without question, but investigators discover the company is fictitious, operating through a P.O. box and untraceable phone numbers. The consistent format of the invoices, the use of common low-dollar charges, and the geographic concentration of victims link the cases as part of an organized invoice fraud scheme.

Exercises

1. A local police department receives reports of elderly residents being contacted by phone about "urgent tax debts." Victims are told to purchase gift cards and provide the card numbers as payment. What fraud variables would you document for comparison across

multiple reports? How could these variables help determine whether the calls are part of a larger organized scheme?
2. Collect three examples of fraud attempts (phishing emails, scam texts, or recorded phone scripts) from public awareness sites or your own spam folder. Identify five consistent elements across these communications (urgency language, grammar patterns, payment methods requested). Create a simple checklist investigators could use to link fraud cases based on communication style rather than content.

Critical Thinking Guidance

Fraud cases often lack physical evidence or traditional crime scene indicators, requiring focus on patterns in offender behavior, communication methods, and victim targeting to identify serial crimes. Think critically about how fraudsters adapt to new technology, how they exploit trust, and how they obscure their identities. Comparing variables such as language used in communications, payment methods demanded, and the demographic profile of victims can reveal links between cases. Fraud also frequently crosses jurisdictions, making information-sharing between agencies essential. Approach fraud as a dynamic system, where offenders adjust tactics as victims and law enforcement respond, may help anticipate shifts in schemes and reduce future victimization.

Bibliography

American Bankers Association Foundation & Federal Bureau of Investigation. (2025). *ABA foundation and FBI release new infographic to help Americans spot and avoid deepfake scams*. www.aba.com/about-us/press-room/press-releases/aba-foundation-and-fbi-joint-infographic-on-deepfake-scams

FinCEN. (2024, November 13). *FinCEN alert on fraud schemes involving deepfake media targeting financial institutions* (FIN 2024 Alert004). U.S. Department of the Treasury. www.fincen.gov/system/files/shared/FinCEN-Alert-DeepFakes-Alert508FINAL.pdf

Internal Revenue Service. (2021). *Internal revenue manuals, 25.1.2 recognizing and developing fraud*. U.S. Department of the Treasury. www.irs.gov/irm/part25/irm_25-001-002

Newman, G. R., & Herbert, J. (2020). *Check and card fraud* (2nd ed., Problem-Specific Guide Series No. 21). Office of Community Oriented Policing Services, U.S. Department of Justice. https://popcenter.asu.edu/content/check-and-card-fraud-2nd-ed

USA.gov. (n.d.). *Scams and fraud*. U.S. General Services Administration. www.usa.gov/scams-and-fraud

40 Identity Theft

Introduction

Identity theft is a pervasive and adaptive crime that involves the unlawful acquisition and misuse of another person's personally identifiable information (PII). Unlike traditional theft, which centers on physical property, identity theft targets the intangible yet highly valuable data that underpins financial, medical, and governmental systems. Offenders use a wide array of techniques to assume the identity of their victims. They range from low-tech methods like mail theft and dumpster diving to high-tech intrusions such as large-scale data breaches, phishing campaigns, and SIM swapping.

The consequences extend beyond financial loss. Victims may face damaged credit, false criminal records, compromised health records, and long-term personal and professional repercussions. For law enforcement, identity theft represents a multifaceted challenge: it often spans multiple jurisdictions, exploits both human and technological vulnerabilities, and can be linked to broader organized crime or fraud networks. Understanding the methods, variables, and evolving tactics used in identity theft is essential for recognizing patterns, protecting vulnerable populations, and identifying serial offenders operating across different domains.

Personal Identifiable Information

Personal Identifiable Information (PII) is defined as any representation of information that permits the identity of an individual to whom the information applies to be reasonably inferred by either direct or indirect means. Furthermore, PII is defined as information: (i) that directly identifies an individual (e.g., name, address, social security number or other identifying number or code, telephone number, email address) or (ii) by which an agency intends to identify specific individuals in conjunction with other data elements, that is, indirect identification. (These data elements may include a combination of gender, race, birth date, geographic indicator, and other descriptors.) Additionally, information permitting the physical or online contacting of a specific individual is the same as personally identifiable information. This information can be maintained in paper, electronic, or other media.[1]

DOI: 10.4324/9781003728733-43

Identity Theft MO Variables

Objective and Motivation

- Financial Gain: The primary objective is often monetary benefit, such as gaining access to bank accounts or credit lines.
- Fraudulent Activities: Use of the stolen identity for activities like securing loans, making purchases, or evading law enforcement.
- Information Sale: Selling the acquired personal information to third parties.

Planning and Information Gathering

- Social Engineering: Methods such as phishing, pretexting, or baiting to trick individuals into revealing personal information.
- Public Records: Gleaning personal information from public databases or social media platforms.
- Surveillance: Physical or digital stalking of the target to gather information.

Tools and Techniques

- Skimming: Employing devices to capture card information at ATMs or during legitimate transactions.
- Phishing Emails and Websites: Creating fake websites or emails that mimic trusted organizations to capture personal information.
- Hacking: Directly breaching databases or systems to obtain personal information on a massive scale.

Execution

- Account Takeover: Using the stolen information to gain control over bank, email, or other personal accounts.
- New Account Creation: Using the stolen identity to open new lines of credit or accounts in the victim's name.
- Document Forgery: Creating counterfeit identification documents like passports, driver's licenses, etc.

Intermediaries

- Data Brokers: Individuals or groups specializing in collecting and selling personal data.
- Mules: People who knowingly or unknowingly help in transferring stolen assets.

Evasion Techniques

- Use of Anonymous Networks: Utilizing networks like Tor to cloak activities.
- Proxy Usage: Employing proxy servers to hide the IP address and location.
- Digital Trails: Deleting or altering digital footprints and transaction logs to cover tracks.

Post-Offense Activities

- Data Laundering: Making the stolen data less traceable.
- Asset Liquidation: Converting stolen or fraudulently acquired assets into cash or other forms.
- Cover-Up: Taking steps to minimize detection and identification, such as constantly changing physical or digital locations.

Identity Theft Example Methods

Physical Theft Methods

These involve direct physical access to documents or information. Methods include mail theft from mailboxes to obtain bank statements or credit card offers; dumpster diving through trash for discarded documents containing personal information; stealing wallets or purses containing identification and credit cards; shoulder surfing to observe PIN entry at ATMs or terminals; theft of employment records from workplace files; and stealing physical identification documents like passports or driver's licenses.

Social Engineering and Impersonation

These exploit human trust and psychology to obtain information. Common tactics include phishing emails pretending to be legitimate organizations; pretexting through creating false scenarios to extract information; impersonating government officials, service providers, or family members; fake job applications and scams requesting personal information; phony charity, sweepstakes, or lottery scams; fake online surveys or contests to collect data; romance scams using fake profiles to exploit victims; and telemarketing calls posing as legitimate companies.

Digital and Technical Methods

These use technology to steal or intercept data. Methods include data breaches targeting financial institutions and databases; hacking and exploiting website vulnerabilities; credit card skimming at ATMs or point-of-sale terminals; SIM swapping to hijack phone numbers and bypass two-factor authentication; password cracking using software or social engineering; fake Wi-Fi networks to intercept user data; online shopping fraud using stolen credentials; and various forms of malware and keyloggers.

Account and Document Fraud

These involve creating false identities or taking over existing accounts. Types include bank and credit card account takeover; creating synthetic identities combining real and fake information; birth certificate and counterfeit ID document fraud; change of address fraud to redirect mail; opening new accounts using stolen identities; and forging documents for loans, rentals, or employment.

Sector-Specific Identity Theft

These target particular systems or benefits. Common types include medical identity theft for services or prescriptions; tax refund fraud filing false returns; social security benefits and number fraud; employment fraud using stolen identities for jobs; education and student information exploitation; utility account fraud leaving victims with bills; rental and car rental fraud; insurance fraud across various policy types; and fraudulent benefit claims.

Targeting Vulnerable Populations

These specifically exploit children, elderly, or dependent individuals. Methods include child identity theft often going undetected for years; elder exploitation through caregiver access or trust; family member impersonation to access accounts; exploitation of deceased individuals' identities before death certificates are filed; and targeting individuals with cognitive impairments or limited English proficiency.

Commercial and Financial Exploitation

These monetize stolen identities through various channels. Activities include selling stolen data to brokers or on dark web markets; using identities for money laundering operations; creating shell companies with stolen identities; conducting auction fraud with fake seller accounts; rental application and property fraud; credit fraud through loans and credit cards; and systematic insurance claim fraud.

Emerging Crime Pattern: Synthetic Identities

A synthetic identity is a fake identity created by combining pieces of real information with fabricated details to make a new, false persona. For example, a fraudster might use a real Social Security number (stolen from a child, a homeless person, or someone who doesn't use credit) but pair it with a made-up name, date of birth, and address. Over time, this synthetic identity can be used to build credit, apply for loans, or open accounts, making it harder for banks or law enforcement to detect because it doesn't belong to a single real person. This type of fraud is one of the fastest-growing financial crimes because it exploits gaps in identity verification systems.[2]

Crime Pattern Scenario

Over a three-month period, dozens of residents across several neighboring suburbs report fraudulent withdrawals from their checking accounts shortly after visiting different branches of the same regional bank. Detectives eventually trace the pattern to a temporary staffing agency employee who worked rotating assignments as a customer-service clerk at multiple branches. The offender, an active member of a regional professional banking association, used her legitimate access to internal systems to capture customer account numbers and partial Social Security data. She then sold the information to accomplices who created counterfeit debit cards and made rapid ATM withdrawals before victims detected the losses. Her association membership and work credentials gave her both the insider knowledge to bypass standard safeguards and a plausible reason to move between branches without arousing suspicion.

Exercises

1. Make a list of all the ways your personal identifiable information (PII) is stored (wallet, phone, social media, online accounts, mail, workplace files). Identify at least three weak points where an offender could steal it.

2. Research one major data breach from the past five years (without accessing actual stolen data). Create a timeline showing: when the breach occurred, when it was discovered, when victims were notified, and when identity theft cases began appearing. Explain the gap between breach and exploitation and what this reveals about how criminals use stolen data.

Critical Thinking Guidance

Identity theft cases often lack clear starting points: there may be no direct suspect description, and victims may not realize the crime until weeks or months after it occurs. Piecing together patterns from fragmented data sources such as bank alerts, consumer complaints, and suspicious activity reports is part of the process of identifying a serial crime pattern. Ask: Are multiple victims reporting account takeovers tied to the same IP addresses, regions, or fraudulent phone numbers? Do different fraud cases share similar techniques, such as phishing templates or counterfeit IDs? Considering these variables systematically can reveal serial offenders or organized groups that would otherwise appear as isolated cases.

Notes

1 U.S. Department of Labor (n.d.).
2 Simons (2023, April 21).

Bibliography

Newman, G. R. (2004). *Identity theft* (Problem-Specific Guide Series No. 25, Problem-Oriented Guides for Police Series). Office of Community Oriented Policing Services, U.S. Department of Justice. https://popcenter.asu.edu/content/identity-theft-0

Simons, T. (2023, April 21). Trends in synthetic identity fraud. *Thomson Reuters Legal.* https://legal.thomsonreuters.com/en/insights/articles/trends-in-synthetic-identity-fraud

U.S. Department of Labor. (n.d.). *Guidance on the protection of personal identifiable information.* www.dol.gov/general/ppii

Vanderford, R. (2025, January 28). GenAI increasingly powering scams, Wall Street watchdog warns. *The Wall Street Journal.* www.wsj.com/articles/genai-increasingly-powering-scams-wall-street-watchdog-warns-a6592d54

41 Counterfeiting

Introduction

Counterfeiting involves the production or distribution of fake goods, official documents, or currency designed to deceive consumers, businesses, or governments. It spans a wide range of products, from luxury goods and pharmaceuticals to identification documents and banknotes, and has significant economic, security, and public health implications. While the motivation is typically financial gain, counterfeit items can also be used to facilitate other crimes, such as fraud, smuggling, or identity theft.

Counterfeiting often operates as an organized system, requiring planning, production, and distribution networks that may extend across borders. Counterfeiters take advantage of gaps in regulation, trade flows, and technology, adapting quickly when enforcement pressure rises. Because counterfeit items often intermingle with legitimate goods, they can be difficult to detect, making the identification of patterns – such as recurring distribution hubs, consistent product lines, or specialized skill sets – essential to linking cases into a broader criminal network.

Counterfeiting Items MO Variables

Objectives and Motivation

- Financial Gain: The primary objective is usually to make money by creating and distributing fake items.
- Market Exploitation: In some cases, the aim is to undercut genuine brands or manipulate markets.

Planning and Target Selection

- Product Selection: The type of goods to be counterfeited is decided on the basis of factors such as demand, production costs, and legal risks.
- Supply Chain Analysis: Understanding how the genuine products are manufactured and distributed to mimic these processes effectively.

DOI: 10.4324/9781003728733-44

Resource Acquisition

- Material Sourcing: Procurement of materials needed to produce counterfeits that are as close to the original as possible.
- Skill Requirements: Identifying or training individuals who have the necessary skills to produce counterfeit items.

Types of Counterfeiting

- High-Quality Fakes: These are almost indistinguishable from the real item and often require specialized skills or machinery to produce.
- Low-Quality Fakes: Easier and cheaper to make but easily distinguishable from genuine items.

Production

- Manufacturing Facilities: Places where the counterfeit items are produced, ranging from small makeshift setups to more sophisticated operations.
- Quality Control: Some operations may include a quality check to ensure that the counterfeits closely mimic the original items.

Distribution Channels

- Direct Sales: Through street vendors, pop-up shops, or direct consumer contact.
- Online Platforms: Utilizing e-commerce websites, social media, or dark web marketplaces.
- Supply Chain Infiltration: Inserting counterfeit items into the legitimate supply chain.

Intermediaries

- Transporters: Individuals or services responsible for moving the counterfeit items.
- Vendors: Those who sell the counterfeit items to consumers or other intermediaries.
- Money Handlers: Those involved in the financial aspect, including collecting payment and possibly laundering money.

Evasion Techniques

- Documentation Forgery: Creating fake invoices, certificates, or other documents to legitimize the counterfeit goods.
- Brand Mimicry: Creating packaging and branding that very closely resembles the original.
- Jurisdictional Hopping: Operating in multiple jurisdictions to evade detection and arrest.

Post-Offense Activities

- Financial Laundering: Converting the revenue generated into legitimate funds.
- Evidence Destruction: Eradicating or altering any evidence that could link back to the criminals involved.

Counterfeit Currency MO Examples

Counterfeiting currency involves the illicit production of fake money with the intention of using it as genuine legal tender.

Objectives

- Financial Gain: The primary aim is to enrich oneself by using counterfeit money in transactions as if it were genuine.
- Economic Sabotage: Rare but possible, the objective might also be to destabilize a country's economy.

Planning

- Target Currency: Deciding which currency to counterfeit, often based on its value and the perceived difficulty of mimicking its security features.
- Research and Reconnaissance: Studying the target currency's design, color, and security features like watermarks, holograms, and embedded threads.

Resource Gathering

- Material Sourcing: Obtaining the paper, ink, and other materials required for the production of counterfeit money. Sometimes specialized suppliers are involved.
- Equipment: Acquiring or fabricating the machinery and tools required, which may include printing presses, inkjet printers, and engraving tools.

Skills and Expertise

- Skill Set: High-quality counterfeiting requires specialized skills in graphic design, printing, and, in some cases, chemistry.
- Technical Knowledge: Detailed understanding of the target currency's security features.
- Production:
- Printing: Actual production of the counterfeit notes, sometimes happening in hidden or underground facilities.
- Quality Control: Checking the final products for defects and similarity to genuine currency.

Distribution

- Initial Circulation: Introducing the counterfeit money into the financial system, often by using them in small transactions where they are less likely to be detected.
- Subsequent Levels: Transfer of the fake money through various levels, including wholesalers and retailers, each taking a cut.

Intermediaries

- Money Mules: Individuals responsible for carrying and distributing the counterfeit money.
- Middlemen: These could include individuals who act as brokers between the counterfeiters and distributors.

Risk Mitigation

- Layering Transactions: Engaging in complex financial transactions to distance the counterfeit money from its source.
- Avoiding Detection: Using tactics such as changing locations frequently and employing technology to cover tracks.

Post-Offense

- Money Laundering: Proceeds from the crime might be laundered through various means, including cryptocurrencies, shell companies, or cash businesses.
- Evidence Destruction: Disposal or hiding of evidence, including printing equipment and materials, to evade capture.

Types of Counterfeiting Operations

Counterfeiting operations vary significantly in their targets, methods, and required expertise. While all share the common goal of creating deceptive replicas for profit, each category presents unique production challenges, distribution channels, and investigative considerations.

Product Counterfeiting

Product counterfeiting encompasses the creation of fake physical goods designed to mimic legitimate branded items. This includes luxury knockoffs such as handbags, watches, and designer clothing that exploit brand prestige; counterfeit electronics including smartphones and computer components often made with inferior materials that pose safety risks; fake pharmaceuticals that may contain incorrect or harmful ingredients, threatening public health; counterfeit auto parts like brake pads and airbags that create serious safety hazards; and fake food and beverages that violate health standards while mimicking popular brands. These operations range from small workshops producing limited quantities to industrial-scale facilities churning out millions of units. Distribution occurs through street vendors, online marketplaces, and infiltration of legitimate supply chains, making detection particularly challenging when counterfeits blend with authentic products.

Document Counterfeiting

Document counterfeiting involves creating false official papers and identification materials. This category includes forged identity documents such as passports, driver's licenses, and social security cards used for identity theft and illegal immigration; falsified financial instruments including checks, bonds, and securities used in fraud schemes; counterfeit academic credentials and professional certifications; and fake business documents such as invoices, certificates of authenticity, and shipping manifests that facilitate other criminal activities. Document counterfeiters often require specialized knowledge of security features, access to specific paper types and inks, and sophisticated printing equipment. The shift to digital verification systems has pushed counterfeiters to develop increasingly sophisticated forgeries that can pass electronic authentication.

Currency Counterfeiting

Currency counterfeiting, while following similar organizational structures to product counterfeiting, presents unique challenges and methods due to the sophisticated security features of modern banknotes and severe legal penalties associated with this crime. The production of fake money requires extensive planning including researching target currency designs, studying security features like watermarks, holograms, and embedded threads, and deciding which denominations offer the best risk-reward ratio. Resource gathering involves obtaining specialized paper with the correct weight and texture, acquiring specific inks that match color-changing properties, and securing printing equipment capable of reproducing fine details. The production process demands exceptional technical skills in graphic design, printing, and sometimes chemistry to replicate modern security features. Distribution follows a careful pattern of introducing counterfeit notes through small transactions where detection is less likely, using money mules to distance producers from circulation, and employing complex layering techniques to obscure the money's origin. Unlike product counterfeiting where quality can vary, currency counterfeiting requires consistently high quality to avoid immediate detection, making it a more specialized and technically demanding criminal enterprise.

Emerging Methods: 3D Printing and Digital Manufacturing

The advent of 3D printing technology has fundamentally altered the counterfeiting landscape. Traditional counterfeiting required specialized equipment, centralized production facilities, and established distribution networks with high barriers to entry. In contrast, 3D printing enables decentralized production using widely available printers and downloadable design files, allowing counterfeiters to produce items on-demand in small batches that reduce detection risk. This technology particularly threatens industries relying on precision parts – automotive, aerospace, and medical devices – where counterfeit components can have catastrophic consequences. The shift from mass production to distributed manufacturing complicates enforcement, as authorities must now monitor countless small producers rather than targeting major facilities. Additionally, the improving quality of 3D-printed items makes visual detection increasingly difficult, requiring new authentication methods based on material composition and microscopic analysis rather than surface appearance.

Crime Pattern Scenario

A local auto repair shop unknowingly purchases counterfeit brake pads produced using 3D printers. The pads are nearly identical to genuine branded parts, complete with copied serial numbers. However, the material quality is inferior, and several customers experience brake failures within weeks. Investigators later discover that the counterfeit parts were printed in small batches overseas, shipped through multiple distributors, and blended into legitimate supply chains. The decentralized production model made it harder for authorities to trace the origin.

Exercises

1. Research how one country's currency has added security features over the past 20 years. Create a timeline showing major security additions and explain what counterfeiting methods each feature was designed to prevent. Discuss how counterfeiters adapt to new security measures and why the "arms race" between security and counterfeiting continues.
2. Create a list of three products in your daily life (medicines, electronics, household items, etc.) that could be vulnerable to counterfeiting. For each item, note: Why it might be targeted (high demand, high cost, difficult for consumers to verify authenticity). What indicators a counterfeit version might have (differences in packaging, unusual performance, missing safety seals).

Critical Thinking Guidance

Counterfeiting presents unique challenges for crime pattern recognition because it often straddles multiple domains: fraud, intellectual property crime, organized crime, and public health. Think beyond individual incidents of fake goods and look for recurring variables, such as distribution hubs, shared production techniques, or similar packaging anomalies. Linking counterfeit cases requires collaboration across jurisdictions, since counterfeit items may be manufactured in one country, shipped through another, and sold in a third.

Remain alert to the evolving tools of counterfeiters. For example, 3D printing and digital design software now allow high-quality knockoffs of consumer products and even security documents, while e-commerce platforms provide anonymous, global reach. A systematic approach includes defining what constitutes a linked counterfeit case, documenting shared features, and integrating intelligence from customs, trade authorities, and financial crime units. This helps distinguish isolated incidents from organized counterfeit networks.

Bibliography

Gerstein, D. M., & Leidy, E. N. (2024, February 15). *Emerging technology and risk analysis: Additive manufacturing* (RR-A2984-1). RAND Corporation. www.rand.org/pubs/research_reports/RRA2984-1.html

Interpol. (n.d.). *Identity and travel document fraud.* www.interpol.int/en/Crimes/Counterfeit-currency-and-security-documents/Identity-and-travel-document-fraud

OECD/EUIPO. (2019). *Trends in trade in counterfeit and pirated goods: Illicit trade.* OECD Publishing. https://doi.org/10.1787/g2g9f533-en

U.S. Currency Education Program. (n.d.). *Learn to authenticate your money.* www.uscurrency.gov

U.S. Department of Homeland Security. (2020, January 24). *Combating trafficking in counterfeit and pirated goods.* DHS. www.dhs.gov/sites/default/files/publications/20_0124_plcy_counterfeit-pirated-goods-report_01.pdf

World Health Organization. (2024, December 3). *Substandard and falsified medical products.* WHO. www.who.int/news-room/fact-sheets/detail/substandard-and-falsified-medical-products

42 Intellectual Property Crimes

Introduction

Intellectual property (IP) crimes involve the theft, reproduction, or misuse of creations such as copyrighted works, patents, trade secrets, and trademarks. These crimes are often financially motivated and exploit digital technologies that make replication and distribution simple, inexpensive, and global. IP theft frequently transcends borders, operating in jurisdictions with weak enforcement. The impacts are broad: eroding consumer trust, undermining innovation, funding organized crime, and posing health and safety risks when counterfeit goods (such as pharmaceuticals or auto parts) enter legitimate markets.

Intellectual Property Crimes MO Variables

Motivation and Planning

- Financial Gain: One of the most common motivations is to profit from the unauthorized use, reproduction, or distribution of intellectual property.
- Competitive Advantage: Corporations may steal intellectual property to gain a competitive edge over rivals.
- Ease of Replication: Digital technologies have made it easier than ever to duplicate and distribute copyrighted or patented material, making the crime more attractive.

Target Selection

- High-Value Targets: Perpetrators often target well-known brands, software, or creative works that are likely to bring them the most profit.
- Vulnerabilities: They may search for targets that have less secure digital protections or lax enforcement mechanisms, making the crime easier to commit.

Pre-Crime Preparation

- Technical Skills: The criminals usually have a good understanding of technologies like hacking, encryption, and anonymization tools to conceal their activities.
- Market Research: They may assess demand for the targeted intellectual property to maximize financial gain.

DOI: 10.4324/9781003728733-45

Execution

- Reproduction and Distribution: This involves the unauthorized copying, adapting, or sharing of intellectual property.
- Misrepresentation: The counterfeit or pirated products are often represented as genuine to deceive consumers.
- Digital Platforms: Various online platforms may be used for distribution, from peer-to-peer networks to dedicated websites.

Intermediaries and Networks

- Supply Chains: Intellectual property crimes often involve a network of manufacturers, distributors, and retailers who might be knowingly or unknowingly involved.
- Digital Facilitators: Individuals or entities may provide web hosting, payment processing, or other services that facilitate the crime.

Avoidance of Capture

- Identity Concealment: Use of fake identities and aliases is common, both online and offline.
- Jurisdiction Hopping: Criminals may operate from jurisdictions with lax intellectual property laws or ineffective enforcement, making capture and prosecution difficult.
- Digital Footprint Erasure: Efforts are made to erase or conceal any digital evidence that could link back to them.

Post-Crime Activities

- Monetization: The proceeds from the crime may be laundered through various channels to make them appear legitimate.
- Obfuscation: After the crime, perpetrators often take steps to disassociate themselves from the illegal activities, such as shutting down websites or disappearing from online forums.

Intellectual Property Crimes Execution Methods

The execution of intellectual property crimes follows distinct patterns based on the type of IP being targeted and the technical capabilities required. Understanding these methods within the framework of broader MO variables helps investigators recognize patterns and link related cases.

Digital Reproduction and Distribution Methods

Digital piracy represents the most common execution method, involving unauthorized copying and distribution of copyrighted content including software, music, movies, and e-books. Perpetrators employ various technical approaches from simple file-sharing to sophisticated DRM circumvention tools. Distribution occurs through peer-to-peer networks, dedicated piracy websites, and increasingly through legitimate-appearing streaming services that mask their illegal nature. The ease of digital replication means a single breach can result in millions of unauthorized copies, with distribution networks often spanning multiple countries and jurisdictions. Criminals frequently monetize through advertising revenue on piracy sites, subscription fees for illegal streaming services, or direct sales of pirated content at reduced prices.

Physical Counterfeiting and Manufacturing

Counterfeiting involves creating physical imitations of branded products, requiring different execution methods than digital piracy. This includes establishing manufacturing facilities ranging from home workshops to industrial operations, sourcing materials that approximate genuine products while minimizing costs, and creating packaging and labeling that mimics authentic brands. Distribution channels infiltrate legitimate supply chains through compromised wholesalers, online marketplaces with limited verification, and street-level vendors in areas with weak enforcement. The execution requires coordination between manufacturers, transporters, and sellers, often involving organized crime networks that handle multiple product lines simultaneously.

Technical Theft and Espionage Methods

Trade secret theft and patent infringement involve more targeted execution methods focusing on specific valuable information. Insider threats use their legitimate access to copy confidential information, often just before leaving for a competitor. External attacks employ hacking, social engineering, or physical infiltration to access protected information. Reverse engineering legally purchased products to extract proprietary information represents a gray area that becomes illegal when patents are violated. The execution often involves sophisticated technical skills and extended surveillance or reconnaissance to identify vulnerabilities in security systems. Distribution of stolen technical information may be direct sale to competitors, incorporation into competing products, or publication to damage the original owner's competitive advantage.

Trademark and Brand Exploitation

Trademark infringement execution involves unauthorized use of protected marks and brands through various methods. Cybersquatting registers domain names containing trademarks to sell them back or redirect traffic. Counterfeiters apply legitimate trademarks to inferior products. Some operations create confusion through similar marks or packaging designed to mislead consumers. The execution requires understanding of trademark law to exploit gray areas, graphic design capabilities to recreate logos and branding, and distribution networks that can quickly move products before detection. Online marketplaces have become primary venues for trademark infringement, with sellers creating multiple accounts to evade suspension.

Hybrid and Evolving Methods

Modern IP crimes increasingly combine multiple execution methods. A single criminal operation might steal trade secrets through hacking, manufacture counterfeit products using that information, distribute them through piracy networks, and launder profits through cryptocurrency. The convergence of different IP crime types reflects organized crime's recognition that intellectual property represents a low-risk, high-reward target. Emerging technologies like 3D printing and artificial intelligence are creating new execution methods, such as AI-generated content that infringes copyrights or 3D-printed products that violate patents.

These evolving methods require investigators to understand both traditional IP crime patterns and emerging technological capabilities that enable new forms of infringement.

Emerging Trends in Digital Rights Management (DRM) Circumvention

A growing trend in intellectual property crimes involves the circumvention of Digital Rights Management (DRM) technologies. DRM is intended to protect digital products such as movies, music, software, e-books, and video games and controls how they are accessed, copied, and distributed. However, criminal groups increasingly exploit vulnerabilities in these systems.

One major pattern is the proliferation of illicit streaming services and devices that bypass DRM protections on subscription platforms. These "fully loaded" devices, often sold online or through informal markets, provide pirated access to premium content while generating revenue streams for organized crime. Similarly, software cracking communities systematically remove DRM protections from high-value software products and resell them through darknet markets or peer-to-peer sites. This not only undermines legitimate businesses but also exposes consumers to malware and data theft, as pirated copies often contain embedded malicious code.

Another emerging trend involves DRM removal tools for e-books, films, and music, which enable large-scale piracy with minimal technical expertise. Criminal groups aggregate stripped content into massive repositories for resale or advertising-driven distribution. Additionally, DRM circumvention in video games has become a lucrative criminal enterprise, with cracked copies circulating rapidly across global networks. These versions sometimes carry malware or spyware that further victimizes users. Finally, industrial DRM attacks – targeting proprietary software embedded in automotive, medical, or industrial equipment – are an emerging frontier. Here, attackers bypass protections not only to pirate technology but also to compromise systems with potential public safety consequences.

DRM circumvention thus reflects a broader shift: intellectual property crimes are no longer confined to counterfeit physical goods, but increasingly occur in digital ecosystems where detection, enforcement, and jurisdictional authority are more complex.

Crime Pattern Scenario

A multinational corporation discovers that its proprietary software has been illegally duplicated and is being sold through multiple online platforms at a fraction of the original cost. Investigation reveals that the pirated software originated from servers located overseas, hosted in a jurisdiction with weak intellectual property enforcement. Payment for the pirated copies is funneled through cryptocurrency wallets, complicating financial tracing. Analysts note that the same seller is also distributing counterfeit versions of related products, suggesting a serial IP crime network rather than isolated incidents.

Exercises

1. Consider a hypothetical small business (restaurant, tech startup, or retail shop). List five types of information that could be considered trade secrets (recipes, customer lists, pricing strategies). For each, identify one way it could be stolen (employee theft, hacking, dumpster diving) and one protective measure. Explain why some trade secrets are more vulnerable than others.

2. Research three legitimate reasons people might want to bypass DRM (backing up purchased content, accessibility needs, format compatibility) versus three illegal uses. Create a brief explanation of why the same technology can have both legal and illegal applications, and how this complicates enforcement.

Critical Thinking Guidance

Linking intellectual property crimes into patterns requires looking beyond single incidents and consider broader networks of production, distribution, and facilitation. Unlike traditional crimes where physical presence ties an offender to a scene, IP crimes often leave digital trails such as server logs, domain registrations, cryptocurrency transactions, and recurring online identities. Distinguish between isolated piracy and coordinated, serial infringement that involves supply chains and organized crime groups. Cross-referencing cases of piracy, counterfeiting, and trade secret theft may reveal shared infrastructure or actors. It is also critical to integrate cybercrime intelligence, customs enforcement data, and corporate reports of infringement to form a more complete picture. Recognizing adaptation (such as shifting from selling pirated movies to counterfeit pharmaceuticals) can be one key to identifying evolving IP crime enterprises.

Bibliography

Crudu, A., & MoldStud Research Team. (2025, January 25). Exploring emerging security trends shaping the future of intellectual property protection. *MoldStud.com*. https://moldstud.com/articles/p-exploring-emerging-security-trends-shaping-the-future-of-intellectual-property-protection

Danaher, B., Smith, M., & Telang, R. (2020). Piracy landscape study: Analysis of existing and emerging research relevant to intellectual property rights (IPR) enforcement of commercial-scale piracy. *SSRN Electronic Journal*. https://doi.org/10.2139/ssrn.3577670

National Intellectual Property Rights Coordination Center. (n.d.). [Homepage]. www.iprcenter.gov

43 Money Laundering

Introduction

Money laundering is the process of disguising the origins of illegally obtained funds, so they appear legitimate. Offenders or groups typically (and repeatedly) integrate laundering into broader criminal enterprises, such as trafficking, fraud, or corruption. The process is often complex and may overlap across three main stages. Placement refers to introducing illicit funds into the financial system or retail economy, often in smaller amounts to avoid detection. Layering involves obscuring the money's origin by moving it through a series of transactions, accounts, or jurisdictions, making it difficult to trace. Integration occurs when the laundered funds re-enter the economy as seemingly legitimate assets, such as real estate, businesses, or luxury goods.

Money Laundering MO Variables

Motivation and Objective

- Concealment of Illicit Gains: The primary aim is to disguise the origin of money derived from illegal activities.
- Asset Protection: To protect assets from seizure by authorities.

Planning and Methodology

- Research and Analysis: Money launderers might conduct extensive research to understand banking laws, tax regulations, and existing loopholes.
- Consultation with Experts: They may consult financial advisors, lawyers, and other experts who can assist in the laundering process, sometimes unwittingly.

Initial Entry: Placement

- Cash Deposits: One common method is to deposit large amounts of cash in banks, often in smaller, less suspicious amounts.
- Use of Cash-Intensive Businesses: Using businesses that generally deal in cash can help blend the illicit money with the business's legitimate earnings.
- Currency Smuggling: Physically moving money across borders to deposit in foreign banks.
- Buying Assets: Purchasing valuable items like property, cars, or art, which can later be sold.

DOI: 10.4324/9781003728733-46

Layering: Disguising Origins

- Wire Transfers: Transferring money between different accounts, often across multiple banks, sometimes including those in other countries.
- Shell Companies: Using fake companies to funnel money creates a web of transactions that obscure its origins.
- Loan Back Schemes: Giving loans to oneself from the laundered money, making it appear as legitimate business earnings.

Final Integration: Making Money Legitimate

- Investment in Legal Ventures: Investing laundered money in legitimate business ventures.
- Real Estate: Buying property with illicit funds, then selling it to turn it into seemingly clean money.

Intermediaries and Facilitators

- Financial Institutions: Banks, cryptocurrency exchanges, and other financial institutions may unknowingly facilitate money laundering.
- Corrupt Officials: Government or banking officials may knowingly or unknowingly assist in the laundering process.

Evasion Techniques

- Digital Currencies: Utilization of cryptocurrencies to further anonymize transactions.
- Offshore Accounts: Use of banks in countries with strict bank secrecy laws.

Post-Laundering Activities

- Wealth Management: After the money has been successfully laundered, the focus shifts to managing and growing the now clean assets.
- Cover-Up: Documentation and other evidence are destroyed or manipulated to minimize the risk of detection.

Detection and Investigation

Understanding how to detect money laundering patterns requires recognizing clusters of indicators that, when combined, reveal systematic criminal activity rather than isolated suspicious transactions. These indicators serve as investigative building blocks that help distinguish legitimate financial activity from disguised criminal proceeds.

Transaction Monitoring Indicators

Financial institutions and investigators track specific transaction patterns that suggest laundering activity. Structuring remains one of the most common indicators – repeated deposits just below reporting thresholds, particularly when made across different branches or ATMs on the same day. Large, round-number cash deposits inconsistent with customer profiles raise immediate red flags, as do sudden unexplained increases in previously dormant account activity. Rapid movement of funds through multiple accounts, especially across different institutions or jurisdictions, indicates layering attempts. Complex transactions without clear business purposes, circular money movements where funds return to original sources through convoluted routes, and frequent transfers to or from high-risk jurisdictions all suggest systematic laundering rather than legitimate business activity.

Customer and Business Behavior Patterns

Behavioral indicators often reveal laundering operations before transaction analysis does. Customer reluctance to provide identification, use of false or forged documents, or inability to explain funding sources signal potential criminal activity. Frequent changes in business or account ownership without clear reasons, accounts opened in names of minors or elderly persons as nominees, and transactions conducted by third parties all indicate attempts to obscure beneficial ownership. For businesses, deposits inconsistent with observable sales volumes, customer traffic, or industry norms suggest commingling of illicit funds. Cash-intensive businesses showing revenue patterns incompatible with their location, size, or market conditions warrant particular scrutiny.

Geographic and Jurisdictional Patterns

Money launderers exploit geographic differences in regulation and enforcement. Frequent routing of transactions through countries with weak anti-money laundering enforcement, use of offshore accounts or tax havens without legitimate business purposes, and funds transferred through multiple jurisdictions in short periods all indicate sophisticated laundering operations. Unusual reliance on money service businesses, hawala networks, or informal transfer systems, particularly when formal banking is readily available, suggests deliberate avoidance of regulated channels.

Digital Asset Indicators

The rise of cryptocurrencies and digital assets has created new laundering channels with distinct indicators. Large or frequent cryptocurrency transfers without legitimate explanation, use of privacy coins designed to obscure transaction trails, and employment of mixing services or tumblers reveal attempts to break the link between criminal proceeds and their ultimate use. In decentralized finance, repeated use of the same protocols for cycling funds, wallet clustering suggesting coordinated activity across multiple identities, and NFT transactions at prices wildly inconsistent with market value all indicate potential laundering. The speed and pseudonymous nature of digital transactions require different detection approaches than traditional banking.

Trade and Commercial Indicators

Trade-based laundering exploits international commerce to move value across borders. Over- or under-invoicing of goods and services, repeated import/export transactions at prices inconsistent with market rates, and use of free trade zones to obscure ownership patterns reveal this method. Documentation anomalies, such as invoices that don't match shipping manifests or payment terms inconsistent with industry practices, often expose trade-based schemes. Shell companies with no real operations but high transaction volumes, particularly when registered in multiple jurisdictions, indicate systematic laundering infrastructure.

Asset and Lifestyle Indicators

Unexplained wealth manifests in recognizable patterns. Purchase of luxury goods, vehicles, or real estate inconsistent with known income sources, particularly when bought with cash or through nominees, signals integration of laundered funds. Rapid buying and selling of properties without clear purpose, loans paid off unusually quickly, and lifestyle expenditures dramatically exceeding legitimate income all suggest criminal proceeds entering the legitimate economy. The use of professional intermediaries to obscure asset ownership, particularly when the same lawyers or accountants appear across multiple suspicious transactions, indicates organized laundering operations.

Money Laundering Examples

Real Estate Money Laundering: Buying property with illicit funds and then selling those properties to make the money appear legitimate.

Cryptocurrency Laundering: Using cryptocurrencies like Bitcoin to move funds anonymously. The digital currency is then converted back into real currency.

Trade-Based Laundering: Over- or under-valuing invoices to move money across borders.

Gambling: Using illicit money to gamble, then cashing out with the "winnings," which appear to be legal earnings.

Cash Businesses: Funneling illicit money through cash-intensive businesses like laundromats or car washes, mixing it with legitimate earnings.

Foreign Bank and Financial Accounts: Using offshore accounts to hide money, often in jurisdictions with strict banking secrecy laws.

Investment in Tangible Assets: Purchasing valuable items like art, gold, or luxury cars to store value, which can be later sold for clean money.

Hawala or Informal Value Transfer Systems: Transferring money through a network of brokers or agents, avoiding formal financial systems. This is common in regions where banking is less accessible.

Tax Amnesties: Taking advantage of government-offered tax amnesty programs to declare hidden funds as previously "unreported income," paying a smaller penalty but legalizing the money.

Double Invoicing and False Invoicing: Manipulating invoices to disguise the movement of money.

Loan Back: Taking out a loan from an offshore entity, using illicit money as collateral, then claiming the loan amount as income.

Emerging Crime Patterns

Decentralized Finance (DeFi) Laundering: Criminal groups exploit decentralized finance platforms, where automated smart contracts process transactions without central oversight, to launder illicit proceeds. Funds are cycled through liquidity pools and decentralized exchanges, often moving across multiple blockchains to obscure their origin.

Elements: offender financial concealment, blockchain-based transactions, anonymity.

Variables: token type, liquidity pool address, smart contract exploited, frequency of swaps, cross-chain bridges used.

Non-fungible tokens (NFTs) are used to disguise illicit funds by artificially inflating the value of digital artwork or collectibles. Offenders create multiple wallets, "sell" the same asset at inflated prices, and then cash out through legitimate-looking sales.

Elements: offender use of digital assets, false value creation, victimized financial systems.

Variables: NFT platform, wallet clustering, transaction price anomalies, repeated buyer/seller identities, geographic location of wallets.

Money Laundering Indicators

Transaction Indicators

- Structuring: Repeated deposits just below reporting thresholds.
- Multiple small deposits made across different branches or ATMs.
- Large, round-number cash deposits inconsistent with customer profile.
- Sudden or unexplained increases in account activity.
- Frequent transfers to/from high-risk jurisdictions.
- Rapid movement of funds through multiple accounts ("layering").
- Use of complex transactions without clear business purpose.
- Dormant accounts suddenly becoming active with high-value transactions.
- Multiple accounts controlled by the same person moving money in a circular fashion.

Account and Customer Behavior Indicators

- Reluctance to provide identification or use of false/forged documents.
- Frequent changes in ownership of businesses or accounts without clear reason.
- Opening accounts in the names of minors, elderly persons, or third parties.
- Accounts with activity inconsistent with customer's stated occupation or income.
- Customers unwilling or unable to explain source of funds.
- Transactions conducted by third parties on behalf of the account holder.

Business Indicators

- Cash-intensive businesses (restaurants, bars, car washes, casinos) with deposits that don't match sales volume.
- Over- or under-invoicing of goods/services in trade transactions.
- Repeated import/export of goods at prices inconsistent with market value.
- Businesses using shell or shelf companies with no real operations.
- Use of professional intermediaries (lawyers, accountants, notaries) to obscure beneficial ownership.

Geographic and Channel Indicators

- Frequent transactions routed through countries with weak AML enforcement.
- Offshore accounts or tax haven involvement without legitimate purpose.
- Funds transferred through multiple jurisdictions in short periods.
- Unusual reliance on money service businesses, hawala, or informal transfer systems.

Digital and Emerging Indicators

- Large or frequent transfers involving cryptocurrency without legitimate explanation.
- Use of privacy coins (like Monero, Zcash) or mixers/tumblers to conceal origin of funds.
- Repeated use of the same DeFi protocols or NFT platforms for transactions.
- Wallet clustering suggesting coordinated activity across multiple digital identities.

Lifestyle and Asset Indicators

- Purchase of luxury goods, cars, jewelry, or art inconsistent with reported income.
- Use of nominees to purchase assets on behalf of others.
- Frequent buying and selling of real estate without legitimate explanation.
- Loans or mortgages paid off unusually quickly in cash.

Real-Life Case

On May 15, 2025, the US Department of Justice charged 12 individuals in a RICO-fueled conspiracy tied to over $263 million in stolen cryptocurrency, a scheme that illustrates how deeply money laundering is intertwined with broader criminal activity. This cyber-enabled enterprise, active from October 2023 through March 2025, originated from relationships forged on online gaming platforms and evolved into a coordinated criminal network comprising hackers, social engineers, money launderers, and home-invasion burglars. After stealing digital assets through database breaches and manipulative contact campaigns, conspirators laundered the proceeds using peel chains,[1] crypto mixers,[2] VPNs, wire transfers, bulk cash, and shell entities. The laundered funds then financed a lavish lifestyle including nightclub blowouts, exotic cars, private jets, luxury real estate rentals – demonstrating that laundering here is both a financial mechanism and a means of sustaining violent and fraudulent criminal behavior. This case reveals how laundering cannot be isolated: it is enmeshed in every phase, from the digital theft to physical violence and extravagant expenditure, making the money-laundering variable pivotal for linkage analysis across cybercrime, fraud, and organized theft typologies.

Crime Pattern Scenario

Investigators reviewing suspicious activity reports (SARs) notice repeated wire transfers between multiple shell companies registered in different countries. Each company lists different industries, but all are linked to the same beneficial owner. The funds, originating from regions tied to narcotics trafficking, are layered through complex cross-border transactions before being used to purchase high-value real estate in the United States. The reuse of shell entities, layering via cryptocurrency exchanges, and repeated purchases of luxury property signal a serial laundering operation rather than isolated incidents.

Exercises

1. Choose and research one common laundering method such as real estate investment, cryptocurrency mixing, or trade-based laundering. Then:
   (1) Identify how offenders disguise the illicit origin of money in this method.
   (2) List three variables (such as transaction size, geographic regions, industries used) that could be tracked to reveal repeated patterns.
   (3) Explain how law enforcement or compliance officers could disrupt this method.
2. List five types of cash-intensive businesses commonly used for laundering (restaurants, car washes, etc.). For each, identify one indicator that revenue might be inflated with illicit funds (deposits inconsistent with foot traffic, unusually high cash percentages, etc.). Explain which type of business would be hardest for investigators to prove is laundering money and why.

Critical Thinking Guidance

When evaluating potential money laundering, identify repeated behaviors across time, actors, and methods. A serial laundering pattern reveals itself through recurrence: the same shell companies, repeated transfer routes, recurring use of certain banks or digital platforms, or consistent movement of money through the same industries (like real estate or casinos). Compare cases across different reporting periods, jurisdictions, and financial institutions to see whether similar techniques appear. Look for consistency in variables such as transaction size, timing, or geographic corridors to distinguish one-off anomalies from systematic criminal strategies. Detecting these repeating structures is central to linking multiple cases to the same offender or network.

The indicators described in this chapter should be evaluated in combination rather than isolation. A single indicator might have a legitimate explanation, but multiple indicators across different categories – transaction patterns plus behavioral anomalies plus geographic factors – create a compelling pattern suggesting systematic laundering.

Notes

1 Peel chain is a money laundering technique in cryptocurrency transactions where large amounts of digital assets are moved through a series of many small transfers. At each step, a portion of the funds is "peeled off" to a new address, while the bulk continues moving through additional wallets.

2 A cryptocurrency mixer (also called a tumbler) is a service that takes in digital coins from many users, blends them together, and then sends back the same amount – minus a fee – to different wallet addresses. The purpose is to break the link between the sender and receiver, making it harder to trace the origin of the funds and often used as a money laundering method.

Bibliography

Akartuna, E. A., Johnson, S. D., & Thornton, A. (2024). Motivating a standardised approach to financial intelligence: A typological scoping review of money laundering methods and trends. *Journal of Experimental Criminology*. https://doi.org/10.1007/s11292-024-09623-y

Basel Institute on Governance. (2022). *Basel AML index 2022: 11th public edition – ranking money laundering and terrorist financing risks around the world*. https://index.baselgovernance.org

Financial Crimes Enforcement Network. (n.d.). *Money laundering prevention: A money services business guide*. U.S. Department of the Treasury. www.fincen.gov/sites/default/files/shared/prevention_guide.pdf

Patel, S., Kasztelnik, K., & Zelihic, M. (2023a). Global overview of modern financing typologies to mitigate financial risks in developed countries. *Socioeconomic Challenges*, *7*(2), 54–66. https://doi.org/10.21272/sec.7(2).54-66.2023

Patel, S., Kasztelnik, K., & Zelihic, M. (2023b). Modern offense typologies to reduce the risk of money laundering and increase financial stability and sustainability in the United States banking system. *Journal of Applied Business and Economics*, *25*(2). https://doi.org/10.33423/jabe.v25i2.6108

U.S. Department of Justice. (2025, May 15). *Additional 12 defendants charged in RICO conspiracy for over $263 million cryptocurrency thefts, money laundering, home break-ins*. U.S. Attorney's Office, District of Columbia. www.justice.gov/usao-dc/pr/additional-12-defendants-charged-rico-conspiracy-over-263-million-cryptocurrency-thefts

U.S. Department of the Treasury. (2022, February). *National money laundering risk assessment*. https://home.treasury.gov/system/files/136/2022-National-Money-Laundering-Risk-Assessment.pdf

U.S. Department of the Treasury. (2023). *Illicit finance risk assessment of decentralized finance*. https://home.treasury.gov/system/files/136/DeFi-Risk-Full-Review.pdf

U.S. Department of the Treasury. (2024). *Illicit finance risk assessment of non-fungible tokens*. https://home.treasury.gov/system/files/136/Illicit-Finance-Risk-Assessment-of-Non-Fungible-Tokens.pdf

44 Illegal Gambling

Introduction

Illegal gambling encompasses betting or gaming activities that operate outside the boundaries of the law. These can take the form of unlicensed betting operations, underground poker games, unlawful online platforms, or betting rings organized around sports or animal fighting. While offenders pursue financial gain, illegal gambling also provides a vehicle for money laundering, loan sharking, organized crime financing, and exploitation of vulnerable populations. Because many of these activities are repeated across locations, seasons, or specific events, illegal gambling often forms serial patterns that analysts and investigators can trace. Identifying recurring features such as the reuse of specific venues, betting platforms, communication methods, or enforcers can be critical to disrupting organized operations.

Illegal Gambling MO Variables

Objectives

- Financial Gain: The primary objective is usually to amass wealth through unregulated betting or gaming.
- Evasion of Regulation: Illegal gambling aims to bypass government restrictions, permits, and taxation.

Planning and Organization

- Concealment: Choosing discreet locations or online platforms that are hard to detect by law enforcement.
- Target Market: Identifying a community or group less likely to report the illegal activity.
- Funding: Money to start the operation is usually sourced illicitly, and transactions are often made in cash or cryptocurrencies to avoid detection.

Operational Framework

- Game Types: Selecting gambling formats that are easy to set up and manage, such as betting rings, card games, or unlicensed electronic gaming machines.
- Rules and Odds: Often skewed in favor of the house and are not transparently communicated to participants.
- Human Resources: Hiring or recruiting people who can be trusted, sometimes from within a criminal network.

DOI: 10.4324/9781003728733-47

Technology and Communication

- Online Platforms: Utilizing encrypted websites or apps for operation to avoid detection.
- Communication: Use of secure, untraceable methods of communication between organizers, intermediaries, and participants.

Security Measures

- Surveillance: Both to watch for law enforcement and to ensure that participants are not cheating.
- Armament: In some cases, organizers employ armed guards or enforcers.

Intermediaries

- Bookmakers: In sports betting, bookies set odds, take wagers, and handle payouts.
- Enforcers: Individuals employed to ensure payments are made and to deal with noncompliance forcefully if necessary.

Financial Transactions

- Money Laundering: Profits are often laundered through various channels to make them appear legitimate.
- Cash Transactions: Dominantly cash-based to avoid financial tracing.

Risk and Cheating

- Violence or Intimidation: Used to enforce rules and ensure payments.
- Collusion and Rigging: Instances where the outcomes are predetermined to benefit the organizers.

Aftermath

- Payouts and Collections: Often done in person and in cash to avoid a paper trail.
- Mobility: Locations or online sites may change frequently to evade law enforcement.

Illegal Gambling Pattern Examples

Illegal Gambling Operations

Pattern: Often set up in areas with weak enforcement or in communities where gambling is culturally accepted.
Example: Underground casinos may repeatedly operate in the same neighborhoods, especially where law enforcement has a limited presence or is easily bribed.

Bookmaking

Pattern: Illegal bookmakers might focus on specific sporting events or seasons.
Example: An illegal bookmaker may target college basketball season every year, leveraging local interest and knowledge of the sport.

Sports Betting Rings

Pattern: These rings might form around major sporting events or leagues.
Example: A criminal organization may regularly set up illegal betting rings during the World Cup, exploiting the global interest in the event.

Online Gambling

Pattern: Operates through websites or applications that might appear legitimate but are unregulated.
Example: A network of websites offer illegal online gambling on horse races, continually changing domains to evade detection.

Use of Slot Machines

Pattern: Illegally operated slot machines might be placed in certain establishments.
Example: Dive bars or convenience stores in a specific area repeatedly host illegal slot machines, targeting local patrons.

Lottery Fraud

Pattern: Consistent in targeting vulnerable populations, such as the elderly.
Example: Scammers might regularly prey on senior citizens with fake lottery schemes, contacting them via mail or phone.

Cheating at Gambling

Pattern: May occur in both legal and illegal gambling establishments, utilizing specific methods or devices.
Example: A group of cheaters travels to different casinos, employing the same card-counting strategy to beat blackjack tables.

Loan Sharking

Pattern: Often associated with gambling venues, providing high-interest loans to gamblers.
Example: Loan sharks consistently operate near illegal gambling dens, offering desperate gamblers short-term loans at exorbitant interest rates.

Money Laundering Through Gambling

Pattern: A method used by criminal organizations to clean illicit funds.
Example: A criminal syndicate repeatedly uses a network of illegal casinos to launder money from drug trafficking, exploiting the cash-intensive nature of the gambling business.

Gambling by Minors

Pattern: Minors are drawn to specific types of illegal gambling, like betting on video games.
Example: An online platform might target minors for gambling on video game competitions, knowing that young people are more engaged with esports.

Animal Fighting for Gambling Purposes

Pattern: May occur in rural or secluded areas where it can be hidden from law enforcement.
Example: Organizers might rotate illegal cockfighting or dogfighting events between various remote farms, attracting a regular and secretive gambling community.

Real-Life Case

In July 2025, federal prosecutors indicted nine individuals connected to a large-scale illegal gambling ring that generated more than $9.5 million in profits. The defendants operated multiple unlicensed game arcades at six locations across Missouri from 2022 to 2025. They promoted the games as lawful entertainment while secretly running them as gambling businesses, repeatedly using deceptive tactics to misrepresent winnings and conceal profits. The group allegedly laundered proceeds through various channels and attempted to hide their involvement by moving money through personal and business accounts. Charges in the 72-count indictment include conspiracy, illegal gambling operations, wire fraud, and money laundering. The investigation began at the local level and expanded into large, multi-jurisdictional case.[1]

Crime Pattern Scenario

Investigators in a mid-sized US city uncover a network of bars and convenience stores hosting illegal slot machines. The same operators move machines from location to location every six months to avoid detection. Profits are collected weekly in cash and laundered through a chain of small retail businesses controlled by the same group. Over time, analysts recognize that every venue is located within a five-mile radius of the same organizer's residence, suggesting a deliberate territorial pattern.

Exercises

1. Compare traditional illegal gambling (in-person betting, physical venues) with modern online operations. Create a chart showing five advantages criminals gain from going digital (anonymity, geographic reach, automated payments) and five new vulnerabilities they face (digital evidence, IP tracking, payment trails). Explain why many operations maintain both physical and digital presence despite the increased complexity.
2. Identify three locations in a typical community that might be vulnerable to hosting illegal gambling (bars with video poker, social clubs, convenience stores). For each, explain what makes it attractive to operators and what prevention measures could reduce vulnerability without harming legitimate business.

Critical Thinking Guidance

Illegal gambling functions as a criminal ecosystem, not a one-off crime. These enterprises rely on steady customers, fixed venues, and predictable cash flows, creating patterns that can be tracked over time. Look for temporal spikes around sporting seasons, paydays, or cultural events, and for geographic boundaries where operators avoid rival territories or police attention.

Follow the Money: gambling's cash-intensive nature produces suspicious deposits, spending that exceeds income, or structured transactions to avoid reporting thresholds. Social networks are equally revealing – trusted enforcers, runners, and facilitators often appear across multiple operations. Illegal gambling typically overlaps with loansharking, money laundering, extortion, and corruption, so evidence of one offense can expose the larger network. As operations increasingly mix online platforms with local cash collection, investigators need both digital forensics and knowledge of traditional organized crime. Careful documentation of repeated operators, methods, and venues is critical, since demonstrating organized, continuous activity elevates charges from minor gambling offenses to federal racketeering.

Note

1 U.S. Department of Justice, U.S. Attorney's Office, Western District of Missouri (2025, July 25).

Bibliography

American Gaming Association. (2022, November). *Sizing the illegal and unregulated gaming markets in the U.S.* www.americangaming.org/resources/sizing-the-illegal-and-unregulated-gaming-markets-in-the-u-s/

Banks, J. A., & Waugh, D. (2018). A taxonomy of gambling-related crime. *International Gambling Studies*, *19*(2), 339–357. https://doi.org/10.1080/14459795.2018.1554084

Green, S. P. (2012). Foreword: Symposium on vice and the criminal law. *Criminal Law and Philosophy*, *7*(1), 3–9. https://doi.org/10.1007/s11572-012-9178-5

Green, S. P. (2013). Vice crimes and preventive justice. *Criminal Law and Philosophy*, *9*(3), 561–576. https://doi.org/10.1007/s11572-013-9260-7

U.S. Department of Justice, U.S. Attorney's Office, Western District of Missouri. (2025, July 25). *Nine indicted in illegal gambling ring worth over $9.5 million* [Press release]. www.justice.gov/usao-wdmo/pr/nine-indicted-illegal-gambling-ring-worth-over-95-million

45 Illegal Pornography

Introduction

Illegal pornography encompasses a range of activities involving the creation, distribution, and possession of unlawful sexual content. This includes child sexual abuse material (CSAM), non-consensual pornography such as revenge porn, coerced or trafficked pornography, and obscene or prohibited content under certain jurisdictions. These crimes involve participants (offenders, distributors, consumers), technology (platforms, storage, encryption), and methods of dissemination. Patterns in these crimes can be identified through repeated offender tactics, technological choices, and victim targeting strategies. Because illegal pornography often crosses borders and involves repeat use of the same platforms or networks, identifying its recurring elements is critical in serial crime pattern identification.

Illegal Pornography MO Variables

Objectives

- Financial Gain: A common objective is financial profit through the sale or distribution of illegal material.
- Sexual Gratification: In some cases, the objective might be personal sexual gratification rather than financial gain.

Planning and Organization

- Sourcing Content: Obtaining illegal material through coercive tactics, surreptitious recording, or exploitation.
- Targeting Victims: Some perpetrators specifically target vulnerable individuals, such as minors or those unable to give consent.
- Secrecy and Anonymity: Perpetrators often use pseudonyms, VPNs, or other methods to conceal their identity.

Technical Framework

- Platform Selection: Opting for platforms where anonymity is possible, such as the dark web, peer-to-peer networks, or encrypted messaging apps.
- File Storage: Storing illegal content in encrypted or hidden folders.
- File Sharing: Using encrypted or otherwise secure methods for sharing files.

DOI: 10.4324/9781003728733-48

Distribution

- For-Profit Websites: Creating or utilizing websites that charge fees for access to illegal material.
- Free Sharing: Distributing illegal content freely in closed or secret online communities.
- Digital Currency: In for-profit cases, payments may be made using hard-to-trace digital currencies like Bitcoin.

Security Measures

- Encryption: Encrypting files and communications to avoid detection.
- Counter-Surveillance: Frequently changing usernames, email addresses, and other identifiers to evade law enforcement.

Intermediaries

- Content Creators: Those who produce the illegal material.
- Distributors: Those who disseminate the content to wider audiences.
- Consumers: Those who view or purchase the illegal material.

Legal Evasion

- Jurisdiction-Hopping: Using servers in jurisdictions where laws may be less stringent or law enforcement is lax.
- Fast Flux: Rapidly changing the DNS records associated with websites to prevent tracking.

Aftermath

- Data Wiping: Deleting or encrypting data if the perpetrators suspect that law enforcement is closing in.
- Asset Transfer: Moving financial assets to different accounts or digital wallets to evade asset forfeiture.

Illegal Pornography Pattern Examples

Child Sexual Abuse Material (CSAM)[1]
Pattern: Often spread through secretive online networks or dark web forums.
Example: A criminal group systematically distributes child pornography through encrypted channels, targeting specific user communities across multiple countries.

Non-Consensual Pornography (Revenge Porn)

Pattern: Can spread quickly through social media or specific websites that host such content.
Example: Individuals engaging in revenge porn might repeatedly target ex-partners, using specific platforms known for hosting non-consensual explicit content.

Obscene Material

Pattern: Occurs in jurisdictions with strict obscenity laws, targeting niche or fringe sexual content.

Example: A region with stringent obscenity laws sees recurring attempts to sell or distribute material deemed obscene, using hidden shops or online networks.

Sex Trafficking and Forced Pornography

Pattern: Often connected with human trafficking networks exploiting vulnerable individuals.
Example: A criminal organization systematically recruits women under false pretenses, forcing them into the production of pornographic material across various locations.

Illegal Distribution and Piracy

Pattern: Involves widespread distribution of copyrighted adult content without proper authorization.
Example: Websites or individuals consistently engage in the unauthorized distribution of paid adult content, creating a network of piracy that harms the legitimate industry.

Sexual Exploitation and Coercion in Pornography Production

Pattern: Can occur within certain sectors of the adult industry where oversight is lacking.
Example: Unscrupulous producers might repeatedly exploit aspiring performers through coercion or deception, creating patterns of abuse within certain niches of the industry.

Possession or Distribution in Restricted Areas

Pattern: Involves consistent attempts to distribute or possess pornographic material in jurisdictions where it is heavily restricted or banned.
Example: In a country with strict laws against pornography, smuggling rings might systematically import and distribute material through clandestine channels.

Use of Pornography for Extortion or Blackmail

Pattern: Can involve the use of explicit content to threaten or manipulate individuals.
Example: A criminal group may repeatedly target individuals through online relationships, coercing them into sharing explicit content, and then using that content for blackmail.

Production or Distribution Without Proper Consent

Pattern: Involves creating or sharing adult content without the proper consent of all parties involved.
Example: A pattern of deception might occur within a certain sector of the adult industry, where producers consistently fail to obtain proper consent from performers for distribution.

Emerging Crime Patterns

AI-Generated and Deepfake Pornography

A growing crime pattern involves the creation and distribution of synthetic explicit content using artificial intelligence. Offenders use deepfake technology to superimpose victims' faces (celebrities, minors, or private individuals) onto pornographic material without their consent.

These files are distributed in closed groups, darknet forums, or commercial websites. The anonymity of AI-generated content makes it harder to prosecute under traditional pornography laws, yet the harms are equivalent to non-consensual pornography. Look for indicators such as repeat offender use of specific deepfake generation tools, recurring file hashes, wallet addresses linked to payments, or clusters of fake videos targeting the same victim groups.

Revenge Porn

Revenge porn, also known as non-consensual intimate imagery, involves the distribution of private sexual images or videos without the subject's consent, often with the intent to humiliate, control, or extort the victim. The problem has grown rapidly due to widespread smartphone use, anonymous online platforms, and the ease of digital sharing. Increasingly, perpetrators use threats of exposure as leverage in sextortion schemes, demanding money, additional images, or compliance from victims. Recently, artificial intelligence has introduced new challenges through the creation of deepfake pornography, allowing offenders to fabricate explicit content featuring individuals who never consented or participated. Identify serial behaviors in repeated use of the same online platforms or forums, the recurrence of usernames or digital wallets, and similarities in file formats, watermarks, or metadata across incidents.

Crime Pattern Scenario

A darknet forum specializing in child sexual abuse material (CSAM) repeatedly resurfaces under different names but is operated by the same administrators. Although domains change every few months, investigators note identical file-sharing protocols, forum rules, and cryptocurrency wallet addresses for payments. By tracking these recurring variables, law enforcement is able to link separate cases across multiple countries to the same organized crime group.

Exercises

1. Consider how technology choices (such as use of encryption, blockchain payments, or darknet forums) can form identifiable serial patterns in illegal pornography cases. Research this subject and develop a list of at least three indicators that investigators could track over time to link cases together.
2. Create a framework for how investigators could coordinate when illegal content is produced in one country, hosted in another, and accessed in a third. Identify three legal challenges, three technical challenges, and three ways international cooperation could be improved. Explain why jurisdictional complexity particularly benefits these criminal operations.

Critical Thinking Guidance

Illegal pornography crimes frequently exhibit serial patterns: offenders reuse networks, platforms, payment methods, or tactics to produce and distribute material. Pay attention to recurring features, such as the same online communities, identical usernames across platforms, repeat payment routes, or reappearances of unique file signatures. Recognizing these repeating elements is vital for linking cases across jurisdictions, especially since these crimes often involve transnational actors and technology.

Note

1 This term is now preferred internationally over "child pornography."

Bibliography

Federal Bureau of Investigation. (2023, June 5). *Malicious actors manipulating photos and videos to create explicit content and sextortion schemes* [Public service announcement]. Internet Crime Complaint Center (IC3). www.ic3.gov/PSA/2023/psa230605

Federal Bureau of Investigation. (2024, January 23). *Sextortion: A growing threat targeting minors* [News article]. FBI Memphis Field Office. www.fbi.gov/contact-us/field-offices/nashville/news/sextortion-a-growing-threat-targeting-minors

National Association of Attorneys General. (2021, November 16). An update on the legal landscape of revenge porn. *Attorney General Journal*. www.naag.org/attorney-general-journal/an-update-on-the-legal-landscape-of-revenge-porn/

Reuters. (2025, March 18). Europol warns AI-driven crime threats, including synthetic pornography. *Reuters*. www.reuters.com/world/europe/europol-warns-ai-driven-crime-threats-2025-03-18/

U.S. Department of Justice. (2023, June). *Child sexual abuse material*. U.S. Department of Justice. www.justice.gov/d9/2023-06/child_sexual_abuse_material_2.pdf

Wortley, R., & Smallbone, S. (2006). *Child pornography on the Internet* (Problem-Specific Guide Series No. 41, Problem-Oriented Guides for Police Series). Office of Community Oriented Policing Services, U.S. Department of Justice. https://popcenter.asu.edu/content/child-pornography--0

46 Prostitution

Introduction

Prostitution, defined as the exchange of sexual activity for money or goods, has long been a recurring element in crime patterns worldwide. It varies in scale and structure, ranging from street-level survival sex work to highly organized brothels or online networks. Crime pattern variables include the type of setting, recruitment methods, payment systems, intermediaries, and the degree of organization, which can involve pimps, madams, traffickers, and facilitators. Because prostitution can intersect with related crimes such as drug trafficking, human trafficking, and money laundering, identifying repeat variables and serial patterns is crucial for law enforcement. Understanding these recurring elements can help distinguish between isolated incidents and organized or serial prostitution networks.

Prostitution MO Variables

Objectives

- Financial Gain: The primary objective is usually economic benefit, either for the individual prostitute, the pimp, or the entire network involved.
- Survival: In some cases, particularly with street-level prostitution, the objective is immediate financial relief to cover basic necessities.

Planning and Organization

- Recruitment: Some prostitutes are recruited, while others enter the profession independently. Recruitment can be through coercion, deception, or voluntary.
- Setting: The environment may vary from public spaces like streets (street-level prostitution) to more organized establishments such as brothels or via online platforms.
- Client Acquisition: This could be through word of mouth, online advertising, or through a pimp or madam.

Technical Framework

- Communication: Various communication channels like cell phones, social media, or encrypted messaging apps may be used for client interactions and appointments.
- Payment Methods: Cash is most common, though digital payment methods are increasingly used for discretion.

DOI: 10.4324/9781003728733-49

Execution

- Service Provision: Sexual services are usually provided in a predetermined location which could be a motel, the client's residence, or a location set by the prostitute or pimp.
- Security Measures: Some prostitutes have personal security measures like carrying a weapon or having someone nearby for protection.
- Time Frame: The duration of the service can vary and may be agreed upon beforehand.

Intermediaries

- Pimps/Madams: Often involved in organizing the prostitution, ensuring payment, and providing "protection."
- Clients: Those who pay for the services.
- Brothel Owners: In areas where brothels are legal or semi-legal, they act as facilitators.
- Online Platforms: Websites or apps that may unknowingly (or knowingly, in some cases) facilitate the setting of appointments.

Legal Evasion

- Loopholes: Exploiting legal gray areas, like advertising "escort services" to bypass prostitution laws.
- Code Words: Using coded language or signals to avoid open solicitation that could attract law enforcement.
- Jurisdiction-Hopping: Moving locations to evade police or operate in areas with laxer laws.

Aftermath

- Payment Division: If pimps or madams are involved, earnings are usually divided according to pre-agreed terms.
- Customer Retention: In some cases, efforts are made to keep clients returning through various means such as loyalty schemes or special offers.

Prostitution Pattern Examples

Street Prostitution

Pattern: Often concentrated in specific areas known for solicitation.
Example: Certain streets or intersections in a city may become known hotspots for street prostitution, particularly during late-night hours.

Brothel-Based Prostitution

Pattern: Operates out of fixed locations, sometimes disguised as legitimate businesses.
Example: A series of massage parlors within a city might covertly offer sexual services, with new establishments regularly opening as others are shut down by law enforcement.

Escort Services

Pattern: Often utilizes online advertising and operates in various locations.
Example: Escort services might advertise on specific websites or social media platforms, shifting locations to avoid detection and regularly updating contact information.

Child Prostitution

Pattern: Occurs in areas where minors are particularly vulnerable to exploitation.
Example: Criminal networks may target homeless or runaway youths in certain urban areas, recruiting them into prostitution through coercion or manipulation.

Human Trafficking for Prostitution

Pattern: Involves the recruitment and transportation of individuals across borders or within countries.
Example: A trafficking ring might systematically bring women from impoverished regions to urban centers, forcing them into prostitution through debt bondage or threats.

Drug-Dependent Prostitution

Pattern: Often found in areas with high drug activity and addiction rates.
Example: Individuals struggling with addiction might engage in prostitution in neighborhoods near drug dealers, with repeat patterns of exchanging sex for substances.

Tourism-Related Prostitution

Pattern: Concentrated in tourist areas, resorts, or entertainment districts.
Example: Certain beach resorts or nightlife districts might become hubs for prostitution catering to tourists, with seasonal fluctuations corresponding to tourism peaks.

Online Prostitution and Cybersex Trafficking

Pattern: Utilizes digital platforms to connect buyers and sellers.
Example: Online forums or websites specializing in adult services might host systematic advertising for prostitutes, continually shifting to new platforms as old ones are policed.

LGBTQ+ Specific Prostitution

Pattern: May occur within specific venues or online spaces catering to LGBTQ+ clientele.
Example: Certain clubs or online communities may become known spaces where LGBTQ+ individuals engage in or seek prostitution, following patterns of social networking within the community.

Survival Sex Work

Pattern: Often involves marginalized individuals engaging in sex work for basic needs.
Example: Homeless or economically disadvantaged individuals might repeatedly engage in prostitution in certain areas, driven by urgent needs for shelter or food.

Emerging Crime Pattern: Online Prostitution via Digital Platforms

A rapidly evolving trend in prostitution is its migration to digital platforms, where social media, messaging apps, and online advertisements increasingly facilitate discreet commercial sex work across geographic boundaries. This shift complicates enforcement, as platforms operate globally and take advantage of jurisdictional gaps, while legislation and regulation struggle to keep pace. Prostitution is moving away from visible street-level solicitation toward dispersed, often anonymous online networks, creating significant challenges in detection and investigation. It is possible to identify serial prostitution networks by tracking recurring online variables such as domain names, advertising language, location references, and encrypted communication patterns. These indicators are becoming critical for adaptation to the changing dynamics of sexual exploitation in the digital era.

Crime Pattern Scenario

A metropolitan police department notices repeated advertisements on a well-known escort website featuring similar wording, photographs, and contact numbers. Over several months, sting operations reveal that the ads lead back to the same network of individuals running multiple "massage parlors" across the city. The network rotates women between locations every few weeks to avoid detection, uses prepaid cell phones and encrypted messaging apps, and launders proceeds through shell businesses. These repeated operational methods allow investigators to link what initially appeared to be separate cases into a coordinated prostitution ring.

Exercises

1. Select two different jurisdictions (e.g., a US state and a European country). Summarize in a one-page brief how their prostitution laws differ and how those differences might affect cross-border investigations. Highlight at least one challenge for each jurisdiction in pursuing online prostitution cases.
2. Write a short essay explaining how prostitution networks can be viewed as a system: include key actors (offenders, intermediaries, consumers), feedback loops (demand, enforcement), and points where intervention might disrupt the pattern.

Critical Thinking Guidance

When looking for links in prostitution incidents, consider whether recruitment methods, communication styles, or payment channels are consistent across cases. Be alert to overlaps with other crimes, such as drugs or human trafficking, that may strengthen linkage analysis. Note that prostitution crime patterns are adaptive: when one avenue is disrupted, offenders often shift to new platforms, jurisdictions, or tactics. Asking whether recurring details are coincidental or indicative of a structured system helps refine investigative priorities and resource allocation.

When assessing prostitution-related crime patterns, go beyond cataloguing incidents to examine the systemic interactions that sustain them. Consider prostitution networks as dynamic systems: multiple actors (offenders, intermediaries, clients, victims) create feedback loops – demand drives recruitment, recruitment fuels profits, profits finance evasion tactics – which in turn shape law enforcement responses.

Legal and Policy Context

Compare how different jurisdictions define and regulate prostitution and trafficking. For example, US federal statutes such as the Trafficking Victims Protection Act (18 U.S.C. § 1591) and international frameworks like the UN Palermo Protocol frame exploitation differently. Examine how these differences complicate cross-border investigations or online enforcement.

Investigative Challenges and Tools

Evaluate which modus operandi indicators – such as recurring advertising language, encrypted messaging handles, or financial transactions through cryptocurrency – are most difficult to track. Determine which investigative techniques (open-source intelligence, financial analysis, undercover operations) are best suited to link cases across platforms or jurisdictions.

Victim-Centered Perspective

While mapping and linking crime patterns, remember that individuals involved may be victims of coercion or trafficking. Explore how law enforcement and service agencies can balance evidence-gathering with safeguarding vulnerable individuals.

Systems-Disruption Strategies

Identify leverage points that can disrupt the pattern – such as targeting digital payment intermediaries, providing exit services for exploited persons, or strengthening cross-border cooperation. Reflect on how interventions at different points in the system might change offender behavior or reduce harm.

Bibliography

Scott, M. S., & Dedel, K. (2006). *Street prostitution* (Problem-Specific Guide Series No. 2, Problem-Oriented Guides for Police Series). Office of Community Oriented Policing Services, U.S. Department of Justice. https://popcenter.asu.edu/sites/default/files/street_prostitution_2nd_ed.pdf

United Nations Office on Drugs and Crime. (2024). *Global report on trafficking in persons 2024*. www.unodc.org/documents/data-and-analysis/glotip/2024/GLOTIP2024_BOOK.pdf

U.S. Government Accountability Office. (2021). *Sex trafficking: Online platforms and federal prosecutions* (GAO-21-385). www.gao.gov/products/gao-21-385

47 Quality of Life Crimes

Introduction

Quality of life crimes – also called nuisance crimes, disorder offenses, or petty crimes – are typically minor infractions that disrupt community order and public well-being. Examples include public intoxication, loitering, vandalism, graffiti, noise violations, and littering. While often classified as low-level offenses, their cumulative impact can erode trust in public safety, lower neighborhood morale, and contribute to the "broken windows" effect, where visible disorder may encourage more serious crimes. Analysts and officers should recognize that while individual quality-of-life crimes may seem isolated, recurring nuisance patterns in specific locations or involving repeat offenders can signal deeper social or criminal issues.

Quality of Life Crimes MO Variables

Objectives

- Motive: The motives behind quality-of-life crimes can be varied, including thrill-seeking, boredom, revenge, or personal benefit.

Planning and Target Selection

- Area Selection: Often occurs in public spaces like parks, sidewalks, or public transportation systems where enforcement is perceived to be lax.
- Timing: Usually carried out during hours of low foot traffic or when law enforcement presence is minimal, although some crimes like loitering can occur in plain sight.

Tools and Equipment

- Tools: Varies by crime. For graffiti, it would be spray paint or markers; for public intoxication, it might involve alcohol or drugs.

Execution

- Method of Commission: Usually simple and opportunistic, requiring minimal planning or skill. Acts are often quick to minimize the chance of being caught.
- Visibility: Varies significantly. Crimes like loitering or public intoxication are overt, whereas graffiti or vandalism might be done covertly.

DOI: 10.4324/9781003728733-50

Evasion

- Escape Plan: Often not sophisticated due to the spontaneous nature of the crime. May involve simply walking away from the scene.
- Evidence Elimination: Limited, as the crimes are often opportunistic and not premeditated. However, some might wear disguises or use aliases.

Aftermath

- Disposition: Perpetrators often don't monitor the aftermath or law enforcement's response, unlike in more serious crimes.
- Frequency: Quality of life crimes often have high rates of recidivism, and offenders may commit the same types of crimes repeatedly.

Adaptation and Variation

- MO Evolution: Typically, there is little evolution in the MO for quality of life crimes unless the individual escalates to more severe criminal activities.
- Accomplices: Usually committed alone, but there can be instances where a small group engages in the activity together, such as in group vandalism or loitering.

Quality of Life Crime Pattern Examples

Vandalism

Pattern: Vandalism may occur in neglected or abandoned areas where there's a lack of oversight.
Example: A specific neighborhood with many vacant buildings might become a hotspot for graffiti and broken windows.

Public Intoxication

Pattern: Often happens around bars, clubs, or entertainment districts.
Example: A street with several bars might see repeated incidents of public intoxication, especially on weekends.

Loitering

Pattern: Common in areas lacking recreational spaces or where youths gather.
Example: Teens may regularly gather at a specific mall or public area, leading to repeated loitering complaints.

Panhandling

Pattern: Tends to occur near shopping centers, tourist areas, or traffic intersections.
Example: Certain busy intersections may become known for panhandling, with individuals returning daily to the same spots.

Graffiti

Pattern: Often associated with specific urban areas or along public transportation routes.
Example: Train or subway stations might become consistent targets for graffiti artists.

Pattern: Occurs in neglected or isolated urban areas, often correlated with gang activity.
Example: Gang-related graffiti may appear systematically in a neighborhood, marking territory and creating tensions among rival groups.

Noise Violations

Pattern: More common in densely populated areas or near entertainment venues.
Example: A street with several nightclubs may experience ongoing noise complaints during late-night hours.

Littering

Pattern: Can be found around public parks, schools, or fast-food establishments.
Example: A park lacking proper trash disposal facilities might become a consistent site for littering.

Public Urination

Pattern: Occurs in areas with limited public restrooms, often near bars or nightlife districts.
Example: An alleyway near a cluster of bars might become a regular spot for public urination, especially during late hours.

Illegal Street Vending

Pattern: Often occurs in busy pedestrian areas or near public transportation hubs.
Example: The area around a major subway station might see regular illegal street vending activities.

Unleashed Dogs

Pattern: More common in urban parks or neighborhoods with lax enforcement of leash laws.
Example: A particular park known for its lax enforcement might become a gathering spot for dog owners who let their dogs off-leash.

Trespassing

Pattern: Tends to happen in areas with vacant properties or construction sites.
Example: A construction site that is known to be unguarded at night might become a regular target for trespassing.
Pattern: Often happens in vacant buildings or properties with low security.
Example: A series of trespassing incidents might occur in abandoned buildings where homeless individuals seek shelter during cold months.

Aggressive Driving

Pattern: May be more prevalent on certain roads known for speeding or during specific traffic hours.
Example: A particular highway stretch without proper speed enforcement might be known for consistent aggressive driving incidents.

Quality-of-Life Crime Indicators Checklist

Location Indicators

Same street corner, transit stop, or park repeatedly involved
Offenses clustering around vacant buildings, alleys, or entertainment districts
Public spaces with low surveillance or weak enforcement regularly targeted

Time Indicators

Repeated activity at the same time of day or week (weekend nights for intoxication, early morning for graffiti)
Seasonal or event-driven spikes (holidays, tourist seasons, festivals)
Incidents occurring in law enforcement coverage gaps (late night, shift change)

Offender Behavior Indicators

Repetition of method (same graffiti style, same panhandling pitch, same loitering behavior)
Consistent tools or props (spray paint colors, shopping carts for street vending, musical instruments for busking without permit)
Group behavior (same individuals or crews appearing together)

Victim/Community Impact Indicators

Same businesses or residents repeatedly reporting nuisance
Fear or avoidance behavior by the public (commuters changing routes, businesses boarding windows)
Growing community complaints to city services or police

Escalation/Adaptation Indicators

Graffiti shifting from stylized tags to gang symbols
Loitering evolving into trespassing or vandalism
Public intoxication linked to disorderly conduct, assaults, or petty theft
Panhandling escalating from passive requests to aggressive demands

Crime Pattern Scenario

Surveillance and community reports show tags (graffiti) from the same group of individuals appearing on train cars, station walls, and surrounding businesses every weekend. The consistency of the tagging style and geographic clustering suggests an identifiable group is responsible. Over time, vandalism escalates to territorial markings associated with gang presence, raising concerns about violent crime emerging in the same area. Recognizing this quality-of-life pattern early enables police to implement targeted interventions, such as increased patrols, rapid removal of graffiti, and community engagement.

Exercises

1. Select local newspaper articles or online news stories about nuisance or disorder offences. Categories the incidents by type (graffiti, noise violations, panhandling, etc.) and by setting

(parks, transit hubs, nightlife districts). Identify any recurring themes or public concerns and discuss how media coverage might influence residents' fear of crime or policy responses.

2. Take a walk in a public space you know well – a neighborhood street, park, or shopping district. Record the date, time, and any signs of nuisance crime: graffiti tags, litter accumulation, loitering groups, loud noise, or public drinking. Look for patterns: repeated symbols in graffiti, recurring trash build-ups in the same corner, or similar times when noise is loudest. Summarize what you observe and consider how these repeated minor infractions might influence residents' sense of safety and neighborhood cohesion.

Critical Thinking Guidance

Detecting serial patterns in quality-of-life crimes requires moving beyond the assumption that these offences are random or inconsequential. Analysts and officers should first consider clustering in time and space. Repeated incidents in the same neighborhood, transit hub, or entertainment district, especially if they occur at predictable hours such as weekend nights, can reveal that the disorder is not merely sporadic but follows a discernible pattern. Mapping incidents and comparing them with environmental features such as vacant buildings or nightlife venues helps to identify areas where minor disorder may repeatedly surface.

A second consideration is offender consistency. Graffiti tags that share distinctive lettering, panhandlers using the same pitch, or loitering groups that appear at the same corner each evening can point to a stable set of individuals or crews responsible for recurring nuisance behavior. Recognizing these repeated tactics and signatures allows law enforcement to link incidents that might otherwise appear isolated.

It is equally important to evaluate the potential for escalation. Minor crimes such as graffiti or trespassing can act as early indicators of territorial disputes, gang activity, or the opening stages of more serious criminal markets. Early recognition of these signals enables agencies to intervene before the problems harden into entrenched crime patterns.

Finally, weigh the community's perception and response. Even when each offense is low-level, persistent disorder can create a fear of crime or reduce public confidence in law enforcement. Understanding how residents and businesses react, whether by avoiding certain areas or making repeated complaints, provides essential context for prioritizing resources and shaping prevention strategies.

Bibliography

Laing, C. (2010). *Aggressive driving* (Problem-Specific Guide Series No. 61, Problem-Oriented Guides for Police Series). Office of Community Oriented Policing Services, U.S. Department of Justice. https://popcenter.asu.edu/content/aggressive-driving-0

Scott, M. S. (2002). *Panhandling* (Problem-Specific Guide Series No. 13, Problem-Oriented Guides for Police Series). Office of Community Oriented Policing Services, U.S. Department of Justice. https://popcenter.asu.edu/content/panhandling-0

Weisel, D. M. (2002). *Graffiti* (Problem-Specific Guide Series No. 9, Problem-Oriented Guides for Police Series). Office of Community Oriented Policing Services, U.S. Department of Justice. https://popcenter.asu.edu/content/graffiti-0

Wilson, J. Q., & Kelling, G. L. (1982, March 1). Broken windows: The police and neighborhood safety. *The Atlantic*, *249*(3), 29–38. www.theatlantic.com/magazine/archive/1982/03/broken-windows/304465/

48 Drug and Alcohol Crimes

Introduction

When focusing on drug and alcohol crimes that exclude trafficking, the types of offenses can range from possession and use to driving under the influence (DUI), public intoxication, and underage drinking.

Drug and alcohol crimes that exclude trafficking generally involve possession, personal use, impaired driving, and behavior in public spaces under the influence of substances. Unlike trafficking, which is often organized and profit-driven, these crimes tend to be opportunistic, situational, and highly influenced by social environments. Patterns emerge in the timing (weekends, holidays), the places (bars, festivals, neighborhoods with open-air drug use), and the offender behaviors (concealment of substances, impaired operation of vehicles). Because these crimes frequently overlap with other offenses (such as assaults near bars or property crimes by drug-dependent offenders) recognizing their variables is helpful for crime analysts, law enforcement officers, and policymakers.

Drugs and Alcohol Crimes MO Variables

Objectives

- Motive: Personal use or recreation, sometimes leading to intoxicated behavior or driving while impaired.

Planning and Target Selection

- Area Selection: Offenses like DUI or public intoxication might not involve planning and are opportunistic, occurring in any area where the individual happens to be. Possession may involve specific locations known for drug availability.
- Timing: DUI and public intoxication are often related to specific times like nights or weekends but can occur at any time.

Tools and Equipment

- Tools: Possession usually involves small containers or baggies for drugs, flasks or portable containers for alcohol. DUI involves a vehicle.

DOI: 10.4324/9781003728733-51

Execution/Method of Commission

- Possession: Concealment is common, whether in a vehicle, on the person, or in a residence.
- DUI: The person drives a vehicle despite being impaired, risking detection by erratic driving.
- Public Intoxication: The individual may behave erratically or disruptively in a public space, attracting attention.
- Consumption Methods: Inhalation, injection, or oral consumption for drugs; drinking for alcohol.

Evasion

- Escape Plan: Often unplanned. In the case of DUI, individuals might try to evade capture by speeding or taking alternate routes.
- Concealment Tactics: For possession, drugs may be hidden in various parts of a vehicle or on the person.

Aftermath

- Disposition: In cases like DUI or public intoxication, there may be immediate legal consequences such as arrest. For possession, the aftermath might involve consumption or sharing of the substances.
- Evidence Disposal: After consumption, evidence like drug paraphernalia or empty alcohol containers might be discarded to avoid detection.

Adaptation and Variation

- MO Evolution: Offenders might adapt methods of concealment or choose different locations for possession or use based on perceived law enforcement patterns.
- Accomplices: Often acts alone but may involve peers or friends, particularly in the context of social drinking or drug use.

Drug Crimes Pattern Examples

Drug Possession

Pattern: May be more prevalent in certain neighborhoods or demographic groups.
Example: Patterns of marijuana possession arrests might align with targeted law enforcement practices in specific urban communities.

Prescription Drug Fraud

Pattern: Illegally obtaining prescription drugs like opioids often involves recurring tactics.
Example: Individuals may systematically doctor-shop, visiting multiple physicians to obtain prescriptions for controlled substances.

Drug Paraphernalia Sales

Pattern: Sales of items related to drug consumption can occur in particular locations or online.
Example: Certain head shops or online platforms may repeatedly engage in selling paraphernalia intended for illegal drug use.

Drug Use and Driving

Pattern: DUI arrests may show correlations with particular areas, times, or events.
Example: Patterns of drug-related DUIs may spike near music festivals or in nightlife districts on weekends.

Alcohol Crimes Pattern Examples

Underage Alcohol Sales and Possession

Pattern: Might occur in specific venues or among particular youth communities.
Example: Certain stores or bars might repeatedly sell alcohol to minors, while specific schools or neighborhoods may see recurrent underage drinking incidents.

Illegal Alcohol Production (Moonshining)

Pattern: Can be found in regions where homemade alcohol production has cultural roots.
Example: Moonshine production might follow historical patterns in rural areas, with specific families or networks engaged in the practice.

Public Intoxication

Pattern: Often concentrated around nightlife areas, festivals, or events.
Example: Urban entertainment districts might see repeated patterns of public intoxication arrests, particularly on weekends or holidays.

Selling Alcohol Without a License

Pattern: May occur where there is demand but limited legal access to alcohol.
Example: Pop-up venues or speakeasies might systematically engage in unlicensed alcohol sales in a specific city or region.

Driving Under the Influence (DUI)

Pattern: DUI arrests may align with particular routes, times, or demographics.
Example: Certain roads near bars or clubs may become hotspots for DUI checkpoints and arrests, particularly late at night.

Alcohol Smuggling and Tax Evasion

Pattern: Often involves established routes and methods to circumvent taxes or regulations.
Example: A network might systematically smuggle alcohol from lower-tax jurisdictions to higher-tax areas, using consistent routes and techniques.

Emerging Crime Pattern: Cannabis-Impaired Driving Post-Legalization

As more US states and other countries legalize recreational cannabis, law enforcement agencies are reporting an increase in drug-impaired driving cases. Unlike alcohol, which can be tested quickly with a breathalyzer, cannabis impairment is harder to measure because THC remains in the body long after intoxication has worn off. This complicates enforcement and prosecution.

Pattern Indicators

DUI arrests increasingly involving poly-drug use (alcohol + cannabis).

Higher crash risks around dispensaries and nightlife districts.

Arrest clusters on weekends and holidays, similar to alcohol-related DUIs.

Recurring difficulties in proving impairment due to lack of standardized roadside THC testing.

Crime Pattern Scenario

A college town police department notes a recurring pattern of DUI arrests clustered around the same four bars within a two-mile stretch. Most arrests occur between midnight and 2 a.m. on Thursdays and Saturdays, following drink specials targeted at students. Several offenders are repeat arrestees, and many use the same two roadways leading back to campus. By examining these indicators – repeat locations, consistent time frames, and offender demographics – the department identifies an emerging hot spot for impaired driving. Collaboration with bar owners and targeted DUI checkpoints on the two main roads results in a measurable reduction in arrests and related accidents over the following semester.

Exercises

1. Open Google (or another search engine). Type in: "DUI arrests [your city/state]" or "public intoxication arrests [your city/state]." Read five recent news articles. Write down: where the incidents happened, when they occurred (time of day/weekend/holiday), any repeated patterns you notice (such as always near bars, late at night).
2. Examine local news or open-source reports of assaults or property crimes near bars or nightlife districts. Identify how often intoxication or drug use is mentioned as a contributing factor. Summarize how substance-related behavior might be a driver of these secondary crimes and propose one policing or community strategy to address the overlap.

Critical Thinking Guidance

Drug and alcohol crimes can appear spontaneous or victimless, yet systematic analysis reveals recurring patterns that are crucial for effective intervention. Time and place are key indicators: incidents often cluster around nightlife districts, music festivals, or university campuses, and arrests commonly rise on weekends or holidays. Recognizing these temporal and spatial trends helps agencies predict when and where enforcement or prevention resources will be most effective.

Equally important is the substance-specific dimension. Different drugs and alcohol-related behaviors generate distinct demographic and social patterns. Opioid possession, cannabis-impaired driving, and binge drinking near college campuses each present unique enforcement and public health challenges. Consider how these differences influence both the type of offence and the appropriate prevention strategies.

Drug and alcohol offences often create linkages to other crimes. Intoxication increases the risk of assaults, disorderly conduct, and property crimes, especially in nightlife areas. By tracking these connections, analysts can identify hotspots where substance abuse and other offences intersect, allowing for comprehensive problem-solving rather than isolated enforcement.

Bibliography

Harocopos, A., & Hough, M. (2005). *Drug dealing in open-air markets* (Problem-Specific Guide Series No. 31, Problem-Oriented Guides for Police Series). Office of Community Oriented Policing Services, U.S. Department of Justice. https://popcenter.asu.edu/content/drug-dealing-open-air-markets-0

Sampson, R. (2001). *Drug dealing in privately owned apartment complexes* (Problem-Specific Guide Series No. 4, Problem-Oriented Guides for Police Series). Office of Community Oriented Policing Services, U.S. Department of Justice. https://popcenter.asu.edu/content/drug-dealing-privately-owned-apartment-complexes

Scott, M. S., & Dedel, K. (2006). *Assaults in and around bars* (2nd ed., Problem-Specific Guide Series No. 1, Problem-Oriented Guides for Police Series). Office of Community Oriented Policing Services, U.S. Department of Justice. https://popcenter.asu.edu/content/assaults-and-around-bars-2nd-ed

Scott, M. S., Emerson, N. J., Antonacci, L. B., & Plant, J. B. (2006). *Drunk driving* (Problem-Specific Guide Series No. 36, Problem-Oriented Guides for Police Series). Office of Community Oriented Policing Services, U.S. Department of Justice. https://popcenter.asu.edu/sites/default/files/problems/PDFs/drunk-driving.pdf

49 Cybercrime

Introduction

Cybercrime refers to criminal activities carried out using computers, networks, or the internet. Unlike many traditional crimes, cybercrime can occur across borders instantly, targeting individuals, businesses, organizations, and governments simultaneously. These crimes include hacking, unauthorized access to systems, identity theft, ransomware attacks, fraud, and the distribution of malicious software. Because offenders can mask their identities, use anonymizing[1] tools, and operate globally, identifying patterns in cybercrime requires specialized analysis. Linking cases often depends on consistent technical indicators, such as repeated IP[2] ranges, malware signatures,[3] attack vectors,[4] or even unique social engineering scripts reused across campaigns. Integrating digital forensics, financial intelligence, and victim reporting assists in determining whether incidents are isolated or part of a larger series.

Scope and Boundaries of Cybercrime

Cybercrime can be divided into two broad categories that help clarify how these offences fit into wider crime pattern identification. Cyber-dependent crimes are offences that exist only because of computers, networks, or the internet – activities such as ransomware attacks, botnet operations, and distributed-denial-of-service (DDoS) assaults that cannot occur without digital infrastructure. In contrast, cyber-enabled crimes are traditional offences that technology has expanded or intensified, including fraud, extortion, identity theft, and elements of human trafficking conducted through online platforms. Recognizing this distinction helps analysts and law-enforcement practitioners classify incidents more accurately and understand how cybercrime variables correspond to those found in conventional crime patterns.

Cybercrime MO Variables

Motivation and Objectives

- Financial Gain: Many cybercrimes are motivated by the potential for monetary profit through various means such as fraud, theft, and ransom.
- Intellectual Property Theft: Stealing proprietary information, patents, or trade secrets.
- Espionage: Obtaining sensitive information for strategic, political, or military advantage.

DOI: 10.4324/9781003728733-52

Planning and Reconnaissance

- Vulnerability Assessment: Conducting a vulnerability scan of the target system to find weaknesses to exploit.
- Social Engineering: Gathering information through deceptive interpersonal tactics, like phishing.
- Technical Research: Studying the target's software, network configurations, and cybersecurity measures.

Tools and Techniques

- Malware: Utilizing malicious software like viruses, worms, and Trojans to gain unauthorized access or damage systems.
- DDoS Attacks: Overwhelming systems with traffic to render them inoperative.
- Exploit Kits: Pre-packaged toolkits designed to perform tasks like finding and exploiting vulnerabilities.

Execution and Attack Vectors

- Phishing Emails: Sending deceptive emails to trick recipients into revealing sensitive information or installing malware. Example: May ask a person to confirm their account and thus fraudulently gain that information.
- Credential Stuffing: Using stolen usernames and passwords to gain unauthorized access to accounts.
- Zero-Day Exploits: Leveraging previously unknown vulnerabilities before they are patched by software developers.

Data Exfiltration and Usage

- Data Harvesting: Collecting valuable data, such as credit card numbers or personal identification.
- Ransomware: Encrypting a victim's data and demanding payment for its release.
- Data Sale: Selling stolen data on the dark web or to other criminals.

Intermediaries and Facilitators

- Script Kiddies: Less skilled individuals who use pre-written software or scripts to conduct attacks.
- Hacker Groups: Organized groups specializing in sophisticated attacks.
- Insider Threats: Employees or affiliates with inside information aiding in or conducting the cybercrime.

Evasion Techniques

- IP Spoofing: Masking the true origin of the attacking system by using a false IP address.
- Encryption and Tunneling: Using encrypted channels to avoid detection while transmitting data.
- Use of Proxy Servers and VPNs: Routing traffic through multiple points to obscure origin and destination.

Post-Attack Activities

- Data Laundering: Making stolen data harder to trace back to the cybercrime activity.
- Asset Liquidation: Converting stolen assets into cash or other forms through cryptocurrencies or other laundering techniques.
- Cover-Up: Deleting logs, using misdirection tactics, or employing other methods to erase traces of the cybercrime.

Cybercrime Example Methods

Phishing

Email Phishing: Sending fraudulent emails that appear to be from legitimate sources, tricking recipients into providing sensitive information or clicking on malicious links.

Spear Phishing: Customizing phishing attempts to target specific individuals or organizations by using personalized information.

Smishing: Sending deceptive text messages to trick recipients into revealing personal information or clicking on malicious links.

Vishing: Making phone calls and impersonating trusted entities to deceive individuals into providing sensitive information.

Malware

Viruses: Infecting computers or systems by attaching malicious code to legitimate files or programs.

Trojans: Disguising malware as legitimate software to gain unauthorized access, steal information, or enable other malicious activities.

Ransomware: Encrypting files or locking computer systems until a ransom is paid to the attacker.

Spyware: Collecting information without the user's consent, including keystrokes, browsing habits, or personal data.

Adware: Displaying unwanted advertisements or redirecting users to malicious websites.

Botnets: Taking control of a network of compromised computers or devices to carry out coordinated attacks or distribute malware.

Hacking

Password Cracking: Guessing or using automated tools to discover passwords and gain unauthorized access to systems or accounts.

SQL Injection: Exploiting vulnerabilities in web applications to manipulate or extract data from databases.

Remote Code Execution: Exploiting vulnerabilities to execute malicious code on a target system or network.

Man-in-the-Middle (MITM) attacks: Intercepting communications between two parties to eavesdrop, alter, or steal information.

Cross-Site Scripting (XSS): Injecting malicious scripts into web pages or trusted applications, allowing the attacker to steal information or manipulate content.

Identity Theft

Credential Theft: Obtaining usernames, passwords, or other credentials through various means, such as keyloggers, social engineering, or data breaches.

Impersonation: Posing as someone else, such as a trusted individual or organization, to deceive others or gain unauthorized access.

Synthetic Identity Theft: Creating fictitious identities using a combination of real and fake information for fraudulent purposes.

Account Takeover: Gaining unauthorized access to someone's online accounts by stealing or guessing their credentials.

Social Engineering

Pretexting: Creating a false scenario or pretext to manipulate individuals into revealing sensitive information or performing certain actions.

Baiting: Leaving physical or digital bait, such as infected USB drives or enticing downloads, to deceive and compromise unsuspecting individuals.

Quid pro quo: Offering something of value in exchange for sensitive information or access, often done under the guise of technical support or assistance.

Denial-of-Service (DoS) Attacks

Flooding Attacks: Overwhelming a target system or network with excessive traffic, rendering it unable to handle legitimate requests.

Distributed Denial-of-Service (DDoS) attacks: Coordinating multiple compromised computers or devices to flood a target with traffic, making it inaccessible to users.

Data Breaches

Network Intrusions: Penetrating a network's defenses to gain unauthorized access and steal sensitive data.

SQL Injections: Exploiting vulnerabilities in web applications to extract or manipulate data stored in databases.

Brute Force Attacks: Repeatedly guessing usernames and passwords until the correct combination is found.

Cyber Extortion

Ransomware Attacks: Encrypting files or blocking access to computer systems until a ransom is paid.

Doxing: Revealing sensitive or personal information about individuals or organizations to coerce or blackmail them.

Cryptojacking

Illegally using someone's computer or device to mine cryptocurrencies without their knowledge or consent.

Cyber Espionage

Advanced Persistent Threats (APTs): Covert and targeted attacks carried out by nation-states or sophisticated threat actors to gain unauthorized access to sensitive information or systems.

Real-Life Case

From June to August 2025, INTERPOL coordinated Operation Serengeti 2.0 with law enforcement in 18 African countries and the United Kingdom, targeting high-impact cybercrimes and fraud that had victimized nearly 88,000 people. The operations exposed several criminal activity patterns: illicit cryptocurrency mining centers powered by illegal electricity stations, generating millions in hidden profits; fraudulent online investment schemes, including fake crypto platforms advertised with promises of high returns, which defrauded tens of thousands of victims and funneled hundreds of millions of dollars; and transnational inheritance scams, where offenders tricked victims into paying fees to claim nonexistent estates, resulting in millions in losses. Together, these cases show how cybercriminals combine modern digital fraud methods with long-standing deception tactics to operate at massive scale.[5]

Emerging Crime Pattern: Attacks on the Internet of Things

A major emerging cybercrime trend involves the exploitation of Internet of Things (IoT) devices for large-scale botnet campaigns, ransomware attacks, and even direct threats to critical infrastructure. Criminals are increasingly leveraging automated tools and dark web services to hijack billions of poorly secured IoT devices such as smart TVs, routers, security cameras, and industrial sensors, turning them into assets for distributed denial-of-service (DDoS) attacks, click-fraud operations, illicit proxy networks, and persistent cyber-espionage. This threat is no longer only about stolen data; attackers now have the power to disrupt essential services, endanger public safety, and cause kinetic damage by compromising medical devices, water treatment plants, or energy grids.

Crime Pattern Scenario

Over a two-month period, several mid-sized law firms across three states report ransomware attacks. Each incident involves the same malware strain delivered through spear-phishing emails disguised as court filings. The ransom demands are nearly identical in wording and request payment in Bitcoin. Forensic review reveals the attackers used the same cryptocurrency wallet clusters and similar phishing domain names that mimic legitimate court websites. By linking these recurring technical variables (malware type, payment method, and spoofed domain themes) investigators identify a coordinated campaign rather than isolated cyber incidents.

Exercises

1. Access the most recent Europol or FBI Internet Crime Report. Choose one cybercrime category (e.g., ransomware or business-email compromise) and list the key indicators investigators use to link multiple incidents. Summarize how these indicators could help identify whether a case in your jurisdiction might belong to a wider series.
2. Identify three types of Internet-of-Things (IoT) devices commonly used in homes or small businesses (such as smart cameras, thermostats, or routers). For each device, describe a potential vulnerability that could be exploited in a botnet or ransomware attack and suggest one mitigation strategy that would reduce that risk.

Critical Thinking Guidance

Cybercrime patterns are often not obvious to victims or first responders. A phishing email that tricks one individual may look unrelated to a malware infection across town, yet both could stem from the same offender group. To detect cybercrime series investigators must rely on digital "fingerprints" such as repeated phishing lures, consistent time-of-day attack launches, or cryptocurrency wallets reused across extortion attempts. Equally important is separating noise from meaningful data since many cyberattacks are copycat techniques, but unique features (such as coding errors, phrasing in ransom notes, or infrastructure reuse) can signal a true serial offender.

Recognize the global nature of cybercrime. Offenders can operate from jurisdictions with limited cooperation treaties, complicating attribution and prosecution. Effective pattern analysis therefore depends not only on technical forensics but also on international partnerships, timely intelligence sharing, and harmonized legal frameworks.

Consider the interplay between technology and human factors. Successful cyberattacks often combine sophisticated technical exploits with social engineering that preys on human trust. Evaluating both the technical traces and the psychological tactics helps build a more complete picture of offender behavior and identify leverage points for prevention.

Notes

1 The process of removing or hiding personal details from information so that it cannot be linked back to a specific individual.
2 Short for Internet Protocol, it is the system that assigns a unique address (called an IP address) to each device on a network so they can find and communicate with each other.
3 Unique patterns of code or behavior that identify a specific malicious program, used by security software to detect and block it.
4 The different paths or methods that hackers or criminals use to gain access to a computer, network, or system.
5 Interpol (2025, February 20).

Bibliography

Correia, S. (2022). Making the most of cybercrime and fraud crime report data: A case study of UK action fraud. *International Journal for Population Data Science*, *7*(1). https://doi.org/10.23889/ijpds.v7i1.1721

Curtis, J., & Oxburgh, G. (2022). Understanding cybercrime in "real world" policing and law enforcement. *The Police Journal: Theory, Practice and Principles*, *96*(4), 573–592. https://doi.org/10.1177/0032258X221107584

Federal Bureau of Investigation. (2022). *Internet crime report 2021*. Internet Crime Complaint Center. www.ic3.gov/Media/PDF/AnnualReport/2021_IC3Report.pdf

Federal Bureau of Investigation. (2023). *Internet crime report 2022*. Internet Crime Complaint Center. www.ic3.gov/Media/PDF/AnnualReport/2022_IC3Report.pdf

Europol. (2023). *Internet organised crime threat assessment (IOCTA) 2023*. Publications Office of the European Union. https://doi.org/10.2813/587536

Europol. (2025). *Steal, deal and repeat: How cybercriminals trade and exploit your data – Internet organised crime threat assessment (IOCTA) 2025*. Publications Office of the European Union.

Interpol. (2025, February 20). *African authorities dismantle massive cybercrime and fraud networks, recover millions*. Interpol. www.interpol.int/en/News-and-Events/News/2025/African-authorities-dismantle-massive-cybercrime-and-fraud-networks-recover-millions

IoTBreakthrough. (2025, July 29). *Is IoT finally secure? What 2025 taught us about cyber risk in connected devices*. https://iotbreakthrough.com/is-iot-finally-secure-what-2025-taught-us-about-cyber-risk-in-connected-devices/

Khalil, M. (2025, August 24). IoT hacking statistics 2025: Threats, risks & regulations. *DeepStrike*. https://deepstrike.io/blog/iot-hacking-statistics

National Crime Agency. (2018). *The cyber threat to UK business: 2017–2018 report*. www.nationalcrimeagency.gov.uk/who-we-are/publications/178-the-cyber-threat-to-uk-business-2017-18/file

Nieles, M., Dempsey, K., & Pillitteri, V. (2017). *An introduction to information security* (Special Publication NIST SP 800-12r1). National Institute of Standards and Technology. https://doi.org/10.6028/NIST.SP.800-12r1

Ribaux, O., Baechler, S., & Rossy, Q. (2022). Forensic intelligence and traceology in digitalised environments: The detection and analysis of crime patterns to inform practice. In M. Gill (Ed.), *The handbook of security* (pp. 101–120). Palgrave Macmillan. https://doi.org/10.1007/978-3-030-91735-7_5

50 Hate Crimes

Introduction

Hate crimes are criminal acts motivated by bias against a victim's actual or perceived race, color, religion, national origin, sexual orientation, gender, gender identity, or disability. Unlike other crimes that may be driven primarily by opportunity or profit, hate crimes are rooted in prejudice and often aim to intimidate not only the direct victim but also the broader community associated with that identity group. Offenders may act impulsively during confrontations or carefully plan attacks on symbolic targets such as houses of worship, LGBTQ+ venues, or ethnic neighborhoods. The presence of hate symbols, derogatory slurs, or ritualistic behavior often distinguishes these crimes from other forms of violence or property damage. Hate crimes also tend to have disproportionate social impact, amplifying fear and insecurity among targeted populations.

Hate Crime MO Variables

Motivation and Justification

- Underlying Bias: Hate crimes are motivated by a deep-rooted bias against a specific group. The form of bias can be racial, religious, sexual, etc.
- Ideological Reinforcement: Perpetrators often engage with material – online or offline – that strengthens their prejudiced views and may justify their actions.

Target Selection

- Target Vulnerability: Victims are usually selected on the basis of their perceived vulnerability and membership in a targeted group. This could be their race, religion, sexual orientation, gender identity, nationality, or any other protected characteristic.
- Symbolic Targets: Locations such as religious institutions, LGBTQ+ clubs, or ethnic neighborhoods may be chosen for their symbolic significance.
- Pre-Crime Surveillance and Planning
- Reconnaissance: The perpetrator may carry out initial surveillance to assess the target's routine or security measures.
- Preparation: This can involve acquiring weapons, creating disguises, or conducting trial runs to test the feasibility of the attack.

DOI: 10.4324/9781003728733-53

Methods of Attack

- Physical Violence: Includes assault, homicide, and other forms of violent attacks.
- Property Damage: Includes vandalism, arson, and destruction of property, often accompanied by hate symbols like swastikas or derogatory slurs.
- Cyber Hate Crimes: Utilizing digital platforms to harass, intimidate or disseminate hate speech against targeted groups.
- Psychological Tactics: Intimidation, stalking, or verbal abuse aimed at instilling fear and suppressing the targeted group.

Communication and Publicity

- Online Forums: Some perpetrators frequent online forums that reinforce their biased views, and they may discuss plans or intentions there.
- Claiming Responsibility: After committing the crime, the perpetrator may leave behind messages or symbols, either at the scene or online, to claim responsibility and express their prejudiced views.

Avoidance of Capture

- Evasion Techniques: These may include switching vehicles, changing appearance, or using fake identification to evade law enforcement.
- Altering Evidence: Attempts to destroy or alter evidence that can link them to the crime, including digital traces.
- Community Support: In some cases, individuals may find safe harbor within communities that share or tolerate their views, complicating efforts to bring them to justice.
- Post-Crime Impact
- Psychological Impact on Community: Hate crimes often have a broader psychological impact on the community they target, instilling a sense of fear and insecurity.
- Media Manipulation: Perpetrators may use media, including social media, to propagate their views further or to claim responsibility and incite further incidents.

Hate Crime MO Examples

Explicit Expression of Bias: Often, hate crimes are accompanied by clear expressions of bias. This could be verbal, such as racial slurs or homophobic language, or it could be symbolic, such as the use of hate symbols or the defacement of religious buildings or symbols.

Pattern of Prejudice: Hate crime perpetrators often have a history of biased attitudes or behaviors. This could include not only previous hate crimes but also more subtle behaviors like the use of hate speech or involvement in extremist groups.

Spontaneous, Impulsive Acts: Some hate crimes are not premeditated but are instead spur-of-the-moment acts triggered by an immediate situation. For example, an argument or confrontation could escalate into a hate crime if the perpetrator has underlying prejudices.

Group Membership: Hate crimes are committed by individuals who are part of a larger group that shares their biases. In these cases, the hate crime may be seen as a way to gain status within the group, or it may be encouraged or organized by the group.

Escalating Violence: Hate crimes can be part of an escalating pattern of violence. A perpetrator might begin with relatively minor acts, like vandalism or verbal harassment, before progressing to more serious crimes like assault or murder.

Online Activity: Some hate crime perpetrators are active online, where they may share and consume hate speech, engage with extremist groups, or plan hate crimes.

Cyber Hate Crimes: With the rise of the digital age, there has also been an increase in hate crimes committed online. This can include things like online harassment, doxxing (publicly releasing private information), or threatening violence against individuals or groups based on their protected characteristics.

Overkill: Hate crimes, especially those that involve violence, often involve a degree of overkill. This means the violence involved is more than what would be necessary to commit the crime, often as an expression of intense hatred or rage.

Ritualistic Behaviors: In some cases, hate crime perpetrators may carry out their crimes in a ritualistic manner or according to a specific symbolic logic. For instance, burning crosses has been used as a method of racial intimidation, and this ritual was adopted by the Ku Klux Klan in the United States.

Use of Threatening Communication: This could be letters, emails, social media messages, or phone calls in which the offender threatens the victim because of their perceived group membership. These are not always immediately preceding a crime, but they can be part of a larger pattern of harassment or intimidation.

Stalking and Surveillance: Hate crime perpetrators may obsessively follow, watch, or harass their victims over a period of time. They may study their routines, habits, and vulnerabilities to exploit.

Mobilizing Community Fear and Tension: Some hate crime perpetrators work to create an environment of fear or hostility in their community. They may seek to exploit existing tensions or stir up fear against a certain group. This could involve spreading rumors, lies, or propaganda.

Territorial Marking: Some offenders mark their territory by painting graffiti, leaving symbols of their hate group, or otherwise damaging property in a way that signals their presence and intent.

Recruiting and Indoctrination: Hate crime offenders associated with a hate group may engage in recruiting and indoctrinating others into their belief system, often through the use of propaganda, social pressure, or coercion.

Use of Dates or Anniversaries: Some hate crime perpetrators commit their crimes on specific dates that have symbolic significance, either to their ideology or to the group they are targeting.

Targeting Public Spaces: Many hate crimes occur in public spaces, such as streets, parks, or public transportation. This can be a way of sending a broader message of fear and intimidation to the targeted community.

Emerging Crime Pattern: Online Radicalization

A new trend in hate crime patterns is the digital radicalization of young men through online misogynistic content. Communities such as the manosphere, including incels, men's rights activists, and other misogynist groups, normalize hate and cultivate a dehumanizing view of women that can evolve into real-world violence. This online radicalization often begins with aspirational or self-help messaging but shifts toward overt misogyny and violent ideology, increasingly amplified by social media algorithms. Notably, in the UK, authorities have raised the alarm over online "com networks" where young men are radicalized to target vulnerable women, often through suicide or eating disorder forums, which has necessitated counter-terrorism involvement to prevent escalation.

Crime Pattern Scenario

Over the course of two months, a suburban community experiences a series of hate-motivated vandalism incidents. Swastikas and racial slurs are spray-painted on a local synagogue, a Black church, and the homes of immigrant families. The incidents occur late at night, in locations close to each other, and the paint and handwriting style appear consistent. Community members report increased fear and avoidance of public spaces, while police analysis of surveillance footage reveals a similar vehicle near each crime scene. These indicators suggest a repeat offender or small group engaging in a bias-motivated crime series.

Exercises

1. Search your local law enforcement website or FBI.gov for hate crime statistics in your state or city. What categories of bias (race, religion, sexual orientation, etc.) are most frequently reported? Compare this with what you see in your own community. Do you think some incidents might go unreported? Why or why not?
2. Select a recent, publicly available report on online extremist movements. Summarize the recruitment and radicalization tactics described. Identify two features that investigators could monitor to detect when online rhetoric begins to translate into real-world hate crimes.

Critical Thinking Guidance

Linking hate crime incidents into a coherent series requires a careful search for repeating bias indicators across events. Investigators should first catalogue every observable sign of prejudice – specific slurs used in graffiti or verbal attacks, the style and color of symbols such as swastikas or other extremist emblems, and any ritualistic features (e.g., cross burnings or the placement of particular objects). Consistency in these elements can signal that separate incidents share a common offender or group.

Temporal and spatial patterns are equally important. Look for incidents that cluster around significant dates – religious holidays, anniversaries of historic events important to extremist movements, or political milestones – as well as locations that hold symbolic meaning, such as places of worship or community centers. Repeated offenses in a defined geographic corridor, or timed to the same calendar events, can strengthen the inference of a linked series.

Digital evidence often provides additional clues. Public posts in extremist forums, repeated phrases in online threats, or the reuse of the same usernames, avatars, or social media handles may reveal connections between seemingly unrelated crimes. Investigators can compare these digital "fingerprints" with physical evidence such as matching spray-paint chemicals or similar construction of incendiary devices.

Evaluate escalation and offender behavior over time. A pattern that begins with hate-motivated vandalism or threatening letters may progress to arson or assault. Detecting this trajectory early allows law enforcement to intervene before violence intensifies. By integrating physical evidence, online intelligence, and the timing and location of incidents, officers and analysts can move from isolated reports to a linked hate-crime series, enabling both targeted enforcement and proactive community protection.

Bibliography

Bureau of Justice Statistics. (1999). *A policymaker's guide to hate crimes.* U.S. Department of Justice, Office of Justice Programs. www.ojp.gov/pdffiles1/bja/162304.pdf

California Office of the Attorney General. (n.d.). *Hate crimes brochure.* https://oag.ca.gov/system/files/media/hate-crimes-brochure-english.pdf

Dodd, V. (2025, April 12). Misogynistic content driving UK boys to hunt vulnerable girls on suicide forums. *The Guardian*. www.theguardian.com/uk-news/2025/apr/12/uk-counter-terror-police-nca-misogyny-com-networks

Federal Bureau of Investigation. (2011). *Variables affecting crime: Uniform crime report hate crime statistics, 2011*. https://ucr.fbi.gov/hate-crime/2011/resources/variablesaffectingcrime_final.pdf

Federal Bureau of Investigation. (2019). *2019 hate crime statistics*. https://ucr.fbi.gov/hate-crime/2019/topic-pages/location-type

Federal Bureau of Investigation. (2023, March 13). *FBI releases supplemental 2021 hate crime statistics*. www.fbi.gov/news/press-releases/fbi-releases-supplemental-2021-hate-crime-statistics

Freilich, J. D., & Chermak, S. M. (2012). *Hate crimes* (Problem-Specific Guide Series No. 72). Office of Community Oriented Policing Services, U.S. Department of Justice. https://popcenter.asu.edu/content/hate-crimes-0

Hunter, K., & Jouenne, E. (2021). All women belong in the kitchen, and other dangerous tropes: Online misogyny as a national security threat. *Journal of Advanced Military Studies*, *12*(1), 57–85. https://doi.org/10.21140/mcuj.20211201003

International Association of Chiefs of Police. (n.d.). *Responding to hate crimes: A police officer's guide to investigation and prevention*. www.theiacp.org/resources/responding-to-hate-crimes-a-police-officers-guide-to-investigation-and-prevention

U.S. Department of Justice. (n.d.). *Learn about hate crimes*. www.justice.gov/hatecrimes/learn-about-hate-crimes

51 Terrorism and Violent Extremism

Introduction

Terrorism is the use of violence or intimidation, often against civilians, in pursuit of political, religious, or ideological goals. Violent extremism refers to the beliefs and actions of people who support or use ideologically motivated violence to achieve radical ideological, religious, or political views. While it's a form of terrorism, violent extremism tends to focus more on the ideological and psychological factors that drive individuals or groups to commit acts of violence.

Terrorism and violent extremism represent some of the most serious threats to national security and community safety. While individual attacks may appear isolated, they often emerge from identifiable patterns of ideology, recruitment, and operational behavior. Like other forms of crime, terrorism follows discernible variables: how offenders are radicalized, how they secure funding and training, the tactics they select, and the symbolic targets they choose. Recognizing these elements as part of a crime pattern enables law enforcement and intelligence professionals to better anticipate threats, link incidents, and intervene before attacks occur.

Terrorism and Violent Extremism MO Variables

Ideological Foundations and Objectives

- Ideological Orientation: The underlying belief system that motivates the terrorists, which could be religious, nationalist, or political in nature.
- Objectives and Targets: The strategic aims, which may include instigating fear, destabilizing governments, or provoking sectarian violence, and the chosen targets that align with these aims.

Recruitment and Radicalization

- Propaganda and Messaging: Use of social media, encrypted messaging services, and other communication channels to spread propaganda and attract sympathizers.
- Vetting and Selection: Processes to identify and recruit individuals who are aligned ideologically and willing to carry out acts of terrorism.

DOI: 10.4324/9781003728733-54

Planning and Financing

- Funding Sources: May include state sponsorship, charitable donations, organized crime, or self-funding methods like running legitimate businesses.
- Strategic Planning: Tactical planning of attacks, including the choice of target, method of attack, and timing, often planned in cells to limit exposure.

Training and Pre-Operation Surveillance

- Skill Development: Training recruits in weapon use, bomb-making, surveillance techniques, and other skills crucial to the planned attack.
- Reconnaissance: Gathering intelligence on the target to identify vulnerabilities, optimal timing, and escape routes.

Execution and Tactics

- Choice of Weaponry: The choice between firearms, explosives, vehicles, or other weapons often reflects both ideological leanings and logistical considerations.
- Coordination: Synchronizing the timing of multiple attacks or activities to maximize impact and media coverage.
- Delivery Method: The tactics used to deliver the attack, whether through suicide bombings, shootings, vehicular attacks, or remote detonation of explosives.

Communication and Media Strategy

- Claiming Responsibility: Public statements or videos released before or after the attack to claim responsibility and outline the ideological rationale.
- Information Warfare: Using misinformation or disinformation to create confusion, distrust, or to mislead investigations.

Security Measures and Counter-Surveillance

- Operational Security: Measures to protect the identities of participants, including the use of aliases, encrypted communications, and safe houses.
- Counter-Surveillance: Techniques to detect and evade law enforcement surveillance, including irregular movement patterns and avoiding technology.

Adaptability and Evolution

- Response to Countermeasures: Adapting methods and targets in response to changes in law enforcement or security protocols.
- Lessons Learned: After-action reviews to understand what went well or poorly, both to celebrate "successes" and to adapt future operations.

Indicators

Identifying signs of terrorism and violent extremism is critical for law enforcement agencies and communities to take preemptive action. However, it's crucial to note that many indicators, taken alone, are not necessarily proof of terrorist or extremist activities. They are signs that should be considered as part of a broader assessment.

Financial Indicators

- Large Cash Withdrawals: Unexplained or large amounts of cash withdrawals could indicate funding for operations.
- Wire Transfers to High-Risk Locations: Money transferred to countries known for extremist activities.
- Multiple Funding Sources: Complex layers of funding sources that make it difficult to trace to the origins.

Behavioral Indicators

- Radicalized Behavior: Sudden change in appearance, ideology, or religious practices.
- Social Isolation: Withdrawal from friends, family, and community.
- Secrecy: Unusual levels of secrecy about activities or whereabouts.
- Hostile Reconnaissance: Unusual interest in security measures of potential target locations.

Online Activity

- Extremist Propaganda: Sharing, posting, or distributing extremist content online.
- Secure Communication Channels: Use of encrypted or untraceable communication methods.
- Suspicious Searches: Searches related to making bombs, reconnaissance, or other attack planning.

Procurement of Material

- Purchase of Firearms: Especially without proper documentation or via unofficial channels.
- Chemical Purchases: Purchase of chemicals that could be used to create explosives.
- Acquisition of Military Gear: Purchase of body armor, camouflage, etc.
- Unexplained Possession of Police or Military Gear: Owning equipment without an evident reason can be a sign.

Tactical Indicators

- Dry Runs: Performing mock operations to test the feasibility.
- Observation and Surveillance: Taking notes, sketches, or photographs of potential target sites.
- Testing of Security Responses: Probing reactions of security services, perhaps by leaving suspicious packages and observing responses.

Logistical Indicators

- Stockpiling: Accumulation of weapons, ammunition, and other supplies.
- Safe Houses: Maintaining residential locations for the purpose of hiding operatives or equipment.
- Unregistered Vehicles: Use of stolen or unregistered vehicles for surveillance or transport.

Travel and Movement

- Unexplained or Secretive Travel: Especially to regions known for terrorist training.
- Multiple IDs or Passports: Possession of false identification or travel documents.
- Frequent Changes in Appearance: To avoid detection during travels.

Community-Based Indicators

- Erosion of Social Cohesion: When community bonds weaken, extremist ideologies can take hold.
- Active Recruitment: Efforts to recruit others into an extremist ideology.
- Community Endorsement: Vocal or tacit community approval or tolerance of extremist viewpoints.

Example Types of Terrorism

Domestic Terrorism: Acts of terrorism carried out by citizens within their own country and directed at their fellow citizens.

International Terrorism: Involves acts of terrorism that transcend national borders in terms of the means by which they are carried out, the individuals they are intended to intimidate, or the locale in which perpetrators operate.

State-Sponsored Terrorism: Governments providing support or resources to non-state actors engaging in terrorism, often against other countries.

Religious Terrorism: Acts of terrorism carried out in the name of religious beliefs, often against religious minorities or secular institutions.

Right-Wing Terrorism: Violence committed by groups or individuals, the motivation of which derives from extremist ideologies often related to white supremacy, anti-government stances, and xenophobia.

Left-Wing Terrorism: Violence committed by groups or individuals aimed at overthrowing capitalist systems and replacing them with socialist or communist regimes.

Ethno-Nationalist Terrorism: Terrorism motivated by nationalism and the desire to create a separate state for a particular ethnic group.

Eco-Terrorism: Acts of violence committed in the name of environmental activism, often against corporations or institutions seen as harming the environment.

Cyber-Terrorism: Attacks on digital infrastructure or systems with the intent to cause harm, steal sensitive information, or disrupt governance and daily life.

Narco-Terrorism: Acts of terrorism funded by or conducted to support drug trafficking organizations.

Suicide Terrorism: Individuals carrying out acts of terrorism by intentionally killing themselves along with their targets.

Vehicle-Based Terrorism: Using vehicles like trucks or vans to ram into crowds or buildings, causing mass casualties.

Lone-Actor Terrorism: Individual terrorists who operate without clear affiliation to a larger group but may be inspired by extremist ideologies.

Hostage-Taking and Kidnapping: Holding individuals hostage or kidnapping them as an act of terrorism, often for ransom or political concessions.

WMD Terrorism: Using weapons of mass destruction like chemical, biological, radiological, or nuclear materials to conduct terrorist attacks.

Example Types of Violent Extremists

Religious Extremists: Individuals or groups that use violence to further their religious ideologies. Examples include radical Islamic terrorists and Christian extremist groups.

Ethno-Nationalist Extremists: Those who employ violence to achieve a separate state or territory for their ethnic group. Examples include the Irish Republican Army (IRA) or the Basque separatist group ETA.

Right-Wing Extremists: Groups or individuals that use violence to create a society that aligns with their ideological beliefs in racial purity, extreme nationalism, and authoritarianism. Examples include white supremacist and neo-Nazi groups.

Left-Wing Extremists: Those who advocate for socialist, communist, or anarchist ideologies and use violence to overthrow capitalist systems and institutions. Examples include groups like the Red Brigades in Italy or the Weather Underground in the United States.

Anti-Government Extremists: Individuals or groups that consider their own government or governing institutions to be illegitimate and use or promote violence to bring about change. Examples include sovereign citizens or militia movements.

Eco-Terrorists: Groups that use violence to advocate for environmental causes. Examples include groups like Earth Liberation Front.

Gender-Based Extremists: Those who use violence to enforce traditional gender roles or to oppose what they see as the "feminization" of society. Examples include "incel" (involuntary celibate) violence.

Animal Rights Extremists: Groups or individuals that use violence to prevent animal exploitation. Examples include Animal Liberation Front.

Issue-Oriented Extremists: Individuals or groups who focus on specific issues like abortion or immigration, resorting to violence to bring attention to their cause.

Cult Extremists: Groups that follow a charismatic leader and who may use violence to bring about a vision described by that leader. Example: The Aum Shinrikyo cult in Japan.

Lone-Actor Extremists: Individuals who act alone in planning and executing extremist violence, often radicalized online and unaffiliated with an organized extremist group.

Emerging Crime Pattern: Use of Commercial Drones

A growing trend in terrorism and violent extremism is the weaponization of commercial drones. Once limited to state militaries, off-the-shelf drones are now being adapted by extremist groups for reconnaissance, smuggling, or delivering small explosives. Patterns are emerging in the use of drones near symbolic locations, with offenders modifying drones for payload delivery or surveillance of critical infrastructure. As these incidents increase, in will be important to incorporate aerial tactics into crime pattern recognition alongside traditional ground-based methods.

Crime Pattern Scenario

A lone-actor extremist in the Midwest begins posting online manifestos echoing themes from international extremist propaganda. Investigators notice that his purchases include precursor chemicals, tactical gear, and firearms from different vendors. In addition, several community members report that he has abruptly withdrawn from social circles, begun practicing at local firing ranges, and made veiled online threats against government facilities. Individually, these behaviors could be overlooked, but taken together, they align with indicators seen in other lone-actor terrorist cases. Linking the digital activity, procurement records, and local surveillance establishes a crime pattern that moves the subject from general concern to an identifiable threat requiring intervention.

Exercises

1. Locate two publicly reported terrorism or violent-extremism incidents (e.g., lone-actor attacks or foiled plots) from reputable news or government sources. Identify at least three common indicators – such as weapon acquisition methods, online propaganda themes, or reconnaissance activity – that could help analysts determine whether the incidents share a common ideological or operational pattern.
2. Select a case study (e.g., from the US National Threat Assessment Center or Europol reports) that details an individual's path to violent extremism. Create a timeline of key behavioral indicators (online postings, travel, purchase of materials). Then identify which indicators, if detected earlier, could have allowed authorities to link the case to other known extremist activity.

How to Create the Timeline

List Key Events – Read the case study carefully and note every important step in the individual's path toward violent extremism (e.g., first exposure to extremist content, major changes in social circle, travel to training areas, weapon purchases).

Add Dates or Time Ranges – Next to each event, write the approximate date or time period when it occurred. If the exact date is unknown, use what the source provides (such as "Spring 2022" or "about six months before the attack").

Arrange Chronologically – place these events in order from earliest to most recent so the sequence of radicalization is clear.

Mark Key Indicators – Highlight or underline warning signs such as online propaganda activity, reconnaissance of targets, or stockpiling of weapons.

Identify Intervention Points – Review the timeline and note where early detection – by family, community, or law enforcement – might have interrupted the process.

Critical Thinking Guidance

Terrorism and violent extremism are high-profile issues, but it is important to resist the temptation to overgeneralize. Many individuals consume extreme content without progressing to violence. The challenge is to distinguish isolated behavior from serial patterns that show mobilization toward an attack. Linking indicators, such as repeated online postings, acquisition of weapons, and reconnaissance of symbolic targets, across multiple domains (digital, financial, physical) helps avoid false positives while still recognizing legitimate threats. A critical mindset requires evaluating whether emerging behaviors fit within established extremist MOs or whether they reflect new adaptations that may serve as indicators, such as the use of cryptocurrency for funding or the adoption of drones as delivery platforms.

Bibliography

Dallas Police Department. (n.d.). *Homeland security.* https://dallaspolice.net/Community/Pages/Homeland-Security.aspx

Europol. (2023). *European Union terrorism situation and trend report.* Publications Office of the European Union. https://doi.org/10.2813/271385

Federal Bureau of Investigation. (n.d.). *Terrorism.* www.fbi.gov/investigate/terrorism

National Counterterrorism Center. (n.d.). *First responder toolbox.* www.dni.gov/index.php/nctc-how-we-work/joint-ct-assessment-team/first-responder-toolbox

National Counterterrorism Center, Federal Bureau of Investigation, & Department of Homeland Security. (2021). *U.S. violent extremist mobilization indicators* (2021 ed.). www.dni.gov/files/NCTC/documents/news_documents/Mobilization_Indicators_Booklet_2021.pdf

Pledger, T. G. (2021). *The role of drones in future terrorist attacks* (Land Warfare Paper No. 137). Association of the United States Army. www.ausa.org/sites/default/files/publications/LWP-137-The-Role-of-Drones-in-Future-Terrorist-Attacks_0.pdf

RAND Center for Terrorism Risk Management Policy. (2007). *Terrorism risk modeling for intelligence analysis and infrastructure protection* (RAND Technical Report TR-386). RAND Corporation. www.rand.org/content/dam/rand/pubs/technical_reports/2007/RAND_TR386.pdf

Schuurman, B., Bakker, E., Gill, P., & Bouhana, N. (2018). Lone actor terrorist attack planning and preparation: A data-driven analysis. *Journal of Forensic Sciences*, *63*(4), 1191–1200. https://doi.org/10.1111/1556-4029.13676

U.S. Secret Service, National Threat Assessment Center. (2025, August). *Aligning behavioral threat assessment and management with a multi-tiered system of support: Building a continuum of prevention and intervention* (Report). U.S. Secret Service. www.secretservice.gov/sites/default/files/reports/2025-08/Aligning-Behavioral-Threat-Assessment-And-Management-With-A-Multi-Tiered-System-Of-Support.pdf

52 Drug Trafficking

Introduction

Drug trafficking is a global illicit trade involving the cultivation, manufacture, distribution, and sale of substances that are subject to drug prohibition laws. It is one of the most complex forms of organized crime because it spans every stage of the supply chain – production, transportation, distribution, and financial laundering. Unlike isolated incidents of possession or use, drug trafficking is inherently serial in nature: organizations and networks repeat methods, routes, and concealment tactics over long periods, refining their approaches as law enforcement adapts.

Trafficking groups rely on well-defined drug corridors, hidden safe houses, and specialized methods such as load vehicles or narco-submarines to move shipments undetected. They recruit mules (couriers) under financial pressure or coercion, often operating on a cycle that reveals patterns over time. Operations also depend on precursor chemicals diverted from legitimate industries, and many networks engage in poly-drug trafficking, shifting substances based on demand and profitability.

Understanding drug trafficking as a repeatable and patterned system, rather than as isolated seizures, helps investigators recognize the consistency in concealment techniques, financial flows, and operational support. Just as a controlled delivery can expose higher levels of an organization, recognizing recurring behaviors across multiple cases is critical to identifying the structure and resilience of trafficking groups.

Drug Trafficking MO Variables

Cultivation and Production

- Choice of Location: Drug cultivators often select remote, hard-to-reach areas for growing crops like cannabis, coca, or opium poppy. Synthetic drugs like methamphetamine are produced in makeshift or specialized laboratories that can range from a residential house to industrial settings.
- Secrecy and Security Measures: Cultivators and manufacturers often use camouflage, guards, and sometimes advanced technology to keep their operations hidden.
- Production Techniques: The methods used for cultivation and drug production can vary significantly, including indoor hydroponic systems for cannabis or rudimentary outdoor plots for coca plants.

DOI: 10.4324/9781003728733-55

Transportation and Distribution

- Transport Routes: Drug traffickers use a variety of routes to move drugs, including land, air, and sea. These routes often go through multiple transit countries before reaching the destination.
- Concealment Methods: Traffickers use numerous tactics to conceal drugs, such as hidden compartments in vehicles, mixing drugs with legitimate cargo, or using drug mules who ingest or carry the substances on their person.
- Intermediaries and Brokers: Middlemen play crucial roles in connecting producers with distributors. They may also be responsible for storing the drugs before further distribution.

Sales and Marketing

- Target Market: Depending on the substance, traffickers identify target markets, ranging from street-level sales in marginalized communities to high-volume sales in affluent neighborhoods or through online platforms.
- Pricing Strategy: Drugs are priced according to purity, demand, and risks involved in production and transportation.
- Marketing and Branding: Some traffickers use branding, packaging, or even social media to create a demand for their specific product.

Financial Transactions

- Money Laundering: The illicit gains are often laundered through a variety of methods, including shell companies, cryptocurrency transactions, or through legitimate businesses.
- Payment Systems: Depending on the scale of the operation, payments can range from simple cash transactions to complex financial instruments or digital currencies.

Support and Protection

- Corruption and Coercion: Drug traffickers often rely on corrupt officials or use intimidation and violence to protect their operations and routes.
- Use of Technology: Technology, including encrypted communication platforms, is increasingly being used for coordination and evasion from law enforcement.

Adaptation and Scaling

- Response to Law Enforcement: Traffickers adapt their routes, methods, and even the types of drugs produced in response to changes in law enforcement tactics or legislation.
- Diversification: Many trafficking organizations diversify into other forms of illicit activity, including arms trafficking or human smuggling, to maximize profit and mitigate risks.

Example Drug Trafficking Elements

Production and Manufacture

- Basement Meth Lab: A makeshift methamphetamine laboratory set up in the basement of a suburban home, where the drug is produced using over-the-counter medications and household chemicals.
- Poppy Fields in Remote Areas: Cultivation of opium poppy plants in secluded areas, often protected by armed guards, and subsequently processed into heroin.

Transportation and Smuggling

- Body Carriers: Individuals swallowing drug-filled capsules to bypass airport security and then excreting them at their destination.
- Hidden Compartments in Cars: Smugglers use specially designed hidden compartments in vehicle dashboards, under seats, or in trunks to smuggle drugs across borders.
- Submersible Vessels: Use of homemade submarines or semi-submersibles to move large quantities of cocaine by sea (narco-submarines).

Distribution and Sales

- Schoolyard Dealers: Adolescents or young adults selling small amounts of drugs, like marijuana or prescription pills, to classmates.
- Online Sales: A vendor on a dark web marketplace offers various controlled substances, shipped discreetly to buyers.
- Drive-through Drug House: A residential property where drugs are sold much like a drive-through, where customers drive up, make an exchange with a runner, and drive away.

Financial Activities

- Bitcoin Laundering: Profits from drug sales are converted into Bitcoin and then moved through multiple digital wallets to hide the source before converting back into fiat currency.
- Real Estate Investment: Drug money is used to purchase property, which is then rented out, effectively laundering the funds through legal income.

Human Trafficking for Drug Trade

- Forced Labor in Cannabis Farms: Trafficked individuals are forced to work in hidden cannabis farms, often in deplorable conditions and without pay.
- Mule Recruitment under Duress: Individuals are coerced or threatened into becoming drug mules, often under threat to their family or loved ones.

Drugs

The following information about drugs (the property in illegal manufacturing of drugs, illegal sales of drugs, and drug trafficking) and their street names is adapted from the 2022 DEA Resource Guide Drugs of Abuse.[1]

Knowledge of street names of drugs can help in searching information for links to possible drug-related crime patterns. This information may be particularly useful for searching social media and other online sites.

Narcotics/Opioids

Synthetic opioids are made entirely in a lab and include meperidine, fentanyl, and methadone. Semi-synthetic opioids are synthesized from naturally occurring opium products, such as morphine and codeine, and include heroin, oxycodone, hydrocodone, and hydromorphone.

General common street names: Smack, Horse, Mud, Brown Sugar, Junk, Black Tat, Big H, Paregoric, Dover's Powder, MPTP (New Heroin), Hillbilly Heroin, Lean or Purple Drank, Oc, Ox, Oxy, Oxycotton, Sippin Syrup

Fentanyl common street names: Apache, China Girl, China Town, Dance Fever, Friend, Goodfellas, Great Bear, He-Man, Jackpot, King Ivory, Murder 8, Tango & Cash

Heroin common street names: Big H, Black Tar, Chiva, Hell Dust, Horse, Negra, Smack, Thunder

Hydromorphone common street names: D, Dillies, Dust, Footballs, Juice, And Smack

Methadone common street names: Amidone, Chocolate Chip Cookies, Fizzies with MDMA, Wafer

Morphine common street names: Dreamer, Emsel, First Line, God's Drug, Hows, M.S., Mister Blue, Morf, Morpho, Unkie

Opium common street names: Ah-pen-yen, Aunti, Aunti Emma, Big O, Black Pill, Chandoo, Chandu, Chinese Molasses, Chinese Tobacco, Dopium, Dover's Powder, Dream Gun, Dream Stick, Dreams, Easing Powder, Fi-do-nie, Gee, God's Medicine, Gondola, Goric, Great Tobacco, Guma, Hop/hops, Joy Plant, Midnight Oil, Mira, O, O.P., Ope, Pen Yan, Pin Gon, Pox, Skee, Toxy, Toys, When-shee, Ze, Zero

Oxycodone common street names: Hillbilly Heroin, Kicker, OC, Ox, Roxy, Perc, and Oxy

Stimulants

Stimulants Include

- prescription drugs such as amphetamines [Adderall® and Dexedrine®], methylphenidate [Concerta® and Ritalin®]
- diet aids [such as Didrex®, Bontril®, Preludin®, Fastin®, Adipex P®, Ionomin®, and Meridia®]
- other illicitly used drugs such as methamphetamine, cocaine, methcathinone, and other synthetic cathinones that are commonly sold under the guise of "bath salts."
- Amphetamines' common street names: Bennies, Black Beauties, Crank, Ice, Speed, Uppers
- Cocaine common street names: Blow, Coca, Coke, Crack, Flake, Snow, Soda Cot
- Khat common street names: Abyssinian Tea, African Salad, Catha, Chat, Kat, Oa
- Methamphetamine common street names: Batu, Bikers Coffee, Black Beauties, Chalk, Chicken Feed, Crank, Crystal, Glass, Go-Fast, Hiropon, Ice, Meth, Methlies Quick, Poor Man's Cocaine, Shabu, Shards, Speed, Stove Top, Tina, Trash, Tweak, Uppers, Ventana, Vidrio, Yaba, Yellow Bam

Depressants

- Barbiturates: butalbital (Fiorina®), phenobarbital, Pentothal®, Seconal®, and Nembutal®
- Benzodiazepines: Valium®, Xanax®, Halcion®, Ativan®, Klonopin®, Restoril®, Rohypnol®
- CNS depressants: Lunesta®, Ambien®, Sonata®, meprobamate, methaqualone (Quaalude®), GHB
- Common street names for depressants: Barbs, Benzos, Downers, Georgia Home Boy, GHB, GrievousBodilyHarm, LiquidX, Nerve Pills, Phennies, R2, Reds, Roofies, Rophies, Tranks, Yellows
- Barbiturates common street names: Barbs, Block Busters, Christmas Trees, Goof Balls, Pinks, Red Devils, Reds & Blues, and Yellow Jackets
- Benzodiazepines common street names: Benzos, Downers
- GHB common street names: Easy Lay, G, Georgia Home Boy, GHB, Goop, Grievous Bodily Harm, Liquid Ecstasy, Liquid X, Scoop
- Rohypnol® common street names: Circles, Forget Pill, Forget-Me-Pill, La Rocha, Lunch Money Drug, Mexican Valium, Pingus, R2, Reynolds, Roach, Roach 2, Roaches, Roachies, Roapies, Robutal, Rochas Dos, Rohypnol, Roofies, Rophies, Ropies, Roples, Row-Shay, Ruffies, Wolfies

Hallucinogens

- Hallucinogens: psilocybin-containing mushrooms, lysergic acid diethylamide (LSD), MDMA (ecstasy), ketamine, peyote, and mescaline
- Common street names: Acid, Fry, Mind Candy, Mushrooms, Shrooms, Special K, STP, X, ecstasy (or XTC)
- Ecstasy/MDMA common street names: Adam, Beans, Clarity, Disco Biscuit, E, Ecstasy, Eve, Go, Hug Drug, Lover's Speed, MDMA, Peace, STP, X, and XTC
- Ketamine common street names: Cat Tranquilizer, Cat Valium, Jet K, Kit Kat, Purple, Special K, Special La Coke, Super Acid, Super K, Vitamin K
- LSD common street names: Acid, Dots, Mellow Yellow, Window Pane
- Peyote and mescaline common street names: Buttons, Cactus, Mesc, and Peyoto
- Psilocybin common street names: Magic Mushrooms, Mushrooms, and Shrooms

Steroids

Anabolic steroids are synthetically produced variants of the naturally occurring male hormone testosterone and include: testosterone, trenbolone, oxymetholone, methandrostenolone, nandrolone, stanozolol, boldenone, and oxandrolone.

Steroids common street names: Arnolds, Juice, Pumpers, Roids, Stackers, and Weight Gainers

Marijuana/Cannabis

Marijuana/cannabis common street names: Aunt Mary, BC Bud, Blunts, Boom, Chronic, Dope, Gangster, Ganja, Grass, Hash, Herb, Hydro, Indo, Joint, Kif, Mary Jane, Mota, Pot, Reefer, Sinsemilla, Skunk, Smoke, Weed, Yerba

Marijuana concentrates common street names: 710 (the word "OIL" flipped and spelled backwards), wax, ear wax, honey oil, budder, butane hash oil, butane honey oil (BHO), shatter, dabs (dabbing), black glass, errl

Inhalants

Inhalants can be dangerously inhaled in over 1,000 common household products including typewriter correction fluid, air conditioning refrigerant, felt tip markers, spray paint, air freshener, butane, and cooking spray.

Inhalants common street names: Gluey, Huff, Rush, and Whippets

Designer Drugs

Baths salts are the name of designer drugs which contain synthetic cathinones, which are central nervous stimulants.

Bath salts common street names: Bliss, Blue Silk, Cloud Nine, Drone, Energy-1, Ivory Wave, Lunar Wave, Meow Meow, Ocean Burst, Pure Ivory, Purple Wave, Red Dove, Snow Leopard, Stardust, Vanilla Sky, White Dove, White Knight, White Lightning

K2 and Spice are synthetic cannabinoids that are being sold as "legal" alternatives to marijuana made of chemicals.

K2/Spice synthetic marijuana common street names: "Spice, K2, Blaze, RedX Dawn, Paradise, Demon, Black Magic, Spike, Mr. Nice Guy, Ninja, Zohai, Dream, Genie, Sence, Smoke, Skunk, Serenity, Yucatan, Fire, Skooby Snax, and Crazy Clown

Common illicitly produced synthetic opioids: acetyl fentanyl, butyryl fentanyl, beta-hydroxythiofentanyl, furanyl fentanyl, 4-fluoroisobutyryl fentanyl, acryl fentanyl, U-47700, benzimidazole-opioids such as etonitazene and isotonitazene.

Emerging Crime Pattern: Autonomous Narco-Submarines

A new pattern in drug trafficking has emerged: the development and deployment of autonomous narco-submarines which are unmanned, semi-submersible vessels outfitted with satellite communications and surveillance equipment. Intercepted off Colombia's Caribbean coast, one such drone-like narco-submarine was found empty but equipped with a Starlink modem and antennas, likely part of a test by the powerful Gulf Clan for future illicit cargo operations. This technological leap eliminates the human courier, markedly reducing risk for traffickers, and signals a shift toward remote, scalable smuggling solutions that law enforcement must urgently adapt to.[2]

Crime Pattern Scenario

A joint task force investigating cross-border crime identifies a pattern of cocaine shipments hidden in commercial produce trucks. Each seizure occurs along the same interstate corridor, with shipments concealed inside refrigerated compartments among legitimate cargo. The traffickers rotate drivers and trucking companies, but the concealment method and route remain consistent. Further investigation reveals that proceeds are laundered through small construction companies owned by associates of the trafficking organization. The repeat use of the corridor, the concealment method, and the laundering strategy point to a serial trafficking pattern tied to a larger cartel network.

Exercises

1. Search online for the 2025 UNODC World Drug Report or your country's most recent national drug threat assessment. Identify one trafficking route, concealment method, or laundering strategy described in the report. Summarize it in three to four sentences and explain how repeated use of that tactic could be detected as a pattern by law enforcement.
2. Review three recent news stories on major drug seizures (e.g., from DEA press releases or national news). List the concealment methods used in each case (hidden compartments, commercial cargo blending, body carriers). Note any similarities and describe how those shared methods might reveal a single trafficking network or a trend in concealment tactics.

Critical Thinking Guidance

Drug trafficking investigations require recognizing how seemingly unrelated seizures or arrests connect to broader systems. A single traffic stop might appear isolated, but when compared with similar concealment techniques, repeated routes, or recurring shell companies, patterns of organization emerge. Analysts and investigators should be cautious of focusing only on the type of drug seized. Instead, examining the methods of concealment, the financial channels, and the travel patterns of traffickers often reveals the repeatable structures of organized crime. Serial trafficking groups tend to innovate slowly – while they adapt to enforcement pressure, they still rely on consistent logistical and financial frameworks that leave behind identifiable traces.

Notes

1 DEA (2022).
2 Barber (2025, July 11).

Bibliography

Barber, H. (2025, July 11). Colombia identifies new threat in drug war: The autonomous narco drone sub. *The Guardian*. www.theguardian.com/world/2025/jul/11/colombia-narco-submarine-cocaine

Drug Enforcement Administration. (2022). *Drugs of abuse: A DEA resource guide* (2022 ed.). U.S. Department of Justice. www.dea.gov/sites/default/files/2022-12/2022_DOA_eBook_File_Final.pdf

Scott, M. S., & Dedel, K. (2006). *Clandestine methamphetamine labs* (2nd ed., Problem-Specific Guide Series No. 16). Office of Community Oriented Policing Services, U.S. Department of Justice. https://popcenter.asu.edu/content/clandestine-methamphetamine-labs-2nd-ed-0

United Nations Office on Drugs and Crime. (2023). *World drug report 2023*. United Nations. www.unodc.org/unodc/en/data-and-analysis/world-drug-report-2023.html

United Nations Office on Drugs and Crime. (2025). *World drug report 2025*. United Nations. www.unodc.org/unodc/data-and-analysis/world-drug-report-2025.html

53 Firearm Trafficking

Introduction

Firearm trafficking involves the unlawful trade, distribution, and transfer of firearms, ammunition, and related accessories. This illicit market fuels organized crime, terrorism, and armed violence by supplying weapons to individuals and groups who are often prohibited from possessing them. Trafficked firearms can originate from thefts, corrupt dealers, straw purchases, or illegal manufacture, and they frequently move across state or national borders to exploit gaps in regulatory systems. Because firearms are durable goods, once they enter illicit markets, they may circulate for years, intensifying long-term risks to community safety. Linking firearm trafficking criminal activity requires attention to the methods of procurement, concealment, distribution, and financial flows, as well as the adaptive strategies traffickers employ to evade law enforcement.

Firearm Trafficking MO Variables

Pre-Crime Preparation: Sourcing and Procurement

- Determining Origin of Firearms: Illicit firearms may come from various sources, such as thefts from legal owners, military arsenals, or illegal manufacture.
- Establishing Point of Contact: Traffickers may establish contact with corrupt officials, rogue elements in military or police forces, or individuals with access to firearms.
- Creating or Obtaining Documentation and Permits: Fake identification, altered permits, or even legitimate documents obtained through corrupt means are often used in the acquisition process.

Execution

Storage and Staging

- Safe Houses and Warehousing: After acquisition, firearms are usually stored in hidden or secure locations, often guarded to prevent unwanted attention or seizures.
- Inventory Management: Sophisticated operations often have a detailed inventory system to track the firearms and ammunition, enabling quicker distribution when demand arises.

DOI: 10.4324/9781003728733-56

Transportation

- Transportation Methods: Various means, such as cars, boats, and even commercial flights, are used for moving firearms. Traffickers may use hidden compartments, disguise methods, or transport firearms in parts to avoid detection.
- Routing and Transshipment: Firearms are often moved through multiple points, sometimes even internationally, to obscure their origin and make tracking more difficult.

Sales and Distribution

- End Users: The firearms may be intended for street gangs, organized crime syndicates, insurgents, or terrorists, among others.
- Channels of Sale: Sales may take place through the dark web, face-to-face transactions, or through middlemen who facilitate the trade.
- Pricing and Payment: Prices are determined by demand, scarcity, and risk involved. Payments may be in cash, barter, or digital currency to leave minimal trace.

Support and Protection

- Corruption and Collusion: Bribes and other forms of corruption may be used to facilitate the trade, from the acquisition phase to the point of sale.
- Security Measures: Traffickers often employ various security protocols, including the use of disposable phones, coded language, and encrypted communications, to evade law enforcement.

Adaptability and Scaling

- Adaptation to Law Enforcement Tactics: Traffickers adapt to law enforcement measures by changing routes, altering methods of concealment, and employing new technologies.
- Networking and Alliances: Traffickers may collaborate with other illicit trades or organized crime groups, sometimes diversifying into other forms of illegal activities.

Firearm Trafficking MO Examples

Straw Purchasing: The trafficker recruits individuals with clean criminal records, known as "straw buyers," to purchase firearms on their behalf from licensed dealers. Sometimes an individual legally purchases firearms on behalf of someone who is prohibited from owning or acquiring them and then transfers the firearms to the prohibited person.

Straw purchasing rings/networks: Firearm traffickers establish networks of individuals who engage in straw purchasing activities, pooling resources, coordinating purchases to acquire large quantities of firearms for resale to distribute them to prohibited individuals or the black market.

Straw purchasing from multiple dealers: Firearm traffickers avoid suspicion by purchasing firearms from multiple licensed dealers to avoid detection or suspicion by authorities.

Straw purchasing from private collectors: Traffickers exploit private collectors or enthusiasts who legally own a significant number of firearms, convincing them to sell or transfer their firearms to the trafficker.

Straw purchasing from gun ranges: The trafficker recruits individuals visiting shooting ranges to purchase firearms on their behalf, taking advantage of the accessibility of firearms and relaxed monitoring at ranges.

Illicit sales at gun shows: The trafficker uses gun shows as a venue to conduct illegal sales of firearms, often exploiting loopholes in regulations and background check requirements.

Trafficking through private sales: Firearm traffickers exploit the loophole in private sales or gun shows to facilitate the illegal transfer of firearms to individuals who are prohibited from owning or acquiring them.

False documentation: Firearm traffickers forge or use fraudulent documents, such as identification cards or background check forms, to deceive sellers and obtain firearms illegally.

Firearms trafficking through mail or shipping: Traffickers conceal firearms in packages or shipping containers to transport them across regions or countries.

Theft and burglary: Firearms are stolen from legal owners, gun stores, shooting ranges, residences, vehicles, or other locations to build their inventory for illegal sales.

Corrupt licensed dealers: The trafficker establishes connections with licensed firearms dealers who knowingly engage in illegal sales or falsify records to supply firearms to the underground market.

Clean transactions: Firearm traffickers use individuals with clean records to purchase firearms legally and then transfer them to criminals or the illicit market.

Interstate trafficking: Firearm traffickers exploit differences in gun laws between states by purchasing firearms in states with lax regulations and selling or transferring them to individuals in states with stricter regulations.

Illegal importation of firearms: The trafficker smuggles firearms into a country or region by circumventing customs controls, utilizing concealed compartments, or exploiting vulnerabilities in border security. Firearms are smuggled across national borders to supply illicit markets where firearms are in high demand or have limited availability.

Conversion of replica firearms: The trafficker modifies or converts replica firearms to make them fully functional and capable of firing live ammunition, enabling the sale of unregistered and untraceable firearms.

Online sales: Firearm traffickers exploit online platforms or dark web marketplaces to facilitate illegal sales or transfers of firearms.

Ghost guns: The trafficker assembles firearms from unfinished receivers or 3D-printed components, creating unserialized and untraceable firearms that can be sold without regulatory scrutiny.

Trafficking from conflict zones: Firearms are obtained from regions experiencing armed conflicts or post-conflict environments and smuggled to other areas for sale or use in criminal activities.

Trade-in schemes: Firearm traffickers use trade-in schemes where individuals can exchange firearms they legally own for new firearms, allowing traffickers to acquire firearms without undergoing background checks.

Firearms theft from law enforcement or military sources: Traffickers target law enforcement agencies, military facilities, or armories to steal firearms, which are then sold or transferred to the illicit market.

Collaboration with criminal organizations/networks: The trafficker operates within established criminal networks, supplying firearms to gang members, organized crime groups, or other illicit organizations involved in criminal activities.

Collaboration with corrupt officials: The trafficker bribes or colludes with corrupt law enforcement officers, customs officials, or other government personnel to facilitate the movement and distribution of firearms.

Front businesses: Firearm traffickers use legitimate businesses as a front to conceal their illegal activities, using them as a cover for acquiring and distributing firearms.

Chop shop operations: The trafficker disassembles firearms and sells the parts individually, making it difficult to trace the origin of the firearms or their components.

Conversion of blank-firing firearms: The trafficker modifies blank-firing firearms to enable them to fire live ammunition, creating seemingly legal firearms that can be sold illegally.

Manufacture of homemade firearms: The trafficker produces firearms from scratch using rudimentary tools and materials, evading regulations and traceability associated with commercially produced firearms.

Straw donations to armed groups or militants: The trafficker disguises the sale or transfer of firearms as charitable donations to armed groups, militants, or terrorist organizations.

Emerging Crime Pattern: Ghost Guns

An emerging trend in firearm trafficking is the rise of "ghost guns." These weapons are manufactured from unfinished receivers or digital blueprints, often assembled at home using widely available 3D printers and parts kits. Because they lack serial numbers, ghost guns are untraceable, bypass background checks, and are increasingly appearing in investigations linked to gang violence and extremist plots. Law enforcement agencies report a sharp increase in ghost gun recoveries, making them one of the fastest-growing sources of illicit firearms in the United States and abroad.[1]

Real-Life Case

"Operation Powder Burn" was an eight-month, multi-agency investigation, led by the Orange County District Attorney's Office, Sheriff's Office, ATF, DEA, and numerous state and local partners, that dismantled the largest gun trafficking network in Orange County's history. The conspiracy involved an "Iron Pipeline" scheme through which handguns and assault weapons from Georgia and Pennsylvania were shipped into New York, often via FedEx deliveries. Investigators executed 55 controlled buys of firearms, corroborated by eavesdropping and surveillance, and recovered an additional 12 firearms during search warrants. The trafficking network was intertwined with narcotics distribution – investigators also seized over 700 grams of fentanyl and cocaine and more than $65,000 in cash. This case underscores the close operational link between illegal gun distribution and drug trafficking, highlighting the multi-faceted nature of violent crime networks.[2]

Crime Pattern Scenario

A regional gun trafficking network operated by a small crew in the Midwest focused on exploiting straw purchasers – individuals with clean records who were paid to buy firearms legally and then transfer them to traffickers. Over a two-year span, the group recruited more than a dozen buyers who purchased multiple handguns at licensed dealers across three states. The firearms were then moved in small quantities hidden inside commercial trucking shipments, ultimately supplying local gangs in urban centers. Investigators later determined that several of the trafficked weapons were recovered at crime scenes involving robberies and assaults. This case illustrates a repeating pattern where seemingly minor, legal purchases, when aggregated and redirected, fuel organized violence and demonstrate how money laundering, interstate travel, and violent crime are tied to firearms trafficking.

Exercises

1. Obtain a publicly available annual firearms-trace report from the ATF or your state. Identify the top two source states or countries for crime guns recovered in your jurisdiction. Discuss how differences in gun laws between those source regions and your own could create a pattern for traffickers to exploit.
2. Search for an article or government bulletin about ghost guns or 3D-printed firearms. Identify the main regulatory challenge described and list two investigative indicators (e.g., online parts sales, use of specific printing materials) that could help analysts flag serial trafficking of untraceable weapons.

Critical Thinking Guidance

To link cases in firearm trafficking, look beyond individual seizures and examine patterns in sourcing, transport, and distribution. Firearms may circulate through multiple hands, but consistent variables (such as the same straw purchaser appearing in multiple cases, repeat use of certain shipping methods, or concentration of recoveries in a specific gang territory) reveal trafficking networks rather than isolated crimes. Consider how traffickers adapt to enforcement: for example, shifting from interstate trafficking to ghost guns when interstate regulations tighten. Linking cases requires combining trace data, ballistics, financial records, and community intelligence to identify serial trafficking behaviors.

Notes

1 Karni and Cameron (2025, March 26).
2 Orange County District Attorney's Office (2025, August 1).

Bibliography

Braga, A. A., Cook, P. J., Kennedy, D. M., & Moore, M. H. (2002). The illegal supply of firearms. *Crime and Justice*, *29*, 319–352. https://doi.org/10.1086/652223

Bureau of Alcohol, Tobacco, Firearms and Explosives. (2023). *National firearms commerce and trafficking assessment: Firearms in commerce*. U.S. Department of Justice. www.atf.gov/firearms/docs/report/national-firearms-commerce-and-trafficking-assessment-firearms-commerce-volume/download

Karni, A., & Cameron, C. (2025, March 26). What are ghost guns? *The New York Times*. www.nytimes.com/2025/03/26/us/politics/what-are-ghost-guns.html

New York State Office of the Attorney General. (n.d.). *Target on trafficking: New York crime gun analysis*. https://targettrafficking.ag.ny.gov/#toppart

Orange County District Attorney's Office. (2025, August 1). *Operation Powder Burn: Largest gun and drug trafficking ring dismantled in Orange County history* [Press release]. Orange County District Attorney's Office.

Police Executive Research Forum. (2017). *The "crime gun intelligence center" model: Case studies of the Denver, Milwaukee, and Chicago approaches to investigating gun crime*. www.policeforum.org/assets/crimegunintelligencecenter.pdf

54 Human Trafficking and Smuggling

Introduction

Human trafficking and human smuggling are terms that are sometimes used interchangeably, but they describe distinct activities: trafficking centers on the exploitation of individuals through force, fraud, or coercion, while smuggling involves the consensual but illegal movement of people across borders, usually for financial gain. Trafficking victims are often exploited for sex, labor, or other forms of servitude, whereas smuggling participants may later become vulnerable to exploitation, creating overlap between the two crimes. Both crimes thrive on global migration pressures, economic inequality, political instability, and organized crime networks that profit from human vulnerability. Recognizing the differences and the ways in which these activities intersect is critical to identifying patterns, protecting victims, and dismantling the criminal enterprises that sustain them.

Human Trafficking Versus Human Smuggling

While the terms are sometimes used interchangeably, these crimes differ in both intent and impact. Human trafficking is the exploitation of people through force, fraud, or coercion for purposes such as forced labor, sexual exploitation, or servitude. Consent is irrelevant once exploitation occurs, and victims are controlled through violence, threats, or deception.

Human smuggling, by contrast, involves the consensual but illegal transport of individuals across borders for financial gain. The relationship between smuggler and migrant typically ends after the border crossing.

The distinction lies in coercion versus consent: trafficking is a crime against a person, while smuggling is a crime against a country's immigration laws. However, the two can overlap when a smuggling arrangement shifts into trafficking – for example, when migrants are later coerced into forced labor or sex work to repay debts. Understanding this difference is essential for investigators to correctly identify victims and apply the appropriate legal and support responses.

Human Trafficking MO Variables

Target Selection and Pre-Crime Preparation: Recruitment Phase

- Target Identification: Traffickers frequently target vulnerable individuals, such as those in financial hardship, or those without a strong support network. The choice of target often depends on market demand and ease of manipulation.

DOI: 10.4324/9781003728733-57

- Recruitment Method: Methods of recruitment can range from fraudulent job offers to kidnapping. Some traffickers employ "groomers" to build relationships with victims before ensnaring them.
- Initial Coercion or Deception: Misleading promises are often used at this stage, such as offers of employment or a better life, to lure victims away from their home environment.

Execution

Capture and Containment

- Transportation: Once recruited, victims are usually moved to a location where they are easier to control. This may be within the same country or across international borders.
- Document Seizure: Traffickers often take away victims' identification documents to make escape and identification more difficult.
- Initial Exploitation: This can involve forced labor, sexual exploitation, or other forms of abuse. The objective is often to break down the victim's will to resist.

Exploitation Phase

- Living Conditions: Victims are often kept in squalid, prison-like conditions where their basic needs are barely met, further weakening their will and ability to resist or escape.
- Systematic Exploitation: This is the phase where the traffickers generate revenue from the victims. This could be through forced labor, sexual exploitation, or even organ harvesting.
- Control Mechanisms: Traffickers use a variety of means to control their victims, from physical violence to psychological manipulation, including debt bondage and threats against the victim's family.

Specific Marketing: Distribution and Sale

- Market Strategy: Traffickers usually have specific markets where they "sell" their victims, or the goods produced by them. These could be brothels, sweatshops, or illegal online platforms.
- Financial Transactions: Payment for trafficked victims or their services usually involves cash or other untraceable means to evade detection.

Intermediaries: Legal and Illegal Support

- Corrupt Practices: Traffickers often rely on corrupt law enforcement officials, border guards, and other authorities to ignore or actively facilitate their activities.
- Use of Technology: Modern traffickers also make extensive use of technology for recruitment, coordination, and exploitation purposes.

Post-Crime Activities: Exit Strategy

- Disposal or Release: Once they are no longer "useful," victims are either discarded, sold to another trafficker, or in rare cases, released.
- Adaptation and Evolution: Traffickers adapt their MO in response to law enforcement activities and public awareness. They update their recruitment strategies, exploitation methods, and transit routes to evade capture.

Examples of Types of Human Trafficking

Sex Trafficking: Victims are coerced, lured, or forced into prostitution and other forms of commercial sexual exploitation.

Forced Labor: Also known as involuntary servitude, victims are forced to work under severe conditions, often in factories, farms, or construction sites.

Bonded Labor or Debt Bondage: Victims are compelled to work to repay a debt and are unable to leave until the debt is repaid. It's a form of coerced labor.

Domestic Servitude: Victims are forced to work in homes as domestic helpers, nannies, or housekeepers, without freedom of movement.

Child Labor: Unlawful exploitation of children for labor. This often happens in exploitative, unregulated, or hazardous working conditions.

Child Soldiers: Children are forcibly recruited by armed groups and used as combatants, informants, or other forms of labor.

Forced Marriage: Individuals are compelled to marry against their will, often under threats of violence or severe social repercussions.

Organ Trafficking: The illegal trade of organs, where victims are forced or deceived into giving up an organ.

Commercial Surrogacy: Women are forcibly impregnated, and their babies are sold, often under the guise of legitimate surrogacy agreements.

Forced Criminality: Victims are forced to engage in illegal activities like drug cultivation, theft, or scams.

Begging Rings: Individuals, often children, are forced to beg on the streets. Their earnings are then taken by the traffickers.

Child Sexual Exploitation: Involves exploiting children for the sexual gratification of others, including child pornography production.

Tourism Trafficking: Victims are exploited within the tourism industry, for either labor or sexual exploitation.

Online Trafficking: Exploiting victims by forcing them into performing non-consensual acts over webcams or other online platforms.

Recruitment Through False Job Offers: Victims are offered employment opportunities in foreign countries but upon arrival are forced into labor or sexual exploitation.

Human Smuggling

Human smuggling involves the facilitation of illegal entry of individuals across international borders, typically in exchange for financial or other material gain. While it differs from human trafficking in terms of the presence of consent and exploitation, the two can often overlap or evolve into each other.

Human Smuggling MO Variables

Target Selection: Recruitment and Organization

- Initial Contact: Smugglers usually establish initial contact with potential migrants through social networks, word-of-mouth, or advertising on digital platforms.
- Screening and Assessment: Smugglers may assess the financial capacity, motivation, and risk factors associated with potential clients before accepting them.

Pre-Crime Preparation: Planning and Logistics

- Itinerary Planning: Smugglers often have detailed plans for the journey, including routes, transportation modes, and rest stops.
- Documentation: False or altered identification documents may be prepared or acquired for use at border checkpoints.
- Financing: Upfront payments, installment plans, or post-arrival payments are usually discussed and agreed upon.

Execution

- Mode of Transport: Various forms of transportation may be used, including cars, trucks, boats, or even commercial flights, depending on the length and complexity of the journey.
- Concealment Techniques: Smugglers employ various concealment methods such as hidden compartments in vehicles or mingling with legitimate travelers.
- Accompanying Persons: In some cases, an "escort" may accompany the individuals being smuggled to guide and assist them through various stages of the journey.

Transportation

- Crossing Points and Border Checks
- Location of Crossing: Smugglers typically have knowledge of less-frequented border points or times when border security may be lax.
- Corruption and Collusion: Bribes or relationships with corrupt officials can be employed to facilitate smoother border crossings.

Arrival and Settlement

- Drop-off Points: Upon arrival, individuals are usually dropped off at predetermined locations, often in proximity to their final destination.
- Post-Arrival Services: Some smugglers offer additional services like accommodation, employment assistance, or further internal transportation.

Communication: Security and Evasion Measures

- Use of Technology: Encrypted messaging apps, disposable cell phones, or GPS devices may be used for secure communication and coordination.
- Code Words and Signals: Smugglers often use a system of code words, hand signals, or other non-verbal cues to communicate with clients and associates to evade detection.

Avoidance of Capture: Adaptability

- Response to Law Enforcement: Smugglers quickly adapt to changes in immigration policies and border enforcement techniques, altering routes and methods as needed.

Example Human Smuggling Methods and Routes

Land-Based Smuggling: Individuals are transported across land borders, often hidden in vehicles or guided by foot through unpatrolled areas.

Maritime Smuggling: Smuggling by sea, often involving dangerous and overcrowded boats. The Mediterranean and Southeast Asia are common regions for this type of smuggling.

Air Smuggling: Use of false documentation to enter another country by plane or sometimes being hidden in cargo.

Visa Overstay: Entering a country legally but staying beyond the permitted time, often facilitated by smugglers who provide false documentation.

Document Fraud: Utilizing forged or altered documents, such as passports or visas, to enter another country.

Safe House Networks: Use of a series of safe houses to move individuals across multiple borders or distances in stages.

Coyote Smuggling: In Latin America, "coyotes" are individuals who specialize in smuggling people across the US–Mexico border.

Mule Operations: Use of "mules" to transport individuals across borders; often these are people who transport both drugs and humans.

Employment-Based Schemes: Offering false job opportunities in another country as a means of smuggling individuals.

Family Reunification: Smuggled under the guise of reuniting families; often involves minors being sent across borders unaccompanied.

Trafficking Corridors: Specific routes that are frequently used for smuggling, often controlled by organized crime groups.

Underground Railways: Coordinated efforts to move people from one safe place to another until they reach their final destination, similar to the Underground Railroad from American history.

High-End Smuggling: Smuggling operations catering to wealthier individuals, offering safer and more comfortable conditions, often for a very high price.

Emerging Crime Pattern: Encrypted Communication Platforms and Cryptocurrency Payments

A trend in human trafficking and smuggling is the integration of encrypted communication platforms and cryptocurrency payments into offender operations. Recruiters now use end-to-end encrypted messaging apps such as WhatsApp, Telegram, and Signal to lure victims with fraudulent job offers or migration opportunities, making monitoring by law enforcement more difficult. At the same time, payments for smuggling services and exploitation profits are increasingly funneled through cryptocurrencies, which offer perceived anonymity and make financial tracking challenging. This dual shift – secure recruitment channels and decentralized financial flows – creates layered barriers to detection while allowing traffickers and smugglers to operate across borders with fewer physical interactions. Recognizing consistent patterns in digital recruitment language, repeated cryptocurrency wallets, and the use of closed-group chats can help analysts detect and link cases across jurisdictions.[1]

Crime Pattern Scenario

A law enforcement task force in a US border state begins noticing a pattern of young women from Central America being discovered in labor trafficking situations at agricultural sites. Interviews reveal that many were first approached with promises of legitimate farm jobs but, upon arrival, had their documents confiscated and were forced to work under threats of violence. At the same time, investigators intercept a group of migrants smuggled through the same route, who report paying coyotes to bring them across the border. The overlapping routes, safe houses, and financial facilitators suggest that the same criminal organization is engaged in both trafficking and smuggling, shifting between the two crimes depending on profit opportunities. This linkage highlights how analyzing recruitment tactics, routes, and financial patterns together can help distinguish and connect cases.

Exercises

1. Review a national or regional assessment (e.g., Europol or Department of Homeland Security) and note one trafficking or smuggling route. Describe the route, the main transport methods, and any repeated concealment tactics. Explain how recognizing those repeated elements would help law enforcement identify a larger criminal network.
2. Using publicly available government or NGO reports (such as UNODC or US State Department), create a simple diagram showing how trafficking and smuggling can intersect. Identify at least two points where smuggling operations can turn into trafficking (e.g., migrants being forced into labor when they cannot pay their smuggling debt).

Critical Thinking Guidance

Human trafficking and smuggling share logistical similarities (routes, facilitators, and methods of concealment), yet they diverge sharply in intent and victim impact. Evaluate whether the situation involves consent that later erodes into coercion (a smuggling case evolving into trafficking) or whether exploitation was the purpose from the outset. Consider whether the victim is free to leave, who profits from the arrangement, and whether force, fraud, or coercion is present. A critical mindset avoids collapsing both categories into one and ensures responses are tailored: immigration enforcement for smuggling versus victim-centered support and prosecution for trafficking.

Note

1 ATII (2020, December 8).

Bibliography

ATII. (2020, December 8). *Special ATII report: Crypto transactions and human trafficking – a non-traditional investigation perspective for traditional financial institutions.* www.acfcs.org/special-atii-report-crypto-transactions-and-human-trafficking-a-non-traditional-investigation-perspective-for-traditional-financial-institutions

Council of Europe. (2022). *Online and technology-facilitated trafficking in human beings: Summary report.* https://rm.coe.int/online-and-technology-facilitated-trafficking-in-human-beings-summary-/1680a5e10c

Department of Homeland Security. (n.d.). *Indicators of human trafficking.* www.dhs.gov/blue-campaign/indicators-human-trafficking

Europol. (2024). *Tackling threats, addressing challenges: Europol's response to migrant smuggling and trafficking in human beings in 2023 and onwards* (European Migrant Smuggling Centre, Public Information). Publications Office of the European Union. https://doi.org/10.2813/203212

Homeland Security Investigations. (2017). *Human trafficking vs. human smuggling.* U.S. Department of Homeland Security. www.ice.gov/sites/default/files/documents/Report/2017/CSReport-13-1.pdf

Newman, G. R., & Corey, J. (2020). *Exploitation of trafficked women* (2nd ed., Problem-Specific Guide Series No. 38). Office of Community Oriented Policing Services, U.S. Department of Justice. https://popcenter.asu.edu/content/exploitation-trafficked-women-2nd-ed

U.S. Department of State. (n.d.). *About human trafficking.* www.state.gov/humantrafficking-about-human-trafficking/

55 Wildlife, Forest, and Fisheries Crime

Introduction

> "Wildlife, forest, and fisheries crime refers to any criminal activity connected with the taking, trading (supplying, selling, or trafficking), importing, exporting, processing, possessing, obtaining and consumption of wild fauna and flora, including timber *and other forest products, in contravention of national or international law.*[1]"

Wildlife, forest, and fisheries crimes represent one of the fastest-growing areas of transnational organized crime, undermining biodiversity, threatening food security, and funding armed groups and criminal syndicates. These crimes span from poaching endangered animals for ivory, rhino horn, or exotic pets, to illegal logging that fuels deforestation, and illegal, unreported, and unregulated fishing that depletes marine ecosystems. Unlike other crime types, detection is especially difficult because victims (animals, forests, or fish stocks) cannot report their exploitation, leaving much of the problem hidden. As Andrew Lemieux (manager of the Problem-Oriented Wildlife Protection program for LEAD Ranger which is an organization that supports wildlife park rangers around the world) notes, this creates a chronic underreporting problem and allows traffickers to operate with relative impunity.[2]

The illicit proceeds of these crimes often rival those of narcotics or arms trafficking, with billions of dollars annually moving through complex smuggling networks that converge with corruption, money laundering, and even terrorism financing. Understanding the modus operandi (MO) of offenders, from subsistence hunters to transnational criminal organizations, is essential for detecting patterns, disrupting supply chains, and protecting ecosystems that communities and economies rely on worldwide.

Scope and Definitions

Wildlife crime involves the illegal taking, trade, or possession of wild animals and their parts – such as poaching endangered species for ivory or capturing exotic birds for the pet trade – in violation of national or international law.

Forest crime refers to unlawful logging, land clearing, or trade in timber and other forest products, including the use of fraudulent permits or corruption to harvest protected forests.

Fisheries crime encompasses illegal, unreported, and unregulated (IUU) fishing and related offenses such as fish smuggling, mislabeling catch, or using prohibited gear, all of which threaten marine ecosystems and legitimate fishing economies.

DOI: 10.4324/9781003728733-58

Wildlife, Forest, and Fisheries Crimes MO Variables

Specific Types of Offenders

- Subsistence Harvesters: Harvesting for household or local use.
- Specialists: Commercially oriented with specific skills or technologies.
- Opportunists: Harvest based on chance encounters.
- Local Guides: Locals aiding non-residents in illegal harvesting.
- Rule Abusers: Individuals knowingly breaking laws such as quotas or protected area restrictions.
- Bycatch Operators: Those unintentionally capturing non-target species.
- Recreational Offenders: Harvesting for enjoyment rather than livelihood.
- Reactionaries: Harvesting in protest against conservation policies.

Pre-Crime Preparation: Harvesting Phase

- Target Identification: Choosing specific animal or plant species that are high-value or easy to capture. Decisions are made on the basis of market demand, ease of access, and risk factors.
- Method of Capture: The type of equipment and techniques used to capture the target species. This can range from high-tech traps and snares to traditional hunting methods. The choice often depends on the expertise of the harvesters and the degree of specialization.
- Location and Timing: Picking specific areas and times that maximize the chances of a successful harvest while minimizing the risk of detection. For example, traffickers may operate during times of low surveillance or in remote areas. Offenses may be committed during specific seasons or times of day.

Transportation

- Smuggling Routes: The choice of routes for transporting the harvested species, often through less patrolled or poorly monitored areas. This might also involve the use of decoy vehicles or diversions.
- Concealment Techniques: Methods for hiding the harvested items during transportation. This could include custom compartments in vehicles, the use of other goods as cover, or mislabeling cargo to disguise its true nature.

Execution: Sale and Distribution

- Market Strategy: Identification of target markets and customers. This could involve direct sale to consumers or through intermediaries like vendors, on online platforms, and in black markets.
- Payment Methods: How transactions are completed, which might range from cash to digital currencies, to evade financial scrutiny.
- Laundering Techniques: The use of various methods to legitimize the illegal products, such as mixing them with legally acquired items or using fraudulent documentation to verify their origin.

Post-Trafficking Activities

- Exit Strategies: Plans for retreating from the operation safely and minimizing traces that could lead back to the traffickers.
- Adaptation: An often-overlooked aspect is the traffickers' ability to adapt their MO based on successes, failures, and changes in law enforcement tactics.

- Specific Markets: Consumers
- Medicinal Users: Individuals using the products for traditional or novel medical practices.
- Ornamental Users: Individuals using products like ivory or shells for decoration.
- Cultural Users: Those involved in long-standing traditional practices, often ritualistic.

Targeted Wildlife Examples

Endangered Species: Species that are endangered or protected by law, such as elephants, rhinos, tigers, pangolins, and sea turtles, are often targeted for their valuable body parts, such as ivory, horns, skins, scales, or shells, which are used in traditional medicine, jewelry, or for ornamental purposes.

Birds: Rare and exotic bird species, particularly parrots, raptors, and songbirds, are illegally captured for the pet trade or for their feathers, which may be used in fashion accessories or traditional ceremonies.

Reptiles: Snakes, lizards, and turtles, including endangered species like tortoises and certain exotic reptiles, are captured, and traded for the pet market or for their skin, which can be used in the production of luxury accessories.

Marine Wildlife: Species like whales, dolphins, sharks, and various fish are targeted for their meat, fins (for shark fin soup), blubber, or other body parts, often for consumption or use in traditional medicines.

Timber and Plants: Illegal logging and trade of timber, as well as the collection and smuggling of endangered plant species, such as orchids and cacti, are also forms of wildlife crime.

Illegal Fishing: Overfishing, destructive fishing practices, and the illegal trade of fish and seafood, including high-value species like sturgeon (source of caviar), are significant wildlife crime concerns.

Bushmeat: The illegal hunting and trade of wild animals for their meat, referred to as bushmeat, occur in many regions, particularly in Africa, Asia, and South America. This includes animals like monkeys, antelope, bats, and various rodents.

Crime Type Examples

Wildlife Crimes

Poaching: Illegal hunting, capturing, or killing of protected or endangered species.

Wildlife Trafficking: Illegal trade in wildlife and their parts, such as elephant ivory, rhino horn, and tiger bones.

Illegal Pet Trade: Capturing and selling wild animals as exotic pets.

Illegal Bird Trading: Capture and sale of protected bird species, often for pet markets or avian products.

Bushmeat Trade: Illegal hunting and sale of wild animals for food.

Conflict With Protected Species: Deliberately killing or capturing protected species due to human–wildlife conflict, often by agricultural communities.

Canned Hunting: The hunting of captive or semi-captive animals in confined areas from which they cannot escape.

Forest Crimes

Illegal Logging: Unauthorized cutting down of trees in protected areas or on public lands.

Land Grabbing: Illegal acquisition of forested land for agricultural or commercial purposes.

Illegal Timber Trade: Unlawful selling or exporting of timber.

Forest Degradation: Actions that reduce the quality of the forest, often as a result of illegal activities.

Wildfires: Deliberately setting fires for land clearance or other illegal purposes.
Non-Timber Forest Products (NTFPs) Crimes: Illegal gathering and trade of products like mushrooms, berries, and medicinal plants.

Fisheries Crimes

Illegal, Unreported, and Unregulated (IUU) Fishing: Fishing activities that violate national laws or international obligations.
Bycatch: The illegal or unregulated capture of non-target fish or marine species during commercial fishing.
Fisheries Fraud: Mislabeling of fish species, weight, or origin to evade regulations or tariffs.
Ghost Fishing: Abandoning fishing gear in the water, leading to uncontrolled and wasteful killing of marine life.
Use of Prohibited Gear: Employing illegal fishing techniques or equipment, such as dynamite or cyanide fishing.
Fish Smuggling: Illegally exporting or importing fish to evade tariffs or regulations.
Aquatic Invasive Species: Illegal introduction of non-native species into water bodies, often from ballast water discharge from ships.

Emerging Crime Pattern: Online Wildlife Trafficking

A significant trend in wildlife crime is the use of social media platforms, encrypted messaging apps, and online marketplaces to facilitate illegal wildlife trade. Offenders now bypass traditional smuggling networks by directly advertising ivory carvings, live reptiles, exotic birds, and even pangolins to global buyers. These transactions often involve coded language using emojis of trees, leaves, or animals to disguise sales, and digital payments, including cryptocurrencies, to obscure money trails. This digital shift broadens offender reach, accelerates transactions, and complicates enforcement, as platforms are global while laws and jurisdictions remain local.[3]

Real-Life Case

In August 2025, a Chinese national pleaded guilty to exporting approximately 850 protected eastern box turtles and three-toed box turtles, valued at around $1.4 million, to Hong Kong. The live turtles were concealed in mailed parcels falsely labeled as "plastic animal toys," tightly bound inside socks. This case reflects a broader pattern in wildlife trafficking where traffickers exploit international postal systems, mislabel protected species, and target high-demand markets in Asia.[4]

Crime Pattern Scenario

During a multi-agency operation in West Africa, customs officials at a coastal port intercepted a shipping container declared as "frozen seafood." Inside, inspectors discovered several hundred kilograms of shark fins concealed beneath layers of legitimately caught fish. Forensic review of shipping records revealed that the same exporter had repeatedly sent nearly identical consignments to East Asia over the past year, each using different shell companies and rotating freight forwarders to mask ownership. Financial investigators later uncovered that profits from these shipments were laundered through a network of small import – export businesses that also moved counterfeit pharmaceuticals. The pattern of mislabeling, recurring shipping routes, and overlapping illicit trades highlighted how fisheries crime can be systematically linked to broader transnational organized crime networks.

Exercises

1. Search online for recent government or NGO reports on illegal wildlife trade (such as INTERPOL, UNODC, or TRAFFIC). Identify one method of concealment traffickers use in wildlife or timber smuggling (e.g., hiding ivory in coffee shipments or mixing illegal logs with legal timber). Write three to four sentences explaining why this method works and how law enforcement might detect it.
2. Write a short paragraph describing one way wildlife, forest, or fisheries crime can converge with other organized crimes (such as drug trafficking, money laundering, or terrorism financing). Suggest one data source or investigative partnership (e.g., financial intelligence units, customs agencies) that could help uncover these links.

Critical Thinking Guidance

Wildlife, forest, and fisheries crimes are often "low visibility crimes." Offenders take advantage of the fact that the immediate victims (animals, plants, ecosystems) cannot report exploitation, and enforcement agencies may lack resources. This makes pattern recognition especially challenging. Ask: What indicators suggest an organized, repeated MO rather than isolated incidents? For example, repeated seizures of mislabeled timber from the same port, or multiple exotic pet advertisements tied to the same usernames, suggest an organized trafficking pattern. Consider how convergence with other crimes (such as drug smuggling or money laundering) magnifies the problem. View these crimes not in isolation but as interconnected nodes in broader illicit supply chains that can be tied to corruption, terrorism, or transnational organized crime.

Notes

1 Homeland Security Investigations (n.d.).
2 Ratcliffe (2023, June 29).
3 U.S. Department of the Interior (2021, April 27).
4 U.S. Department of Justice (2025, August 11).

Bibliography

Homeland Security Investigations. (n.d.). *Wildlife trafficking campaign partner social media toolkit.* U.S. Department of Homeland Security. www.ice.gov/toolkit/wildlife

Phelps, J., Biggs, D., & Webb, E. L. (2016). Tools and terms for understanding illegal wildlife trade. *Frontiers in Ecology and the Environment, 14*(9), 479–489. https://doi.org/10.1002/fee.1325

Ratcliffe, J. (Host). (2023, June 29). *#60 Andrew Lemieux* [Audio podcast episode]. Reducing Crime. https://soundcloud.com/reducingcrime/60-andrew-lemieux

United Nations Office on Drugs and Crime. (2022). *Wildlife and forest crime analytic toolkit* (2nd ed.). United Nations. www.unodc.org/documents/Wildlife/Toolkit_e.pdf

U.S. Department of the Interior. (2021, April 27). *Online wildlife trafficking marketplace.* Office of Law Enforcement. www.doi.gov/ocl/online-wildlife-trafficking-marketplace

U.S. Department of Justice. (2025, August 11). *Chinese national pleads guilty to exporting protected turtles*. U.S. Attorney's Office, Western District of New York. www.justice.gov/opa/pr/chinese-national-pleads-guilty-exporting-protected-turtles

van Uhm, D. P., & Nijman, R. C. C. (2020). The convergence of environmental crime with other serious crimes: Subtypes within the environmental crime continuum. *European Journal of Criminology*, *19*(4), 542–561. https://doi.org/10.1177/1477370820904585

56 Environmental Crimes

Introduction

Environmental crimes encompass the unlawful release, disposal, or mismanagement of pollutants and natural resources that cause harm to ecosystems, communities, and public health. These offenses include the illegal dumping of hazardous waste, unauthorized industrial emissions, unlawful mining or logging, and fraudulent handling of chemicals or carbon credits. Unlike more visible crimes, environmental violations are often hidden within routine industrial activity, making them harder to detect until widespread damage occurs. Organized crime groups and corrupt officials frequently play a role, profiting from illegal dumping, resource theft, and cross-border waste trafficking. Because the impact of these crimes can span years and affect entire populations, analyzing crime patterns (such as recurring discharge locations, falsified permits, or repeated ecological damage) offers law enforcement and regulators critical insights for identifying systemic offenders and preventing further harm.

Definitions

Pollution and Waste Crime: Illegal disposal or release of hazardous materials, including industrial emissions and dumping.

Resource Exploitation Crime: Unlawful extraction of timber, minerals, or water resources that depletes ecosystems.

Climate and Energy Fraud: Manipulation of carbon credits or renewable energy schemes to obtain illicit profit.

Environmental Crime MO Variables

Motivation and Planning

- Cost Savings: One of the primary motivations for companies or individuals to commit pollution crimes is to avoid costs related to proper disposal or treatment of waste and emissions.
- Regulatory Loopholes: Perpetrators might exploit gaps or ambiguities in environmental regulations to argue that their actions are not explicitly illegal.
- Industrial Secrecy: Industries may hide behind trade secrets to avoid disclosing the full extent of pollutants they release.

DOI: 10.4324/9781003728733-59

Target Selection

- Vulnerable Locations: Sites with limited surveillance or near economically disadvantaged communities are often targeted, as the likelihood of detection and public outcry may be lower.
- Natural Water Sources: Rivers, lakes, and oceans may be targeted for the illegal dumping of pollutants due to their ability to dilute substances, making detection more challenging.

Pre-Crime Preparation

- False Documentation: Offenders may prepare fake permits, licenses, or waste disposal records to show compliance with regulations.
- Corrupt Networks: Building relationships with corrupt officials can help perpetrators avoid inspections or fines.

Execution

- Timing: Crimes are often committed during off-hours or holidays to evade detection.
- Concealment Methods: Specialized containers, vehicles, or other means may be used to store and transport the pollutants covertly.
- Deceptive Labeling: Hazardous materials may be mislabeled as non-hazardous to avoid scrutiny.

Intermediaries and Distribution Networks

- Third-Party Contractors: Some companies employ third-party contractors to handle waste, thereby distancing themselves from direct involvement in the crime.
- Shell Companies: Fictitious companies may be used to disguise the real entity behind the pollution.

Avoidance of Capture

- Monitoring Evasion: Offenders may have knowledge of environmental monitoring schedules and locations, planning their activities to evade detection.
- Data Falsification: Emission data or waste disposal records may be falsified to present a compliant image.
- Bribes and Kickbacks: Offering bribes to regulatory officials or inspectors is a common tactic to avoid penalties.

Post-Crime Activities

- Asset Movement: Financial gains obtained from the crime might be moved to different accounts or different countries to avoid asset forfeiture.
- Disinformation: Public relations campaigns or biased studies may be employed to cloud public perception and deflect attention.

Indicators

Indicators of possible environmental violations according to the Environmental Protection Agency:[1]

- strong, offensive, or unusual chemical odors
- large numbers of dead birds, fish, or other animals

- pipes or valves appear hidden or bypass waste treatment systems
- tank trucks discharging into drains, manholes, or bodies of water
- oily slicks on bodies of water
- drums or containers dumped at odd hours in out-of-the-way places
- corroded, leaking waste containers

Environmental Crime Examples

Pollution and Waste Disposal

- Illegal Dumping: Unlawful disposal of waste in unauthorized locations often to avoid disposal fees or regulatory oversight.
- Air Pollution: Emission of harmful substances into the atmosphere in violation of regulations often from industrial sources. Water Pollution: Illegal discharge of pollutants into water bodies often from factories or agricultural run-off. Chemical Waste: Improper disposal or handling of hazardous chemicals often from industrial processes.

Natural Resource Exploitation

- Illegal Mining: Unauthorized extraction of minerals and ores.
- Unregulated Sand Mining: Illegal extraction of sand from rivers and beaches, often causing significant environmental degradation.
- Illegal Water Extraction: Unauthorized removal of groundwater or surface water, often for agricultural or industrial use.

Chemical and Substance Crimes

- Illegal Pesticides and Fertilizers: Use or sale of banned or restricted chemicals in agriculture.
- Ozone-Depleting Substances: Production, trade, or use of substances that are known to deplete the ozone layer, in violation of international agreements like the Montreal Protocol.

Corporate and Institutional Crimes

- Environmental Fraud: False representation of environmental compliance, often by companies to evade regulations.
- Environmental Corruption: Bribing or otherwise influencing public officials to overlook or permit environmental violations.

Climate and Energy Crimes

- Carbon Credit Fraud: Falsification of carbon offset credits, either by misrepresenting emissions reductions or by selling the same credits multiple times.
- Renewable Energy Scams: Fraudulent schemes related to the generation or sale of renewable energy.

Crime Pattern Scenario

In a rural area, residents notice a strong chemical odor near a small river where fish and other wildlife have begun dying in large numbers. Local farmers also report that their crops near the riverbanks are wilting. Investigation reveals that a nearby manufacturing facility has been discharging untreated chemical waste into the river at night and during weekends to avoid detection. To conceal the crime, the company falsified its wastewater treatment logs and paid bribes to a local inspector. The consistent timing of the discharges, combined with falsified documentation and the use of tanker trucks at night, demonstrates a clear pattern of environmental crime that links the facility to ongoing ecological damage.

Exercises

1. Research online for a recent case of illegal dumping, industrial pollution, or hazardous waste disposal reported in your country or region. Summarize the case in a few sentences. Identify two MO variables (such as concealment, corruption, falsified permits) that align with the framework described in this chapter. Reflect on how those indicators could have been detected earlier by regulators, communities, or investigators.
2. Search online for two recent news stories on different types of environmental crimes (e.g., illegal logging and hazardous waste dumping). In a paragraph, compare the offenders' motives and methods. Highlight at least one similarity in how the crimes were concealed or profited from.

Critical Thinking Guidance

Environmental crimes often remain hidden because they are carried out by legitimate-seeming businesses that falsify records or use intermediaries to distance themselves from direct involvement. Analysts and investigators must critically assess whether patterns of ecological harm – such as repeated fish die-offs or clusters of illness – could signal deliberate illegal activity rather than accidental contamination. Cross-referencing environmental data (air and water quality reports, health complaints, satellite imagery) with regulatory records can help identify inconsistencies that point toward intentional violations. A key challenge is distinguishing between lawful but harmful industrial practices and outright illegal acts, requiring a careful balance between regulatory knowledge, scientific evidence, and investigative reasoning.

Note

1 Environmental Protection Agency (n.d.).

Bibliography

Environmental Protection Agency. (n.d.). *Criminal investigations.* U.S. Environmental Protection Agency. www.epa.gov/enforcement/criminal-investigations

Nellemann, C., Henriksen, R., Raxter, P., Ash, N., & Mrema, E. (Eds.). (2016). *The rise of environmental crime: A growing threat to natural resources, peace, development and security.* United Nations Environment Programme & Interpol. www.unep.org/resources/report/rise-environmental-crime

U.S. Department of Justice, Environment & Natural Resources Division. (2023). *FY 2023 accomplishments report.* www.justice.gov/enrd/media/1348776/dl?inline=

57 Cultural Property Crimes

Introduction

Cultural property crimes involve distinct sets of techniques, strategies, and patterns that offenders use to commit offenses such as art theft, artifact smuggling, or illegal excavation of archaeological sites. These crimes go beyond theft of property; they strip communities of their heritage, erase history, and often fuel broader networks of organized crime

Criminals and terrorists are turning more frequently to cultural property crimes in order to fund their activities because they are less risky and sometimes more lucrative than human, drug, and firearm trafficking.[1]

Definitions

Cultural property crime: Theft, illicit trade, or destruction of objects of historical, artistic, or archaeological significance.

Art crime: A subset focusing on fine art and high-value cultural objects.

Antiquities trafficking: Smuggling of archaeological artifacts, often from conflict or excavation zones.

Cultural Property Crimes MO Variables

Motivation and Planning

- Financial Gain: The primary motivator for most criminals in this sector is the high monetary value of cultural property.
- Collectors' Demands: Often, items are stolen or looted to fulfill the demands of private collectors.
- Research and Reconnaissance: Offenders might carry out extensive research to identify valuable items and their locations.

Target Selection

- High-Value Items: Preference for artifacts, artworks, or historical items with significant cultural or monetary value.
- Vulnerable Locations: Targeting museums, galleries, private collections, or archaeological sites with inadequate security measures.

DOI: 10.4324/9781003728733-60

Pre-Crime Preparation

- Forgery and Documentation: Preparing fake documentation and certificates of authenticity for the stolen or smuggled items.
- Tools and Equipment: Obtaining special tools for breaking in, disabling security systems, or excavating sites.

Execution

- Stealth Techniques: Use of sophisticated or discreet methods to avoid detection during the act of stealing, excavating, or smuggling.
- Teamwork: Often involves a group with specialized skills: lock-picking, hacking security systems, or experienced handling of fragile artifacts.
- Transportation: Immediate and well-planned transportation of the stolen or smuggled items to a secure location, often using unmarked or stolen vehicles.

Intermediaries and Distribution Networks

- Brokers and Middlemen: These are individuals or groups specializing in the illegal sale and transportation of cultural property.
- Online Platforms: Use of the dark web or open online platforms for sales, auctions, or trades.
- Global Networks: Connections with international smuggling rings for moving the stolen artifacts across borders.

Avoidance of Capture

- Altering Identity: Offenders may manipulate the appearance or historical description of stolen items to prevent identification.
- Offshore Storage: Utilizing overseas storage to keep items away from local jurisdictions where the crime occurred.
- Layered Transactions: Multiple buy-sell operations to make tracing the original theft more difficult.

Post-Crime Activities

- Money Laundering: Profits from the sales are often laundered through complex financial arrangements.
- Retaining Anonymity: Criminals typically operate under aliases and utilize encrypted communication channels.

Cultural Property Defined

The United Nations Education, Scientific and Cultural Organization (UNESCO) defined cultural property in the following list:[2]

> The term 'cultural property' means property which, on religious or secular grounds, is specifically designated by each state as being of importance for archaeology, prehistory, history, literature, art, or science and which belongs to the following categories:

rare collections and specimens of fauna, flora, minerals, and anatomy, and objects of paleontological interest

property relating to history, including the history of science and technology and military and social history, to the life of national leaders, thinkers, scientists, and artists and to events of national importance

products of archaeological excavations (including regular and clandestine) or of archaeological discoveries; elements of artistic or historical monuments or archaeological sites which have been dismembered

antiquities more than one hundred years old, such as inscriptions, coins, and engraved seals

objects of ethnological interest

property of artistic interest, such as: pictures, paintings and drawings produced entirely by hand on any support and in any material (excluding industrial designs and manufactured articles decorated by hand); original works of statuary art and sculpture in any material; original engravings, prints and lithographs; original artistic assemblages and montages in any material

rare manuscripts and incunabula, old books, documents, and publications of special interest (historical, artistic, scientific, literary, etc.) singly or in collections

postage, revenue, and similar stamps, singly or in collections

archives, including sound, photographic and cinematographic archives articles of furniture more than one hundred years old and old musical instruments

Cultural Property Crime Examples

Theft and Looting

Museum Theft: The theft of objects from museums, often involving art pieces, artifacts, or valuable historical documents.

Archaeological Looting: Unauthorized excavation and removal of artifacts from archaeological sites.

Library Theft: Stealing rare or significant books, manuscripts, or documents from public or private libraries.

Religious Relic Theft: Theft of religious icons, relics, or texts from places of worship.

Illegal Trade and Trafficking

Art Trafficking: Illegally buying and selling artworks, often across international borders.

Antiquities Trafficking: Unlawful trade in ancient artifacts, usually removed from archaeological sites or museums.

Illegal Export/Import: Moving cultural property across borders without proper documentation or in violation of export/import restrictions.

Vandalism and Destruction

Historic Site Vandalism: Deliberate defacing, damaging, or destruction of buildings, landmarks, or sites that hold historical significance.

Iconoclasm: The deliberate destruction of religious icons, images, or monuments, often for ideological reasons.

Art Vandalism: Defacing works of art displayed in public or private settings.

War Crimes Involving Cultural Property

War Looting: Looting of cultural property during armed conflict, often considered a war crime under international law.

Targeting of Cultural Sites: Deliberate destruction or damage of culturally significant locations during armed conflicts.

Real-Life Case

Operation Pandora VI, conducted from June 1 to September 30, 2021, resulted in 52 arrests and the seizure of 9,408 cultural artifacts across 28 countries and targeted sophisticated criminal methods employed in cultural goods trafficking.

Criminal Methods Identified

Archaeological Site Looting: French Customs seized 4,231 archaeological objects which included approximately 3,000 coins, as well as bells, buckles, rings and pieces of pottery which were looted from archaeological sites by a single individual using a metal detector. The operation also revealed that 90 metal detectors destined for illicit use at archaeological sites were recovered.

Online Market Exploitation: Criminals increasingly utilized digital platforms to market stolen artifacts. Special focus was placed on the monitoring of online markets. To that end, a cyber patrol week was organized by the National Police Force of the Netherlands to identify suspicious sales online.

High-Value Theft and Distribution: The Spanish National Police recovered a treasure consisting of 91 gold coins from the Roman Empire worth an estimated half a million euros on the black market.

Multi-Channel Operations: Law enforcement authorities in 28 countries carry out checks and controls in airports and at border crossing points, as well as in auction houses, museums and private indicating criminals operated through various legitimate and semi-legitimate venues.

The operation demonstrated the international scope of cultural trafficking networks, with over 170 investigations still ongoing at the time of reporting.[3],[4]

Crime Pattern Scenario

A theft occurs at a regional museum where several rare Mesopotamian tablets are stolen overnight. Security cameras were disabled, suggesting insider knowledge. Within weeks, the tablets appear for sale through a private broker in another country with falsified documentation claiming they are from a "private collection." Law enforcement links this case to a larger smuggling ring that has moved dozens of artifacts from conflict zones, through similarities in modus operandi modus operandi, highlighting how local theft can connect to global trafficking networks.

Exercises

1. Search the FBI National Stolen Art File. Develop two fictional scenarios involving two different stolen art objects, describing how they might have been stolen incorporating basic elements of crime patterns as well as those patterns specific to cultural property crimes.
2. In one paragraph, describe how the theft or destruction of a local historical artifact could affect your community's identity or tourism economy. Explain why these crimes are far from "victimless."

Critical Thinking Guidance

Cultural property crimes are often seen as "victimless" because the harm is not always immediate or visible. Yet these crimes erode cultural identity, destabilize communities, and fuel organized crime. Consider how stolen artifacts move through layered networks, how demand from wealthy collectors drives supply, and how cultural heritage crimes intersect with terrorism financing. Treat these crimes not as isolated thefts, but as possibly part of broader transnational organized crime systems.

Resources

FBI. National Stolen Art File. Available at: https://artcrimes.fbi.gov
Interpol. ID-App. Available free on Apple and Android devices.

Notes

1 Organization for Security and Co-operation in Europe (2023, April 13).
2 United Nations Educational, Scientific and Cultural Organization (1970).
3 Interpol (2022a, March 10).
4 Interpol (2023).

Bibliography

Charney, N., Denton, P., & Kleberg, J. (2012, March). Protecting cultural heritage from art theft: International challenge, local opportunity. *FBI Law Enforcement Bulletin*, 1–8. https://leb.fbi.gov/file-repository/archives/march-2012-leb.pdf/view

Interpol. (2022a, March 10). *52 arrests in operation across 28 countries targeting trafficking in cultural goods.* www.interpol.int/News-and-Events/News/2022/52-arrests-in-operation-across-28-countries-targeting-trafficking-in-cultural-goods

Interpol. (2022b). *Assessing crimes against cultural property: Survey of Interpol member countries.* www.interpol.int/en/Resources/Documents#WPS

Interpol. (2023). *International art trafficking operation leads to 60 arrests and over 11,000 objects recovered.* www.interpol.int/en/News-and-Events/News/2023/International-art-trafficking-operation-leads-to-60-arrests-and-over-11-000-objects-recovered

Organization for Security and Co-Operation in Europe. (2023, April 13). *Cracking down on illicit art trade to improve security – the OSCE's critical role.* www.osce.org/stories/cracking-down-on-illicit-art-trade-to-improve-security

United Nations Educational, Scientific and Cultural Organization. (1970). *Convention on the means of prohibiting and preventing the illicit import, export and transfer of ownership of cultural property.* https://unesdoc.unesco.org/ark:/48223/pf0000133378

United Nations Office on Drugs and Crime. (2016). *Practical assistance tool to assist in the implementation of the international guidelines for crime prevention and criminal justice responses with respect to trafficking in cultural property and other related offences.* United Nations. www.unodc.org/documents/organized-crime/trafficking_in_cultural/16-01842_ebook.pdf

U.S. Immigration and Customs Enforcement. (n.d.). *Cultural property, art and antiquities investigations.* U.S. Department of Homeland Security. www.ice.gov/features/cpaa

Part IV

Moving Forward

58 The Implications of Generative Artificial Intelligence

Introduction

Artificial Intelligence (AI) is not a single tool but a collection of technologies that simulate aspects of human cognition: recognition, prediction, and decision-making. In policing, AI's value lies in its ability to process vast datasets, detect hidden patterns, and accelerate investigative work. For crime analysts, this does not mean replacement but transformation: agencies will need more analysts, not fewer, as their role shifts from manual data review to guiding AI systems, validating results, and translating findings into strategy.

AI's value lies not only in analyzing vast datasets but also in improving the front end of data collection. AI-enabled reporting tools can prompt officers to record critical details consistently, reducing missing or vague information and producing higher-quality inputs for analysis. Strong reporting practices and trained analysts will determine whether AI becomes a reliable partner in crime pattern recognition or simply a fast processor of flawed inputs.

This chapter examines how generative AI can enhance both data collection and analysis, the new responsibilities analysts will assume in this partnership, and the challenges law enforcement must address to ensure these tools are accurate, ethical, and operationally useful.

The Potential

For crime analysts and students of criminal justice, AI's potential lies in its ability to dramatically enhance pattern recognition. It can process far more variables than a human analyst could, across vast datasets of crime reports, surveillance footage, social media, and more. For example, AI systems can be trained to flag similarities in modus operandi across jurisdictions, detect spatial-temporal clusters[1] of crimes, or identify subtle trends in victim targeting that might otherwise go unnoticed. These capabilities align closely with the goals of crime analysis: to detect emerging series, help allocate resources strategically, and support investigative linkage of related crimes.

However, the utility of AI depends on the quality of the data it is given. Poorly written reports, missing fields, vague descriptions, or inconsistent coding of variables will undermine AI's ability to detect meaningful patterns. AI cannot infer what was never recorded. Just as traditional crime analysis relies on clear and complete data to find connections, AI requires well-structured, accurate, and detailed information. Smart data collection practices, enhanced by AI-powered report templates and officer training, will be essential to ensure the reliability of future AI systems in law enforcement. This book can serve as part of the necessary training to collaborate with AI effectively.

DOI: 10.4324/9781003728733-62

AI will serve as a powerful partner to police officers, investigators, analysts, and researchers, an "intelligent assistant" that can process more information faster and flag connections that merit deeper investigation. For this partnership to succeed, law enforcement must invest in both the technology and the foundational work of improving data literacy and report quality. The future of crime pattern recognition depends not just on smart machines, but on smart inputs from the field.

The Importance of Modus Operandi Nuances

One of the most consistently underdeveloped aspects of crime pattern recognition and identification is the failure to document and interpret nuanced aspects of modus operandi (MO). These micro-patterns are essential in linking cases, identifying offenders, and understanding their decision-making processes.

When Nuanced MO Data Are Captured

Linkages between seemingly unrelated cases can emerge.

Escalation or de-escalation in offender behavior becomes traceable.

Behavioral consistency or experimentation patterns can be identified.

Theoretical models become testable and meaningful.

AI tools that assist in collecting or inferring these nuances, such as LLM-based interview prompts, pattern-extraction engines, and case linkage algorithms, could dramatically enhance the quality and utility of crime data. But for these tools to function effectively, the foundation must be built; officers must be trained to observe and document these nuances, and reporting systems must be built to capture them.

New Tools

New and emerging AI tools are transforming the ability of law enforcement to collect, structure, and analyze detailed crime pattern data. These innovations are aimed at solving the long-standing issue of missing, vague, or inconsistently recorded variables.

Some Examples of Tools that may Become Widespread in the Future

Smart Report Writing Assistants

AI prompts officers in real-time while writing reports to ensure they enter critical elements like method of entry, point of contact, time windows, and property details.

Capability: AI systems embedded in report writing platforms prompt officers for specific crime pattern details in real time.

Application: Prompts officers with tailored follow-up questions based on crime type; auto-suggests structured fields for variables like time range, target type, and MO descriptors; flags vague or incomplete entries and suggests clarifications

Impact: Creates structured, searchable pattern variables at the point of data entry while reducing analyst time spent interpreting narratives.

Narrative Extraction Tools

NLP (Natural Language Processing) scans free-text narratives and extracts key pattern variables such as suspect behavior, location features, and MO.

Capability: Natural Language Processing tools that read officer-written narratives and extract crime pattern variables into structured formats.

Application: Extracts and codes elements such as point of entry, suspect approach, targeted items, environmental context; tags potential linkage cues and maps them for analysts; retrofits older reports for pattern analysis

Impact: Enables automated pattern flagging across thousands of reports while creating structured data from unstructured narratives.

Auto-Linkage Detection

In voice-to-structured reporting, officers can speak reports in the field; AI transcribes and tags important variables. AI compares new reports with past incidents and flags likely matches.

Capability: AI models trained to detect repeat elements in new incident reports and flag likely pattern matches.

Application: Runs similarity scoring based on MO, location, victim type, or time window; alerts analysts to "near match" cases even when different terminology is used; connects cases across jurisdictions with different reporting practices

Impact: Connects cases sooner, encourages proactive investigation, and enables coordinated responses.

Field Suggestion Tools (in development)

On-scene guidance via mobile devices to help officers ask better questions and observe variables relevant to crime linkage.

These tools collectively enhance the quality of crime data, making it more consistent, analyzable, and valuable for linkage, prevention, and accountability efforts.

Critical Limitations

Law enforcement agencies worldwide will invest billions in AI systems promising to revolutionize crime pattern analysis. It is important to think critically when dealing with vendors who promise that their technology can replace humans.

AI systems may be inadequate if they're trained on fundamentally inadequate data. AI systems are only as good as their training data. If current data collection is flawed, AI perpetuates and amplifies those flaws.

Bias Amplification: AI may amplify existing biases in data collection and systematically miss patterns in underreported crime types or communities.

Over-Reliance Risk: Humans may become dependent on AI and lose critical observational and analytical skills.

AI can flag patterns, detect correlations, and summarize unstructured text, but it cannot determine investigative relevance, legal sufficiency, or operational feasibility on its own. Human analysts will still be required to:

- Confirm whether flagged cases are truly linked.
- Interpret behavioral nuances AI may misread.
- Prioritize cases based on real-world context.
- Prevent false positives or bias in algorithm outputs.

Ethical Risks in Crime Pattern Classification and AI

Bias amplification: Historical data often reflect enforcement practices rather than actual offending, and if these biases are built into AI or typologies, they may unfairly reinforce disparities. Regular review of data inputs and AI models helps detect and correct bias before it distorts investigative results.

Overgeneralization and mislabeling: Complex behaviors may be forced into rigid categories, leading to misclassification of incidents or wrongful suspicion of individuals. Human oversight must remain central, validating AI findings and applying professional judgment rather than deferring to automated outputs.

Privacy and surveillance concerns: Expanding structured data collection increases the volume of personal and situational information, raising the potential for misuse or breaches of confidentiality. Agencies should define the investigative purposes of these tools and prevent their expansion into broad surveillance of lawful activity.

Stigmatization of communities: Designating neighborhoods or populations as crime "hot spots" can harm trust and perpetuate cycles of suspicion. Engaging with affected communities and making classification practices visible helps reduce stigmatization and maintain trust.

Over-reliance on technology: Treating AI outputs as objective truths rather than probabilistic assessments may create false positives or wasted investigative effort. Agencies should be able to explain how classifications are made and how AI systems reach their outputs, avoiding "black box" decision-making.

Mission creep: Systems built for narrow investigative purposes may expand into broad surveillance of lawful behavior without proper oversight. Only information relevant to law enforcement responsibilities, including crime pattern information, should be collected, and strong safeguards must be in place to prevent misuse or unauthorized access.

Accountability gaps: As AI and classification tools influence decision-making, responsibility for errors becomes harder to assign, creating ethical and legal challenges. Policies should specify who is accountable when errors occur, ensuring that accountability is not lost in the handoff between human decision-makers and technological systems.

Judgment and Context

AI is better at recognizing repetitive patterns, such as burglaries or vehicle thefts. But for complex, low-frequency, or evolving crimes, like stalking patterns, emerging cybercrime tactics, or multi-crime series, human investigators and analysts are irreplaceable. These cases often require:

- Interview analysis
- Interpersonal dynamics interpretation
- Theory-informed hypothesis testing
- Cross-agency collaboration

Human analysts will play an increasing role in:

- Designing AI queries and selecting relevant data fields
- Training AI models (supervised learning) using labeled pattern[2] examples
- Auditing AI performance to prevent drift,[3] error, or bias
- Adjusting AI systems as crime tactics evolve

This adds a technical and ethical layer to the analyst's job, expanding rather than reducing the skillset needed.

As AI automates time-consuming tasks, such as sifting through hundreds of reports, human analysts will be freed up to:

- Focus on crime prevention strategies
- Support command-level decision-making
- Lead interagency pattern analysis initiatives
- Conduct research and policy development

This will shift analysts from "data retrievers" to strategic advisors and knowledge integrators. AI generates possibilities; analysts provide judgment and context.

A Partnership

As digital evidence, smart surveillance, online reporting systems, and interagency data sharing grow, the volume of information will exceed human capacity to review manually. AI will help filter and triage this data, but analysts will still be needed to handle the complex cases, manage interdepartmental coordination, and translate findings into tactical or policy decisions.

The partnership between crime analysts and artificial intelligence will function as a collaborative system, where AI enhances but does not replace human judgment. AI will serve as a force multiplier, identifying hidden connections, reducing data overload, and enabling faster, more informed decision-making.

AI functions as a rapid processor and pattern enhancer, while the crime analyst retains the role of interpreter, strategist, and communicator. The success of this partnership will depend on accurate data entry at the source, appropriate AI training, and strong analyst oversight to distinguish meaningful patterns from statistical noise. Together, AI and analysts will extend the reach and speed of modern crime pattern recognition.

Exercises

1. Locate an online news article about a series of crimes. In a brief paragraph, list the key crime pattern variables (time, location, MO) you detect. Then describe in a second paragraph how you think an AI system might extract the same variables and what it could miss without human judgment.
2. Imagine an AI system trained primarily on burglary data from affluent neighborhoods. Write a short paragraph discussing how this could bias crime pattern recognition across the entire city and suggest one mitigation strategy.
3. Create a one-paragraph checklist (three to five items) of safeguards your local police agency should implement before deploying an AI-based case linkage system, focusing on privacy, transparency, and accountability.

Notes

1 A spatial-temporal cluster is a concentration of events that occur close together in both location and time.

2 A labeled pattern is a recognized and named arrangement of events that share similar characteristics, where the "label" is the descriptive tag used to identify that specific type of pattern (like a "burglary series" or a "drug market hotspot") drift.

3 In AI, drift is the change in data patterns over time that causes a model's performance to decline because the data it sees in the real world no longer matches the data it was trained on.

Bibliography

Barrington, S., & Farid, H. (2023). A comparative analysis of human and AI performance in forensic estimation of physical attributes. *Scientific Reports*, *13*(1), Article 31821. https://doi.org/10.1038/s41598-023-31821-3

Coleman, S. (2025). Early adoption of generative artificial intelligence in law enforcement: A mixed-methods study of policy, practice, and perception. *CrimRxiv*. https://doi.org/10.21428/cb6ab371.7d66c9e6

Dando, C. J., & Adam, C. E. (2025). Collecting initial accounts using ChatCharlie chatbot improves eyewitness memory in later investigative interviews. *Scientific Reports*, *15*, 9456. https://doi.org/10.1038/s41598-025-93281-1

Guler, A., Kula, S., & Boke, K. (2025). Examining public support for AI in policing: The role of perceived procedural justice. *Police Practice and Research*, 1–23. https://doi.org/10.1080/15614263.2025.2516535

Hajkowicz, S., Karimi, S., Wark, T., Klugman, S., Schleiger, E., & Sinha, R. (2019). *Artificial intelligence: Australia's ethics framework* (Discussion paper, p. 15). Data61, CSIRO. https://consult.industry.gov.au/public/5cd282da

Horsefield, O., Lightowlers, C., & Green, M. (2025). Drunk and disorderly data: Applying natural language processing to identify alcohol-related crimes in police data. *Police Practice and Research*, 1–30. https://doi.org/10.1080/15614263.2025.2508275

May, B. (2025). Are we DrAIfting? The role of large language models in police investigative interviewing. *Articles II:RP*, *15*(1). https://iiirg.org/wp-content/uploads/2025/09/IIRP_20250506_May_Final.pdf

59 Next

Introduction

Crime pattern analysis has not developed a diagnostic framework in the way medicine or psychology has. This is not because its value has not been fully recognized. Other fields moved forward decades ago with structured diagnostic systems – The Diagnostic and Statistical Manual of Mental Disorders (DSM) in psychology and the International Classification of Diseases (ICD) in medicine. These models show how complex problems can be described using common language, categories, and criteria. They allow professionals to compare observations, test hypotheses, and reach consensus.

Crime patterns operate the same way. Offenders are not infinitely creative. They are limited in how they approach, conceal, and escape, just as investigators are limited in the ways they record and describe cases. Behaviors repeat, and those repetitions can be documented. A structured ontology (a framework that organizes concepts and relationships) gives law enforcement a way to capture this recurring knowledge. It turns what officers and analysts already know into a more robust sharing of usable information.

The real gap is not in ability but in documentation. We have relied heavily on tacit knowledge – intuition and experience – but have not built the structured systems that make that extensive knowledge durable and transferable.

Diagnosing Crime Patterns

In medicine, diagnosis begins with gathering descriptive information such as symptoms, test results, and patient history. Professionals use agreed-upon criteria to group observations into meaningful categories. These systems work because they capture both what is seen and what is understood through experience.

Crime pattern analysis can apply the same approach. Reports, witness statements, and physical evidence are our "symptoms." Analysts compare recurring elements (methods of entry, times, locations, victim types) and test competing explanations, much like doctors rule out conditions. Confirmation comes through further evidence, and the "treatment plan" is the policing strategy that follows.

Both processes are iterative: they require collecting, testing, and refining information as new evidence comes in. Both rely on professional expertise and standardized language to ensure consistency. And both carry ethical responsibilities: medicine protects patient privacy, while law enforcement protects individual rights and fair treatment.

DOI: 10.4324/9781003728733-63

Example: Diagnostic Approach in Action

A city experiences several late-night robberies over two weeks. Each involves a masked offender, a small firearm, and a convenience store target. Initially, the cases are logged separately. An analyst compares the details, identifies the recurring elements, and rules out other robberies that don't fit. The result is a confirmed series, a working diagnosis that helps anticipate future targets and direct resources.

Taxonomy, Typology, Ontology

Law enforcement already uses classification every day, though usually without naming the system behind it. In research, three kinds of classification are especially useful for making sense of complex domains: taxonomy, typology, and ontology. Each plays a role in organizing knowledge about crime patterns, and each fills a different gap.

A taxonomy is a hierarchical classification system that arranges concepts from general to specific, much like the branches of a tree. Crime reporting is already built on taxonomies. At the broadest level, we distinguish violent crimes from property crimes. Within violent crime, we separate robbery, assault, and homicide. Within robbery, we may note whether it was armed, and if armed, what type of weapon was used. At the most specific level, we might describe a single case as an armed robbery with a handgun at a gas station. This kind of structure is familiar to anyone who has filled out a police report or coded a case for UCR or NIBRS. Its strengths are in consistency, comparability, and trend analysis – it allows agencies to aggregate data across jurisdictions and track changes over time. Its limitation is that it tells us what happened, but not necessarily how or why it happened, and it may oversimplify cases.

A typology is different. It is not about hierarchy but about grouping events by shared features, motivations, or circumstances. In homicide research, for example, cases are often grouped as gang-related, domestic, serial, or felony-related. Burglary can be broken down into crimes of opportunity, drug-motivated offenses, or professional, organized jobs. Fraud can be divided into identity theft, investment scams, or corporate embezzlement. Typologies provide meaning beyond the legal label, helping explain differences within a category and guiding investigative or prevention strategies. They allow us to say not just that a homicide occurred, but that it was domestic in nature and therefore requires a different approach than a gang-related shooting. The limitation is that typologies can overlap, and categories are not always sharply defined.

Ontology goes further still. Rather than stopping at categories, it maps the relationships between behaviors, settings, and variables. For example, in burglary, taxonomy tells us the case is a burglary. A typology might classify it as a residential nighttime burglary. Ontology connects the full set of elements: the method of entry, such as forcing a rear window with a pry tool; the time of occurrence, perhaps between midnight and 4 a.m.; the target, such as single-family homes near highway access; the offender behavior, such as selective theft of electronics without ransacking; and the environmental conditions, such as poor lighting and easy escape routes. By linking these variables, ontology builds a structured knowledge map that can be used by both human analysts and machine systems. Its strengths are in integration, transparency, and adaptability. It allows tacit and explicit knowledge to be joined in one framework, makes investigative reasoning clearer, and provides a foundation for advanced analytical tools. Its limitations are that it requires agreement and continual updating as offender behavior and environments change.

These three systems are not in competition but complement one another. Taxonomy provides structure by telling us what kind of crime it is. Typology offers interpretation by showing us what the crime resembles in terms of behavior, motivation, or circumstance. Ontology integrates both by showing how all the elements fit together into a recognizable and testable pattern. Other fields have already demonstrated this progression. Medicine and psychology began by naming and counting disorders (taxonomy), then grouped them into themes (typology), and ultimately developed diagnostic ontologies that connected symptoms, causes, and treatment options. Crime pattern analysis can take the same path, building a shared knowledge framework that supports both practitioners and researchers.

Using Crime Elements as an Ontology

Elements of crime – offender, victim, place, time, method, protective measures, and sequence – are often presented as separate categories. Ontology brings them together into a system by showing how each part connects to the others. An offender chooses a victim, the victim is tied to a place, the place is shaped by protective measures such as lighting or surveillance, and the crime unfolds in time and sequence.

When these connections are mapped, incidents stop appearing as isolated events and begin to reveal patterns. A series of burglaries may suddenly be seen as linked by method, timing, or location. This makes it possible to predict where the next incident might occur or to design interventions at weak points in the system, such as poorly lit areas or repeat victimization sites.

Ontology also prepares officers, analysts, and students to work with artificial intelligence. Future AI systems will rely on structured, relational data to connect offenders, victims, places, and times. By learning to think in terms of ontology now, practitioners will be able to understand how AI systems reach their conclusions, recognize when important connections are missing, and make better-informed decisions based on AI outputs. This ensures that human expertise and machine analysis complement one another rather than working at cross purposes.

Ontology in Practice: A Mini-Framework

An ontology shows how pieces of information relate. Instead of treating each detail as separate, it links offender behavior, environmental context, and victim characteristics into a recognizable pattern that stretches across the preparation, commission, and aftermath of crime. Using residential burglary as an example, the elements can be described as an interconnected whole.

Before the crime, offender behavior often reveals routines that shape opportunities. Pre-crime activity may include scouting neighborhoods, observing homes for signs of absence, or checking for visible security measures such as alarms or cameras. These preparatory actions, although subtle, are crucial because they link the offender to the environment and demonstrate how familiarity and routine awareness shape the eventual decision to offend. The choice of target is rarely random; offenders may return to areas they have passed through before or select properties that resemble those they successfully victimized in the past.

During the crime, the method of entry provides important detail. An offender who forces a rear window with a pry tool demonstrates access to specific equipment and a willingness to take the risk of leaving physical evidence. Another who slips through an unlocked door shows reliance on opportunity rather than preparation. Time of offense also adds meaning. Burglaries committed between midnight and four in the morning indicate different offender routines and levels of risk-taking compared to those that occur during daytime hours when residents are absent at work. These temporal choices can help distinguish between juvenile and adult offenders, as well as between opportunists and more practiced burglars.

After the crime, offender behavior continues to shape the pattern. The stolen property itself tells a story: electronics may be quickly resold for cash, jewelry may be exchanged within informal markets, and firearms may be funneled into criminal networks. How stolen goods move through these channels links the burglary not just to the victimized household but to larger systems of trafficking and profit. Post-crime conduct inside the property also matters. Some offenders move carefully, taking only what they came for, while others ransack rooms in a hurried or careless manner. These differences point to levels of planning, control, and experience that distinguish types of burglars.

Environmental context ties the sequence together. Poor lighting, unmonitored alleys, and low levels of police visibility create the backdrop in which these pre-crime, crime, and post-crime behaviors unfold. They are not just passive conditions but active parts of the ontology, shaping offender choices and offering points of intervention for prevention.

When these elements are linked, they form more than a timeline or checklist. They reveal a structured crime pattern that stretches from preparation to aftermath. A burglary involving pre-crime scouting, rear-window entry with a pry tool, theft of electronics, and resale through known markets is not an isolated event – it is part of a connected system of behaviors and contexts. Even if details differ across cases, such as the exact items stolen or the type of house targeted, the relational framework highlights an offender "signature" and enables analysts to compare incidents meaningfully.

This is what an ontology does. It connects the dots between who, what, when, where, how, and why, before, during, and after the event, allowing crime patterns to be recognized as structured systems rather than counted as separate cases.

Concluding Reflections

Crime pattern recognition and identification sit at the intersection of art and science. Practitioners rely on intuition developed through years of experience and the need to work quickly to address community threats, while researchers and policymakers seek structured systems that allow patterns to be documented, tested, and shared. This book has tried to bridge that divide by presenting crime pattern recognition and identification as both a practical skill and an emerging discipline. It requires intuition and experience AND careful documentation, ethical reflection, and a commitment to continuous learning.

Crime patterns exist within limits. Human behavior, environmental conditions, and social context constrain the choices available to offenders. Recognizing these constraints makes it possible to build taxonomies, typologies, and ontologies that give shape to what might otherwise seem like endless variation.

Technology will expand what is possible, but it cannot replace human judgment. Artificial intelligence and other analytical tools are best understood as force multipliers. They can process vast amounts of information, extract subtle details from reports, and highlight connections across jurisdictions. Yet their accuracy depends on the data they are given, and without human guidance, they risk amplifying flaws or biases already present. The enduring role of the human will be to gather relevant data, design effective queries, guide AI training, interpret results, and translate findings into actionable strategies.

Systems of classification, whether in medicine or in policing, carry risks of misuse. But the absence of structure carries its own risks: undiagnosed patterns, unlinked offenders, and communities left unprotected. The responsible course is not to avoid classification but to build systems transparently, apply them fairly, and refine them continually through practice and research. The long-term goal is a reproducible, shareable diagnostic framework that lets any agency describe, link, and test crime patterns the same way.

The next generation of officers, investigators, analysts, and researchers will face challenges of unprecedented complexity but also unprecedented opportunity. By documenting what is known, clarifying how it is known, and creating tools that combine human expertise with machine assistance, timely crime pattern recognition and identification can only improve. The ongoing work of defining, diagnosing, and interpreting crime patterns will evolve as practitioners, scholars, and communities contribute their knowledge in the shared effort to build a safer world.

This book is simply a beginning. It is up to the readers to decide what to do next.

Bibliography

Barrett, L. F. (2009). The future of psychology: Connecting mind to brain. *Perspectives on Psychological Science*, *4*(4), 326–339. https://doi.org/10.1111/j.1745-6924.2009.01134.x

Heilbron, M., Armeni, K., Schoffelen, J., Hagoort, P., & de Lange, F. P. (2022). A hierarchy of linguistic predictions during natural language comprehension. *Proceedings of the National Academy of Sciences*, *119*(32), e2201968119. https://doi.org/10.1073/pnas.2201968119

Luczak, A., McNaughton, B. L., & Kubo, Y. (2022). Neurons learn by predicting future activity. *Nature Machine Intelligence*, *4*(1), 62–72. https://doi.org/10.1038/s42256-021-00430-y

Lum, C., Telep, C. W., Koper, C. S., & Grieco, J. A. (2012). Receptivity to research in policing. *Justice Research and Policy*, *14*(1), 61–95. https://doi.org/10.3818/jrp.14.1.2012.61

National Academies of Sciences, Engineering, and Medicine. (2022). *Ontologies in the behavioral sciences: Accelerating research and the spread of knowledge* (Digest version). The National Academies Press. https://doi.org/10.17226/26755

Pareschi, R. (2023, July 17). Abductive reasoning with the GPT-4 language model: Case studies from criminal investigation, medical practice, scientific research. *Sistemi Intelligenti*, arXiv preprint arXiv:2307.10250. https://doi.org/10.48550/arXiv.2307.10250

Police Executive Research Forum. (2018). *The changing nature of crime and criminal investigations.* www.policeforum.org/assets/ChangingNatureofCrime.pdf

Rossmo, D. K. (2006, September). Criminal investigation failures: Avoiding the pitfalls. *FBI Law Enforcement Bulletin*, *75*(9), 1–8.

Sherman, L. W. (2015). A tipping point for "totally evidenced policing". *International Criminal Justice Review*, *25*(1), 11–29. https://doi.org/10.1177/1057567715574372

World Health Organization. (n.d.). *International statistical classification of diseases and related health problems (ICD)*. WHO.

About the Author

Deborah Osborne is a retired US Secret Service Investigative Analyst and a former Crime Analyst for the Buffalo Police Department. As a crime analyst, she read and analyzed the narratives of over 100,000 police crime reports. She co-authored the book Introduction to Crime Analysis: Basic Resources for Criminal Justice Practice and wrote Out of Bounds: Innovation and Change in Law Enforcement Intelligence Analysis as a research fellow for the Joint Military Intelligence College. Ms. Osborne was the co-chair of the International Association of Crime Analysts' certification committee when it developed certification standards for the profession. She trained analysts and taught this subject at the college level for over six years. She has won awards from the International Association of Crime Analysts and the International Association of Law Enforcement Intelligence Analysts for her contributions to the field.

Comparative Vocabulary of Everyday Terms in Crime Reports: US to UK/Commonwealth

Transportation Related

truck: lorry, trailer truck: articulated lorry, station wagon: estate car, convertible: cabriolet, RV (recreational vehicle): caravan/motorhome, minivan: people carrier, motorcycle: motorbike, hood (car): bonnet, trunk (car): boot, license plate: number plate, windshield: windscreen, tailpipe/muffler: silencer, turn signal: indicator, truck bed: lorry bed, parking lot: car park, parking meter: ticket machine, gas station: petrol station, rest area: services/service station, car dealership: garage, dumpster: skip

overpass: flyover, beltway/freeway: ring road/motorway, intersection: crossroads, traffic circle: roundabout, crosswalk: zebra crossing/pelican crossing

Clothing and Accessories

sweater: jumper, vest (outer garment): waistcoat, pants: trousers, underwear: pants

sweatpants: tracksuit bottoms/jogging bottoms, sneakers: trainers, rain boots/rubber boots: wellingtons/wellies, suspenders (trousers): braces, suspenders (underwear): garter belt, undershirt: vest, sweatsuit: tracksuit, mittens: hand warmers, zipper: zip, backpack: rucksack, purse (woman's): handbag, jewelry: jewellery

Residence and Buildings

apartment: flat, apartment building: block of flats, main street: high street, restroom/bathroom (public): toilet/loo, restroom (private): bathroom, mailbox: postbox, closet: wardrobe, yard: garden, trash/garbage can: rubbish bin/dustbin, address/zip code: postcode

Shopping and Retail

shopping cart: trolley, shopping basket: basket, cash register: till, grocery store: supermarket/grocer, drugstore: chemist, strip mall: parade of shops, store clerk: shop assistant, mall: shopping centre, fast-food restaurants: takeaway restaurants, downtown: city centre

Household

trash bag: bin liner, band-aid: plaster, eraser: rubber, thumbtack: drawing-pin, clothespin: clothes peg, flashlight: torch, backpack: rucksack, scotch tape: sellotape, lightbulb: bulb, mini blinds: venetian blinds

Technology and Objects

cell phone: mobile, flash drive: memory stick, antenna (tv): aerial, faucet: tap, thermos: flask, commodities: goods

Miscellaneous

allowance: pocket money, one-way ticket: single, round trip: return, schedule: timetable,

line (queue): queue, restroom key: toilet key, collect call: reverse charge call, Social Security Card: National Insurance Card, counterclockwise: anticlockwise, trash collector: dustman, sports equipment: sports kit

Index